The Programming Approach and the Demise of Economics

Franco Archibugi

The Programming Approach and the Demise of Economics

Volume II

Selected Testimonies
on the Epistemological 'Overturning'
of Economic Theory and Policy

Franco Archibugi
Rome, Italy

ISBN 978-3-319-78059-7   ISBN 978-3-319-78060-3   (eBook)
https://doi.org/10.1007/978-3-319-78060-3

Library of Congress Control Number: 2018945553

© The Editor(s) (if applicable) and The Author(s) 2019
This work is subject to copyright. All rights are solely and exclusively licensed by the Publisher, whether the whole or part of the material is concerned, specifically the rights of translation, reprinting, reuse of illustrations, recitation, broadcasting, reproduction on microfilms or in any other physical way, and transmission or information storage and retrieval, electronic adaptation, computer software, or by similar or dissimilar methodology now known or hereafter developed.
The use of general descriptive names, registered names, trademarks, service marks, etc. in this publication does not imply, even in the absence of a specific statement, that such names are exempt from the relevant protective laws and regulations and therefore free for general use.
The publisher, the authors and the editors are safe to assume that the advice and information in this book are believed to be true and accurate at the date of publication. Neither the publisher nor the authors or the editors give a warranty, express or implied, with respect to the material contained herein or for any errors or omissions that may have been made. The publisher remains neutral with regard to jurisdictional claims in published maps and institutional affiliations.

This Palgrave Macmillan imprint is published by the registered company Springer Nature Switzerland AG
The registered company address is: Gewerbestrasse 11, 6330 Cham, Switzerland

Preface
to the Second Volume of the Trilogy
on the Programming Approach

This is the second volume of a Trilogy of books concerning the Programming approach, a totally different and alternative approach, with respect to the traditional approach that is practised, with a continuous sense of failure and guilt—in Economics—by most authors, who have the 'invisible hand' as the basis of their discipline and who have also constituted the history of the discipline.[1]

So, in this volume, I considered it useful and interesting to offer readers a selection and synthesis of some authors, economists, and others from other social sciences, (some well known, others less so), who—even not achieving the same systematic clarity, advances and *explicit vision* of the authors examined and relocated on the scene in **Vol. I**—deserve to be considered. This is a preparatory support, in some way, to that critical conscience (without particular radical theoretical effects, but full of innovative effects) of contemporary Economics thinking, which—even if acknowledged as 'mainstream'—would intend the adoption of the *Programming Approach*.

In this sense, in this volume of this work (edited in the form of a Trilogy), I have selected and gathered from the vast world of *Economics* and social research, those *testimonies* which—in my opinion—have manifested, in an interesting way, attention and arguments *towards the overturning* of the determinist into the programming approach, without yet drawing from it any explicit and useful conclusions.

v

Testimonies Contrasting with *'Mainstream'* Economics

It is a question of a selection of examples of critical scholars that oppose the 'positivist' approach, in a new and brilliant way, often through a radical critique, drawing attention to, in any case, the insufficiencies of the traditional approach, even if not completely aware of the contributions of Frisch's followers, and of the series of proposals from the scholars evoked in **Vol. I** who have provided strong arguments for the concept of the epistemological overturning, which is the main focus of this book.

It is my conviction that many of the economists taken into consideration in this volume of this trilogy have perceived how the positivistic approach has trapped economic thinking within a system of generic a-prioristic postulates; and therefore within limited, debatable, conceptual and behavioural 'rationalism'. A 'rationalism', furthermore, that influences the same economists (and other social scientists of the time) by the evolving habits, customs, uses and 'modernities' of their epoch. It is, however, a 'rationalism' itself 'evolutionist' and ready at any moment to be outdated, demanding to be permanently 'scrapped' and renewed.

In which direction? This is another question.

Since, in a simple vision of differentiated evolutive stages, we need to arrange these stages chronologically, we must update what happened before, and at the next stage, update again from the previous stage.

This determines a series of unparallel situations mutually influential, but in different and asymmetric ways. The asymmetry is greater when between different stages there are increasing interdependencies and forms of communication which produce an integrative process among stages that have anthropological and ideological characteristics.

This occurs in some directions with slow changes or developments—more in the most advanced countries (economically but also in other cultural, technical, human/social), or anthropological-ideological-sociological-sensibility, and less in later developed countries in the twentieth century, which nearly disappeared in the early twenty-first century. There is an accompanying proportionally parallel sequences of events in each country towards a minimum standard unified model of progress, so as to facilitate an acceptable imperative of management for planetary interests.

The Influence of Technical-Scientific Discovery on Economic Development Policy

There are many factors in this trend. (1) Far from being universal, independent of any geographical, religious, racial, environmental, linguistic, limiting factor. (2) I do not believe that we can forget that economics, when it first began (in the eighteenth century) as a reflection (or 'science', or discipline) and when somebody looked to building a kind of rational knowhow in the mind and capacities of the operators in the field of economic activities (teachers, colleagues or students, as well as practical operators and actors in some sectors of the public service), the world was very different in structure and thought, and the economic research was reflective of beliefs, values, desires and customs of the human world 'thinking' in respect to the natural world, inert and non-thinking of the epoch.

From the epoch when economics arose, the scientific approach to the natural sciences was achieving very significant progress. Thus, economics has been influenced by examples of research in the fields of the natural sciences, and has been easily intended like that based on a situation where economics was still 'rough' and less developed than in its modern form, and where the available capital on the 'market'[2] (an essential factor of development) was much more abundant in the private sector than in the public sector. It was advantaged by pyramidal injustices of the older times when property, possession and power were continuing to be legitimated by extreme minorities of the populations.

The private initiative was much less complex, more efficient, and more productive (the true k factor of the growth rate registered in the 1800s, two or three centuries after an equilibrium without any growth had been stabilised for two to three millennia in human history); it was easier and more 'productive' than the public one, which still had not been studied, measured and evaluated like the private one.

In such a way the modern developed in last century, constituting the 'original sin' of economics until today. And this has not helped the natural consistency trends of modern situations.

Rome, Italy   Franco Archibugi

Notes to the Preface to the Second Volume of the Trilogy

1. In spite of the dissent generated by more pragmatic economists and by public opinion, less available to accepting the academic sophistry, but nevertheless predominant (so called 'mainstream' economics).

2. This abstract concept of the 'market' (the result of the 'negotiating' of goods in local squares in the Middle Ages) has today become almost a 'metaphysical' concept, mostly after the dozens of enquiries (by universities or study centres in the modern 'free' market economies of different countries) on how the so-called 'market prices' are actually established in reality. They revealed that around 80–90% of all prices, of each type and nature (salaries, capital, goods, services, taxes, interest, public services, etc.) are no longer 'market prices' (unless for sake of expression), but—in the largely public economies, in the widespread structurally existent monopolies and monopsonies—are prices fixed by sellers and producers and so are considered 'administrative', vaguely public or under public control.

Contents

1 The Programming Approach: As Epistemologically Based, Futuristic Decision and 'Rational Utopia' — 1

  1.1 The Logical Foundations of the Decisional Models — 1

  1.2 The Epistemological Basis of Economics (*According to Ludwig von Mises*) — 3

      1.2.1 The Activistic Basis of Knowledge — 4

      1.2.2 The Logical Structure of the Human Mind and of History — 6

  1.3 Programming Versus Forecasting, the Crucial Point of the Overturning Approach to the Future (*According to Jan Tinbergen*) — 10

  1.4 The 'Utopia' Role as Requirement in Economic Theory (*Viewpoints by Bruno de Finetti*) — 15

      1.4.1 Risk of Misleading Conceptualisation — 17

      1.4.2 Critique of Over-Simplification in the Abuse of the Language of Mathematics — 19

  1.5 Economic Theory as 'Fiction' — 20

      1.5.1 'Four Bridges Towards Reality' — 23

      1.5.2 An Impasse — 23

      1.5.3 Rationality or Time? — 25

      1.5.4 An 'Interpretative' Economic Theory (*According to Bell*) — 26

x   Franco Archibugi The Programming Approach and the Demise...

1.6   A Pragmatic 'Realism' as a Way Out from the Impasse   29
Bibliographical References to Chapter 1 (Vol. II)   34

2   The Programming Approach and the Old, Unresolved Debate on 'Decision Theory'   35

2.1   The Traditional 'Methodological' Debate on Economic Decision and Its Inconclusiveness   36

2.2   How the Descriptive Versus Normative Dichotomy Is Raised?   36

2.2.1   The 'Logical Confusion' Concerning 'Value-free' Judgements and 'Scientific' Propositions   38

2.2.2   Methodological Judgements Versus Value Judgements (*According to Ernest Nagel*)   39

2.2.3   Others Steady Attempts to Bypass Controversial Terms (*the Max Weber Trial*)   43

2.2.4   Last Trial (*by Myrdal*)   45

2.3   The Descriptive and Normative Approach in Modern 'Decision Theory'   49

2.4   A New Trichotomy in Modern Decision Theory, Its Inner Interactions (*and Its Tribulations*)   53

2.4.1   The Ambiguities of the Dichotomy Between the 'Descriptive' and 'Normative' Approaches   54

2.4.2   Again, the Illogicality of the 'Realistic' Validity of Behavioural Projection   60

2.5   Conclusions: The Common Pragmatic Bases of the Prescriptive and Programming Approaches   63

Bibliographical References to Chapter 2 (Vol. II)   67

3   The Programming Approach in the Collective Decision and 'Action-Centred' Analysis   69

3.1   Programming and the Knowledge: Action Nexus   69

3.1.1   'Positive' Knowledge and 'Programming' Knowledge   70

3.1.2   The Damage Done by the 'Positivist' Approach   71

3.2		The Unexpected but Significant Contribution of Land and Urban Planners (*the 'Planning Theory' Movement*)	74
	3.2.1	The DNA of 'Planning Theorists'	74
	3.2.2	A Look at the 'Gestation Period' of Planning Theory (*the 1960s*)	75
	3.2.3	A List of Planning Theorist Authors Deserving of More Attention	77
	3.2.4	Limits and Carelessness in the Community of Planning Theorists	79
	3.2.5	What Hope for the Future of the Planning Theorists?	82
	3.2.6	The Need for the Integration of 'Proceduralism' and 'Substantivism' in a Unique Methodology	83
3.3		Toward a Methodology of the Rational Planning (*Faludi's Original Contribution*)	86
	3.3.1	From Planning Theory to Planning Methodology	87
	3.3.2	Some Previews of Planning Methodological Definitions: The Concept of Effectiveness	90
	3.3.3	From Decisions to Programmes and Plans	95
	3.3.4	The Achievement of an Advanced Vision of Consequences: From Decision to Plan (*Frisch's Pyramid Question*)	96
	3.3.5	An Indispensable Ingredient of Rationality in the Planning Methodology: Collective Bargaining	98
	3.3.6	A Cogent-Approach to Flexibility	99
	3.3.7	A Final Summary of Planning Methodology, in the Spirit of Critical Rationalism (*According to Faludi*)	100
3.4		Further Steps Toward a New Methodology of Planning	103
	3.4.1	The Main Requirements of a New Planning Methodology	104

	3.4.2	A Plain Memory again of Some Critical Points and Postulates of the Programming Approach	107
	3.4.3	A Basic Postulate in the Restarting: The Programming Approach as an Action-Oriented Analysis	109
	3.4.4	The Operational Requirement of Planning: Quantification	110
	3.4.5	Evaluation Ex Ante and Evaluation Ex Post in Planning Methodology	112
Bibliographical References to Chapter 3 (Vol. II)			125

4 The Programming Approach and the Mainstream Economic General Theory (*from the Isard's 'General Theory'*) — 131

4.1	Some Needs of 'Realism' in the Economic 'Neo-Classical School' of Thought	131
4.2	Isard's 'General Theory'	132
	4.2.1 In Search of the 'Concept of More Realism'	132
	4.2.2 The 'Relaxation' of Assumptions and the Multiplication of 'Casuistics'	134
	4.2.3 The Extension of the Objective Function to 'Non-Economic Commodities'	137
4.3	'Non-Economic Commodities' (*from Walter Isard*)	137
	4.3.1 Borrowing the 'Social Acts'	138
	4.3.2 From Social Acts to 'Non-Economic Commodities'	139
4.4	The Isard 'General Theory' and the Planning Accounting Frame	142
4.5	Isard's 'General Theory' Between a 'Positivist' Methodology and the Programming Approach (*An other Interesting Proposal by Isard for an Even More General Theory*)	144
Bibliographical References to Chapter 4 (Vol. II)		148

Franco Archibugi General Index of the Whole Work **xiii**

5   The Programming Approach and the Management Sciences   151
  5.1   The Programming Approach and the Administrative
       Sciences: Neglected Interrelations   151
       5.1.1   Management Sciences as Context   151
       5.1.2   Organisational Science as a 'Results-Based'
              Discipline   154
  5.2   The 'Cultural' Origins of Managerial Planning in the
       Public Sector   155
       5.2.1   The Role of the 'Systemic' Approach   156
       5.2.2   Management Sciences: Between Rationality
              and Romanticism   162
  5.3   The Political and Administrative Sciences and the
       Concept of Bounded Rationality   163
       5.3.1   The Imprecision and Relativity of the
              Concept of Bounded Rationality   163
       5.3.2   The Concept of Bounded Rationality in the
              Case of the Programming Approach   166
       5.3.3   The Optimisation Principle and the
              Programming Approach   167
  5.4   Conclusion: The Political and Administrative Sciences
       and the Programming Approach   169
  Bibliographical References to Chapter 5 (Vol. II)   176

**6   The Programming Approach, the Crisis of Traditional
Economics and the Unavoidable 'Post-Capitalism', Leading
to a 'Global Sovereignty' (*A Peculiar Analysis of George Soros*)**   179
  6.1   'Crisis'? For Who and About What?   179
  6.2   The Global System of Capitalism   180
  6.3   Can Economics Manage Economic Crises? (*According
       to the Vision of I. Wallerstein and Associated*)   183
  6.4   A New *Tabula Rasa*?   184
  6.5   From *Logical Positivism* to a *Theory of Reflexivity*   186
       6.5.1   Social Phenomena and Natural Phenomena   186
       6.5.2   Thinking and Reality   187

6.6	The 'Theory of Reflexivity' (*According to George Soros*)	190
	6.6.1 The Sense of History	191
	6.6.2 Does Reflexivity Oblige Us to Accept 'Indeterminacy'	192
	6.6.3 Does 'Reflexivity' Oblige Us to Revise Our Confidence in a Continuous Capacity and Effectiveness of Public Planning?	194
6.7	Design and Political Participation	194
6.8	Reflexive Concept of Truth (*According to George Soros*)	196
	6.8.1 An Interactive Vision of Reality	196
6.9	*Fallibility* and Recognised *Reflexivity*	201
6.10	The 'Feasibility of the Plans'	202
	6.10.1 The 'Feasibility of Plans' as a Pivot Around Which to Rebuild the Programming Approach and the Methodology of Planning	202
	6.10.2 A Reflexive Concept of the Truth, but with an Interactive Vision of Reality	203
	6.10.3 The Program's *Feasibility* and Its Relationship with the Logical Positivism	205
6.11	From the '*Fallibility*' to the '*Feasibility*'	207
6.12	A Radical Criticism of the *Economics* as Studied and Practiced	212
6.13	The Criticism to the Global Capitalism Without Public Planning, and Criticism of the 'Market Fundamentalism' Which Supports it	213
6.14	The Global Capitalist System: An Incomplete Regime	214
6.15	The Future of Global Capitalist System	216
	Bibliographical References to Chapter 6 (Vol. II)	228

7	**A Project for a New Worldwide, Strategic Methodology for Planning (*Under the Sponsorship of a Renovated University of the United Nations*)**	229
7.1	The Construction of the 'Planning Accounting Framework' (*PAF*)	229
	7.1.1 Insufficiency of Purely Methodological Criticism	229

	7.1.2	A New Political Decisional System Consistent with the 'Strategic' Approach (*and—in the Same Time—Fully 'Systemic', Spatially and Multi-structurally*)	231
7.2		The Ridiculous Incapacity of the Current National and International, Economic Policies (*and the Irresponsibility of Governments in 'Navigating in the Fog'*)	233
7.3		Organising a Political Consensus on the Planning Process and in Respect of the Practical Impossibility of Current Economic Policies to Govern the Situation	235
	7.3.1	The Role of the PAF	235
	7.3.2	Using Knowledge to Plan Political Action	236
7.4		New Forms of Capital Formation	237
7.5		A New, Universal Income Policy?	240
	7.5.1	The Income Policy from Endogenous to Exogenous Concept	240
	7.5.2	Connecting Income to Better Job Evaluation	241
7.6		Towards a 'New' Economic Paradigm?	242
	7.6.1	The Dispute Between the 'Growth Models'	246
	7.6.2	The Issue of Expections in Traditional Economic Policy, More or Less Followed by the Competents Operators	249
	7.6.3	So, What May We Intend—Then—with 'New Paradigm'?	250
7.7		New Results Re-discovering Operational Theorems of Economic Policy (*Based on Frischian and Tinbergenian Methodology*)	254
	7.7.1	The Essence of the Lucas Critique	256
	7.7.2	Deep Parameters and Rational Expectations: A Resolution?	257
	7.7.3	Overcoming the Critique	258
Bibliographical References to Chapter 7 (Vol. II)			270

8 The Economics as Tool for Measuring and Improving the Communities Performance Towards a New *Social Accountability* (*in Public and Private; Economic and Social; National and Global*) — 271

8.1	Public and Private Performance: A New Economic Language	271
	8.1.1 The 'Un-Priced Value' Question	272
	8.1.2 Other Directions in the Social Accounting Progress (An Interesting Proposal, Not yet Adequately Assessed, by Karl Fox)	276
8.2	Performance Measuring and Monitoring as the Main Implementation Factors in the Programming Approach	277
8.3	A Return to Strategic Planning?	280
8.4	An Overview of the Steps Ahead in the Researches of Social Accounting	281

Bibliographical References to Chapter 8 (Vol. II) — 289

9 Improving Human Activities and Values as a Strategy to Save Economic Performances and Improvements — 297

9.1	A Great Opportunity: 'Reinventing Government' in the USA	297
	9.1.1 The USA's GPRA Federal Law	298
	9.1.2 The Starting 'Universal' Glossary of the GPRA	300
	9.1.3 Importance and Feasibility of the GPRA	304
	9.1.4 The Public Support for Reform of GPRA	305
9.2	The Successful Federal 'Performance Budgeting'	306
	9.2.1 What Is a 'Performance Budget'?	306
	9.2.2 What Data Must Be Included in the Performance	308
	9.2.3 What Is the Relationship Between the Performance Budget and the Strategic Plan?	309
	9.2.4 Improving the Evaluation Within the 'Performance Budgeting'	310

9.3		A Glance at Current Success and Failure of Strategic Planning	312
	9.3.1	The Unhappy Case of the British and French Experiences	312
	9.3.2	Other OECD Countries	317
	9.3.3	The American Reinvention of Government	317
9.4		The Increased Role of the United Nations	318
9.5		The Essentials Content of the Strategic Planning Process: General Principles	318
	9.5.1	The Strategic Planning Process: Phases or Cycles	318
	9.5.2	Uncertainty in the Planning Process	319
	9.5.3	Flexibility in the Planning Process	322
	9.5.4	Iteration in the Planning Process	323
	9.5.5	Planning and Evaluation	324
	9.5.6	Conditions and General Limits of Strategic Evaluation	325
		Bibliographical References to Chapter 9 (Vol. II)	334

Appendices from the United Nations Organization   337

Bibliography   407

Index   441

Brief Introductory Note to the Chapters of Vol. II

In **Vol. II** of this trilogy, I have selected—as stated in the preface—some testimonies from the vast world of economics and social research (traditional or not, in my opinion) which have manifested attention towards the overturning of the determinist in favour of the programming approach, without drawing from it any explicit conclusions.

Such a matter has been examined by a group of rival scholars of the positivist approach, who, even though not following in the footsteps of Frisch and the other scholars revisited in the first part of the book, have nonetheless offered strong arguments in contribution to the idea of an epistemological overturning—the focus of this book.

The Need for 'Realism' in the Traditional Approach of Mainstream Economics

First of all, Chap. 1 of **Vol. II** is dedicated to some authors that have engaged, under one form or another, with economics with the aim of liberating this from the positivistic approach in order to go directly to the programming approach—or who have considered its problems as problems of action addressed to the action and consequently to the future of actors, in any possible case: the individuals, the social group or political communities, any kind of operating institution representative of the common citizen.

I have described—in Chap. 1—three authors that have recommended a changed approach in economics, with respect to future actions of three different attitudes (non-positivist and purposeful).

The first chapter of this volume (see Sect. 1.1.) is dedicated to the special case of Ludwig von Mises—a curious case of extreme methodological contradiction. In fact, nobody can deny that von Mises made a great epistemological contribution to 'liberate' the social sciences (which he calls the 'sciences of the human action', or praxeology[1]) from the positivism and the methodological imitation of natural sciences. Thus, he also made a similarly important contribution to the epistemology of economics, emptying it of 'empiricism'. In this way, von Mises also participated in the 'crusade' against determinism and positivism in the social sciences, arguing that mankind can be master of his own actions and can freely decide his goals, objectives and destiny, without accepting his own existence as only subjected to 'naturalist', 'historical' or 'experimental' laws.

But then, at the same time, von Mises—influenced by the political, social, and popular circumstantial debate at his time, regarding 'ethical' or 'collectivistic' philosophies, and, perhaps negatively biased by discussions with the theorists of the authoritarian 'ethnic state' (the state of fascism, Nazism and soviet communism and other similar dreadful forms of totalitarian and liberticidal regimes)—set himself up as extreme defender of the absolute 'individual' freedom of choice (in order to affirm the freedom of choice and the decisional programming autonomy of mankind), until assigning only, and absolutely only to the single individual the right to choose one's own destiny.[2]

In fact, von Mises—haunted by the political events of his own time—arrived at denying consequentially the possibility and the right to make choices and to 'formulate preferential solutions'—in the ambit of the conquered liberal and democratic societies—to any other kind of social entity or subject (family, group, association, public agencies and state and republic, or the common good).[3]

But reserving the 'freedom' only to the single individual, we must believe that the maximum effect of utility and personal satisfaction for each one can derive only from the maximum *laissez faire* of the individuals, when operating freely in the 'market', without any rule or restriction. This postulate—this kind of a-priorism—however, is reduced for any kind of community into a 'casual' solution, in a stochastic result, smuggled in as a 'spontaneous order';[4] it is a concept which ends up acting on humanity and on freedom of choice as a law much more mechanical and positivistic than any other 'natural' law. This intrinsic contradiction between the inherent positivism of the natural market behaviour with respect to the capacity of intentional action of the problem solving will be examined more fully in Chap. 1.

In later chapters we shall mention some other visions that are very similar in nature to the perception of the 'overturning' of the approach, which constitutes the leitmotiv of this book. These visions have been selected from those that have sensed in some way the 'overturning' approach, and the demise of the positivistic economics, even originating from distant areas of thought.

Also in Chap. 1, I refer to some testimonies concerning the sharp distinction between programming and forecasting, as presupposition of any correct planning activity approach (again as with Tinbergen, Leontief, or Frisch himself).

At the same time (and also in Chap. 1), I have dealt with the vision of economics as a 'utopia', in the sense described by Bruno de Finetti;[5] or as 'utopic fiction', as described by Daniel Bell,[6] intended as an area of 'future' analysis, one still unmarked by past 'facts', non-existent—insofar as it is 'nowhere'—having its main basis in the programming approach methodology. This is a utopia that knows, of course, limits, bounds and constraints, which are valid only if applicable for the future, and drawn from the programming approach, even if extracted from the present; it is a fiction that is not very expressive of the 'reality' and, therefore, should be verified case by case, and should be used only cautiously in the policy intention. I have also added a reference to the vision of economics as operative science, as a science of doing, and to the contribution given into that sense by the so-called 'Sociology of Knowledge' and to the work of Karl Mannheim.

Then (in Chap. 3) I have tried to update the methodological debate (which has occupied economics from its origins), on whether it is possible to have a social science or theory, free from value judgements; this is a sterile debate, and has never reached a satisfactory conclusion, for at least two centuries.

It is a debate, however, that in some of its more critical aspects in the field of some modern reflections about the 'decision theory' seems to have proposed some new support that validates the programming approach method.

Consequently, I have sought to deliver (in Chap. 5) a critical panorama of some trends in emerging studies on management and planning studies (in various sectors of public administration) under the form (and vision) of 'planning based on a decision-centred analysis'. This vision has emerged and developed in the last decades of the twentieth century, over all in the ambit of the physical, regional and urban planning (now called also 'territorial' or 'spatial') schools.[7]

It is a vision which deserves to be recalled as a privileged field of reflection for an endless range of other decisional fields, interesting for the decision-making of groups and public entities at any kind of communitarian level.

From this ambit was developed, with Andreas Faludi and other fellows, a discourse on a 'planning theory', originally integrated with many different specialties; this was even 'innovative' but later swamped—in my opinion—in a poorly and scarcely constructed debate of the 'political-scientist' type, one inconsistent and inconclusive—a debate where the research of a methodology of comprehensive approach was absent. A methodology that would have been useful in advancing the integrating programming approach at the lower, as well as at the higher, operational level.[8]

Moreover, from the other side, in Chaps. 5 and 6, I wanted to recall and comment on two extreme cases of positivist approaches to economics, which are very far from the awareness of the 'overturning' (which this book intends to support).

In fact, both cases are emblematically imbued with precisely the determinist, or positivist, approach. However, they well represent—each with regards to its correlated subjects—the points by which on the contrary, the overturning is operating, that furthermore constitute a splendid occasion to reveal the reasons for such an overturning.

Thus, these two cases complete, in a provisional way—in negative terms—the picture of the testimonies which have predicted the overturning itself.

The first of the two cases (Chapter II-5), on the 'General Theory' of Walter Isard, is a typical case of the positive theory of neo-classical economics. All the main postulates of the traditional theory of economics are present and accepted in this extensive work, which I consider among the most regular, updated, systematic and exact of the neo-classic economic doctrine.

However, in the effort to come out of its narrow limits, Isard's work also includes 'non-economic goods' in the framework of the same neo-classical logic, as well as the schemes of the structural social theory (by Talcott Parsons, for instance) in the same frame as the neo-classical 'General theory'. This constitutes a challenge that cannot be ignored by scholars who postulate the integration between 'social' and 'economic' problems, in a unified 'approach to analysis and planning'. (The essential description of this challenge and our proposed answer can be found in Chap. 5).

The second of the two cases (Chap. 5) is that represented by the so-called 'bounded rationality' in the theory of decision (referring mainly to the very famous work of Herbert A. Simon).

This case is set up through an epistemological misunderstanding, exactly at the point of intersection and separation between the positivistic, or deterministic, approach, on the one hand, and the programming approach, on the other hand. In effect, in the positivist approach (deduced ex post) it would be impossible to deny the validity of the Simonian arguments concerning 'bounded rationality'. But in the programming approach (ex ante planning analysis), it is impossible to determine *a priori* a satisfying solution, different from an optimising one, because both are undeterminable. The difference between them is measurable only ex post. Consequently, it would be illogical to admit, ex ante, a 'satisfying' solution in respect to the optimal one, only for formal consistency, only because it will exist *ex post*.

The need to clarify this aspect, which is one of the pivots on which planning science and praxeology itself is based (seen in the context of the vast culture of the organisational and managerial sciences) is discussed in Chap. 5.

But it is especially in the work of George Soros, analysed in Chap. 6, that I have found an expression of full awareness regarding the epistemological insufficiency of the traditional positivist approach (even in regard to Karl Popper's 'logical' positivism); this, through varied channels and experiences, has developed in parallel to those matured in this book. The premises, on the one side, and the implications, on the other, connected by the programming approach (as explained in this book) have found indirect and 'oblique' support from the presentation and sharp argumentation of the 'reflexivity theory' by George Soros. This has driven me to add to this book a further chapter on Soros's recent work, whom I consider myself lucky to have met in the latter stages of my research, and whom I consider not sufficiently well-known and received in the academic world.

In Chap. 7, the last of this long sequence of testimonies, announcers of the epistemological overturning, I wanted to refer to the more contemporary self-critical problems which are present today within the economist's profession, against the profession itself. These problems have reached an extreme level of intensity, whether within the profession or outside of it, from the potential or effective users of it. They are problems which also reveal some contradictions: they have not yet arrived at formulating a systematic and 'holistic' abandonment of the positivistic approach but are also a good measure of the crisis of ideas and methods within the profession. A crisis of ideas and methods, reflecting the demand for a radical change of methods (like this book itself, one based, however, on the critical return to the teaching of a group of great economists, who have been rightly 'celebrated', without being strictly followed).

It is a crisis which is reflected in the superficiality of improvised 'experts' and, through them, also of political decision-makers less prepared to understand to what extent and why, without the support of a vision and methodology, that they 'are driving in the fog'.[9]

On the contrary, they have been ignored by the profession.[10]

The state of affairs, today, has not changed. The personalities (economists and politicians) indeed have, but go along the same useless roads, which are ambiguous and ineffective for a serious conception of public management. But there is always a time to re-launch and enrich the experience of a new systematic methodology of planning in the footsteps of

Frisch and associates. This book would be a small contribution to give back to Frisch et al. the attention that they deserved, and still deserve, in trying to move towards this new scientific methodology.

They should dedicate themselves to a true technical cooperation with political decision-makers, on the quality of the decisional methods (such as the development of the Planning Accounting Framework, with which this book is concerned), which would contribute to making the political debate more advanced and informed, using safer and always more valid instruments of evaluation (elaborated with specialised experts) even for policy-makers.

As true experts, they should move public opinion to react against the political men who do not use their cooperation with the result of deceiving on current institutional policies that do not solve problems—as Leontief used to say—except in the short term, navigating without nautical instruments, at random; this, as well as being ineffective, is also very dangerous. Who will take the responsibility for the government's political-scientific evasion?

It would be necessary to give a guarantee, a technical-contractual one, which could represent a 'hand well visible' and transparent in decision-making, not trusting the 'invisible hand' based on theoretical assumptions and decisional models.

This is the only way to oppose the 'invisible hand' and to implement some relationship between actions and effects, with a certain determination of accounting and accountability.

Furthermore, the accounting relationship would be based on 'decisional' schemes and models (like the 'Oslo' models), which offer to the politicians the choice—with the technical support of technicians, in relative certainty—of which roads to take, at times unavoidably alternative, since the product of trade-offs inherent to the same system of preferred objectives.

In Chap. 7, I tried to give an insight into the most recent good intentions found in the academic world for a radical renewal of economic thinking.

In the hope that the programming approach, outlined at the time by Frisch and associated, and re-launched in the intentions of this trilogy, could be re-discovered with interest for that acclaimed renewal, I also directed attention to the initiative of the Institute for New Economic Thinking of which Joseph Stiglitz recently became promoter and supporter.

I think that, for an effective role of interventions in the life of international organisations and many national governments, the movement of economists and other integrative disciplines would need greater unitary cohesion, armoured against the unavoidable, personal rivalries that certainly will not fade. It would be difficult to find an equally suitable personality who has encompassed similar visibility in his role in the field of economics as Joseph Stiglitz. So, an allusion, even critical, to his work, seems to me appropriate, as a scholar among the more representative for the introduction of a new methodology of planning.

What in this volume I have called 'testimonies' of the methodological overturning, is described in single chapters.[11] Thus I have limited myself here to a thematic anticipation of what can be found in each of the eight chapters of this volume, in respect to all intentions and the central theme of the trilogy.

In such a way, the entire this volume can be considered an interlude, which is inserted between the first and the third part of the trilogy, just to not lose contact with rumours between the end of economics in the late twentieth century and the late revival of attention toward the philosophy and methodology of the great economists analysed in **Vol. I**.

Moreover, considering **Vol. III** of this trilogy, some further methodological steps to understanding the message of **Vol. I** are introduced, to be applied in the new implementation of planning steps and a new general (or potentially globally oriented vision) of the programming approach.

Performance Revolution in the Economic and Political Thinking

The real pillar of the anthology of authors which we have called as a witness of the programming approach and of the reform of accountability needed for a more significant and conscious use of the economic decisions is the recommendation by our economists described and quoted in

Brief Introductory Note to the Chapters of Vol. II   xxvii

chapters of **Vol. I** (Myrdal, Frisch, Tinbergen, Leontief, Johansen and others): the recommendation of associating more and more in the programmes and plans, a monetary accounting with a 'real' accounting (physical or technical accounting).

This gives a basis for a kind of 'revolution' in economic analysis and decisions: in order to manage the economic flows more strictly connected with their performance and results, in a word that have increasingly characterised material production and consumption, and the welfare of people derived, only in terms of 'relative prices' between commodities exchanged. From all this a greater attention is paid to the performances of the expenditure, investments, consumption, labour remunerations and capital measurements, all give the quality of the economies and societies that we live and we want to plan.

The most important argument of the programming approach is those performances of the actions: how to measure them, how to improve them, how to evaluate their impact or effect on the fields of the citizen welfare, and so on.

Consequently, I have decided to close this volume of the trilogy with a panorama of some lasting advancements in economic thinking around the world, to which I dedicated—calling them, in some ways, 'witnesses' of the change in economics—**Vol. II**, Chap. 9, such as the way to pick up some pathways that have just appeared, and selected in different new disciplines, ones still not mature, on which I wish stimulate much colleagues and re-direct their studies of different field.

Briefly the fields are as follows. (1) The social accountability and social indicators as instrumental tools for planning activities and decisions; enlarging the field of phenomena out of the market of traditional production and commodities exchange; with a defined classification of non-priced commodities. A construction of a relative system of accounting integrated with the System of National Account (SNA). (2) The non-profit area of the public and non-public sectors, with special attention to the 'strategic planning' of their activities and the 'engineeringisation' of programme management. (3) The programming initiative aimed at reinforcing and strengthening the cooperative increase of the exchanges between the countries and governments of primary, secondary and tertiary stages, with a communitarian philosophy and objectives, leading to a better exchange of men, women, religious needs and traditions, with tolerant integration, and organised bilateral migrations and technical assistance largely applied under the appropriate role of the United Nations Organization reinforced and reorganised to be more efficient.

Notes to the Brief Introductory Note

1. 'Praxeology' was a term often used at the end of the nineteenth century, in referring to the 'science of human action', variously employed in its history. It was widespread in some scientific works of classification (Louis Bourdeau, *Théorie des sciences: Plan de Science intégrale* 1882; and others). However, the most intense and well-known use was by some authors of the Economic School of Vienna in order to distinguish the sciences of nature from those of 'human action'.

2. See Geoffrey M. Hodgson, 'Can Economics Start from the Individual Alone' in Edward Fullbrook ed., 2005.

3. Ludwig von Mises (and his followers), overall, made use of such argument, not devoid of ambiguities and misunderstandings, which we will mention later in this book, in Chaps. 1 and 2 of the **Vol. I**, dedicated to Myrdal's work, or also in Chap. 1, **Vol. II**, dedicated to the work by von Mises, *Grundprobleme der Nationaloekonomie*, (1933); [translated into English: *Epistemological Problems of Economics* (1960)], as well as in Chap. 4, dedicated to 'decision-based analysis'.

4. The linguistic oxymoron was coined by Karl Menger and—used constantly by von Mises and von Hayek and others—became a brand of the 'Austrian economics'. Von Hayek, was, however, more moderate than von Mises in his radical individualism. Furthermore, I wonder if this had a role in the fact that the first was awarded a Nobel and the second was not.

5. Bruno de Finetti (1906–1985) was an Italian mathematician, wellknown internationally (he was very critical about the mathematics applied to the positivist approach in economics). Bruno de Finetti was a friend and supporter of the 'programming approach' introduced by Ragnar Frisch.

6. Daniel Bell (1911–2011), a well-known American sociologist, one of the first anticipators of the 'post-industrial' society analysis.

7. The associative movements raised within this kind of attention were the American Association of Collegiate School of Planning, the Association

Brief Introductory Note to the Chapters of Vol. II   xxix

of European Schools of Planning and other world-regional associations of Planning Schools, connected in a Global Planning Education Association Network. The main basin of such movement was at the College of Architecture and City Planning.

8. A critical analysis of the 'planning theory' school (of which I consider myself a fellow) was developed in one of my recent books (*Planning theory: from the political debate to the methodological reconstruction*, Springer 2008). In this work, I outlined a methodology that, in my opinion, could lead the school again towards a useful technical-scientific operativity after an 'orgy' of polity, borrowed by sociology, with scarce critical sense. I presented my criticism regarding this enormous quantity of 'positivistic' papers at the first World Congress of those Planning Schools, in Shanghai (China), 2001.

9. An expression much used by Frisch and Leontief some decades ago, when they wanted to affirm how useless and dangerous it would be to economists to venture into public action decisions without these evaluation instruments, such as in the designing of 'decisional models', of a holistic nature, better for organising the agreement and the cohesion—at the highest information level between political and social parties—and at making known, with concrete 'effectiveness,' the expected and shared results, direct and indirect, as feasible. (See many quotations of the texts by the authors indicated above and see also one essay of mine from 1957 on *Economic planning and collective bargaining* in *Studi economici*. In that essay the benefits of a collective bargaining based on a wider framework of structural interdependencies of a national economy is examined.)

10. Frankly, it is difficult for me to find understandable reasons or motivations here.

11. I recommend to the reader that, in this volume, he/she may find it more suitable and useful to go directly to the reading of each author and each argument (as closer to his own study interests), so that he/she does not lose sight of the connection between authors and arguments covered, because they are essential to the understanding of the characteristics of the citations and references for the entire thesis of the trilogy, and not sufficiently significant for the general work of each author introduced in the field.

1

The Programming Approach: As Epistemologically Based, Futuristic Decision and 'Rational Utopia'

1.1 The Logical Foundations of the Decisional Models

We have seen Frisch's insistence on the distinction between *decisional models* and *growth models*: he is very clear on the importance of this distinction.[1]

A second observation concerns an elementary relationship, one between a decisional model and common sense. Frisch is also very clear on this point.

This logical condition is satisfied in asserting that decisional models for use in any and all circumstances, place and time do not exist; there are only *relative* decisional models, which we could call 'situational', that is, tied to the circumstances, places and times that justify them.

In brief, the authors of the paths exhibited (Frisch, Leontief, Tinbergen and others) have been, by their own nature, vision and work, predisposed to blur (so not to see clearly and explicitly) the distinction between the *determinist* or *positivist* approach and the *programming* approach. Therefore, we owe it to them, if we can, to design a clearer planning methodology (one we could call 'planology') as a more radical, alternative,

---

© The Author(s) 2019

F. Archibugi, *The Programming Approach and the Demise of Economics*,

https://doi.org/10.1007/978-3-319-78060-3_1

2   Volume II. Selected Testimonies on the Epistemological...

more effective and less misleading guide to public management (of which this trilogy could constitute one of the first handbooks).

This does not mean, however, that we also have to acknowledge that the authors of these steps have uniformly applied the *programming approach*; even the authors selected in **Vol. II** (regardless of the sector to which they belong), who have perceived the difference in the approaches, may not have always drawn all the theoretical consequences which they should have done.

We will discuss this by using examples that we consider more significant, but certainly not exhaustive.[2]

Let us briefly analyse the evolution performed by the scholars of the *theory of decision* under the following three aspects:

1. that of the relationship between *decisional analysis* and *forecast analysis*; in other words, between the 'programming' approach and the 'forecasting' approach; this concludes in a logical, increasingly clear distinction between *forecasting* and *planning* (1.1);
2. that of the relationship between empirical and theoretical analysis, a relationship that has tormented entire generations of economists and has been the basis of many commonplaces on the crisis and decline of economics itself (1.2);
3. that of the relationship between *descriptive* (deterministic) and *normative* (or prescriptive) analysis, and their role in the development of decision theory, game theory, operational research, problem solving, praxeology and so on.

The first aspect concerns the difference—or the multiple differences—between *programmatic activities* and *predictive activities*, or more simply, between predictions and plans.

The second aspect concerns the relationship between *positive* and *normative* analysis in the decisional processes, that is, the policy (or programmatic)-oriented element of the analysis itself.

The third is that of *operational research* and *system engineering*, and their epistemological foundations, which have contributed to the maturity of the problems of meaning and interpretation in the determinist crisis.

All three aspects have contributed—sometimes in contradictory ways—to establishing the basis of a *meta-disciplinary* approach. Let us call it *programmatic*, one which is dialectically juxtaposed to the *determinist* approach. (The first two aspects are examined in this chapter and the third in Chap. 6, **Vol. II**)

1.2 The Epistemological Basis of Economics (*According to Ludwig von Mises*)

We cannot ignore Ludwig von Mises[3]—the twentieth-century economist who provided an extreme and tenacious defence of economics as an autonomous science which has its basis in itself (in doctrine and practice, with respect to many other attempts to find other genetic, but also structural and methodological bases)—as the first among testimonies of **Vol. II**, in which I had intended to select some critical aspects in the works of some interesting and perhaps unaware forerunners of the *programming approach*, as recommended in this reconsideration of the same basis of economic awareness and this approach.

We already mentioned this when I introduced the advanced and more directly motivated settings by Gunnar Myrdal, which had a completely different origin and influence on the institutional basis in economics, but also on other social sciences. We denied that one can, for these sciences, construct a theory based on rational *a-priorisms*, one valid for use in pragmatic situations for translating efficient actions and preferred objectives from the political economy of every type and genre into collective and decisional processes.

I also highlighted in **Vol. I**, Chap. 1, how much Ludwig von Mises worked towards liberating the progress of social sciences from the epistemology and methodology valid for all other natural sciences, broadening the possibilities and the virtues of praxeology, and totally impeding the great advantages that praxeological and programming approaches—if adopted on a large scale and most of all a 'collective' decisional scale (family, collective community of all types, founded on deep values, shared methods and democratic solidarity)—could have had for all of humanity; approaches that would have obtained respect in regards to the most serious problems of mankind and the search for finding solutions.

4   Volume II. Selected Testimonies on the Epistemological...

This paragraph explains the merits (but also the motives for its failure) of the testimonial work of von Mises in respect to the programming approach; we cannot ignore his contribution in this trilogy.

1.2.1 The Activistic Basis of Knowledge

I will try to reconstruct, in a synthetic way, the system of thought of von Mises (1881–1973) using one of his works, from 1962, which he produced at the end of his working life, and in which it seems he wanted to re-set the methodology of all notable productions, firmly inspired by a liberal vision of economics and political life.

A first step towards a new conception of a general epistemology was made when the epistemology gained a 'permanent' role in human and social sciences. The starting point for this type of epistemology of human sciences is discussed here.

With this preliminary introduction to all his work, von Mises discovered and claimed 'logic and prasseologic' structures of the human mind.

(a) Epistemology without praxeology

> Epistemology deals with the mental phenomena of human life, with man as he thinks and acts. The main deficiency of traditional epistemological attempts is to be seen in their neglect of the praxeological aspects. The epistemologists dealt with thinking as if it were a separate field cut off from other manifestations of human endeavor. They dealt with the problems of logic and mathematics, but they failed to see the practical aspects of thinking. They ignored the praxeological a priori.
>
> [...] The most characteristic trait of modern epistemology is its entire neglect of economics, that branch of knowledge whose development and practical application was the most spectacular event of modern history. (von Mises 1962, pp. 2–3)

(b) The starting point of praxeological thought

> The a priori knowledge of praxeology is entirely different—categorically different—from the a priori knowledge of mathematics or, more precisely, from mathematical a priori knowledge as interpreted by logical positivism.

The starting point of all praxeological thinking is not arbitrarily chosen axioms, but a self-evident proposition, fully, clearly and necessarily present in every human mind. An unbridgeable gulf separates those animals in whose minds this cognition is present from those in whose minds it is not fully and clearly present. Only to the former is the appellation man accorded. The characteristic feature of man is precisely that he consciously acts. Man is Homo agens, the acting animal. (Von Mises, ibid, p. 4)

(c) Critique of Logical Positivism

The essence of logical positivism is to deny the cognitive value of a priori knowledge by pointing out that all a priori propositions are merely analytic. They do not provide new information, but are merely verbal or tautological, asserting what has already been implied in the definitions and premises. Only experience can lead to synthetic propositions. There is an obvious objection against this doctrine, viz., that this proposition that there are no synthetic a priori propositions is in itself a—as the present writer thinks, false—synthetic a priori proposition, for it can manifestly not be established by experience. (von Mises 1962, p. 5)

(d) The reality of the external world

From the praxeological point of view it is not possible to question the real existence of matter, of physical objects and of the external world. Their reality is revealed by the fact that man is not omnipotent. [...]

If he wants to succeed, he must proceed according to methods that are adjusted to the structure of something about which perception provides him with some information. We may define the external world as the totality of all those things and events that determine the feasibility or unfeasibility, the success of failure, of human action. (Von Mises 1962, p. 6)

(e) Causality and teleology

Action is a category that the natural sciences do not take into account. The scientist acts in embarking upon his research work, but in the orbit of natural events of the external world which he explores there is no such thing as action. There is agitation, there is stimulus and response, and, whatever some philosophers may object, there is cause and effect. There is what appears to be an inexorable regularity in the concatenation and sequence of phenomena. There are constant relations between entities that enable the scientist to establish the process called measurement. But there is nothing that would suggest aiming at ends sought; there is no ascertainable purpose.

The natural sciences are causality research; the sciences of human action are teleological. In establishing this distinction between the two fields of human knowledge, we do not express any opinion concerning the question whether the course of all cosmic events is or is not ultimately determined by a superhuman being's design. The treatment of this great problem transcends the range of man's reason and is outside the domain of any human science. It is in the realm that metaphysics and theology claim for themselves.

The purpose to which the sciences of human action refer is not the plans and ways of God, but the ends sought by acting men in the pursuit of their own designs. (von Mises 1962, pp. 6–7)

(f) The categories of action

All the elements of the theoretical sciences of human action are already implied in the category of action and have to be made explicit by expounding its contents. As among these elements of teleology is also the category of causality, the category of action is the fundamental category of epistemology, the starting point of any epistemological analysis.

The very category or concept of action comprehends the concepts of means and ends, of preferring and putting aside, viz., of valuing, of success and failure, of profit and loss, of costs. As no action could be devised and ventured upon without definite ideas about the relation of cause and effect, teleology presupposes causality. (von Mises 1962, p. 8)

1.2.2 The Logical Structure of the Human Mind and of History

(a) The *a-priori* categories

The a priori categories are the endowment that enables man to attain all that is specifically human and distinguishes him from all other beings.

The Programming Approach, As Epistemologically Based...   7

Their analysis is analysis of the human condition, the role man plays in the universe. They are the force that enables man to create and to produce all that is called human civilization. (von Mises 1962, p. 14)

(b) The man and the action

The characteristic feature of man is action. Man aims at changing some of the conditions of his environment in order to substitute a state of affairs that suits him better for another state that suits him less. All manifestations of life and behaviour with regard to which man differs from all other beings and things known to him are instances of action and can be dealt with only from what we may call an activistic point of view. The study of man, as far as it is not biology, begins and ends with the study of human action.

Action is purposive conduct. It is not simply behaviour, but behaviour begot by judgments of value, aiming at a definite end and guided by ideas concerning the suitability or unsuitability of definite means. It is impossible to deal with it without the categories of causality and finality. It is conscious behaviour. It is choosing. It is volition; it is a display of the will. (von Mises 1962, p. 34)

(c) The environment

The category of action is the fundamental category of human knowledge. It implies all the categories of logic and the category of regularity and causality. It implies the category of time and that of value. It encompasses all the specific manifestations of human life as distinguished from the manifestations of man's physiological structure which he has in common with all other animals. In acting, the mind of the individual sees itself as different from its environment, the external world, and tries to study this environment in order to influence the course of the events happening in it. (von Mises 1962, pp. 35–36)

(d) Valuation

The failure of the attempts to apply the methods and the epistemological principles of the natural sciences to the problems of human action is caused by the fact that these sciences have no tool to deal with valuing. In the sphere of the phenomena they study there is no room for any purposive behaviour. The physicist himself and his physical research are entities outside the orbit he investigates. Judgments of value cannot be perceived by the observational attitudes of the experimenter and cannot be described in the protocol sentences of the language of physics. Yet they are, also from the viewpoint of the natural sciences, real phenomena, as they are a necessary link in chains of events that produce definite physical phenomena. (Von Mises 1962, pp. 37–38)

(e) Two branches…

Praxeology is a priori. It starts from the a priori category of action and develops out of it all that it contains. For practical reasons praxeology does not as a rule pay much attention to those problems that are of no use for the study of the reality of man's action, but restricts its work to those problems that are necessary for the elucidation of what is going on in reality. Its intent is to deal with action taking place under conditions that acting man has to face. This does not alter the purely aprioristic character of praxeology. It merely circumscribes the field that the individual praxeologists customarily choose for their work. They refer to experience only in order to separate those problems that are of interest for the study of man as he really is and acts from other problems that offer a merely academic interest. The answer to the question whether or not definite theorems of praxeology apply to a definite problem of action depends on the establishment of the fact whether or not the special assumptions that characterize this theorem are of any value for the cognition of reality. To be sure, it does not depend on the answer to the question whether or not these assumptions correspond to the real state of affairs that the praxeologists want to investigate. The imaginary constructions that are the main—or, as some people would rather say, the only—mental tool of praxeology describe conditions that can never be present in the reality of action. Yet they are indispensable for conceiving what is going on in this reality. Even the most bigoted advocates of an empiricist interpretation of the methods of economics employ the imaginary construction of an evenly rotating economy (static equilibrium), although such a state of human affairs can never be realized. (von Mises 1962, p. 41)

(f) Praxeology: finality is the fundamental category

According von Mises, the natural sciences do not know anything about final causes.

For praxeology, finality is the fundamental category. But praxeology abstracts from the concrete content of the ends humans are aiming at. It is history that deals with the concrete ends. For history, the main question is: What was the meaning the actors attached to the situation in which they found themselves and what was the meaning of their reaction, and, finally, what was the result of these actions? The autonomy of history or, as we may say, of the various historical disciplines, consists in their dedication to the study of meaning.

We should emphasise again that when historians say 'meaning', they refer to the meaning that individual men—the actors themselves and those affected by

> their actions or the historians—saw in the actions. History as such has nothing in common with the point of view of philosophies of history that pretend to know the meaning that God or a quasi-God—such as the material productive forces in the scheme of Marx—attaches to the various events. (Von Mises 1962, p. 43)

(g) Logical character of praxeology and history

> Praxeology is a priori. All its theorems are products of deductive reasoning that starts from the category of action. The questions whether the judgments of praxeology are to be called analytic or synthetic and whether or not its procedure is to be qualified as "merely" tautological are of verbal interest only.
>
> What praxeology asserts with regard to human action in general is strictly valid without any exception for every action. There is action and there is the absence of action, but there is nothing in between. Every action is an attempt to exchange one state of affairs for another and everything that praxeology affirms with regard to exchange refers strictly to it. In dealing with every action we encounter the fundamental concepts end and means, success or failure, profit or loss, costs. An exchange can be either direct or indirect, i.e., effected through the interposition of an intermediary stage. Whether a definite action was indirect exchange has to be determined by experience. But if it was indirect exchange, then all that praxeology says about indirect exchange in general strictly applies to it.
>
> Every theorem of praxeology is deduced by logical reasoning from the category of action. It partakes of the apodictic certainty provided by logical reasoning that starts from an a priori category.

Into the chain of praxeological reasoning the praxeologist introduces certain assumptions concerning the conditions of the environment in which an action takes place. Then he tries to find out how these special conditions affect the result to which his reasoning must lead. The question whether or not the real conditions of the external world correspond to these assumptions is to be answered by experience. But if the answer is in the affirmative, all the conclusions drawn by logically correct praxeological reasoning strictly describe what is going on in reality. (Von Mises 1962, p. 44)

Experience is always experience of the past. There is no experience and no history of the future. It would be unnecessary to repeat this truism if it were not for the problem of business forecasting by statisticians, about which something will be said later. (Von Mises 1962, p. 45)

1.3 Programming Versus Forecasting, the Crucial Point of the Overturning Approach to the Future (*According to Jan Tinbergen*)

It has been noted that one of the direct consequences of the programming approach (a consequence or a determining factor?) is that of making a clear distinction between forecasting and planning.

Both terms, before this distinction was made, were confusing enough in their relation to each other, though not in their nature (everybody was ready to acknowledge a certain difference between the two types of activity). As Frisch clearly states repeatedly of the 'types' of forecast, the attitude of the observer (or *onlooker*, as Frisch calls him) was interwoven with that of the decision-maker in a technically (and logically) improper way, creating what he called 'half-logic' (see **Vol. I**, Chap. 5, Sect. 5.6.3).

We will now see how other authors have felt the need to mark a distinction between forecasting and programming. We do so in order to separate the planning process, and therefore the programming approach, from the mixed approach to a positivist analysis of forecasting, a technology based on methods predicated on standard models and parameters, where the arbitrary nature of decision-makers has not been taken into account.

In fact, a less qualified but more widely disseminated scientific literature (see, for example, many—but not all—of the reports of the 'Club of Rome') did not take proper account the clear separation between forecasting and programming models, which has been—thanks to Frisch's work—a 'canonic' principle of the programming approach.

This is one of the factors (though probably not the most important one) for the credibility crisis of programming studies and of their decline.

Frisch was not alone in highlighting the reasons why the programming approach should be preferred to an approach which merely forecasts. Jan Tinbergen developed the argument in two very important essays which are relevant to our discussion but not easily accessible.[4] The substance of his argument is that while both approaches have to work with unknowns, the unknowns in programming are more easily controllable than those in forecasting.

> I defend the thesis that planning constitutes a better approach to the future than forecasting. In this context planning is characterized by setting targets for the future and considering the instruments to attain the targets as the unknowns of the planning problem. In contrast, forecasting will be understood to mean that the instruments of socio-economic policy are given and are not changed; here the target variables are the unknowns of the problem. (Tinbergen 1971a, p. 1) PSC Special reprints and Permission

It is well known that the 'operational' relationship targets or instruments are at the root of Tinbergen's decisional model.

In Sect. 6.5 of **Vol. II**, however, we recalled the widespread reserve (in particular by Frisch and Leontief) about the 'fixed-objectives' approach adopted by Tinbergen in general and in advance.[5] On the other hand, there is a legitimate concern that creating instruments without defining their targets is not an appropriate basis for planning.

Returning to the theme of programming versus forecasting, in the second of the texts cited (1971b), Tinbergen expressed his reservations regarding long-term forecasting in a more explicit manner.

> A growing number of scientists understood that a profound study in the future could significantly contribute to the future wellbeing of mankind.

And from some time now, it has been defined that to govern is to prevent, to avoid a certain number of characteristic inconsistencies of improvisation. Today, a single question is asked: how to study the future. And this, as of today, has never been agreed upon unanimously. Firstly, there are already two types of research in practice, whose products can be respectively called predictions and plans. The predictions share the common fact of being based on the hypothesis of no change in regards to the regime; that is, that the means of the political socio-economy will not change. The plans are characterized as the best development among alternative possibilities.

Our first theory will be for prolonged periods, let's say, greater than five year periods, the predictions that do not possess a very reduced utility. This reduction resides in the same nature of the predictions. The hypothesis that no change in a regime can be useful for a period of a few months or a few years, but it does not justify the periods that we are interested in. [...] After this inconvenience, another one is added: that of the weakness of our knowledge of socio-economic mechanisms over long periods of time. In general, it is much more simply to identify the operating forces in a short time period that determine the forces, whose effects do not demonstrate that, progressively, a circumstance that often hinders us to distinguish the effects of the multi-faceted influences which determine the movements of the socio-economic variables—not even speaking of those psychological ones, cultural ones, etc…

Consequently, the future study with the help of plans, instead of estimates, is needed, despite how difficult it may be. In other terms, we are forced to take into account ourselves, as essential components of our research of the future, of the necessary changes of regime [...]. And, at least in a structural category, the principal figures of a plan will be less imprecise than those of an estimate: in other words, the unpredictable component of the key figures will be more weak for a plan than for an estimate [...] (Tinbergen 1971b, pp. 1–2)

On this point Leontief too is a very clear logician:

In its published form a national economic plan, or rather the statistical appendix to its text, can be visualized as a detailed, systematic annual survey of manufacture and agriculture, of transportation, and of trade and the federal and local budgets. However, it describes the state of the economy not for a given past year—as does the *Statistical Abstract* or the *Census of Manufacture*—but rather for five years in advance and, in a more summary form, for a much longer interval of time stretching into the future. This does not mean that a plan must be rigidly adhered to over the entire period of say, four or five years. On the contrary, the plan should be revised each year in the light of past experience and newly acquired information and pushed out as a moving average one year ahead.

A plan is not a forecast. The whole idea of planning assumes the possibility of choice among alternative feasible scenarios. Feasibility is the key word. (Leontief 1977, pp. 150–152)

Later, after other considerations about the degree of disaggregation to be preferred in the Programming Accounting Framework (see pp. 150–152 of the *Essays in Economics* (Vol. Two, 1977) by Leontief), he concludes:

Choice among alternative scenarios is the clue to rational national economic planning rather than crystal-ball gazing that, with the rise of general uncertainty, became a marketable product of the economic forecasting industry. [...]

The important practical difference in making a choice between alternative national economic plans and selecting an appropriate set of national goals can best be explained by the following example:

A friend invites me for dinner in a first-class restaurant and asks that I supply him with a general description of my taste so that he can order the food in advance. Unable to describe my—or anyone else's—tastes in general terms, I prefer to see the menu and then select, without hesitation the combination of dishes that I like.

Confronted with alternative national economic plans—each described in great detail, particularly which respect to items they are likely to affect my own well-being and my personal assessment of equity and fairness of the whole—I would have no difficulty in designing which of them I would prefer or, at least consider not inferior to any other. I could do this, despite my inability to describe my preferences, my predilections and my prejudices in general terms. A philosopher, a social psychologist, or an historian might succeed in arriving at such a generalization by inference based on an interpretation of my utterances or, even better, of specific choices I have actually made before. But this, of course, is an entirely different matter.

This, I submit, is the reason why a planning process should start out not with the formulation of what theoretical economists refer to as the general 'objective function' but with elaboration of alternative several possible future state of the economy. (Leontief, ibidem, 1977, p. 153)

14   Volume II. Selected Testimonies on the Epistemological...

This is a difference that, in principle, may be obvious. While forecasting tries to anticipate the future organisation of an economic system resulting from its undisturbed advance, a product of the interaction between constants and variables which the analyst will try to guess, planning, on the other hand, fixes in the future the desired organisation of such an economic system and searches for the modifying interventions which will be necessary to bring the system from condition A (the status quo) to condition B (the desired condition).

In short, the differences between planning and forecasting, as different approaches to the future, concern the following four points:

- the admission/non-admission of changes in what Tinbergen calls the 'regime' of the economy;
- the management of the 'uncertainty' component, or the instrumental nature (in planning) or the substantial one (in forecasting);
- the presence/absence of a search for optimality;
- the degrees of freedom (the number of possible future alternatives) recognised in the system in its evolution.[6]

Frisch is not only interested in underlining the total diversity of approach between forecast and programming but is also engaged in denigrating forecasting activity in practice.

> The various econometric attempts at macroeconomic forecasting that have been made in the last decades, have in general not been so successful as many had hoped they would be. The same pessimistic conclusion cannot be drawn with regard to the use of macroeconomic decision models. Personally I have always been somewhat sceptical about the possibility of macroeconomic forecasting of the evolution that will follow from given initial conditions (because this evolution may depend on individual decisions too big to be covered up in the behaviour of averages). I have believed that analytical effort would pay better dividends—now and in the immediate future—if it were directed into the field of decision models where the reasoning runs: 'If such and such measures are taken and such and such conditions are fulfilled during the time considered, one will most likely create a tendency in such and such a direction'. (Frisch 1957, pp. 1–2)

1.4 The 'Utopia' Role as Requirement in Economic Theory (*Viewpoints by Bruno de Finetti*)

By other means we have come to perceive a clear demarcation between deterministic analysis ('what is') and programming analysis ('what ought to be or could be'). It is a question of understanding the disengagement of a possible future from any reference concerning the past (seen as unique 'reality'). In other words, how do we create the concept of the 'utopic future', that is a future that is still non-existent, but not impossible?

This way of perceiving the still non-existent but strongly feasible, possible future—a *utopia*, literally a 'nowhere'—is the approach of 'scientific utopism'. As such, it is similar to the programming approach and historically has represented a premise and an important starting point for it.

On this point, it may be of interest to recall two authors who, though coming from very different disciplinary backgrounds, both arrive at the same conclusion: 'utopia' is a revision and reconstruction after the crisis of economics as a science.

Even this approach may be considered a step towards the epistemological separation between knowledge and programming that this book intends to identify and advocate.

The first of the selected authors, Bruno de Finetti,[7] is a well-known Italian mathematician interested in the methodology of economics.[8] He consciously began to prefer the word 'utopia' to other less risky and misleading words to radically define a concept of epistemological planning, and also as an 'escape route' for economic science from its crisis, which is due essentially to the 'determinist' approach.

Bruno de Finetti, in his essay 'Utopia as an essential requirement for any significant approach in economics',[9] feels that we lose something in the mere relationship between descriptive and normative sciences: we lose the capacity to transcend the existent, which he considers necessary for discovery and progress. And he also explains the reasons for utopian approach, through a discussion of the relationship between 'descriptive' and 'normative' concepts.

He argues for his thesis thus:

In a certain sense, we can say that to speak about 'utopia' is useless. In effect, it would be sufficient to speak [...] about the distinction between descriptive sciences and normative sciences (*Marschak*), and sustain the interpretation of economics as normative science.[10] However, using these aseptic terms, the distinction, pertaining to abstract discussions on the place of economics in the vault of sciences, seems irrelevant; its actual, revolutionary meaning is not perceived, or—sometimes—it is considered to be applicable only to marginal questions and aspects of economic activities rather than to the situations and structures of the economy as a whole.

In order to break the circle of such misunderstanding (innocent or interested as it may be), it is worthwhile to proclaim the need and the intention to found economics on utopia. [...]

But, what is it a utopia? And what are the motives which cause it to be strongly appreciated or mocked?

It could be a simple fantasy about the way to be and the way the world works, according to somebody's wishes; in that case it can, at the most, be a cue, a push or a mirage.

However, the fact that it is fruit of a daydream should not be condemned: all new or useful (or not) things, every discovery and form of progress, are first of all the fruit of fantasy. (de Finetti 1973b, pp. 39–40, English tr. Archibugi)

Coming to the core of the problem, de Finetti continues:

The utopian approach of economics consists exactly in examining the possibility of effective working of imagined systems as mental 'utopian' schemes.

Its specific task of economics consists, preliminarily, in analysing the *aims and ideologies at the basis of the studied utopian model*. This serves only to see to which 'value judgements' it corresponds, so that everyone (scholar or layman) can take a stand according to his/her own preferences. These tastes and preferences (mainly social or moral) can be influenced, but this is the task of propaganda of concepts, be they philosophical, social, political, humanitarian, religious, educational, and so on: these also have an essential role, but in a distinct and separate sphere.

The specific task of economic science, in the utopian approach that is urgent to promote, consists, on the contrary,

The Programming Approach, As Epistemologically Based...   17

(a) in translating into a precise form the *desiderata* initially expressed in a more or less vague and indeterminate way, evaluating their intrinsic consistency and suggesting—if necessary—how to modify or integrate them;

(b) in outlining some forms of social organisation which aims to lead to desired situations, assessing and comparing their capacity to work in a simple, concise and effective way, tending towards stability rather than breaking up and favouring the rise of dysfunction, trouble and abuse. (de Finetti 1973b, pp. 40–41)

This task—de Finetti acknowledges—is not easy.

Evidently, the functionality, demonstrated in the paper, does not guarantee good functionality in practice: this can be impeded by many general causes, which are difficult to convert into an abstract framework, or contingent causes (such as people's immaturity to understand, accept or implement a new and perhaps better system, in respect of that familiar one).

The utopian point of view—in this sense—does not intend to deny or underestimate these difficulties; it affirms, rather, that these difficulties must not become prejudicial, and that the purpose of studying and promoting renewed and improved forms of socio-economic organisation must be encouraged as far as possible in compatibility with effective implementation difficulties. (de Finetti 1973b, pp. 41–42)

He concludes:

A utopia will almost never be a model to be executed in a practical form. Vice versa, none of the many and varied possible radical improvements needed by today's very poor forms and structures could really be conceived and implemented without having first been conceived, studied and examined in the form of a utopia. It would be like trying to build a complex machine without first drawing up some designs. (de Finetti 1973b, pp. 41–42)

1.4.1 Risk of Misleading Conceptualisation

From this vision, de Finetti draws some implications regarding the concept of economic theory itself. First, he outlines three possible attitudes towards economics, considering that:

- it could be subject to immutable concepts and laws;
- it could be subject to concepts and laws deterministically dependent on historical circumstances which are not controlled by the will of man;
- it could be open to "all solutions which are not technically contradictory" and therefore to any possible solution. (de Finetti 1973b, p. 43)

He then offers this reasoning:

It is clear that, in leaning towards the first two attitudes, any attempt to put economics at the service of, rather than as a tyrant over, mankind, and indeed any examination of this theme would be like a foolish academic and 'utopian' ambition, in the most disparaging sense of the term 'utopian'. On the contrary, an inclination towards the third, the mere construction of a 'utopia' (in the sense of a model we must strive to create), constitutes a useful and constructive effort in the field of economy, so that any innovation or reform logically conceived should be studied as a feasible project. Thus we cannot deny nor ignore that any change can meet difficulties because of 'misoneism', conflict of interests, etc., but we can exclude the possibility that change be stopped by preclusions attributed to alleged and self-styled *economic principles*. (de Finetti 1973b, pp. 43–44, emphasis added)

In this way, de Finetti refuses the possibility of searching for objective laws, without prejudices or judgements of worth. The idea of an economy free from judgements of worth, and the search for a 'neutral' or 'positive' working principle, for him means the end of economics as a useful science.

Being inclined to the third attitude, de Finetti believes in:

the clear *overturning* of a principle that many economists have sustained (and perhaps some still sustain) as a requirement for 'science': the exclusion of value judgements.

On the contrary, if we accept the aforementioned attitude, 'value judgements' are the first indispensable premise. Starting from the preference criteria inspired by them, and bearing in mind the objective confining circumstances (availability of the resources) and seeking the best technological theoretically achievable solutions (and the absence of institutional constraints, after which, the institutional structure remains to be identified) and the set of organisational-juridical-accounting conventions that are not based on preconceived or traditional ideas, this proves to be the most suitable and practical method of achieving an almost perfect situation.

The Programming Approach, As Epistemologically Based...   **19**

In other words, we should introduce *institutional constraints* that are the least damaging possible (nearly non-existent) towards the *achievement of the selected socio-economic objectives* (de Finetti 1973b, p. 44, emphases added)

Here it is difficult not to recognise the same Myrdalian, Frischian and Leontefian spirit and atmosphere (set out in **Vol. I**):

- a clear distinction between the descriptive approach and the programmatic one (even from the analysis of reality itself);
- a concern for the importance of clearly separating the question of preference, taking into account the limiting circumstances, from that of identifying the institutional structure capable of implementing the optimal solution in the most practical way;
- the 'overturning' of the scientific concept of economics (as a social science) in so far as it is related to the presence of goals to be achieved and social purposes to be evaluated and chosen, and not to alleged objective laws to be assumed with 'neutrality'.

If, in the quotations of de Finetti that I have selected, we replace the expression 'utopian approach' with that of 'programming approach', it seems to me that we could extract an excellent introduction to the latter.

On the other hand, the above passages from Bruno de Finetti's essay contain a series of mathematical arguments supporting the criticism of the conventional paradigms of economics, which demonstrate how Frisch and de Finetti had similar ideas here.[11]

1.4.2 Critique of Over-Simplification in the Abuse of the Language of Mathematics

Notwithstanding, de Finetti does not lose the opportunity to criticise, as a mathematician, the lack of utility in employing the formal mathematical language in economical reasoning, and the danger of falling into error, over-complexity and over-simplification by so doing.

The usual application of mathematics to economics—those that appear the most obvious for those closed within the scope of current systems—consists in the immediate consideration of what is already expressed in quantity (i.e. prices, monetary values, aggregate macro-economic quantities, etc.). From this comes the illusion that such quantities play a central role and are meaningful in absolute terms. (de Finetti 1973b, ibidem, pp. 21–22)

While for de Finetti the engagement of an autonomous re-thinking of the problems, free from conditions and contaminations,

consists in acquiring the critical awareness of innumerable deformations deriving, in economics and in economic life, from thinking and acting in terms of prices, money and derived notions […] a linear function (value = sum of product quantity per prices) is useful for accounting purposes, but much less significant for economic purposes (in the case of effective or 'shadow' prices) (de Finetti 1973b, pp. 44–47)

De Finetti also deals with a series of criticisms of the meaning of current economic accounting, which we will not comment on here because they have been widely discussed and shared. Even though they have not been abandoned in current analysis, these 'deformations'—as de Finetti calls them—continue to be ignored in practice in political decisions. Thus, they have not found a way of overturning the approach to economic analysis and the analysis of economic policies.

1.5   Economic Theory as 'Fiction'

The next author I wish to reference is Daniel Bell (a well-known sociologist from Harvard). Bell also arrives at his utopian conception through a critique of the entire historical path of economics, offering it as an escape from its organic crisis (which, in his opinion, had reached radical dimensions). He comes to that conclusion in a superb, relatively unknown essay, 'Models and reality in economic discourse' (1981),[12] which goes beyond his other, justifiably famous works.[13]

Revisiting the historic debate of whether economics is a descriptive or normative science, he raises the question of the substance of the social sciences as 'sciences' (this is related to our discussions on the work of Myrdal in Chaps. 1 and 2).

He wonders:

if the general equilibrium that is defined in theory, is a *fiction, a normative standard* against which to judge an +, or a description of how economic exchanges (if unhampered) take place in accordance with the 'laws' of economy. Can theory 'model' reality? (Bell 1981, p. 53)

And in another part of the same text, he says:

Yet the crucial question is whether the opposite of rational is irrational or non-rational, and whether or not non-rational motivations can provide a valid assumption for clear economic behaviour i.e., the behaviour which seeks to enhance the wealth and welfare of mankind. (Bell 1981, pp. 70–71)

Daniel Bell poses the question of the 'fiction' of economic theory through an interesting and rapid excursus into economics itself, which merits a quick digression.

In his view, the history of economics presents at least four different ways of defining its own substance while, however, indifferently using the same terms: 'nature', 'natural rate/degree/level' of 'economic laws', and 'economic science'.

The first way, and the 'Smith's way' is individualistic, but not egotistic, and therefore 'economics […] is inextricably normative and moral' (p. 56).

As for Marshall, 'moral impulses are still evident', but 'morals and money are separate'; 'economic laws are just those generalizations—those regularities—about human behaviour which can be measured in money terms, because men perform the ordinary business of life, seeking the best advantages for themselves'; 'economics […], according to Marshall, deals with the maximization of utility' [in a framework in which] '(1) the distinction between "needs" and "wishes" […] is eliminated and all requests are treated as desires; (2), social welfare is defined only in terms of individual welfare; (3) every individual is the best judge of his own welfare; and (4) the welfare of individuals should not be comparable' (Bell 1981, p. 56).

Walras' idea of *tatonnement*, where individuals feel their way in response to external signals, is applicable here. Here society is like nature (Darwinian nature) in which 'adaptation is the natural process through

22 Volume II. Selected Testimonies on the Epistemological...

which selection takes place. No single group of persons can control it, for the number of desires are so vast and different that no one could match these coherently, like a giant switchboard or computer' (Bell 1981, p. 57).

Then Bell recalls Austrian economist Karl Menger, for whom 'society is an evolutionary system in which a "spontaneous order" arises out of the mutual adaptation of individuals, and the whole is integrated by means of natural processes, quite similar to biological processes.' And according to this, 'human calculations alone cannot anticipate and prepare for diversity which is the dominant characteristic of creative natural forces. Planning is therefore restrictive and self-defeating, limiting the ability of individuals to make their own adaptive responses.'

Bell adds that, according to von Hayek, 'economics, while integral to freedom, has little relation to virtue. This view is almost diametrically opposed to that of the ancient philosophers.'

[My text written in the previous paragraph is my interpolation from that of Bell, from *Models and Reality in Economic Discourse*, 1981, pp. 54–58].

Finally, Bell deals with the model of general equilibrium in the formulation perfected by Arrow, Debreu, Koopmans and others, defining this as:

A precious set of movements, a celestial clockwork—to use the old image of Laplace—in which perfect competition and optimal allocation of resources operate like an Invisible Hand, except that this Invisible Hand is neither God, the origin of benevolence, nor the spontaneous adaptation of Nature, but a Mathematical Theorem, a set of 'coefficients of transformation' which are sublimely indifferent—as by Barone earlier and Lange and Lerner later pointed out—to the private ownership of the means of production or to a decentralized price system of market socialism. It is a work of art, so compelling that one thinks of the celebrated painting of Apelles who painted a cluster of grapes so realistic that birds would come and pick at them. (Bell, ibidem, ed. it. 1981, pp. 57–58)

Thus, Bell asks himself: 'Is this model real?' He continues:

Walras had thought of his model as actually describing how competitive markets would become into equilibrium. He thought that the trading prices in actual markets would be the same, eventually, as those which would solve the system of simultaneous equations. Yet the problem of

The Programming Approach, As Epistemologically Based...   23

disequilibrium in different kinds of markets—such as labor markets – is too obviously a real-world problem. The conclusion is inescapable. There is no empirical guarantee that the blind 'groping' of the market produces a set of 'clearing prices' that are identical with the underlying set of equations. If the model, as elaborated by Arrow, et al., has validity, it is only as a 'fiction'—logical, elegant, self-contained, but a fiction nonetheless. (Bell 1981, p. 58)

1.5.1 'Four Bridges Towards Reality'

After having divided the great periods of economic evolution, Bell provides another interesting and unconventional classification of the effort that economists have made to connect theory to reality. He calls this the 'four bridges towards reality'. These 'bridges' are:

1. the quantity theory of money (empirical studies on the relationship between short-term variations in the quantity of money and prices);
2. the theory of monopolistic competition;
3. the Keynesian 'revolution';
4. the Phillips curve.

Each of these four bridges is considered by Bell an attempt to communicate between the land of theory and the land of reality—a sort of compromise between theory and empiricism.

The four bridges make great use of statistical observations, managed by econometric models, in the hope of finding evaluation tools (ex post) for policy interventions and decisions (ex ante).

This is the 'crucial' point on which Bell rightly questions himself, (but, in my opinion, without giving the right answers).

1.5.2 An Impasse

Bell, and with him many others who have perceived the 'impasse' that economics has reached, are not content merely to find the equilibrium between theory and empirically observed facts.

But, according to Bell, there are two fundamental problems—one might even say fallacies—in the utilization of economic models to understand the ups-and-downs of economic activities. One is that economic theory, in Marshall's opinion, is not a generalization about human behaviour, but, according to Pareto, derives from an 'ideal type' of one kind of action, a so-called 'logical action'. And these may well be a minority of economically significant actions.

The other is that an economic system is not an economy; it is an analytical abstraction, an ideal, a closed world where resources flow freely in response to price, where comparative advantage dictates the shift in resource utilization, where labour is not people but units of skill (or lack thereof), where there are no political boundaries, and where machinery, capital, and commodities distribute themselves to the maximum benefit of 'mankind'. This is a utopia […]

In short, economic theory is a convenient fiction, an 'as if', against which to measure the habitual, irrational, logical, egoistic, self-interested, bigoted, altruistic actions of individuals, firms or governments—but it is not a model of reality. But even as a fictional ideal, it is inherently problematic. (Bell 1981, pp. 69–70)

However, we must ask ourselves, if it is not a model of reality, what use is it? What is the purpose of economic theory?

Thus, even if we agree with Bell's 'crucial point', that economics is no more than a 'fiction', a utopia, what is the advantage of having ascertained this? I repeat, if it is not a model for reality, what use is it? Does economic theory have a purpose? Indeed, if it does not work as a model for reality, it will be ill equipped to interpret or describe that reality. And then what? Does it matter?

We do not need to know what the reality is, but what it could be according to certain programmatic purposes.

Like Myrdal (and many others before), Bell too perceives that economics, from its beginnings, has been founded on a mistaken epistemological basis. It has been unable to catalogue its evolution.

Economics has, throughout its history, pursued a false reality, a non-existent 'positive' reality, laws of reality which do not exist, a chimera. It has pursued and researched a 'positive' rather than a 'purposeful' reality.

1.5.3 Rationality or Time?

Consistently with the whole evaluation of the journey of economic thinking, Bell asserts:

> The economic theory, that developed in the West in the last 200 years…has been a-historical and abstractly analytic. But that is precisely the point. Economic theory, by and large, is based on the model of classical mechanics and operates in the image of natural science. The model leads to the idea of an 'equilibrium' the fulcrum of which is 'perfect competition'. The result is a basically mechanistic view of human behaviour, and when discordances occur, there ensues a series of desperate and twisted efforts to square the 'nominal magnitudes' (i.e. the irrational) with the 'real' magnitudes (the rational) that underlie the system…. How Hegelian!
>
> But this enterprise ignores a crucial distinction. Classical mechanics are constitutive of nature, seeking to discern the intrinsic order which is hidden in the property of the system. Economics is not constitutive. It is a constructed logic, at best an 'as if' model of how certain resources would be distributed if individuals acted in a specific logical way.
>
> But there is no single 'underlying structure' in society. Since men act variously by habit and custom, irrationally or zealously, by conscious design to change institutions or redesign social arrangements, there is no intrinsic order, there are no 'economic laws constituting the 'structure' of the economy; there are only different patterns of historical behaviour. Thus, economics, and economic theory, cannot be a 'closed system'. Social sciences are necessarily partial 'prisms' selecting out different facets of behaviour, in order to understand the causes of change and its meaning. And what sets their boundaries are not the 'essential' properties of the subject matter, but the different questions put, which is why they are so permeable.
>
> Keynes himself—we may recall—raised doubts about the possibility of predicting human behaviour, especially when such behaviour is based on variable expectations. To put it more formally, as G.L. Shackle does in his book, *Epistemics & Economics*, the economic theorist can choose either 'rationality' or 'time'. The theory which rejects time can set forth propositions such as subjective marginalism, partial or general equilibrium. But the introduction of time not only produces uncertainty; it also necessitates understanding 'non-rational' behaviour if it is to deal with the choices human beings make. (Bell 1981, pp. 76–78)

1.5.4 An 'Interpretative' Economic Theory (*According to Bell*)

Bell concludes with an 'interpretative' economic theory which anticipates the epistemological arguments of the programming approach, but without a clear acknowledgment of this.

> What are the roads to reconstruction? What ultimately provides direction for the economy, as Veblen pointed out long ago, is not the *price system* but the *value system* of the culture in which the economy is embedded. The price system is a mechanism for the relative allocation of goods and services, not in accordance with human nature (or utility maximization), but within the framework of the existing distribution of income and the cultural patterns of social wants. Accordingly, economic guidance can only be distributive as equitably as the cultural value system which shapes it.
>
> An 'interpretative' economic theory might have to consider that its own analysis only makes economic sense when joined to sociology. For the hard-nosed economist, this is a fate feared worse than the pox, yet one finds, pleasantly, that even so rigorous a theorist as Robert M. Solow, in his presidential address to the American Economic Association (December 1979), seeking to formulate a theory of wage stickiness to fill in the chinks in Keynesian theory, resorts to explanations such as 'social conventions' and 'codes of good behaviour enforced by social pressure' to explain the 'persistence of disequilibrium in the labor market'. And he concludes, 'Economic man is a social…category.' That, too, is a modest start toward the reconstruction of economic theory.
>
> An economic theory has to understand its underpinnings not only in relations to politics, but to political theory. The great paradox of all modern social theory is that political philosophy, going back to Machiavelli, Hobbes, and Rousseau, saw men as being ruled by appetite, passions, or will, while economic theory has defined human actions as rational behaviour—albeit such rationality is defined in purely instrumental and functional terms. Only Max Weber, among modern theorists, has sought to sketch a theory of social action that takes into account the rational and the non-rational, and to look at economics and administration, politics and religion, in terms of the two modes.
>
> Within that context, economic theory has to integrate political practice within its body of understandings. Price theory is distributive. Resources

flow to the most profitable (or least costly) places. Necessarily, some persons lose; what Schumpeter has called 'creative destruction' or, more recently, Lester Thurow has called the *zero-sum game*. But political practice is redistributive, responding to the weights (votes, money, power) of the different interest, functional, ethnic, advantaged and disadvantaged groups in the society.

And, finally, economic theory has to return to time (in the logical sense) and to history (in the empirical fact) in order to be responsive to the complex new social arrangements that derive from the widening of scales and new arenas of economic and social actions. The world of Adam Smith was one of thousands of small family firms, of visible merchants and customers, so that Smith could look to civil society, not government, as the arena in which competition would be regulated by custom and ethics, rather than by contract and law. A post-industrial order is one in which eco- nomic innovation is ruled by the codification of theoretical knowledge, yet contemporary economic theory, rooted in a world of agriculture and industry, has no means of measuring the 'output' of science, or little, even, of technological change. Yet without such understandings, how effective can economic theory be as guidance, let alone as a 'model' of the economic reality?

The crux of my argument is an epistemological one. Economic theory, unlike physics, is not constitutive of a single underlying reality. Nor can it be, pace Alfred Marshall (and Gary Becker), timeless generalizations about human behaviour. In consequence, economics cannot be, as its model in classical mechanics, a 'closed I system' which ignores change or the effort to discern specific patterns of change.

Does this mean the abandonment of the powerful logical engine, of rationality and equilibria, of maximization and markets, to the vagaries of sociology and the unrestrained wiles of politics? Not at all. 'At least from the time of the physiocrats and Adam Smith', Paul Samuelson has observed, 'there has never been absent from the main body of economic literature, the feeling that in some sense perfect competition represented an optimal situation'. We have also seen, in recent years, the growth of a large body of literature in welfare economics which, deriving from Pareto-optimality, defines a set of optimal outcomes for allocations of resources and distributions of incomes. But this is a divergence, and a necessary one, from the positivist tradition which has ruled economic theory. The corollary of all this is that economic theory should not be taken as a 'model' (or template) of how human beings behave, for these will always be inadequate, but as a 'Utopia', a set of ideal standards against which one can debate and judge different policy actions and their consequences. That, it seems to me, is the meaningful role of any social 'science' in theorizing about human affairs. (Bell 1981, pp. 78–80)

Bell's conclusion is certainly convincing, but not completely satisfying. The attempts made by economic theory, throughout the centuries of its history, and even more recent developments (the four versions examined by Bell, which he calls the four bridges laid between economic 'theory' and reality) do not seem to have given a 'realistic' response. They attempt to fix reality itself in an ahistorical, static position, and, in doing so, lose any sense of realism.

These are 'theories' that are founded on an analysis and evaluation of reality ex-post. However, reality is always in movement; it is dynamic, and the factors that have configured it thus can always be modified, in the past that is known to us. Many of those theories have been criticised over time for seeming extremely heavily influenced and conditioned by circumstances of time. Their ability to regain validity exists in the attempt to connect them to the circumstances that have influenced and prompted them, not in a positive way (as is the norm for the existent) but in a programming way (or teleological, praxeological, finalistic, planning, or any other term one may prefer to use), as an opportunity for a future which does not yet exist, that is, a 'utopian' one.

Bell thus attempts to legitimise the theoretical construction of behavioural models, assuming them to be archetypes of rationality, regardless of the realism they contain.

The operation is interesting because it is very similar to a programming approach, on the condition that it is not simply applied to situations of positive analysis (e.g. 'how do people behave in relation to a rational behavioural model?') and not in situations of effective decisional analysis (e.g. 'how should people behave to obtain this or that result?'; 'what can/should public decision-makers do to obtain this or that result?').

In this way, the 'utopian rationality' of which Bell speaks is identified with programmatic rationality, which will therefore have to consider all the constraints and conditions which, in the exercise in question, are present in the implementation of the objectives or preferences of the decision-makers.[14]

1.6 A Pragmatic 'Realism' as a Way Out from the Impasse

If this is the situation, 'realism' is achieved by directly projecting 'what is to be done', in the future without carrying the weight of the heavy, uncertain and perhaps already obsolete baggage of 'positive' theories.

We are dealing with the transition from the analysis of the factors that determine the way things are generally carried out, on the basis of ex-post observations (which produce theories), to the analysis of the factors that are directly necessary, on a case-by-case basis, to achieve determined results in the future, accomplish fixed objectives, or obtain certain goals. Obviously, this considers certain conditions and constraints, especially over available resources, which are quantitatively and objectively measured, and scarce by definition.

In order to plan and decide actions, economic theories are of very little use. It would be useful, instead, to disregard them, and perhaps 'theorise' actions in the field, measuring their feasibility and effects, with bespoke inquiries and evaluations, measuring them against the historic contingencies of the community for which and on which they operate, its culture, involvement, skills and abilities; testing the effective preferences of its citizens, ruling classes and operators, measured using such inquiries; and so on.

If this is the situation, 'realism' consists in joining intentions and results, in the exact process of planning and operational research. It consists in the constant transition from the evaluation of past actions to the evaluation of decisions or actions to be taken. This also means that any ex post analysis or evaluation should always and only refer to an ex ante analysis and document, in a vision totally oriented towards doing and towards the examination of results, as opposed to the programmed expectations, as the basis for the orientation and research of new actions.

In other terms, this would be the substitution of economic theory with a 'theory of planning'.

Moreover, in this last theory, it would be easy to find a place for non-economic visions and evaluations, which have always undermined economic theories (despite the numerous attempts to clearly distinguish one from the other, in formal, logical exercises, which reduced the former to that 'fiction' of which Bell writes).

In effect, the evolution of 'theoretical' economic thought is full of 'paradoxical' presumptions. These paradoxes were generally used to refute the realism of theories, and often to refute the excesses and even errors of rationality, or to affirm the existence of something that is in itself different from it.[15]

However, the scepticism generated from contesting such paradoxes is limitless. It is a fertile ground for a sort of irrationalism, even if it takes on the academic form of a so-called 'progressive dialectic of ideas'. In reality, as opposed to a rationality without history, and not 'historicised', it leads to a sort of eclecticism—a 'nirvana' for critical thought.

Paradoxes—if suitably historicised—are nothing more than mere rebuttals of previous theories, preludes to new theories founded on new observed data; these new theories are susceptible—in their turn and over time—to being refuted by new data and, therefore, by other new theories.

Therefore—in terms of the themes of economic theory—would it not be much simpler to recognise that the only way to break a sequence is to ignore it? That is, to create a hiatus—a pause, an interruption—between the 'empirical' ex post evaluation and 'theoretical' ex ante evaluation, a hiatus founded on the conviction that facts observed ex post do not necessarily determine the evaluation ex ante.

It does not follow that the observation of facts should be overlooked or ignored. However, this must not be the only basis for action, as it risks being 'irrational' (or, in the best case, 'casual', which is merely another form of irrationality). The knowledge for action must always be founded on rationality and on calculation in order to be coherent and efficient.

In contrast to knowledge for action, one should counterpose knowledge in action itself, or from action and from the ways and methods of action (as we will set out in the next two chapters).

Hence, it is my conviction that planning elaboration can only be founded on theoretical evaluation ex ante, regardless of each evaluation ex post, except that linked to and, I would say, 'generated' from its very own evaluation ex ante.

The Programming Approach, As Epistemologically Based...   31

According to these conditions, then, theoretical evaluation can be amply based on facts and conditions, detected and treated in a rational way (when not influenced by 'theory'—of a 'positivist' or 'prejudicial' nature—on past facts and conditions).

The facts and conditions, which are of interest to those who plan (and decide) ex ante, are the available resources on the one hand and people's aspirations or desires on the other (most likely giving priority to those who institutionally represent the community). Other factors naturally include opinions regarding the behaviour (examined using conventional methods) of citizens and of defined groups of interest. In other words, it is necessary to free ourselves from the prejudice that theory must be based on 'facts'. It should rather have its own life, based on desires and forward-looking attitudes directed towards the future.

We are speaking, here, of that anti-positivist or anti-deterministic emancipation, which we have discussed from the very beginning of this book.

Notes to Chapter 1 (Vol. II)

1. See again the citations offered by Frisch in Chap. 7, **Vol. I**.
2. Limited to a selection of the most significant examples among a vast literature on this subject; it is further limited by what the authors themselves have read and, sometimes, casually selected.
3. Ludwig von Mises (1881–1973), a Viennese economist who emigrated to the USA, will be considered in more detail in Chap. 1 (**Vol. I**) of this trilogy.
4. Tinbergen J., *Two Approaches to the Future: Planning vs. Forecasting* [mimeograph] 1971a, and *Comment faut-il etudier l'avenir?* [mimeograph], 1971b. These two papers, the first in English the second in French, are both dated 1971, and I was lucky enough to receive them from the hands of Tinbergen himself. However, I ignore the circumstance of their preparation and the press form they subsequently assumed. In fact, I ignore the fact that these papers—now preserved in the Library of the Planning Studies Centre—have never been officially published. They are not included in the bibliography of Tinbergen works edited by Kol and de Wolff (1993), two of his colleagues (Kol was also his successor as head

of the Dutch Central Planning Bureau) and published in the reprint of the "Erasmus Centre for Economic Integration Studies" of the University of Rotterdam. I thank Prof. Kol for having sent me a complimentary copy at the time. In any case the two papers were also reprinted in the "Reprints" series of the Planning Studies Centre in 1984.

5. One of the best reconstructions of such controversy between Frisch and Tinbergen is by Leif Johansen in the cited work, *Lectures etc.* (in Sects. 3.10 and 3.11, pp. 234–255).

6. For a deeper definition of the concepts of 'projections', 'forecasts' and 'plans', see Johansen 1977–78, Vol. 1, pp. 125–6. He adds two specific concepts: 'conditional forecasts' and 'indicative forecasts', which, though interesting, add little to the type of critical consideration developed here about the clean distinction between the two approaches. Further developments on this subject can also be found in (Theil 1961; Theil et al. 1964).

7. Bruno de Finetti (1906–1984) is best known for his important studies on the 'theory of probability' (*Theory of Probability*, 1974).

8. One of his volumes of various critical essays is entitled *A mathematician and the economy* (1969a) (unfortunately available only in Italian).

9. I consider this essay one of the most important Italian contributions of recent decades to the progress of theoretical and methodological ideas in economics. The essay was published in a volume edited by the same author with the title *Requirements for an Economic System Acceptable in Relations to the Needs of the Collectivity* (1973b) (*Requisiti per un Sistema economico accettabile in relazione ai bisogni della collettività*) ed. Bruno de Finetti, Milano Franco Angeli, 1973b, (unfortunately available only in Italian). Republished recently in Amari and de Finetti, eds., *Bruno de Finetti, Un matematico tra Utopia e Riformismo*, EDIESSE, 2015. (Quotations in English in this trilogy translated by Archibugi, from the last edition).

10. The quotation of Jakob Marschak is the most relevant expression of the distinction between descriptive and normative sciences and is at least restrictive, because it dates back to another time and other authors (see Chap. 6). Marschak did not abandon a positivist approach in his vision of economist of collective behaviour, as shown in many of his studies, his promotion in the USA as chairman of the Cowles Commission and in his last important and meaningful work, *Economic Information, Decision and Prediction* (1974) (see bibl. ref.).

11. This essay originated from a long report presented by de Finetti to a seminar promoted by the Italian CIME (Mathematical Economics) in

Urbino (20–25 September 1971), six years after another CIME Seminar in L'Aquila (1965), where Ragnar Frisch gave two lectures presenting his 'General outlook on a method of advanced and democratic macroeconomic planning' (as recalled in several chapters of the first two parts of this book). The epistemological 'overturning' here argued for by de Finetti is, compared to Frisch, supported by a series of negative considerations on the use of mathematics in economics, although not limited and conditioned by a precise and predetermined planning system, that is, by some achievable objectives of a political preference function. This essay by de Finetti was practically ignored in Italy (and outside Italy even more, of course) and it deserves to be republished and revisited in English by young economists of the new generation (as do Frisch's lectures of the same CIME seminar in 1965).

12. Published in a collected volume edited by Bell himself in cooperation with I. Kristol under the title *The Crisis in Economic Theory* (1981).

13. The best-known books by Bell are *The End of Ideology* (1960), *The Coming of Post-Industrial Society* (1973) and *The Cultural Contradictions of Capitalism* (1976). According to information from Wikipedia, the first and third of these books have been listed in the *Times Literary Supplement* as among the 100 most important books of the second half of the twentieth century. Daniel Bell died in January 2011, after having expressed his final non-conformist ideas on contemporary society in a rather perturbing compilation book, *The Winding Passage*: *Sociological Essays and Journeys* (1980).

14. More arguments on why Bell can be considered a good representative of a critical 'non-positivist' sociology are contained in another of my works, in which I have discussed structural changes in the economy and in contemporary society and where I have outlined a critical survey of the shortcomings typical of many traditional approaches to change (the technological, economic, historic, institutional and sociological approaches), due to their common positivist 'vice' (see Archibugi, *The Associative Economy* etc., Macmillan, 2000a, pp. 106–111).

15. The term can be clarified by reference to its Greek etymon (and has also been absorbed into Latin): *para* = *against*; *doxa* = opinion. The dictionaries define it as: 'a statement contrary to accepted opinion' (Oxford); 'contrary to received opinion' (Webster); 'affemazione che è in contrasto con l'opinione dei più' (Garzanti/Cusatelli); 'pensée, opinion contraire à l'opinion commune' (Larousse).

Bibliographical References to Chapter 1 (Vol. II)

Bell, Daniel. (1981). Models and Reality in Economic Discourse. *The Crisis of Economic Theory*. D. Bell and I. Kristol. New York, Basic Books.

de Finetti, Bruno. (1973b). 'The Utopia as necessary presupposition, etc.' in *Requirements for an acceptable economic system etc.* [ed. de Finetti, pp.13–15].

Frisch, Ragnar. (1957). *Oslo Decision Models*. Oslo, University of Oslo Institute of Economics.

Kol, J. and de Wolff, P. (1993). 'Tinbergen's Work: Change and Continuity.' *De Economist* 141 (No. 1): 1–28. [Includes a bibliographic catalog of the works of J. Tinbergen] (Reprint, by 'Erasmus Centre for Economic Integration Studies', University of Rotterdam).

Theil, H. (1961). *Economic Forecasts and Policy*. Amsterdam, North-Holland.

Theil, H. et al. (1964). *Optimal Decision Rules for Government and Industry*. Amsterdam, North-Holland.

Tinbergen, J. (1971a). *Two Approaches to the Future: Planning Vs. Forecasting*, [mimeo].

Tinbergen, J. (1971b). Comment faut-il étudier l'avenir?, pp. 1–2.

von Mises, L. (1962). *The Ultimate Foundation of Economic Science. An Essay on Method*. Van Nostrand, (Princeton, etc, 1962).

2

The Programming Approach and the Old, Unresolved Debate on 'Decision Theory'

An interesting contribution to the 'overturning' process to be achieved in the programming approach can be found in the field of studies currently referred to as 'decision theory'.

In previous chapters, we have seen how and why it would be logical to accept what can be defined as a *decisional use of descriptive models* in the programming approach. This issue, which is directly connected to the programming approach, and is one of the oldest debates on decision theory, regards the dichotomy between the 'descriptive' and 'normative' models of decision-making.

However, before exploring how the programming approach impacts modern decision theory, we cannot but recall the fact that the same dichotomy between descriptive and normative models, which fascinates modern decision theorists today—as we will see, in the second part of this chapter—has, for a long time, been a stumbling block for economic theory itself, as it searched for a safe base on which to exist independently from its first methodological steps. Even now, according to the most hardened historians of economics, this dichotomy has been the stumbling block on which many certainties have been shattered, and about which we still have not attained satisfying clarity.

© The Author(s) 2019
F. Archibugi, *The Programming Approach and the Demise of Economics*,
https://doi.org/10.1007/978-3-319-78060-3_2

2.1 The Traditional 'Methodological' Debate on Economic Decision and Its Inconclusiveness

Decision theory would actually appear to be regulated by theories which have developed outside of decision theory[1]: theories and rules which come from other disciplines, such as the theory of law, of politics, and possibly also of planning (even if this is at an underdeveloped stage).

But despite the fact that this issue has been debated by economists—even those who are methodologically oriented—for a long time, creating an impressive amount of literature on the subject, no conclusion has ever been reached and much confusion has been generated. It seems to me that the programming approach tends to bypass this debate. And in so doing, the debate becomes obsolete and useless.

The positive–normative dichotomy has occupied such a permanent place in economic literature that we cannot avoid making rapid reference to its tortuous reasoning; nor can we avoid explaining why it seems obsolete from a programming viewpoint, and why it seems to be an old, slow and unfruitful path, compared to the main road represented by the epistemological and praxeological solution of the programming approach itself.

2.2 How the Descriptive Versus Normative Dichotomy Is Raised?

With regard to modern 'decision theorists', we cannot deny that past economic theory may not be better than current theory but is certainly no worse.

I have made use of the vast panorama provided by the economics historian Mark Blaug in one of his better works, *The Methodology of Economics*,[2] (namely in Chap. 5 of his book—'The distinction between positive and normative economics'—in which he gives a critical survey of the relevant specialist literature).

He begins by reminding us that this distinction is more than 150 years old, dating back to the writings of Nassau Senior and of John Stuart Mill and to statements by David Hume in his *A Treatise of Human Nature*

The Pogramming Approach and the Old, Unresolved Debate...

(1739), such as that 'one cannot deduce ought from is'. These purely factual, descriptive, subjective affirmations can only result in other purely factual, descriptive statements, but never in norms or provisions to do something. To clarify this distinction, Blaug gives us a sequence of antonyms[3]:

- positive versus normative
- is versus ought
- facts versus values
- objective versus subjective
- descriptive versus prescriptive
- science versus art
- true/false versus good/bad

After having so broadly defined the different modalities of distinction, Blaug begins to list the various controversial aspects or, more precisely, the various complex (confusing) problems which have emerged in the relevant economics literature from a generic and poorly articulated comprehension of the distinction itself.

In particular, he highlights the very contradictions that were raised when trying to apply the distinction to different cases of assessment and decision. The case that seemed most emblematic to Blaug is that of the *new* welfare economics:

[I]n the 1930s, the 'new' welfare economics came along to provide a normative economics that was allegedly free of value judgments, after which it appeared that the distinction between positive and normative economics was one between noncontroversial facts and values, on the one hand, and controversial values, on the other. The result was to enlarge traditional, positive economics to include the whole of pure welfare economics, leaving normative economics to deal with specific policy issues, where nothing much can be said about values or ends apart from what politicians tell us. What is involved here are some horrible, logical confusion that laid economists open to whole-sale attack on the very idea of value-free, positive economics. There is clearly much sorting out to be done here, after which we hope to reinstate the positive-normative distinction as yet another Popperian methodological norm peculiarly relevant to a policy science like economics. (Blaug 1992, p. 112)

2.2.1 The 'Logical Confusion' Concerning 'Value-free' Judgements and 'Scientific' Propositions

In effect, the 'logical confusion' to which Blaug refers is the outcome of many ambiguities and unsatisfying answers brought about by the debate on the distinction between descriptive and prescriptive, facts and values, the subject and issue of which is the very cognition of economics as a *positive* science. In my view, we have to go back to this debate to find the sources of that 'logical confusion' (as Blaug calls it) which prompts the logical and epistemological overturning of the programming approach advocated in this book. The basic questions that animated this debate from the start are:

- Is it possible to conceive of economics as independent from values, as 'pure' economics?
- Is there room in economics for it to be free of the impact of values?

A huge debate developed around these questions in the evolution of economic theory. The debate was implicitly based on the desire to preserve, as a scientific discipline, a corpus of principles and laws within economic science, to be used to support political decisions and, in consequence, the various recommended values (ethical, political and philosophical) incorporated in those decisions.

The first question raised was: 'how can we tell whether a given utterance is an *is-statement* or an *ought-statement*?' The first answer was:

- An *is-statement* is simply one that is either materially true or false: it asserts something about the state of the world—that it is such and such, and not otherwise—and we can employ interpersonally testable methods to discover whether it is true or false.
- On the contrary, an *ought-statement* expresses an evaluation of the state of the world—it approves or disapproves, it praises or condemns, it extols or deplores—and we can only employ arguments to persuade others to accept it.

But Blaug lists the initial objections and doubts concerning these definitions, which are considered too simple:

> Surely, it will be objected, the normative proposition that we should not eat babies can likewise be tested by interpersonally testable methods, say, by a political referendum? But all that a political referendum can establish is that all of us agree that eating babies is wrong; it cannot establish that it is wrong. But it will again be objected, this is just as true of every interpersonally testable verification or falsification of an is-statement. Ultimately, a factual, descriptive is-statement is held to be true because we have agreed among ourselves to abide by certain 'scientific' rules that instruct us to regard that statement as true, although it may in fact be false. To say that there are 'brute facts' that we must accept whether we like it or not is to commit the inductive fallacy, and besides, the Neyman-Pearson theory of statistical inference should have taught us by now that the acceptance of every fact in science necessarily implies a risky decision made under uncertainty, involving a definite, but unknown, chance of being wrong. Thus, we accept or reject is-statements on grounds that are themselves conventions and in this sense even 'the scientist qua scientist makes value judgements' to cite the title of a well-known methodological paper (Rudner 1953). Moral judgments are usually defined as prescriptions enjoining a certain kind of behaviour, which everyone is supposed to comply with in the same circumstances. But are assertions about facts not exactly the same kind of judgments, enjoining certain kinds of attitude rather than certain kinds of behaviour? (Blaug 1992, pp. 113–114)

Furthermore, Blaug reminds us that there have been persistent doubts among moral philosophers in recent years about the is-ought dichotomy, largely along the lines that moral judgement are not simply expressions of feelings, or imperatives commanding someone to act, but are actually special kinds of descriptive statements about the world.[4]

2.2.2 Methodological Judgements Versus Value Judgements (*According to Ernest Nagel*)

Thus, on the positive–normative dichotomy regarding decisional processes in the economic field, methodological doubts and dis-satisfaction have spread so much that they compromise the validity of the dichotomy itself.

Most critical analysis has been directed at value judgements, splitting them up and eradicating their clarity and precision.

Ernest Nagel, looking at the dichotomy from the viewpoint of the philosopher of science,[5] stated that such judgments can be classified into at least two main categories. The first involves the choice of subject matter to be investigated, the mode of investigation to be followed and the criteria for judging the validity of the findings, such as adherence to the canons of formal logic, the selection of data in terms of reliability, explicit prior decisions about levels of statistical significance, and so on—in short, everything that Blaug prefers to call 'methodological judgments'.

The latter, on the other hand, refers to evaluative assertions regarding the state of things (of the world), including the desirability of certain kinds of human behaviour and the social outcomes produced by that behaviour; thus, all statements on 'good society' are value judgments (in other words, they evaluate).

Nagel contends that science, 'as a social enterprise', cannot renounce methodological judgments, but it can free itself, at least in principle, from any evaluative or normative commitment of the second kind.

I fear that Nagel's attempt to save scientific objectivity with this distinction from the influence of value judgements, creating distinctions inside those same value judgements between 'methodological' judgements and the more excessively 'partisan' ones, is surely commendable, but technically impossible. Between the seemingly more 'neutral' (but not mechanical) judgements and the more subjectively extreme ones, there is an infinite range of subtleties that are difficult to explain using taxonomies.[6]

Perhaps, in what is commonly called the 'scientific' field (that of the natural sciences), a distinction between value judgements and normative judgements could work: 'methodological' judgements are retained, as they are needed by the natural sciences, and the most significant 'falsifications' of history (in the sense made popular by the Popperian approach) are based on them.

But even in the field of social sciences, where experimentation is never convincing—because of the unpredictability of human behaviour (whether experimental or not)—we have to wonder: what is the point of maintaining a semblance of objectivity by rescuing the possibility of maintaining 'positive' judgments if it is not possible to implement it? How can we maintain positive judgments when we know that they can never be completely positive? Would this not be a scientific deceit transformed, as often happens, into social deceit?[7]

In this regard, Blaug himself, although inclined to defend the historically orthodox dichotomy, perceives, with intellectual honesty, the inefficacy of Nagel's proposal:

> At a deep philosophical level, this distinction [proposed by Nagel] is perhaps misleading. Ultimately, we cannot escape the fact that all non-tautological propositions rest for their acceptance on the willingness to abide by certain rules of the game, that is, on judgments that we players have collectively adopted. An argument about facts may appear to be resolvable by a compelling appeal to so-called objective evidence, whereas an argument about moral values can only be rest on certain definite techniques of persuasion, which in turn depend for their effectiveness on shared values of one kind or another. But at the working level of a scientific inquiry, Nagel's distinction between methodological and normative judgments is nevertheless real and significant in the social science field. (Blaug 1992, pp. 114–115)

Blaug's observation could have been written by one of the so-called 'sociologists of knowledge'. Absolute truths are the product of cognitive social evolution, cultural and epistemological conventions, and are subject to all the variations determined by the dialectics of individual but also of social, collective thought.

Blaug tends to analyse problems that are, indeed, evaluative and normative in their logical nature, but are more open to a kind of compromise to obtain a better knowledge of (apparent) positivity; this also implies that the positivist opens up to alternative, more flexible visions concerning an extended plurality of behaviours.

> We have overstated the case in suggesting that normative judgments are the sort of judgments that are never amenable to rational discussion designed to reconcile whatever differences there are between people. Even if Hume is right in denying that 'ought' can be logically deduced from 'is,' and of course 'is' from 'ought,' there is no denying that 'oughts' are powerfully

influenced by 'ises' and that the values we hold almost always depend on a whole series of factual beliefs. This indicates how a rational debate on a disputed value judgment can proceed: we pose alternative factual circumstances and ask, should these circumstances prevail, would you be willing to abandon your judgment? A famous and obvious example is the widespread value judgment that economic growth, as measured by real national income, is always desirable; but is it, we might ask, even if it made the bottom quartile, decile, quintile of the size distribution of personal incomes absolutely worse off? Another example is the frequently expressed value judgment that capital punishment is always wrong. But if there were incontrovertible evidence that capital punishment deterred potential murderers, we might ask, would you still adhere to your original opinion? And so on.

In thinking along these lines, we are led to a distinction between 'basic' and 'non-basic' value judgments, or what I would prefer to call pure and impure value judgments: 'A value judgment can be called 'basic' to a person if the judgment is supposed to apply under all conceivable circumstances, and it is 'non-basic' otherwise' (Sen 1970, p. 59). So long as a value judgment is non-basic or impure, a debate on value judgments can take the form of an appeal to facts, and that is all to the good because our standard methods for settling disputes about facts are less divisive than those for settling disputes about values. It is only when we finally distill a pure value judgment—think of a strict pacifist opposition to any and all wars, or the assertion that 'I value this for its own end'—that we have exhausted all the possibilities of rational analysis and discussion. There is hardly any doubt that most value judgments that are expressed on social questions are highly impure and hence perfectly amenable to the attempt to influence values by persuading the parties holding them that the facts are other than what they believe them to be. (Blaug 1992, pp. 115–116)

This reasoning by Blaug seems to me more acceptable than the purely 'positivistic' because it brings practical solutions through conventional evaluations and makes dialogue more profitable.[8]

However, whatever the position on a clear distinction between positive/descriptive judgements and normative judgements, on the problems there is a lack of clarity. And Blaug is a good witness, commenting on further debates in the field of economists.

2.2.3 Others Steady Attempts to Bypass Controversial Terms (*the Max Weber Trial*)

Considering all these limits, is it still possible to imagine a 'value-free' social science—a '*Wertfreiheit*' to use the German expression which ignited the traditional debate?

In this regard, Blaug says, turning back somewhat in respect of his previous admission:

> Once we have cleansed the impurities in impure value judgment by a rational debate, we are left with factual statements and pure value judgment between which there is indeed an irreconcilable gulf on anyone's interpretation of the concept of 'facts' and the concept of 'values.' Even if we leave value judgments to be as impure as they usually are, we have so far only demonstrated that the difference between the methods of reaching agreement on methodological judgments and value judgments is one of degree, not of kind. Nothing that we have said should imply that this difference in degree is not worth bothering about.
>
> To argue that the difference is so small as to be negligible takes us straight into the camp of certain radical critics who assert that absolutely all propositions about social phenomena are value-impregnated and hence lack 'objectivity.' […]
>
> The doctrine of value-free social science asserts, first of all, that the logical status of factual, descriptive is-statements is different in kind from that of normative, prescriptive ought-statements, and second, that the methodological judgments that are involved in reaching agreement on is-statements differ in important ways from those used to reach a consensus on normative value judgments. The claim that social science can be value-free in this sense does not deny that ideological bias creeps into the very selection of the questions that social scientists investigate, that the inferences that are drawn from factual evidence are sometimes influenced by values of a particular kind, nor even that the practical advice that social scientists offer is frequently loaded with concealed value judgments, the better to persuade rather than merely to advise. The argument does not rest in any way on the supposed impersonal detachment of individual social scientists but rather on the social aspects of scientific activity, on the critical tradition of a scientific community that constantly weeds out the competing biases of individual scientists.

44   **Volume II. Selected Testimonies on the Epistemological...**

> Max Weber made all this perfectly clear over fifty years ago when he laid down the doctrine of *Wertfreiheit* (freedom from value) and there is really no excuse for misunderstanding of his meaning at this late stage. (Blaug 1992, pp. 116–17)

Weber—obviously—never denied that social science, as it is actually practised, is ruined by political bias. It is precisely for this reason that he preached the possibility of a value-free social science. But Blaug maintains that Weber's *Wertfreiheit* did not, in his opinion, mean that subjective evaluations of human beings, groups or communities could not be analysed rationally. On the contrary, he insisted that *Wertungsdiskussionen* ('discussions on values') were not only possible but of the greatest utility. There stands his great contribution to the rationalisation of political action by means of social research. According to Weber,[9] the discussion on values should have: (1) examined the internal coherence of the premises of value, from which divergent value judgments could be drawn; (2) deduced the implications of those value premises in the light of the practical circumstances to which they are applied; and (3) traced the factual consequences of alternative ways of achieving normative judgments.

Nevertheless, even Weber (like many of his successors), in his best writings, is far from finding a way out from the impasse between the wish to make a clear distinction between objectivity and subjectivity in social science (and consequently the possibility of value-free judgments) and the need to begin the rationalisation of 'no-value-free' judgments (through the analysis of different typologies of judgments influenced by value judgments) to ensure that social action has its own specific rationalisation and 'objectivity'.

This tortuous ambiguity induced Blaug, as a careful observer of the debate on sources of evaluation—both historical and contemporary—to declare, in drastic terms:

> Few of those who attack the doctrine of *Wertfreiheit* have the courage of their own convictions [!]. After marshaling all the standard arguments against the *Wertfreiheit* camp, they usually end up by saying that we are all in favor of objective truth and 'impartial science,' although how there can be such things if 'ises' are inextricably tied up with 'oughts' is not made

clear. If there are not at least some descriptive, factual assertions about social uniformities that are value-free (apart from the characterizing value judgments implied in methodological judgments), it seems difficult to escape the conclusion that we have the license to assert whatever we please.

The denial of objectivity in social science is more common in sociology than in economics. Indeed, economists are traditionally complacent about the is-ought dichotomy, believing apparently that it needs only to be stated clearly to be self-evident (see Klappholz 1964). It has not been easy, therefore, to find examples of economists tripping over themselves by first denying that economics can be value free and then affirming that some economic opinions are nevertheless more valid than others. But perhaps a single, instructive example will suffice. (Blaug 1992, pp. 117–118)

2.2.4 Last Trial (*by Myrdal*)

On this point, however, let us not forget the attempts by Gunnar Myrdal to solve the issue of the impossibility of *Wertfreiheit*.[10]

Although Myrdal's arguments stem from an epistemological analysis of the 'political element in the development of economic theory',[11] they matured after careful reflection on and experience of social research. Perhaps it is not by chance that these arguments have practically been forgotten or ignored by Blaug in his sophisticated debate on the dichotomy between the positive and the normative.[12]

The same happened with Myrdal's arguments, which were developed in a little-known booklet that provides a rich summary of the theme of objectivity in social research.[13] Myrdal's arguments seem to me to be the most advanced in comparison to all those used and criticised by Blaug in his book.

Myrdal's well-known solution regarding the difficulty of ensuring *Wertfreiheit* is not the logically impossible solution of suppressing every value judgment in the interest of a presumed 'scientific objectivity' (in social science); nor does he want to clarify at what point these judgments can be discussed, thus dividing positive judgments from normative. His intention, rather, is to declare them clearly at the start of the analysis. In this way, according to Myrdal, the result would be imbued with a true objectivity. Myrdal says:

At this point of the argument it should be stated most emphatically that the fault in most contemporary is, well as earlier, social science research is not in its lack of 'objectivity' in the conventional sense of independence from all valuations. On the contrary, every study of a social problem, however limited in scope, is and must be determined by valuations. A 'disinterested' social science has never existed and, for logical reasons, can never exist.

However, the value premises that actually and of necessity determine social science research are generally hidden. The student can even remain unaware of them. They are then left implicit and vague, leaving the door open to biases.

The only way in which we can strive for 'objectivity' in theoretical analysis is to expose the valuations to full light, make them conscious, specific, and explicit, and permit them to determine the theoretical research. In the practical phases of a study, the stated value premises, together with the data (established by theoretical analysis with the use of the same value premises) should then form the premises for all policy conclusions. (Myrdal 1970, pp. 55–56)

According to Myrdal, in other terms, it is impossible to distinguish *positive* economics from *normative*, and to attempt this distinction can lead only to self-deception.

Blaug, however, objects, wondering whether it is vain to try to separate the empirical testing of economic theories (without giving free rein to our hopes and wishes, as if this were an ideal to aim for) from the approval or disapproval of certain states of things.

This objection makes sense.

Starting from the inevitability of the distinction in question and the inevitability of the need to find some sort of compromise between the two logical (and epistemological) attitudes, we end up with unsolved problems. The proposals by the authors that Blaug honestly discusses in his broaden critical survey end up in the same position.

But why are we so sure about the inevitability of the distinction? Blaug's question could be useful to pilot us towards a way out from the distinction. It could prompt us to totally eliminate the is-judgement or is-statement from social sciences; praxeologically, it could push us, merely on the basis of the ought-judgment or ought statement, to start defining objectives and their connected ties, and to produce plans and projects in

The Pogramming Approach and the Old, Unresolved Debate... 47

the logic of problem-solving, 'operational research', system engineering and strategic planning.

This simplification, which requires the overturning of 'scientific' logic and a broadening of the 'pragmatist' vision in social science,[14] was not even proposed by Myrdal, who came very close to doing so.

This simplification should see strategic planning take the place of economics and the other social sciences, which deal with humanity's plans and group decisions at every level of the political community, and, moreover, with humanity's constraints, as studied and analysed, in their intrinsic, organic and structural connection, and managed as instruments or goals, according to circumstances.

Within this framework, it no longer makes sense to speak of necessary 'empirical tests'. Tests of what? The point is that empirical testing should examine whether suppositions, principles, proposals or simply hypotheses which are theoretical and universal follow legal or natural norms and respond to testing, with particular attention to their general repetitiveness (as is normal in natural science). These principles and rules in so-called 'positive' economics would transform themselves into 'normative' propositions (anything but 'positive').

But in social science, in our imagined case, things would not work like this. There would be no need to 'empirically' check what corresponds to rational, theoretical assumptions. It would be sufficient to carry out a 'feasibility analysis', in given circumstances, which could not be reproduced under the same conditions. We are dealing with the feasibility of solutions that, starting from objectives, must be compared with the availability of the means.

In our case, rationality is the congruence between ends and means. It would only be a matter of verifying the feasibility of plans and projects, their congruence and compatibility, especially compared to the means and tools available. And this comparison can only be guaranteed by strategic planning and its methods.

A 'situational' opportunity is brought about by a selective process of 'problem solving', by actions chosen to solve problems and by the intentional achievement of specific *objectives* (which are rooted in our hopes and wishes but are obtained feasibly)—that is, by the concrete and practical relation of the objectives to the available conditions, restrictions and resources.

Myrdal was trying to achieve objectivity or a system of rules of conduct derived from a programming (or praxeological) approach, not from an approach based on pure knowledge, abstract theorems and universal standard behaviour by humans who are also abstract with respect to real and concrete historical and environmental situations, within which the problems to be solved are set.

In this sense, the programming approach, in overcoming or denying the positivist approach (because they are bound together with value judgements and the search for praxeological solutions), seems to me to make the logical distinction between positive and normative irrelevant with regard to preferential objectives and their related decisions. Thus, the endless discussions caused by this distinction (in the official methodology of inherited economics) and the ways of avoiding it and gifting the expected and apparent independence of the natural sciences to the social sciences appear pointless to me.

In the same way, the programming approach tends to melt away the last methodological ambiguities which we have observed in Myrdal (in **Vol. I**, Chap. 2).

In my view, Myrdal's great contribution to overcoming 'positive' economics deserves to be remembered even here on the last insightful page he wrote (the final considerations on the theme of his life in the pamphlet mentioned above), even though the 'egalitarian principle', which, he declares, is the principle or value that intrigues him most, is not pertinent to the theme of his pamphlet ('the objectivity of social research'), but is only an idea for further reflection.

> Conventional economic theory is still far from having liberated itself from the metaphysic assumptions it inherited from the moral philosophies of natural law and utilitarianism. Nor has our science yet out-grown the devices used to protect it from its own radical premises. This is why an intensive critical analysis—in terms of the type of logic barely hinted at in the preceding section—is of the continuing importance.
>
> But when this is accomplished, a great number of problems are open to empirical research.
>
> Why and how did early social scientist—like proponents of the great religions and moral philosophies attached to the religions—adopt and give such a central position in their theories to the egalitarian principle?

The escapist tendencies of economic theory in regard to the egalitarian postulate are more easily understandable. They were an adjustment to conditions concerning prevalent valuations and to the political power situation in the countries in which this theory developed. Once one places oneself outside the main trend of economic speculation and looks at the development of theory as a part of social and political history—all of which needs to be explained in terms of causes and effects—there is little mystery about it. Karl Marx—himself involved in the metaphysical pre-conceptions of the old philosophers, as evidenced, for instance, in his theory of 'real value'—never carried out this explanation, although in his empirical, historical, and sociological excursions there are many hints towards such an explanation. These are buried, however, in his teleological doctrine.

The real mystery, which I am not in the position to solve in this context, is the continuous presence in clear form of the egalitarian principle. Where did this lofty ideal come from? And how could it continuously preserve its position at the basis of abstract economic reasoning in Western (and Communist) civilization?

Another problem for empirical research is whether and to what extent the development of the welfare state in the advanced countries was promoted by the position given to the egalitarian principle in all economic thought. Also, what role does this ideological heritage play today in our adjustment in the rich countries to the radically changed postwar political conditions in the underdeveloped countries and our relations to them.

On these questions I would like answers founded upon empirical research, much of it of a historical nature following an institutional approach. Fortunately, I do not need these answers in order to come to terms with the methodological problem raised in this essay. (Myrdal 1970, pp. 109–111)

2.3 The Descriptive and Normative Approach in Modern 'Decision Theory'

Regarding the issue we are facing—the epistemological overthrow of the deterministic approach by the programming one—the positive–normative dichotomy, whose long history we examined in the previous paragraph, is completely surpassed by the fact that very little of the ancient quarrel about that dichotomy remains in modern decision theory.

This is simply because decision theory has developed exclusively in a direction and in an ambit where nothing 'normative' but only the 'positive' remains. Yet normative problems remain at the root of decision theory itself and belong to different disciplinary and scientific areas.

Academically, the most distinguished decision theorists still accept that a decision is composed of two distinct moments: the descriptive and the normative. But the dichotomy is applied to substantially different contents, both in the descriptive and normative versions.

In the old quarrel, one sought to discover:

- whether value-judgments influenced decision-makers (positive version), or
- whether they should be influenced or not.

In today's decision theory, the questions to be resolved are:

- How are decisions are actually taken (positive version)?
- How should decisions be taken (normative version)?

But we must also take into account that the normative 'should' can be interpreted in many ways. Many believe that there is virtually full agreement among scholars of decision that this 'should' refers to the prerequisites of rational decision-making. As such, it exits the field of decision theory, that is, the field of rational decision making, which is regulated independently of normative choices. In other words, the normative decision theory is a theory about how decisions should be made, in order to be rational, regardless of the reasons for making them and regardless of the field to which they are applied.

So what happens to the dichotomy?

As Sven Ove Hansson observes in an essay introducing decision theory (1994):

> Norms of rationality are by no means the only—or even the most important—norms that one may wish to apply in decision-making. However, it is practice to regard norms other than rationality norms as external to decision theory. Decision theory does not, according to the received opinion,

enter the scene until the ethical or political norms are already fixed. It takes care of those normative issues that remain even after the goals have been fixed. This remainder of normative issues, consist to a large part of questions about how to act in when there is uncertainty and lack of information. It also contains issues about how an individual can coordinate her decisions over time and of how several individuals can coordinate their decisions in social decision procedures.

If the general wants to win the war, the decision theorist tries to tell him how to achieve this goal. The question whether he should at all try to win the war is not typically regarded as a decision-theoretical issue. Similarly, decision theory provides methods for a business executive to maximize profits and for an environmental agency to minimize toxic exposure, but the basic question whether they should try to do these things is not treated in decision theory.

Although the scope of the 'normative' is very limited in decision theory, the distinction between normative (i.e. rationality-normative) and descriptive interpretations of decision theories is often blurred. It is not uncommon, when you read decision-theoretical literature, to find examples of disturbing ambiguities and even confusions between normative and descriptive interpretations of one and the same theory.

Probably, many of these ambiguities could have been avoided. It must be conceded, however, that it is more difficult in decision science than in many other disciplines to draw a sharp line between normative and descriptive interpretations. This can be clearly seen from consideration of what constitutes a falsification of a decision theory.

It is fairly obvious what the criterion should be for the falsification of a descriptive decision theory.

(F1) A decision theory is falsified as a descriptive theory if a decision problem can be found in which most human subject perform in contradiction to the theory.

Since a normative decision theory tells us how a rational agent should act, falsification must refer to the dictates of rationality. It is not evident, however, how strong the conflict must be between the theory and rational decision-making for the theory to be falsified. I propose, therefore, the following two definitions for different strengths of that conflict.

(F2) A decision theory is weakly falsified as a normative theory if a decision problem can be found in which an agent can perform in contradiction with the theory without being irrational.

52   Volume II. Selected Testimonies on the Epistemological...

(F3) A decision theory is strictly falsified as a normative theory if a decision problem can be found in which an agent who performs in accordance with the theory cannot be a rational agent.

Now suppose that a certain theory T has (as is often the case) been proclaimed by its inventor to be valid both as a normative and as a descriptive theory. Furthermore suppose (as is also often the case) that we know from experiments that in decision problem P, most subjects do not comply with T. In other words, suppose that (F1) is satisfied for T.

The beliefs and behaviours of decision theoreticians are not known to be radically different from those of other human beings. Therefore it is highly probable that at least some of them will have the same convictions as the majority of the experimental subjects. Then they will claim that (F2), and perhaps even (F3), is satisfied. We may, therefore, expect descriptive falsifications of a decision theory to be accompanied by claims that the theory is invalid from a normative point of view. Indeed, this is what has often happened. (Hansson 1994, pp. 7–8)

If all that Hansson says, in the opening of his introduction to decision theory, is right, there is little new in the most recent developments in the field.

There is, however, the sensation that where everything becomes descriptive, and the 'true' normative belongs in a separate moment, everything that is descriptive automatically becomes normative in some way.

I think, however, that this sensation comes from an insufficient epistemological analysis of the scientific approach, in the field of social sciences, and is still related to a positivistic rather than a praxeological approach to human behaviour (individual and societal).

Certainly, for this type of development we must take into account that the studies and experimentations of the decision theorists to date have been developed within the ambit of typically individual behaviour. Reference is constantly made to humanity in its individual subjectivity, as regulated by reflections of 'methodological individualism'.[15]

As we have already seen when commenting on the praxeology defended by von Mises (Chap. 1, Sect. 1.2), 'methodological individualism' has imposed positivism and determinism on economics and sociology, but also on decision theory.

Here *Homo economicus* is replaced—but with the same method and the same theoretical assumptions—with *Homo diiudicantis*. This too is an abstract, unreal man, one who responds to abstract rules of rationality in decision-making. This figure—in order to be a real participant in the decisions made in any social group to which he belongs (a family, a group of relatives, a profession, an association, a city, a region, a country, an international community, a religious community or, finally, a global community)—must accept as unique the representative delegation of such a multiple regrouping, be it political, institutional, societal or civil. It is this sociability which makes such a figure human.

Without any personal or collective organised representation, if we take single individual actions alone, mankind is condemned to regress. This *Homo*—from the use of the expression itself—is presumed to be collective, in several forms, minus that 'individual'.

Even the individual rights that must be guaranteed to the single members of any society, group or organisation, given belief in the existence of society, in social, collective action and in the protection of these.

This leads to the conclusion that decision theory cannot be reserved to an aseptic, neutral 'rationality', one independent of any assessment of merit. Decision theory needs to distinguish the presence of decisional autonomy for decision-makers, the presence of respect for decisional rights and the existence of those who exercise decisional rights, which in its turn constitutes decisional legitimacy. One cannot disregard the political context within which decision theory operates.

Thus, even in more modern decision theory, the impasse that has divided and distressed the minds and souls of scholars in the history of economics is reproduced: is a *wertfrei* economics, free from value-judgments, possible? (We saw the complexity of this issue in Chap. 1, Sect. 1.2).

2.4 A New Trichotomy in Modern Decision Theory, Its Inner Interactions (*and Its Tribulations*)

Going back to the origins of decision theory, we must assess the development of the interaction between the descriptive and normative aspects, which have always been at the core of decision theory.

In this further step, we will be supported by the latest developments in studies on decision theory. For this purpose, I will use a significant collection of essays by David E. Bell,[16] Howard Raiffa and Amos Tversky (1988)[17] presented at a conference held at the Harvard Business School in Boston in 1988.[18] These essays all aim to elaborate on the 'descriptive, normative and prescriptive interactions of decision-making'.[19]

2.4.1 The Ambiguities of the Dichotomy Between the 'Descriptive' and 'Normative' Approaches

In spite of the fact that decision theory has, for a long time, based its reasoning on the dichotomy between the 'normative' and 'descriptive' approaches to decision-making (*ought to be* as opposed to *is*), Bell, Raiffa and Tversky—after 20 or 30 years of developments in (neo-classical) decision theory—question the validity and even the utility of this traditional dichotomy.[20]

They introduce a 'realistic' and 'pragmatic' critique of decision-making that leads to a third approach, the 'prescriptive' one, which is in many ways similar to the programming approach, but with the inclusion of some necessary objections and additions.

Let us see how Bell-Raiffa-Tversky (BRT) develop their reasoning, examining what is behind the concepts of both approaches. BRT say:

Let us start with descriptive analysis because this is easiest. How do real people think and behave? How do they perceive uncertainties, accumulate evidence, learn and update perceptions? How do they learn and adapt their behavior? What are their hang-ups, biases, internal conflicts? How do they talk about their perceptions and choices? Do they really do as they say they do? Can they articulate the reasons for their actions? How do they resolve their internal conflicts or avoid such resolutions? Do they decompose complex problems, think separately about component parts of problems, and then recompose or integrate separate analyses? Or do they think more holistically and intuitively? What are the differences in types of thought patterns for people of different cultures, of different experience levels? What is the role of tradition, imitation, and superstition in decision making (or non-making)? How can 'approximate' real behavior be described? How good are various mathematical models in predicting future behavior?

In short, descriptive analysis is concerned with how and why people think and act the way they do. At times it may involve intricate mathematical modeling and require sophisticated statistical analysis. It is highly empirical and clinical activity that falls squarely in the province of the social sciences concerned with individual behavior. Scholars can study the domain without any concern whatsoever of trying to modify behavior, influence behavior, or moralize about such behavior. (Bell et al. 1988, p. 16)

Even this first definition of the approach is perplexing. We have the impression that something is rendering the reasoning incongruous.

If the descriptive approach (by decision scholars) concerns the question of how real people think and behave, with all the modalities described above, and with all the differentiations, articulations and conditions that these modalities entail (and that are recalled in the above passage by BRT), should it not be evident that any generalisation on how and why people think and act the way they do is quite impossible?

And, if this is impossible, does this not compromise the validity, on one hand, and the utility, on the other, of 'descriptive analysis' itself, except for the conclusion (which we reach logically), that it is generally invalid and useless?

And does this not also imply the invalidity and uselessness of that 'highly empirical and clinical activity' that—BRT say—'may involve intricate mathematical modelling and require sophisticated statistical analysis' and that—still according to BRT—'falls squarely in the province of the social sciences concerned with individual behavior'?

Moreover—if the syllogism still makes sense—should that not mean that 'the social sciences concerned with individual behavior', with a tendency to generalise the same behaviour on the basis of empirical analysis (while maintaining the specifications of a complex case history) are losing their object, goal and utility?

Does this not then mean that scholars who 'study the domain without any concern whatsoever of trying to modify behavior, influence behavior, or moralise about such behavior' are wasting their time?

This sequence of interrogatives is intended to seriously question the sense of descriptive analysis.

56   Volume II. Selected Testimonies on the Epistemological...

But when we move on to normative analysis, the authors maintain that this activity is 'more difficult to characterise since it presents different facets', and that the 'classic' dichotomy between what is descriptive and what is normative in decision theory is overturned. BRT, in fact, argue:

> First, there is the notion that normative theory has something to do with the way that ideal, rational, super-intelligent people should think and should act.
>
> Such analyses abstract away known cognitive concerns of real people, their internal turmoils, their shifting values, their anxieties and lingering post-decisional disappointments and regrets, their repugnance (or zest) for ambiguity or danger, their inabilities to do intricate calculations, and their limited attention span.
>
> The 'hallmarks' of such normative analyses are 'coherence' and 'rationality' as captured usually in terms of precisely specified desiderata or axioms of the form: if the decision maker believes so and so, he should do such and such. As usual in any mathematical system, the power of any set of desiderata comes from their logical, synergistic, joint, implications'.
>
> Axioms, basic principles, and fundamental desiderata are motivated by what some investigator thinks is logical, rational, intelligent behavior. Then like any mathematical axiom system (such as sets of axioms for geometry) the academic researchers play variations on the themes: what happens if this axiom is dropped, or if this axiom is modified in such and such a way?
>
> This exercise is rewarding if exercise if the mathematical implications are profound or aesthetically pleasing. The exercise can also be rewarding if the researcher can see a better concordance between the abstract system and some aspects of behavior that is empirically verifiable or that the researcher imagines is verifiable. Thus there is a dynamic interaction between the real world, imaginations about the real world, and the abstract mathematical system. There are extant a host of abstract models of decision making bearing some relation to decision making as it is, or as it is perceived to be, or as it should be in someone's mind. (Bell et al. 1988, pp. 16–17)

BRT's definition and description of the normative approach is already more coherent and logical. At the same time, it is more complex and difficult because it is full of variable and temporary elements and factors.

We cannot help but wonder why a scholar—and/or any other person making a decision—would not want his/her decision to be the best and the most worthwhile for the decision-maker him or herself? It is well-known that decision-makers often do not make rational decisions, but are frequently motivated by factors which, on the whole, we can simply define 'non-rational'. Thus, we often arrive at the practical and cognitive inadequacy of some decisions. But what does this mean?

Does it perhaps mean that the decision-maker should always seek to improve his/her decisions, in the sense of making them more 'rational'? Does it not mean that the scholar who counsels the decision-maker should do the same?

Thus, 'decision theory' only makes sense if it is the outcome of and, at the same time, the motivation for an improving normative approach.

On the other hand, 'normativity' (and the search for norms) is implicit and intrinsic in the very existence of professionalism in all fields of the decisional life of the people who decide (whether they are individuals or collective entities). If the desire to improve the rationality of one's own decisions were not implicit, decision-makers would not ask consultants to assist them in their decisions.

We must take into account that the 'non-rationality', or 'irrationality' largely established and evoked in the literature on the descriptive approach, and the demand for 'realism', have an evident twofold origin. (1) From a certain point of view, this is due to the fact that the decision has taken into account implicit factors (inputs) that are not made explicit, and are therefore ignored, within the parameters of the 'rationality' used to measure the rationality itself. This says little about the 'rationality' of the decision-makers but says much about the rationality of the expected parameters of rationality. In this case, empirical enquiries aimed at broadening the knowledge of 'implicit factors', and, consequently, their ability to be explicit, would contribute to improving plans and the effective evaluation of the decisions made by the decision-makers. However, such 'descriptive enquiries' would always be in doubt, and we must wonder whether it would not be better to implement them only ex ante, on a case-by-case basis, regarding future decisions—that is, enquiries regarding 'oriented' or 'centred' decisions (as we will see in the next chapter). (2) From another point of view, irrationality is due to an effective misinformation or a wrong and misleading judgment on the part of the decision-maker.

58   Volume II. Selected Testimonies on the Epistemological...

In both cases, there should not be excessive indulgence of irrationality in 'real' behaviour, but rather an opportunity to improve decisions in normative terms, taking into account the vast range of existing restrictions and their feasibility.

BRT observe:

> In the usual parlance, an abstract system that purports to describe or predict behaviour is called a descriptive model; an abstract system that attempts to capture how ideal people might behave is called a normative model. There is little difficulty in categorising some models as clearly descriptive or normative.
>
> One trouble is that some normatively motivated models are often used, as mentioned above, as first-cut descriptive models. Other clearly normatively motivated models go through successive modifications that try to make them more and more useful for descriptive and predictive purposes and then it may be difficult to say whether these modifications should be classified as normative or prescriptive. On the other hand, some descriptively motivated models are occasionally modified to come a bit closer to what some analyst believes is a proper norm for wise behaviour. And then the model falls into the grey area. Is it descriptive or is it normative? (BRT 1988, p. 17)

Within this motivational framework, BRT rightly recognise that there is a noteworthy logical confusion on the subject and that the concepts need to be tidied up. Moving on to the prescriptive approach, they ask:

> What should an individual do to make better choices? What modes of thought, decision aids, and conceptual schemes are useful—useful not for idealized, mythical, de-psychologized automata—but for real people? And since real people are different, with differing psyches and emotions, capabilities, and needs, good advice has to be tuned to the needs, capabilities, and emotional makeups of the individuals for whom the prescriptive advice is intended. It becomes even more complicated when individuals who think one way have to interact with experts who think along different paradigmatic lines, as, for example, between a rational decomposer and a holistic intuiter. (BRT 1988, p. 17)

Thus, BRT come to a sort of definition for each of the approaches:

> Descriptive models are evaluated by their empirical validity, that is, the extent to which they correspond to observed choices. Normative models are evaluated by their theoretical adequacy, that is, the degree to which they provide acceptable idealizations or rational choice. Prescriptive models are evaluated by their pragmatic value, that is, their ability to help people make better decisions. To be sure, all three criteria are difficult to define and evaluate, as any student of the philosophy of science knows well. It is evident, nevertheless that the criteria are different; an argument against a normative model need not be an argument against a descriptive model and vice versa.[21] (BRT 1988, pp. 17–18)

It is cause for rejoicing to hear acknowledged the importance of a pragmatic approach to decisions from decision theorists accustomed to developing behavioural axioms and theorems. There is also irony from the same decision (and also game) theorists in the regime of high uncertainty, which is—in fact—elaborated only for potential decision-makers, idealised, mythical, de-psychologised. This recalls strongly Frisch's criticism of econometrics (as seen **Vol. I**).

But in two directions it would be wise to proceed in a clearer way, even within the ambit of a definition of the approaches of decision theory. This acknowledges, as stated above—that the descriptive approach—became largely superfluous as an experimental verification of the validity of the theorems. Consequently, it would be much more convenient to address the programming efforts, with the use of behavioural objectives, directly in the moment of a programmatic decision with verification of the behavioural feasibility, selecting, case by case, the solutions, according a criterion of a pragmatic approach, in the sense of an approach adherent to the understanding, the evaluation and the availability of the decision-makers. This policy is as useful and effective as it is applied not in single and individual cases of decisions, but to decisions that imply a high degree of inter-dependence between them, and to public decisions cases (at the different institutional levels concerned) from decision-makers, bearers of a political preference function. In these cases, the use of authoritative experts—bearers of evaluation and computation technologies even more sophisticated, but always operating as collaborators of operational programs of public and collective interest—becomes even more important. This policy can probably employ candidates or potential decision-makers with learning and evaluative capacities and methods greater than those of single, private, disassociated decision-makers.

This approach also avoids putting into the field methods that can achieve academic validity, but only that, and no one practical validity and implementation. But at same time, they do not deflect from an decisively 'programmatic' approach inserted into a system of that is objectives coordinated and planned, related to a system of decisions, based on a careful assessment and bargaining with all the interested participants (as stakeholders) of the development planning of the community concerned, and at the same time as operators of the implementation of the same planning process.

Seen in this light, and with provisos that policies based on behavioural analysis *ex post* or on the decisional use of descriptive models are quite unreliable, there is a need for the introduction of an 'prescriptive' approach, especially in the case of public entities. This approach is analogous to Frisch's programming approach, which gives substance to this book.

2.4.2 Again, the Illogicality of the 'Realistic' Validity of Behavioural Projection

In the studies that (we might say) belong to the programming approach, and not to decision theory, a certain order in the concepts has been established. The surpassing of the ambiguous descriptive-normative dichotomy has allowed for more elaborate concepts in the typological classification of the 'econometric' relationships between plan model variables. For example:

- Doubts have been expressed about the validity of the estimation of coefficients founded on historic series.
- Distinctions have been developed in conceptual differentiation and, above all, in the use of equations (definitional, structural and behavioural).

- The concept of 'autonomous' relationships has been introduced.
- The quantification in 'observed' and 'programmed' values has been articulated, and so on.

In short, a methodological area has been developed that some have thought to call 'planometrics'.[22] The elaboration of these themes falls—obviously—beyond the scope of this work, even if it constitutes—as one can easily understand—an epistemological premise.

Let us for a moment leave aside the problem of cases in which a 'hybriding' of normativeness and descriptiveness takes place. And let us emphasise, in the passages quoted, the radically different nature of the two approaches, less for their intrinsic quality, than for the different meaning that is assumed with respect to the purpose of the analysis.

If, in fact, our purpose is that of extracting from reality objective behaviour (leaving aside its ethical or rational value) which has the characteristic of (relative) scientific certainty, in order to construct upon it projections (for future replication) of this same behaviour as a constraint on our (even 'free') decisions for the future, then our duty would be that of conforming to descriptive analysis alone and—although imperfect—of taking on only the behaviour indicated ex post. In this case, however, everything rests on an assumption: that the behaviour—so 'real' and so 'irrational'—has the ('rational') gift of replication. This assumption seems even more heroic than many 'rational' assumptions that render the normative models so 'unreal'.

If, on the contrary, our purpose is to understand the reality and behaviour that we have recorded ex post in terms of their raison d'être and motivations, and if we do not worry about using the said knowledge because of the improbable future discounts, in a decision process for the future, we will in this case try to be so 'rational' in replicating reality in all its details, in simulating it in all its conditions, constraints and states, as to become highly unrealistic in wishing to project it in improbable and uncertain future states.

The two types of analysis, normative and descriptive, and the respective models that derive from them, must serve two completely different purposes: the descriptive one is a type of analysis that can serve 'decision-making' purposes, and the normative one is a type that can serve 'scientific' purposes.

62   **Volume II. Selected Testimonies on the Epistemological...**

The programming approach overcomes the persistent equivocation that has developed in economics, sociology, psychology and political science, as well as in many derived disciplines which are also very close to decision and planning processes (for example, regional science) but which have a positivist imprint: the idea that one can deduce from human behaviour of man and social groupings 'laws' or 'norms' of behaviour, upon which an aprioristic theory and behaviour paradigms can be constructed and perhaps translated into parameters between behaviour variables in the so-called decision models.

On this fallacious idea Gunnar Myrdal and Ragnar Frisch made some masterly observations a while ago that deserve to be recalled here.[23] I will reproduce only one insightful passage by Frisch on the subject of the 'half logic' which underpins the use of predictive models in planning.

> In most countries the shift of viewpoint is, however, based on a kind of *half-logic* which I have never been able to understand and which, I think, will never be able to yield fundamental solutions. On the one hand one still retains the on-looker viewpoint, and tries to make projections on this basis (*growth models* of the current types). And on the other hand one will afterwards try to use such projections as a *basis for decisions*. How can it be possible to *make a projection without knowing the decisions that will basically influence the course of affairs*? It is as if the policy maker would say to the economic expert: 'Now you, expert, try to guess what I am going to do, and make your estimate accordingly. On the basis of the factual information I thus receive I will then decide what to do'. The shift from the on-looker viewpoint to the decision viewpoint must be founded *on a much more coherent form of logic*. It must be based on a decision model, i.e. a model where the possible decisions are built in explicitly as essential variables. (Frisch 1961, p. 44, emphases added)

Unfortunately, in current usage 'decision model' has ended up meaning any model that is useful for taking decisions. At the same time, in order to avoid the 'half logic' about which Frisch writes, it would be necessary to define as decision models only those constructed on the basis of variables (and on the hypothesised behaviour of such variables) that are strictly linked to the decision process and are not antecedent to it.[24]

Moreover, in order to avoid that half logic, the general equilibrium, of which it is certainly useful as a theorisation, should be conceived in such a way that decisions are founded on the operational awareness of the complexity of the decision problems, not as a pre-condition, but rather as an outcome of the decision process itself.

2.5 Conclusions: The Common Pragmatic Bases of the Prescriptive and Programming Approaches

Returning to BRT's main arguments, the authors themselves—on the basis of some acute observations on descriptive and normative models—conclude, as has been said, that there is a third approach to be favoured in the planning processes, one which greatly resembles what we call the 'planological': the 'prescriptive' approach.

It is clear that decision theory, which is anchored in the socio-psychological foundations of decision behaviour, tends to model logical decision processes on the 'individual', rather than on decisions made by groups, organisations, institutions and even governments, with their range of representativeness. Decision theorists as targets (and clientele) for their consultancy work have in mind mainly managers, whether private or public.

But this does not create great differences in approach between the prescriptive and the programming approach, which is principally aimed at conceiving and assisting decisions in complex systems of social and community planning and at decision-makers with political responsibility.

Let us underline some interesting elements of decision theory, having affirmed the trichotomy, because it converges with the need to overturn the approaches in the ways they have followed each other in the relationship between 'positive science' and 'planning science'.

The *normative* models are evaluated on the basis of their theoretic adequacy, that is, to the degree to which they supply acceptable idealisations or rational choices.

The *prescriptive* models are evaluated on the basis of their pragmatic worth, that is, according to their capacity to help people to make better decisions.

In conclusion, I reaffirm that the task of building 'decisional-type models', in particular in order to assist political decision-makers to take better decisions, is that of planology—a 'true' planology which has been critically and methodologically liberated from the undue assumptions of the neo-classical theory on economic behaviours, but also from the other, even less 'classic' theories of 'positive economy'.

Notes to Chapter 2 (Vol. II)

1. As affirmed by Sven Ove Hannson in an *Introduction to the Decision Theory* (see complete citation in Sect. 15.2), 'the decision theory does not, according to the received opinion, enter the scene until the ethical or political norms are already fixed'.
2. M. Blaug, *The methodology of Economics, or how economists explain*, second edit., Cambridge Univ. Press, 1992.
3. This distinction has been called 'the Hume guillotine', a complete logical separation between the kingdom of facts and the kingdom of values.
4. We will do this with the help of Blaug and his book on the methodology of economics.
5. Blaug quotes Hudson (1969), Black (1970) (Chap. 3).
6. Nagel, in his most important work *The Structure of Science* (1961).
7. Perhaps one could be so pedantic as to develop an elaborate taxonomy and, for each item listed, develop an equally rich case study of the behaviours and legitimacy of the more or less acceptable influences of values and evaluations, which would end up making the whole effort unfeasible and useless.
8. Even with trust in the facts (as products of positive affirmations) much less than mine, for strictly epistemological reasons. Since the relation between 'facts' and 'truth' in the field of social sciences—as seen with Myrdal in **Vol. I**, Chap. 2—it is not so obvious and indisputable as the positivist approach would claim.
9. In his *Methodology of Social Sciences,* an excellent English language collection (1949), selected and edited by E.A. Shils and H.A. Finch, of the methodological writings of Max Weber.

The Pogramming Approach and the Old, Unresolved Debate... 65

10. Conversely, where does the search for 'positivity', trying to guarantee an 'is-judgment' versus an 'ought-judgment', come from, if not from forcing a normative judgment? That cannot avoid inducing the thought that, having been thrown out of the door, we are trying to re-enter through the window.

11. An author that I placed, in this book, as one of the first aware of the epistemological overturning which is at the basis of the programming approach (**Vol. I**, Chaps. 1 and 2).

12. As mentioned in Chap. 1, this became the later English title (1993) of the original Swedish book, which in its previous German edition (1933) was *The political element in the formation of the doctrines of pure economics.*

13. Blaug (in his work on methodology) mentions Myrdal only when dealing with the subject of the objectivity of economic research (Blaug, op. cit. pp. 120–121). I think this is a reprehensible failing, especially for an historian of economic theory.

14. Chronologically, *Objectivity in Social Research* (Duckworth, London, 1970) is the last of his published books. See p. 86, note 40 (where Myrdal summarises the different parts of his previous works on the argument of 'objectivity', which are laid out in the final sections of this work).

15. Reflections that operate mainly in the field of behavioural theory, which, in their turn, deal specifically with the theory of individual behaviour based on methodological individualism. See the objections to methodological individualism in discussing the praxeology badly approached by Ludwig von Mises (Chap. 1, Sect. 1.2).

16. This is David E. Bell, scholar of Operational Research and Decision theory at Harvard Business School and not the sociologist Daniel Bell, discussed in **Vol. II**, this chapter, nor another well-known David E. Bell, who worked with President J.F. Kennedy, and was the director of the Office of Management and Budget (1961–62) and of the Agency for International Development (1962–66).

17. Bell, Howard Raiffa and Amos Tversky are three influential decision-making theorists, who followed many years of developments in (neoclassical) decision theory during, which von Neumann and Morgenstern, Simon, Luce and Raiffa, and Ackoff, to name but a few, stand out. The reference here is to *Decision Making: Descriptive, Normative and Prescriptive Interactions,* edited by D.E. Bell, H. Raiffa, and A. Tversky, Cambridge University Press, 1988.

18. This collection of essays, published by Cambridge University Press, edited by the said authors, who also coordinated the conference, is over 600 pages long and includes 30 papers by authors who are undoubtedly the best researchers in decision theory of the second half of the last century (such as J.G. March; Herbert A. Simon; P.C. Fishburn, Amos Tversky and Daniel Kahneman; Ralph L. Keeny; Kenneth J. Arrow; and Chris Argiris).

19. The way the three editors presented the work deserves to be taken into account, in their own words:

We found the following taxonomy useful:

Descriptive

1. Decisions people make
2. How people decide

Normative

1. Logically consistent decisions procedures
2. How people should decide

Prescriptive

1. How to help people to make good decisions
2. How to train people to make better decisions

Observe that we have moved from the usual dichotomy (descriptive and normative) to a trichotomy by adding a 'prescriptive' category. We have done this primarily because so much of what two of us (David and Howard) do professionally is not adequately captured in the usual descriptive/normative breakdown. One of us (Amos) feels, however that, although the prescriptive category has been useful for our internal discussion, it may not be necessary in proselyting for this more elaborative breakdown if we were to clarify further the normative category [...] Of course, the lines are blurred and even in our own conference papers into descriptive, normative and prescriptive parts (Bell, Raiffa and Tversky, eds, *Decision making; etc*, cited, pp. 1–2).

20. This approach partly recalls the distinction, into two categories, of the value judgments proposed by Nagel, which we mentioned in Sect. 2.4 of this chapter.

21. Here the authors give an example: the property of stochastic dominance. Since this condition is considered as a cornerstone of a rational choice, each theory that does not obey it is considered unsatisfying from a normative point of view. From another side, a descriptive theory is expected to take into account the violations observed of the stochastic dominance. A prescriptive analysis can develop procedures intended to eliminate and reduce these violations. A failure of dominance therefore can serve as a counter-example for a normative model, as an observation to be explained with a descriptive model and as challenge for a prescriptive model.

22. Thus, Zauberman with his *Aspects of Planometrics* (1967). For a wide-ranging 'planological' examination of these distinctions, see the vast bulk of work by Ragnar Frisch, and, in particular, the essays from the last period of his life. Above all, see the systematic treatment on the 'use of models' in planning and decision contained in the fundamental work on macroeconomic planning (1977–78) by Leif Johansen.

23. See the essay by Myrdal: *How Scientific are the Social Sciences?* (Myrdal 1972) amply discussed in **Vol. I**, Chap. 1.

24. Here I recall the typological profile of the models for planning, reproduced already in **Vol. I**, Chap. 7. See also further considerations concerning the analysis of planning centred on the decision, in **Vol. II**, Chap. 8.

Bibliographical References to Chapter 2 (Vol. II)

Bell, D.E., Raiffa, H. and Tversky, A. (eds.) (1988). *Decision Making: Descriptive, Normative and Prescriptive Interactions.* Cambridge, Cambridge University Press.

Blaug, Mark. (1992). *The Methodology of Economics: Or, How Economists Explain.* Cambridge: Cambridge University Press.

Frisch, Ragnar. (1961). The Oslo REFI Interflow Table. Memorandum, Oslo, University of Oslo Institute of Economics.

Frisch, Ragnar. (1976a). *Economic Planning Studies.* A Collection of Essays edited posthumous, by Frank Long, D. Reidel Publishing Company.

Frisch, Ragnar. (1976b). 'From Utopian Theory to Practical Applications: The Case of Econometrics'. In *Economic Planning Studies*, ed. by F. Frank Long, Reidel Publishing Company.

Hudson, W.D. (1969). 'The Is-Ought Question'. *A Collection of Papers on the Central Problem in Moral Philosophy*. London: Macmillan, 1969.

Klappholz, K (1964). Value Judgements and Economics, *British Journal for the Philosophy of Science*, 15 reprinted in Hausman, 1984; pp: 267–292.

Max Weber. (1949). *Methodology of Social Sciences*. Routledge, reprinted in 2017.

Myrdal G. (1972). 'How Scientific are the Social Sciences?' *Cahiers de l'ISEA, Serie H.S. 14*.

Myrdal, Gunnar (1970). *The Challenge of World Poverty; a World Anti-Poverty Program in Outline*. New York, Pantheon Books.

Nagel, Ernest. (1967). Preference, Evaluation, and Reflective Choice. *Human Values and Economic Policy. A Symposium*. H. Sidney. New York, New York University Press.

Sen, Amartya. (1970). "The impossibility of a Paretian Liberal." *Journal of Political Economy* 78.1: 152–157.

Shils, Edward A., and Henry A. Finch. (1949). Max Weber on the Methodology of the Social Sciences. *Glencoe* 111: 73rT.

Zauberman, Alfred. (1967). *Aspects of Planometrics*. London, University of London, The Athlone Press.

3

The Programming Approach in the Collective Decision and 'Action-Centred' Analysis

3.1 Programming and the Knowledge: Action Nexus

What I have described up to this point on the epistemology of economics, in my view, recalls a line of thought that considers it impossible to separate—at least in the social sciences—the moment of *knowledge* from the moment of *action*.[1]

The line of thought to which I refer has very old roots, and has been formulated, in more general terms, as a 'nexus between knowledge and action': the nearer and more explicit roots are in the philosophical stream of pragmatism[2] (Charles S. Peirce, 1839–1914), (William James, 1842–1910), John Dewey (1859–1952), George H. Mead (1863–1931), then in the so-called 'sociology of knowledge' (Mannheim)[3]; many aspects can also be found in the debate[4] between Popper and the Frankfurt School.[5] Its oldest roots can be found in the philosophies of the past (beginning from Plato and Aristotle), which have systematically enhanced the life and activities of mankind in its social relations (the ethics of knowledge and the ethics of action). There is no doubt and it is of little surprise that the programming approach outlined so far in this book could find some of its roots, and discover a basis, precisely in the debate

© The Author(s) 2019
F. Archibugi, *The Programming Approach and the Demise of Economics*,
https://doi.org/10.1007/978-3-319-78060-3_3

on the relationship between knowledge and action—more specifically on the 'knowledge–action nexus'.

It is also unsurprising, then, if within the cognitive/operational sphere where we have placed ourselves (the problems of socio-political management, administrative policy and programming of the public system, and also economic policy) that the knowledge–action nexus presents itself as a nexus between cognition of social facts and political and social action—or, more simply, between action (operational) analysis and planning decisions of action.

Thus, such a nexus involves any kind of action and concerns all social sciences in their operational version, as oriented towards decision and action. Again, we find this discussed at the basis of all modern versions (whether conscious or not) of rational and strategic planning.[6]

Therefore, discussing the programming approach, it is impossible to miss the nexus between cognitive analysis and intentional action.

3.1.1 'Positive' Knowledge and 'Programming' Knowledge

The knowledge–action nexus—in the evolution of modern scientific thought—has been examined through the prism of the saying 'knowing to act (or to decide)'. The prevailing and wiser version is 'knowing before acting or making a decision.'

It is probable—at least in the more modern versions of the idea, especially if related to social questions—that the nexus has been conceived under the radical influence of the behavioural vision called 'positivistic' (or deterministic).

However, no one could deny that, in principle, there is a kind of substantial interaction between both terms of the nexus—that the first can influence the second and the second can influence the first, and even that a kind of reciprocal influence can exist. Nonetheless, in the positivist vision it seems far more acceptable that the moment of knowledge precedes that of action, or could have a kind of priority, logical or temporal, in respect to the action. (Consequently, this is in respect to all of the operational derivations: analysis/decision; programme/design, and so on).

Thus, in this vision, the 'science'—which is also 'knowledge'—identifies itself in that attitude to know and to discover (natural) laws, including those of human behaviour, individual or collective and 'social', in such a way as to render the actions and the decision-making of men, participants and social groups, more rational, compatible and feasible with the laws discovered.

But the programming approach, which is the best protagonist actor of **Vols. I** and **III** of this trilogy (while it is the best non-protagonist actor of **Vol. II**), although it also acknowledges the essential interaction in the knowledge–action nexus, does not consider the laws and norms called 'rational'; these we must identify and discover, as they constitute a universal scientific heritage. It is based on a kind of priority of action in relation to knowledge, in the sense that the possible knowledge finds its start-up, source and motivation in action and in its hypothetical consequences for the facts and reality.

The programming approach thus finds its sole and exclusive matrix in the problems to be solved and in the best decisions to take for the solution of these problems. It is a matter that groups and communities currently have to face with action focused towards the future, without prejudices or theoretical invalid assumptions; or, better, to face with new problems, the solution of which will provide, in turn, new and more advanced knowledge. With the programming approach the binomial of the nexus, therefore, would be the inversion of action/knowledge, action for knowledge (with all the analogous operational derivatives indicated above).

So, within the planning theory itself, we can distinguish the programming approach from the positivistic one.

3.1.2 The Damage Done by the 'Positivist' Approach

At this point, I would like to focus attention on the dangers of, or the damage done by, the positivistic approach. I choose to do so with a particular controversial and provocative tone, in the hope of sufficiently affecting the wall of determinism that has become too heavily consolidated, in a critical silence and in a logical hardening into habit, which seems to be 'implicit'—I am sorry to note—even in the field of planners, whose DNA should be resistant to positivistic influence.

Social positivism (the flat application of the behavioural criteria of the analysis of natural phenomena to social and human phenomena), which still imbues the modern social sciences, has entered into the open field of actual reality with its behavioural 'theories'.[7] The 'naturalist' support has invaded many fields in behavioural research on social and political reasoning and thought, which, while from one side it has enlarged the opportunities for obtaining interesting information and ideas, from the other side has reduced drastically the field of sociology and policies of a normative or programming nature.

From another viewpoint, the 'naturalist support' invasion has found comparisons only in the short term (and with some difficulty), not in the long term, with that which concerns in particular the field of socio-economic planning and even the field of territorial or physical planning.

In effect, a significant level of research (defined as 'scientific') has flooded many parameters (observed or virtual; meaningful and meaningless) and behavioural relations (more or less linear), restricting the freedom of exploration and the flexibility of experimentation.

When those parameters are not contradicted by the data (and are, consequently, disproved), the answer that the experts of social positivism are able to provide, can be reduced and condensed into one word: paradox.

But a paradox of what?

Paradox with respect to the 'laws' and parameters constructed through that 'implicit theorisation' and that excessive 'indirect' statistical inference (as we examined through the arguments of Wassily Leontief in **Vol. I**, Chap. 8), the 'paradox' exists due to all of this.

But if we cancel all this, the paradox disappears as well.

This indirect inference, called 'empirical', is that used to measure the quantification of the model, in the hope of predicting a priori, and conditioning, the phenomenon's repetitiveness. The risk, in that case, is that we build a logical instrument to falsify 'scientifically' what we wish to deny—repetitiveness that in most cases loses its meaning as evidence if we do not use the erroneous hypothesis or conceptual parameters. Any experiment loses certainty and validity if performed in different situations, conditions, time and, above all, with different participants.[8]

Faced with the easy and recurrent denial of the presumed behavioural relations, another attitude of the social positivists, who continue to view social phenomena as analogues to natural phenomena, is to accuse excessively simple or rigid assumptions of the theoretical approach (the *coeteris paribus* abuse). For this, endless papers and formulas have been created to 'relax' the models from their primary assumptions, moving forwards into an endless line of case studies that are absolutely ungovernable.[9]

All of this occurs due to the obstinate trend for seeking laws or 'norms' within the nature of things, before knowing how these things can be seen in relation to the problems to solve or of aspirations or preferences to establish, and consequently in relation to the decisions to be taken.[10]

This happens also because of the resistance to accept that, in the social and human field (where the free choice of humans exists in spite of social limitations and restrictions), there is a lack of support for choices (for individuals, for social groups, for the communities as a whole), other than knowing what those restrictions, the required means, are to make those choices 'rational'.

More recently, partly due to the above-mentioned historical rejections (the various presumed paradoxes) and partly for similar changes that have occurred in the epistemology of the natural sciences,[11] people have begun to justify the predictive failure by employing another trick: 'complexity' and the catastrophic forecast of its governance. The 'mathematical theory of the catastrophe' employed in the field of social events, appears as an attempt to explain the presumed paradoxes of classical social positivism.

All this leads to a justified crisis of a reliance on the methodology of planning, if managed with the simplified and non-critical social (and also economic) positivism, compromising and discrediting all planning that has been confused with those misleading approaches. These situations, in which the methodology of planning could appear—instead of the difficult and innovative steps forward for the organisation of our societies and communities—rather than being built on sand, are ready to leave mankind in the hope only of some natural automatism and fortuity of the 'spontaneous order' (the oxymoron preferred by the optimist Frederick von Hayek).

I do not believe that it is right to mistrust the capacity of formulating the rational behavioural hypothesis simply because this 'rationality' is based on an approximate and mechanical idea flattened by abstract individualistic economic rational behaviour (presumed and non-existent).

74 Volume II. Selected Testimonies on the Epistemological...

In fact, in this context, it is not only 'rationality' itself that is in crisis, but also the rationality of those using it in such a way. And therefore, irrationally—in order to answer also to another family of arguments—it is not a question of using 'hard' or 'weak' thoughts,[12] but it is a question simply of 'critical or non-critical' thought.

3.2 The Unexpected but Significant Contribution of Land and Urban Planners (*the 'Planning Theory' Movement*)

However, it is not so much in the field of economic theory that pragmatism and the problem of the inversion of the knowledge–action nexus are developed. It is developed rather in the field of physical planning (territorial, environmental, infrastructural, urban, socio-medical, and so on) considered in managerial and organisational terms and connected to operational research and decision theory.

It is rather in the field of the system engineering designer or planning designer,[13] in any field of substantive knowhow, where vast methodological reflection on the method of advancing progress has been developed. Physical design, rather than economic theory, is the cultural ground most predisposed to this development.

3.2.1 The DNA of 'Planning Theorists'

In contrast to economic theory, planning theory is totally geared to the 'doing', and not to the 'being', of things. The doing (which represents the idea of change and improving things from what they are into what they should be) is already incorporated into the profession of the engineer or designer, in any field of activity and knowhow.

We could say, briefly, that the 'programming approach' already exists in the DNA of the designer or planner.[14] Here there is no 'passage' that we have to tread from a positivist approach to a programming approach.[15]

In spite of that, urban planning is not divided, as are other sciences, into two parts: the first of a preliminary analytical-descriptive character; and the second of a subordinate, normative-prescriptive one.[16]

Urban planning is, in itself, based from the outset on the logical normative-prescriptive.

Therefore, by its nature, from its starting point, planning is also the analysis of the things, situations and management, made by the designer/planner, from the point of view of the decisions needed to be taken, in order to change things for the better, according to the defined objectives. There would be no need for a special method of connection between 'spatial' behaviour and 'spatial' designing.

If during the planning process we encounter descriptive moments (perhaps it would be better to call them 'cognitive'), they are only subsequent and subsidiary to the definition and elaboration of the operative finalities of land-use planning.[17] And if land-use planning leans too heavily on those descriptive and cognitive aspects, it would be a mistake because such could condition the 'pure' normative (or better, 'programmatic') essence of planning, and pollute it with prejudices and '*a-priorisms*' that would be irregular and 'non-scientific'.

It should find its 'scientificity' (as Myrdal proposed; see **Vol. I**, Chap. 2) in its operational feasibility, in its practicality, or in the liberty of planning (as Frisch said; see **Vol. I**, Chap. 4), and in the method of the optimal preferential selection of that choice, which already includes an analysis of the limits, conditions and bounds of every perceivable action.

This explains how a reflection on how people operate and on how they could operate better has been developed more directly and implicitly in the field of urban planning than in all other social sciences (at least as they have been considered to date).

3.2.2 A Look at the 'Gestation Period' of Planning Theory (*the 1960s*)

From this idea, during the 1960s, what was to become the community of planning theorists was born.

This community emerged spontaneously, with the contribution of scholars of different extractions and backgrounds (political scientists, urban economists, sociologists and their technical colleagues, such as management scientists, system analysts, engineers and operational researchers), but all linked to an operational sphere related to territory and urban management and its schools of urban, regional and land planning. In general, it has been a question of scholars that have been able to meet to discuss problems of method, and to seek a way out from their relatively homogeneous backgrounds in order to be open to new questions of an interdisciplinary or transdisciplinary character.

These scholars felt limited in their professional activities and began to reflect upon, to comment on, to discuss and to debate the methods to be used in their job as planners; that is, the settling and transforming of designs, projects, programmes, plans and policies on land, environment, cities, and any kind of object in the physical world. This approach was given different names, such as Systems Analysis and Engineering, Policy Science, Management Science, Operation Research, Praxeology, Strategic Planning, Planning Theory and others.

In my opinion, this approach was mainly due to a European scholar in Oxford, Andreas Faludi,[18] (whose thinking I will examine below), who put together a critical sample of selected writing from amongst the most meaningful and problematic of those different but emerging disciplines,[19] and edited them under the title of *A Reader in Planning Theory* (1973), publishing them with the aim of offering a form of comparison.

Faludi accompanied this anthology in the same year with a new volume, in which he tried to implement a systematic order for the comparison of this undefined area of literature and proposed a systematisation of the matter, giving to this publication the title of *Theory of Planning*.

The Faludi books were well received as a unitary theoretical interpretation of planning (mainly in its 'procedural' form), one valid for the fields of work and study indicated above.

I think it is suitable here—as I did earlier in **Vol. I**, Chap. 2, Sect. 2.8—with another area of study, which is perhaps less professional than planning, in terms of the methodology of scientific research—to carry out a rapid purely bibliographic review of the main works published by the most well-known scholars of this group. This would serve to send a meta-disciplinary message, to open a window of dialogue with the world of socio-economic planning, within the limits of the methodological aspects. It represents a trial of exchange and development motivated by the same spirit of cultural integration that has pushed me to dedicate a chapter in this book to the group of planning theorists.

3.2.3 A List of Planning Theorist Authors Deserving of More Attention

Moving on from the authors included by Faludi in his readings, a first group is of scholars that share an urban planning experience.[20] Others have a background in political and administrative sciences.[21] Some were sociologists interested in the sociology of the change.[22]

I would like to add some economists (not selected in Faludi's anthology) as influential and potential participants in the club of planners.[23]

Others have experience in strategic programming, system engineering, operational research, decision theory and cost-benefit analysis, on many scales of compatibility and of external economies and dis-economies; others have experience in disciplines connected to renewal in the large-scale management of either private or public machineries services (all emergent disciplines in the post-Second World War period).[24]

It is question a professional figure often evokes in the cultural debates and fields of action and social design as 'social engineering'. However, this status not yet has been translated into an integrated system of work, nor ratified by a common nomenclature or lexicon and—overall—a methodology, accompanied possibly by common experimentation.

Unfortunately, the debate developed by the planning theorists did not go in such direction in the subsequent decades.

First of all, the debate did not concern them alone, as a group educated almost exclusively at the schools and faculties of engineering and architecture, for the most related to the 'profession' of the land- and city-use planners. It has been, alas, a clamorous limitation.

The planning 'problems' of people encompassed by, say, Faludi in his *Reader*, and so on, dealt with much more. They concerned theoretical and methodological problems not limited only to these, but also problems of other scholars, educated in other problems, coming from others schools, special university courses, and faculties or departments: political science, social welfare and organisation planning, economic and development planning, public expenditures, budgeting, social accountability in educational and technological organisation, and any other subjects that play a very important part in our current common and daily life and in its planning and management.

78   Volume II. Selected Testimonies on the Epistemological...

The planning problems have been not only ignored by most from those who had been following that debate (taking the name—as said—from the limited matrix of land- and city-use planners).

Thus, from the departure, it has been disappointing to see that the hope of a new dialogue that from Faludi's initial works it seemed possible to develop—on the problems of an integrated and unified planning on a vaster field of sectorial applications—was cut off in the 1970s and never re-opened again.[25]

The main interest inside the real community of planning theorists was already divided by the predominance of planning positions in land-use planning rather than the relevance of the problem of a unified approach.

The window of dialogue with other planning competences from other faculties (economics, management, political science, and so on), and many other new competences and methods singularly attached to this or that university branch, remained closed.

On the contrary, the initiative of the planning theorists could and should be of interest even to many other types of professional connected to land-use planning activities, of which people for some time have voiced the need for creating a single forum, one not deriving from one of its various components (economics, sociology, accounting, political science, and so on). This would respond, however, in some measure, to the traditions and progress achieved by those components, but establishing the aim which is at the basis of its specific mission: how to develop better plans aimed at multiple strategic ends and on multiple scales, as a technical problem in itself.

Thus, we should ask: was the planning theorists' movement able to satisfy all of these requirements?

It was able to give a body and personality to this planned need for integration (already announced by the United Nations in one of its invited government members and its agencies, particularly in reference to the United Nations Development Programme programmes of aid and development).

But it seems to me that the answer should be no since the window for dialogue with other competences in planning deriving from other disciplines is still too closed.

The most plausible and probable cause lies in the fact that the origin of associations of planning theorists can be found in the classrooms of the engineering and architecture departments, which had—as already said—the great merit of posing problems aimed at inducing action towards the improvement of those problems to be faced. They gave the scholars and professionals trained in those rooms an education aimed at obscuring any problem that surpassed localised planned action, and a physical solution, circumscribed for localised interventions linked to the area of these. It was necessary to find and construct a method, not only procedural but also substantial, only and most of all functional for problems which had the possibility of being dealt with on different scales from those usually defined as 'territorial'—for example, 'national' or for great sectoral and typological divides, energy, chemical use, health innovation, military defence and future archaeology.

In both those ways anticipated by Faludi (see Sect. 3.3), and the ulterior proposals that I permitted myself to make following his trail (Sect. 3.4), which is just as important to consider, it is hopeful that the orientation expressed by Faludi since the end of the 1980s for decisively choosing to work on the technical plan around the construction, still non-existent, of a planning methodology will prevail.

There is a lot of work to do and it would be best to have a greater and more aware commitment and participation from the community of planning theorists concerning the large discourse for preparing public action for facing, on a global scale, the vast and systematic construction of a strategic and systemic nature, of the programming approach in all fields coordinated with the public management.

3.2.4 Limits and Carelessness in the Community of Planning Theorists

The outcome, as I have said, was a vast and dense arena of debate, one which sought to encounter all aspects of contemporary problems of planning and, with great versatility, researched its own roots in all streams of thought of contemporary culture (sometimes with great superficiality).

During the 1980s, the community of planning theorists expanded in many directions and in search of the roots of planning theory, either the remote origins of the modern Western cultures by means of the monumental work by John Friedmann,[26] or the care by some editors of anthologies of selections of writings, which were among the most meaningful in comparison to those of contemporary debate.[27]

More positive and useful was—within the movement of the planning theorists—the engagement of Ernest E. Alexander in his critical and updated exposition of the 'approaches to planning', and a critical 'introduction to the planning theories, concepts and current problems'.[28] His is a very useful textbook for disentangling ourselves from the multiple directions, visions and experiences of the planning theorists, developed in the subsequent decade to that of Faludi's initial books and to the output of the 1960s.[29]

Both, Faludi and Alexander—it seems to me—researched during two different periods, more than ten years apart, and with reference to totally different literature, in order to construct operative reordering schemes of methods and a different approach for a potential new methodology for planning.

However, I doubt that the debate reached a clear conclusion on a new methodology.

The debate has pursued many different roads, reducing the possibility of reaching a common methodology. It vanished, giving place to a series of non-conclusive outcomes that did not give the idea of making plans better, more 'operational' and 'consistent' with the context, nor capable of being guided toward efficient implementation, nor capable of creating a code or protocol for good management, and so on.

In such a way, the debate was developed behind the facade of the name planning theory and it was not consolidated into an explicit methodology to be followed by teachers and practitioners, as a body of rules, steps and suggestions corresponding to the most agreed-on aspects of the community of planning scholars.

In spite of many declarations about the will to approach and integrate methods in different fields of work (this seemed really the aim of the first managers of the multilateral approach *à la* Myrdal and of the first efforts of the United Nations), the planning theorists were de facto even more 'armoured' in their original field of 'city design' without researching methodological dialogues with other disciplinary fields of planning.

Despite being at an advantage due to their predisposition towards *doing* (instead of *being*), and towards projecting and improvement and towards the rational aim of what *ought to be*, the movement could not liberate itself entirely from behavioural analysis and a scientific approach that I define as 'positivistic' (and one that is very poorly 'positive' in reality).

Such a community of planning theorists (and its linked literature) opened and extended its roots and legacy (as dealt with in the book by John Friedman referenced above), but closed within it its unique cultural background, one that has not improved nor increased disciplinary integration (nor meta-disciplinary integration) between different social sciences, as Myrdal and the United Nations deliberations had wished for such a methodology for two decades in the 1950s and 1960s.

The planning theorists in effect, thanks to their natural epistemological predisposition to lead a wider operation-renewal of the scientific approach for social sciences, find themselves in some way, in advance, as capable of understanding and putting in place the movement from a determinist approach to a programmatic one.[30]

In spite of this—as said—they were not able to develop, in a clear way, an integrated planning discipline of systematic character, which focusing on that what makes all other political and social sciences useful to adequately re-use those aspects naturally proposal-based, before 'deterministic' and now 'programmatic'.

This epistemological overturning—as we have seen—has its origin in the 'sociology of knowledge', in 'pragmatism', in the 'praxeological approach', and elsewhere. But, more recently, it has found its more natural assertion in a new methodology of planning.[31]

At this point, a real convergence of a disciplinary approach would be needed for a new unitary methodology of planning and connected experiences. A general methodological convergence, beginning from radical reflections of the entire field of the social sciences (based on the main matrices of economics, politics, sociology and environmental sciences and individual sub- or supporting disciplines) would be necessary where all of these would be functionally oriented towards planning operations.

82   Volume II. Selected Testimonies on the Epistemological...

This would involve a convergence of schools of economics, sociology, operational research, analysis and system engineering, organisational and administrative sciences, spatial planning (at global, European, multinational regional and local level, and so on), in consonance with a number of other streams of thought and applications, arising from different points ('specialisations') without the need for a 'unified approach to planning'.

In other words, it would be an enlarged vision of the 'planning sciences', or planology, as already proposed by Myrdal and by the United Nations[32]; and re-proposed by myself at the scientific Conference in 1992, promoted by the Planning Studies Centre of Rome, in Palermo (Italy) in November 1992.[33]

3.2.5 What Hope for the Future of the Planning Theorists?

The planning theorists, without preparing themselves consciously for this new unified management, which is technically and politically oriented, risk exacerbating the lack of coordination in the world and in international political and administrative life, and risk increasing the degree of randomness and operational disorder, and finally risk seriously eroding confidence in the (Myrdalian) coordination of planning.

Even the expression, theory of planning, is beginning to be interpreted in an 'uneasy' way.

In effect, what does 'theory' mean? It means 'supposition or system of ideas explaining something', and in 'the sphere of abstract knowledge or speculative thought' (according to the *Concise Oxford Dictionary)*. But in our case what could the *theory of planning* mean?

Perhaps we should explain what planning consists of? Perhaps also, we should ask what the principles, conditions or methods are to make plans that deserve to be called 'plans'.

A 'positivist' approach to planning would tend to explain what it means to plan and to describe how planners outline plans and how they manage these, and the methods by which they conduct the plans towards their implementation and success.

A 'programming' approach would tend to be more interested in defining methods or procedures to build and manage plans in order to make plans as meaningful, consistent, rational, operative, feasible and effective as possible in relation to their stated objectives.

Perhaps it is a question of distinctions, but I have personally developed the impression that the first approach, the 'positivist', is more open to a general debate on desired outcomes that remain abstract, various and difficult to define in practical ways and are orientated towards an acceptable implementation. The second approach, the 'programmatic', could limit its objectives only to what is possible to plan, given the constraints and conditions available to the planner. The plans find their 'rationality' in the possibility of being implemented, and—for that purpose—under the opportunity of being pursued and guaranteed by the policy decision-makers, who are also their political and technical authors.

It is in any case within the vast arena of the political representatives that the bargained contribution to the change of approach from positivist to programmatic must be found, indicated as an overturning of the relation between analysis and decision, which is assumed to be at the basis of the change.

3.2.6 The Need for the Integration of 'Proceduralism' and 'Substantivism' in a Unique Methodology

First of all—even before proposing the movement (above) from the theory of planning into a methodology of planning—Faludi's ideas seemed to be revised by a clean distinction established at the basis of 'planning theory' between a 'proceduralist' approach (which he himself declared to be his greater concern) and a 'substantialist' (to use Faludi's own words).

Following the vast and confused debate surrounding the first book, it seemed, in some writings, Faludi would doubt the opportunity to maintain that clean distinction between 'proceduralism' and 'substantialism', in planning theory, especially in fields of application, such as that of the environment. In one of his writings (1985), he declared it preferable to transcend the 'substantivist' versus 'proceduralist' controversy by proposing:

> a theory of environmental planning combining understanding of procedures with understanding of features of the environment that make for a need for

planning. It notes common elements in the views of the environment and environmental planning held by authors from divergent intellectual traditions: (a) they all conceive of the environment as, amongst other things, institutionally determined in the sense of legal barriers forming an important element of it; (b) they see the environment as the object of both private and public decision-making; (e) they see the environment as forming the object of conflict. […].

On this basis, [this essay] identifies land decision units as the foci of public and private decision-making concerning the environment. They are characterised by (a) the resources on them, (b) the channels linking them to other units, (c) the land regime providing barriers against intrusion, (d) land titles identifying the primary decision makers concerned. Public environmental measures taken because of externalities can aim at changing each of these attributes. Land decision units cover jurisdiction like seamless garments, and there is much interaction between what happens on them. Much as with measures of private actors, public environmental measures can mutually enhance each other or get in each other's way. Where this occurs, the article speaks of externalities of the second order. Environmental planning stands for the preparation of environmental plans taking care of such externalities, so that public environmental measures are taken with full knowledge of all their implications. A theory of environmental planning must combine awareness of the element of decision-making in planning with an understanding of the externalities of the second order arising out of the nature of environmental measures as being addressed to land decision units with definite locations in a spatial- temporal expanse. A case study of Dutch urbanisation policy illustrates the notion of externalities of the second order. (Faludi 1985, pp. 239–40)

Here Faludi seems to recognise that it is the same planning method, intended as a conceptual object, which should integrate the procedure and substance of planning; this emerges not from reality but only from a static analysis of the concepts and the fields of planning on which the above-mentioned dichotomies risk (as actually happened) their sterilisation.

But it still does not provide a clear idea of how we should structure this integration.

The idea of focusing attention on the 'externality' of the analysis of the most insidious consequentiality of the structural interdependence is less evident when we explore definite second-order relations of in the accounting structure for planning: it seems to me a very intelligent idea (especially if formulated by an economist). The area of 'externality' constitutes an area of great uncertainty in the processes of planning.

I have allowed myself, however, to add my own personal comments so to further these theories: these are negative on the continuation of the debate of planning theorists, especially concerning the part of the debate relating to the controversy between the 'substantialists and the proceduralists', which, frankly, has never convinced me. My purpose is to highlight the opportunity to overhaul the interpretation totally.

1. What use is there in this, if not the mere acknowledgement of a logical sophistry, in proceeding into the type of activity called 'planning', with the distinction of a proceduralist theory from a substantivist theory? If we wish to introduce 'rationality and method' into these activities, where can we find the instrument if not in a declared melting pot between the two modes in two separate theoretical terrains? Does this not, therefore, break the conceptual dichotomy it provokes by distancing it too radically rather than bringing the two closer together?

2. Will their integration not depend on how much the arguments of the proceduralists come into contact with the concrete problems of the substantivists and vice versa, in each of the operative sectors? And will it not depend on how much one or the other sectors will be able to convince the others that integration is possible and will be of great use for everyone to study the principles and common methods in an ordered way without improvisation?

3. Is it not necessary today to clarify too the methods with which the decisions or the actions are considered in the substantive problems of different operative fields? Must they respect some limits and functions that are applied through proceduralist planning? And would this method not benefit from being extended to substantivist planning in order to allow the appropriate level of measures of compatibility, and the capacity for coordination and methodological integration between the different visions and experiences? Does the methodology not concern perhaps problems also of substance in the single operative fields and not only problems of procedure?

4. Faludi was also, as we have already seen, a critical point of arrival and coordination that the literature (especially American) of urban planning and connected disciplines had produced up to that time. But the undeniably vast debate provoked by his book in 1973 developed without order or method in a number of different directions; it became multi-referenced, losing the well-defined direction of its method. Unfortunately, I do not believe that it created serious disadvantages for the operators of substantial plans due to its limited nature and the extremely partial situations susceptible to a 'consequentialism', which, in spite of being widespread, had a limited scope.

As in Frisch's metaphor on the 'pyramidisation' (see **Vol. I**, Chap. 7—Sects. 7.3.1–7.3.4), in order to be authentically systemic and rational, the methodology of planning needed not to ignore, but to keep virtually present all of its constituent dimensions—that of the collection of affinities, such as those of single constituent elements (the plans and the projects). It needed to be able to have as a potential reference all of the terms and countable relationships of different dimensions of the whole, not only in those closed points of departure or of arrival (micro-centric, mesocentric or macro-centric); in their substance and in their identical nature and validity, they can also be in the procedure.

Are not substance and procedure actually strictly interdependent?

3.3 Toward a Methodology of the Rational Planning (*Faludi's Original Contribution*)

Before asking how it would be possible to correct the situation, as yet enmeshed by the great debate—rather inconclusive from the methodological point of view—in the ambit of the planning theorists, I would like to comment on the contribution which was made in the same direction by Faludi on the specific aspect of planning methodology.

In fact, Faludi (who was overburdened—as we have said in the last section—with so many of the responsibilities of cultivating the movement of the planning theorists) was also the first to be aware that the debate that followed his first book (1973a) provoked a 'hotchpotch' of free words—called 'theory'—that lacked any clear working direction and, moreover, used a concept that risked creating significant confusion about the subject.

Thus, Faludi, a good 13 years after the publication of his first book on planning 'theory' decided to abandon the plural and dispersive arguments on planning and proposed to continue the debate, in a stricter and more focused way, passing from the theory of planning to the methodology of planning. Thus, he dedicated a new book to this movement: *Critical rationalism and planning methodology* (1986a).[34]

In fact, the first chapter of the new book was consequently called 'From Planning Theory to Planning Methodology'. And much of the tone of the observations it contained concerned the concept of an epistemological overturning, which this book supports, as the basis of an effective application of the programming approach.

Indeed, when I think again of the multiplicity of the directions to emerge from the debates of the 'planning theorists', following its brilliant emergence (first in the 1960s and then in the 1970s), I would like to change the name to a more ordinary one, such as the 'methodology of planning', in order to anchor the matter to concepts and solutions that are more practical and operational and less 'volatile' and 'speculative'.[35]

Faludi's ideas are very near to those of the programming approach described by the economists who are at the basis of this trilogy; it represents an interesting testimony to the possibility of a new integrated way of managing socio-economic activities and territorial and environmental projects, plans or programmes, of any substantial type.

3.3.1 From Planning Theory to Planning Methodology

The impetus for Faludi's 1986 book was that some of his colleagues accused him of not having taken into account Popper's methodological work on the larger field of the scientific research methodology. Faludi organised his answers about the Popperian work (that he declared he shared) in his book of 1986.

88   Volume II. Selected Testimonies on the Epistemological…

But in this new book, Faludi expressed his methodological vision of planning, with something extra, with respect to the previous citations, better configuring how certain 'positivistic' and scarcely 'voluntarist' as well as scarcely 'normativist' discourses could be at the heart of the new methodology.[36]

In fact, Faludi, for his part, was able to expand upon some methodological aspects of planning that are directly pertinent to the epistemological developments put forward in this book.

For this reason, some of his discourses of a methodological nature deserve to be included—and also with an abundance of citations (at least equal to the very discursive style of the author)—in the selection of anticipated components, and also some explanatory ones for the 'programming approach', as based on the results from political life and from public planning, to which this book is dedicated (in particular, **Vol. III**).

Thus, he established the change in relation to previous positions:

> In my previous work (Faludi 1973a), the emphasis is on procedural planning theory. Since then, I have come to view my problem as methodological. The purpose of this book, etc. as stated in the preface, is to develop a *planning methodology* in the spirit of the critical rationalism of Sir Karl Popper.
>
> This chapter shows that this step towards planning methodology is a natural one. It also clarifies what to expect of planning methodology. I begin with distinguishing procedural from substantive, as well as positive (or empirical) from normative planning theory, both of which concentrated in rationality in planning.
>
> Ten years after my proposing how to develop empirical planning theory of the procedural type, still no such theory has gained common acceptance. This warrants scepticism concerning the strategy proposed for developing it. In my empirical research since, 'methodological reflection'—the reconstruction of what decision makers and their planning advisers do in practice in the light of some norm of reasonableness—comes to the fore as an alternative. […]
>
> Critics challenge me for clinging to rationality even though planning practice is far from rational. But whether it is borne out by practice is irrelevant

The Programming Approach in the Collective Decision...   89

to its validity. 'Rationality' is not like a hypothesis. By showing how decisions should be critically taken and assessed, it answers to Popper's view of a methodological rule. As we shall see, its philosophical roots can be found in a secular view of humans as the makers or themselves, similar also to Popper's one. Knowledge is not sufficient for making plans. Rather, it must be applied to some purpose, and there must be organisations and procedures for coordination and implementation. This leads to the distinction between theory *in* planning (substantive theory) and theory *of* planning (procedural planning theory). My work relates to the latter.

Next to the procedural/substantive distinction, I make one between positive and normative theories of planning:

[Faludi quotes here a text from his old 1973's book]: '... normative theory is concerned with how planners ought to proceed rationally. Behavioural approaches focus more on the limitations which they are up against in trying to fulfil their Programme of rational action'.

This distinction is not rigid. Improvements to planning must be based on knowledge of practice. Indeed, research is often guided by the desire to improve practice. 'Empirical' planning theory—as I now prefer to describe 'positive' theory—seeks knowledge about the organisation and procedures of planning but, in so doing, it usually aims at improving practice. (Faludi 1986a, pp. 3–4)

Faludi distanced himself somewhat from the debate on dualism in *Planning Theory* which had produced, however (as I have already asserted), a large discussion on planning, its possibilities, its difficulties, its merits and its failings, and on its abstractness and its tangibility.[37] This, in fact, served little to improve plans or to make them more integrated with the context in which they were designed to have an impact; nor did it make them more feasible or more methodologically 'rational', efficient, technically controlled and, therefore, more valid or efficient.

Faludi had—as we have said—a point of critical arrival, and of coordination, in terms of what the literature (American especially) of urban planning and connected disciplines had achieved until then. But the undeniably vast debate provoked by his first book (1973a) developed without order and method in a direction that made it multi-referenced, losing it a precise direction. I think that the debate did not produce any advantage or help to the planning operators (experts or decision-makers).

In effect, in the debate nobody has asked how plans should be made or what methods should be used.[38]

Maybe Faludi also induced too much from the impulse to comment, critique and answer many (even too many indeed) single interlocutors of his book to strengthen the method of a 'rational planning' that for a long time was recommended by those planning theorists recalled above (Sect. 3.3.2).[39]

However, Faludi, by his own part, in spite of time spent in answering the rigmarole arising most from the wrong and tortuous comments to his original book, was able to deepen some methodological aspects directly pertinent to the epistemological change and to devise support through this book. On these aspects, I would like here focus my attention recalling above all the concept that Faludi wanted express as first step toward a new planning methodology.

Assuming the new role of suggesting a methodology to propose to planning colleagues, Faludi chose as his first point to ensure that planning was not considered an exercise based on the objectivity of the behaviour of the operators in the field of the decision-makers. But turning the order on its head, it is an exercise oriented towards the future and the feasibility of the operations, and the availability of technical factors valid for the achievement and compatibility of the pre-selected objectives.

I would like to focus my attention on this subject, briefly recalling the concept that Faludi wanted to express as a first step towards a new methodology for planning.

3.3.2 Some Previews of Planning Methodological Definitions: The Concept of Effectiveness

How should we measure the feasibility and the compatibility of decisions? In reality, these measurements are what make decisions 'operational'.

Without such 'operationality', the decisions would not be so rational. Therefore feasibility, the possibility of measuring decisions as compatible with the means sufficient to implement them, their operationality and compatibility are the conditions *sine qua non* decisions would lose their rationality and their effectiveness; they would remain words, and only words, and would lose any kind of rationality.

It seems to me that decisions, plans, programmes and effectiveness should start—from the outset of the construction of a planning methodology—first from norms and rules, principles and postulates concerning the possibility for measuring the actions and for making them accountable in order to make these plans and programmes 'feasible'.

So, the qualification of an 'operational decision', as the operational basis for a planning methodology, is very important and must be assigned to the decisions which have been measured—as said—as *feasibility* and *compatibility*, together with other system decisions. In other words, these measurements make the decisions 'operational'.

Without operational decisions are not rational because they are ineffective, losing any capacity to be controlled in their implementation; their occurrence becomes casual or random—the opposite of rational.

Encompassing a sample of the conditions requesting rationality in planning, we can state:

1. AN OPERATIONAL DECISION IS WHEN A DECISION-TAKER CAN CERTIFY:

   — THE MEASURABILITY AND ACCOUNTABILITY OF THE SUFFICIENT MEANS INCLUDED IN THE DECISION, AS COMPATIBLE WITH OTHER CONCOMITANT DECISIONS
   — A SELECTION AMONG AVAILABLE ALTERNATIVE DECISIONS
   — A PRIORITY TIME RANGE OF OBJECTIVES AND RELATIVE PROGRAMMES
   — AVAILABLE LEGITIMATE USE OF SUPPORTING MEANS FOR IMPLEMENTATION OF THE DECISION AND CONSECRATION OF DECISION-TAKERS, BY A COMPLEX SOCIAL COLLECTIVITY.

These are the measurements that make decisions 'operational'.

As a complement to the formulated, multi-functional-type key postulate, Faludi employs some arguments which deserve to be remembered. Among them are, for example:

Knowledge is not sufficient for making plans. Rather, it must he applied to some purpose, and there must be organisations and procedures for coordi-

92   Volume II. Selected Testimonies on the Epistemological...

nation and implementation. This leads to the distinction between theory *in* planning *(substantive* theory) and theory *of* planning (*procedural* planning theory). My work relates to the latter.

Next to the procedural-substantive distinction, I make one between *positive* and *normative* theories of planning:

> [...] 'normative theory is concerned with how planners ought to proceed rationally. Behavioural approaches focus more on the limitations which they are up against in trying to fulfil their programme of rational action.

> This distinction is not rigid. Improvement to planning must be based on knowledge of practice. Indeed, research is often guided by the desire to improve practice. Empirical planning theory—as I now prefer to describe positive theory—seeks knowledge about the organization and procedures of planning but, in so doing, it usually aims at improving practice. (Faludi 1986a, pp. 3–4)

Thus, Faludi introduces, through statements of methodological kind, with a concise definition, some postulates concerning the alternative evaluation. For instance:

2. An operational decision is a pronouncement committing a decision-taker to perform a certain activity.

Development can be viewed as an on-going stream of decisions. Developers decide to acquire land. Its owners decide to put it onto the market. Investors decide to provide capital. Architects decide on the shape of buildings. The authorities decide to grant subsidies and to give planning permissions. They, too, take investment decisions: sewage and road works, schools and parks. Finally, people decide to take up residence in new housing, vacating some other property, etc, etc.

Why this emphasis on operational decisions? [...]

Operational decisions entail commitments and use resources and affect the lives of people. Once taken, they foreclose other options. The danger is that important decisions cannot be taken any more as and when required. This is because resources are scarce, attention needs to be focused on one issue at a time, and precedents need to be watched.

Operational decisions are acts of volition. Where public authorities are involved, their proposals to enter into commitments must be supported by argument. This does not mean to say that individuals do not act responsibly. Individuals may equally be called upon to account for their decisions. Sometimes they even put their motives into writing so as to keep a record for the future. For public authorities though, this is of paramount importance.

For decisions to become a matter of public concern and criticism, proposals must be publicly announced. In this way, *standards* can be applied to them. Think about any ordinary decision requiring some deliberation, for example whether to change jobs. In it, standards play their part. This is even more true for discussions held in the public arena.

Considerations might concern the relations of the decisions in question to other decisions, past, present, and future [...].

Planning is simply the attempt to do this thinking systematically. [...] But an authority is under an obligation to demonstrate that it knows what it is doing. It must make statements concerning the overall context within which it takes its decisions. Public authorities therefore formulate and adopt budgets, land-use plans, and other documents stating their policy.

The accountability of public authorities for their operational decisions is the most fundamental norm from which the decision-centred view of planning starts. How can one account for one's decisions? There must be a general rule for answering this question, to which all those concerned can refer. Obviously, my proposal is to regard rationality as such a rule. (Faludi 1986a, pp. 19–21)

Another meaningful object of methodological definition about planning, dealt with by Faludi, is the comparison with possible alternatives:

3. A DECISION IS RATIONAL IF IT RESULTS FROM AN EVALUATION OF ALL ALTERNATIVES IN THE LIGHT OF ALL THEIR CONSEQUENCES

It will be evident that this is a rule for *assessing* decisions once they have been formulated. Nothing is assumed about the process by which the decision has been formulated.

To be able to meet the requirements of rationality, one must know all feasible alternatives and their expected consequences. But in dynamic situations, the identification of consequences is difficult.

94   **Volume II. Selected Testimonies on the Epistemological...**

Add to this that their evaluation implies attaching weights to them. Also, any evaluation bears the stamp of whoever has the ultimate say. In the case of public authorities, many questions arise about the manner in which various interests are reflected in the authority's decisions. Nevertheless, in principle, public authorities can be held accountable by various interests. Many evaluation methods attempt to deal with this problem. Their outcome is the object of political conflict. Since this is even more true for plan-making, I shall defer the discussion of this topic until later.

Difficulties notwithstanding, every effort must be made to identify alternatives and to evaluate their consequences. They add up to what I call the definition of the decision-situation. (Faludi 1986a, p. 21)

Thus, Faludi formulates a kind of third postulate too:

4. A DEFINITION OF THE DECISION-SITUATION IS A DESCRIPTION OF THE ALTERNATIVES WHICH A DECISION-TAKER HAS WITH RESPECT TO A CERTAIN DECISION, TOGETHER WITH THEIR EXPECTED CONSEQUENCES WEIGHED IN THE LIGHT OF HIS/HER VALUES.

Seen in this way, the definition of the decision-situation embodies everything that one must know before taking a decision. It forms the essential premise of any rational decision. Faludi observes:

In a manner of speaking, it represents a complete image of the world as seen by the decision-taker at the moment of being confronted with it. The definition is subjective, as well as time-specific. Limitations on his/her freedom of choice are taken into account by including only those alternatives which he/she is both able and willing to consider. Here, the pragmatic orientation of the decision-centred view comes to the fore yet again. Limitations of knowledge may even lead to the rationality-rule itself being modified so as to minimise the risk of error. Many such variations have been proposed in statistical decision-making. They fall under the more general heading of *uncertainty management* but need not concern us here.

Limitations arising from power constellations must also be taken into account. They prestructure definitions of decision-situations. Also, one takes account of only those consequences which one deems to be relevant. This is the only way in which we may conceive of all alternatives being evaluated in the light of all their consequences. Thus, defining decision-situations involves many decisions in its turn. Again, this will be discussed below in relation to plan-making.

Preparing every one of the operational decisions of public authorities in the way described above is impossible. Consequences of decisions are most diverse. They extend far beyond the area of competence of operational decision takers. As indicated, there is the danger that decisions will conflict with each other, and such consequences must also be figured out. This requires us to formulate *frameworks for operational decisions*. This is what a *plan* is, nothing more and nothing less.

In focusing on *plans*, the level of argument changes to sets of individual decisions viewed in combination. The adoption of a plan concerning such a set is a planning decision. It must be taken in the same manner as operational decisions. (Faludi 1986a, pp. 21–22)

3.3.3 From Decisions to Programmes and Plans

Faludi does not fail to comment on how it is possible to move from single decisions to programmes and plans, and how to respect a due integration between decisions, programmes and plans.

He does so in Chap. 5 of that book we are examining. He does so too by refreshing our memories on Popper's position concerning planning, which most of us had largely forgotten (another great merit of the work of Faludi).

How should it move from a single decision to the plan decision? How can an obligatory integration between different levels of the planning structuring be respected? Should this be horizontally by sectorial interdependences, within single communitarian unities, or vertically, by territorial interdependencies between the different territorial levels to which they, the decision and the decisional plan, should be proposed?

What are we discussing? Are we not by chance referring to the same 'framework' which we consider rational (or better, we feel we can ensure and guarantee with a judgement of rationality)?[40] How compatible and coherent is this in terms of the effects or consequences of possible contrasting decisions—in other words, of accepting or promoting or organising in any decision-making situation a process of systemic planning?[41] Is this not what is driving us (the so-called experts) forward to invent,

96   Volume II. Selected Testimonies on the Epistemological...

propose and obtain the institution of some informative systems that allow us, and through us the political institutional decision-makers, to better understand the effects that single decisions could have on their choices of the lowest decision-making situation? Is it precisely to be better able to evaluate, at a higher level—also a deeper level—the analysis of individual interventions?

And finally, is it not because of all of this that we ask, still as so-called experts, the political representatives (as the final decision-makers) to establish and enrich processes of technical information capable of creating a sufficient awareness of reality—a sufficient 'systemic' awareness? Is such widespread awareness intended to be a tangible example of the sought-for integration between the problems on any territorial level of Frisch's pyramid? That should not be the first requisite of a socially and collectively committed 'methodology of planning'.

3.3.4 The Achievement of an Advanced Vision of Consequences: From Decision to Plan (*Frisch's Pyramid Question*)

In Faludi's book on critical rationalism and the methodology of planning, there are some further points to reference here—they are not sufficient to be called descriptions. As we are examining this in the chapter on planning theorists, we should mention what Faludi states on the subject:

> The need to account for planning decisions means that in plan making, too, the advantages and disadvantages of all alternative proposals need to be considered before opting for one. Rationality again applies as a norm. A definition of the decision-situation is an equally necessary premise. But it is a more complex affair, because planning decisions relate to sets of operational decisions. In other words, the volitional act, which the adoption of a plan also represents, presupposes much intricate cognitive work.
>
> This gives rise to even more problems than is the case when defining operational decision-situations. The consequences of a plan must be calculated via the effects of the plan on operational decision making and action. So, cause-and-effect-chains become longer, and uncertainty increases: there is uncertainty as to whether operational decision takers will implement a

The Programming Approach in the Collective Decision... 97

plan as they should. This quite apart from the inherent uncertainty attached to any prediction of consequences for the environment and people's lives.

For instance, the adoption of a green bell policy in order to prevent individual settlements from merging and so losing their identity is based on the following: (a) such a policy prevents development in designated areas, (b) preventing settlements merging with one another indeed preserves their identity. Green belts are under constant pressure, however, simply because they are adjacent to urban areas, and whether something as elusive as the identity of settlements depends on their physical separation remains open to doubt. In this way, the evaluation of a green belt policy involves a chain of, more or less uncertain, expectations concerning its consequences. (Faludi 1986a, p. 22)

In such way, Faludi expresses, through an example, what he intends as the relation between an individual operational decision and a larger 'segment' of the plan-making. But in an authentic methodology, such examples—between planning and decisional-situations—will be in the thousands.

Moreover, he adds an interesting observation:

Add to these uncertainties the large number of alternatives and consequences, and the need to attach weights to them, and the desire comes naturally for great selectivity in plan-making. Therefore, one must be grateful for any political signals, for any statement of a philosophy from which to define the decision-situation in planning. Otherwise, plan-making becomes a hopeless affair dealing with a hotchpotch of information which no conceivable planning agency has the capacity to assimilate.

Operational decisions and plans are similar. As we have seen, both are acts of volition. To take them in deliberate fashion means that one must take cognisance of the situation at hand. The distinction between volition and cognition is purely conceptual, of course. In reality, volition does not occur separately and after cognition, but occurs throughout decision-making or plan-making. Thus, the definition of the decision-situation is itself the result of choices concerning the range of alternatives and of consequences considered, including how they pertain to various interests. Simple distinctions, such as that between the preparation of plans by experts and their adoption by politicians, are insufficient, but this is where I let this matter rest for the time being. (Faludi 1986a, pp. 22–23)

3.3.5 An Indispensable Ingredient of Rationality in the Planning Methodology: Collective Bargaining

Faludi touches upon an argument that merits a careful and more profound planning methodology: the *negotiations.*

> Ultimately, problems in defining decision-situations stem from the nature of human knowledge. We are unable to grasp reality completely, let alone decision-situations involving considerations on an uncertain future. One reason is physiological. Information needed for action is stored in the so-called short-term memory. This is extremely limited in capacity. Potentially relevant information at our disposal needs to be reduced before it can be brought to bear.
>
> Now, the principles involved in such a reduction can themselves not be derived from observations of reality. There is more than one way of perceiving reality. This is why definitions of decision-situations are subjective. They are themselves the results of a number of decisions. The subjective nature of definitions of decision-situations becomes evident when there is more than one actor involved, as is invariably the case in planning. Thus, an authority might think in terms of improving traffic flow in an inner-city area, whilst its inhabitants consider traffic as a hazard; the authorities might consider a slum as a potential area for expanding a shopping area, whilst the inhabitants see the housing as in need of rehabilitation, etc. Mutual adjustment of these views requires *negotiations.*
>
> In *negotiations*, the partners can threaten each other by calling into question their respective definitions of the decision-situation. This is the painful experience of planners whose legitimacy in dealing with issues from an overall point of view (just think of comprehensive road proposal) has been challenged. A powerful actor may therefore conclude that negotiations are not worth his while. He will impose *his* definitions of decision-situations on others.
>
> How can we live up to the demands imposed by rationality? This rule does not seem to allow for any compromise. The answer is that we take account of existing limitations. They form, so to say, part of the definition of the decision-situation. In this respect, practice is often more advanced than theory. As the research on Dutch planning referred to above shows, exaggerated demands are simply ignored: in theory, all building permits

should be issued in accordance with plans previously adopted, but in practice this requirement is flouted. In theory, statutory plans should be reviewed every ten years, but no such review is attempted unless there is an independent reason for doing so; etc. (Faludi 1986a, pp. 23–24)

3.3.6 A Cogent-Approach to Flexibility

Here Faludi is induced to introduce into the methodology a very important element, one that should feature in a methodological future to be 'normalised' (also see Sect. 3.4): a cogent-approach to flexibility.

An important result of my decision-centred view has been the development of a cogent-approach to flexibility (see Thomas and Healey 1991). Briefly, flexibility may be seen as a response to the problem of bridging the gap, in terms both of organisational and temporal distance, between operational decision-making and plan-making. Time heals many wounds, it is said. It certainly removes some uncertainties. Also, the further down we go in organisational hierarchies, the more detailed the knowledge concerning operational decision-making. A recurrent answer to uncertainty is to delay and/or delegate decisions. This increases flexibility. But there are limits to the extent to which this can be done, beyond which the advantage of planning is lost. […]

This presentation of the decision-centred view of planning should allay any fear concerning the 'technocratic', or 'positivistic' connotations of rationality. The idea that it has anything to do with misconceived views of objectivity, or the common interest, and the like, should disappear. It takes account of the subjective nature of decisions and of the elusive one of any search for a common denominator of various interests. However, these difficulties relate to defining the situation to which the rationality rule applies. They do not suggest that this rule itself, straightforward as it is, needs to be modified. Therefore, I cannot help feeling that critics of rationality in planning might usefully redirect their attention to how decision-situations are defined, rather than to dwell over rationality. Rationality underlies their concern for broadening considerations in planning to include more and more fundamental, issues. (Faludi 1986a, p. 24)

3.3.7 A Final Summary of Planning Methodology, in the Spirit of Critical Rationalism (*According to Faludi*)

I wanted to extend the quotations from Faludi's book because I found there an abundant anticipation—following in the tracks from the work of Popper and from the epistemological debate he inherited—of what I have defined as the *overturning* of the programming approach sustained in this book. From such an *overturning* approach, planning and its still non-existent 'methodology' should be the crux of a transformation of the entire field of the social sciences; it should be aimed at responding to the necessity for a new cooperation between the renewed expertise and the hopefully technically and ethically renewed *political operators*.

What is desired in this work is the formation of a new and autonomous discipline derived from the unification of older disciplines (yet to be unified among many post-Second World War disciplines), as multiplied in the social sciences.[42] This new discipline could be functional in terms of providing a new system of political, economic, administrative and managerial support, for any kind of political community or collective institution.[43] We already have in the world important examples of how we ensure and measure effectiveness and accountability that important and meaningful experiences exist (see Chap. 8 in **Vol. II**).

Though still to be implemented, the new critical-rationalist methodology, at its time outlined by Faludi (in the spirit of the Popperian philosophy), in this selection includes many quotations in the words of the author (since it is more useful for the reader and more respectful towards the author).[44]

The same Faludi, in one of his last chapters of the book, wrote a brief summary of the work in order to give a conclusion to his overly complex argument aimed at promoting a new methodology.[45]

I will limit myself here to reporting, with a few critical annotations, the 'summary' provided by Faludi at the end of his book (which we have already covered in Sect. 3.3).

The first step taken by Faludi is to express what he intends by *planning* and what he intends by *methodology*.

> Planning has many meanings depending on the problem which one wants to tackle. For better or for worse, I have opted for a view of planning as decision-making. More in particular, planning stands for efforts to relate our so-called operational decisions (implying definite commitments to action) to each other. This view of planning is identical with that of the *Institute for Operational Research*.[46] After all, strategy choice stands for exploring the wider implications of decisions. The mainspring of their efforts, and mine, is the quest for rationality, that is far comprehensively evaluating possible actions in the light of their consequences. So, they and l wish to broaden the range of consequences which we consider to include the consequences on other decisions with which we are, or may be, confronted, now and in the future. (Faludi 1986a, p. 115)

Such preliminary consideration on both essential concepts in a methodology of planning obviously should be the basis of an evaluation of actions, as decided by consequences; it constitutes an essential principle of a general method, one which is absolutely paradigmatic.

What is stated above on interdisciplinary cooperation stems from an essential condition for the methodology of a proper planner, who aims to explore ever larger spaces (just 'interdisciplinary') on the consequences of the actions that stem from such a 'disciplinary methodology'.

Thus, it re-organises the sense of the first sentence of the cited passage by Faludi as well, according to whom 'planning has many meanings depending on the problem which one wants to tackle'.

Can it not produce the misunderstanding that could be so many meanings of planning so much are the substantial plans with which the planner is dealing? That is not the contrary of what is said in the last part of quotation reported—that is, from the melting pot among the substantial disciplinary contributions comes the enhanced attention (and of 'rationality') of a unique general planning methodology, as based on disciplinary interdependence, which can change the substantial sectorial approaches of a traditional disciplinarity.

How much time is the apparent optimality in the passage changed from a territorial scale to a different one? From a vision only 'economicistic' (as the fans of 'social' everything proclaim without recognising the bounds of reality would prefer) or a vision only 'juridicistic' (as the fans of total legality proclaim would prefer) without concrete modifications of the opposed preferences of people? Or for a vision that compares 'juridicist' and economic aspects? And to be open to accept concrete solutions according to a mix of prevailing bias or ideologies from different decisional situations (as the fans of generic and insufficient definition would prefer, such as 'economicism' versus 'juridicism', or 'individualism' versus 'collectivism', 'environmentalism' versus 'socialism', 'utilitarianism versus ethicism', and so on)?

As a methodology, on the contrary, the quality of our decisional system could not be improved, from a methodology with the maximum consolidated only with the maximum of experiences, extension and comparison—as Faludi says—through the maximum possible of acquisition of knowledge 'on the consequences [of our decisions] on other decisions with which we are (or could be, or would could be), engaged, today and in the future'.

Do we already have some concrete experiences to which we can apply some of the methods of interdisciplinary cooperation of this kind? I fear that on this matter we are still at ground zero.

In any case, let us cite what Faludi says in regard to the concept of methodology 'inspired from the spirit critical-rationalist'.

Methodology is the theory of method. Method relates to the way in which we can, and should, justify our arguments. It does not dictate how we should formulate them. (But it does, of course, suggest methods of work by which we can arrive at acceptable conclusions! The many planning methods which we know are indeed such methods of work.) The emphasis on argument and its justification stems from respect for others. It conceives of our fellow humans as our equals, whom we have a duty to take seriously. In particular, we have to take seriously their *criticisms*. This is the root of the attitude, inherent to methodology, of rationalism.

Rationalism, properly conceived, turns upon itself. It recognises that all argument starts from assumptions which, questionable though they may be in themselves, cannot all be questioned at once if we want to avoid being stifled into inaction. In particular, it recognises that there needs to be a fundamental commitment to rationalism, to resolving issues by argument instead of by force. Rationalism which does not recognise these limitations is uncritical, and ultimately self-defeating. *Critical* rationalism recognises that it rests on commitment, and it respects the boundaries of the possible. (Faludi 1096, pp. 115–116)

Despite sharing the set of arguments on rational behaviour in constant conflict between rationality and strength, I would not be so reductive as to see the methodology only from this point of view. The methodology serves most of all to suggest the constant and lasting improvement of the choice of method, and to make us understand that no method, in time, can be the best. The progression of methods, in all fields, guarantees progress; similarly, as in social life, the progress of this activity is always moving. Hence, it is not the arguments that the methods must serve, but the results.

3.4 Further Steps Toward a New Methodology of Planning

I had lost contact with the field of research on territorial planning, which had become for me a period of a few years one of four vital sectors of study, research and teaching in both my home country and other inter-national organisations,[47] even if I was informed of the shift towards prob-lems of territorial organisation, in the process of 'substantial' politics for a greater 'territorial cohesion' in the growth of the EU (Faludi and Waterhout 2002).

It seems to me that we are always and very much within a certain indefinite state of the old, conceptually muddled 'theory of planning', in its preferred 'proceduralist' expression.

In order to configure an authentic 'methodology' of planning, we must go much further in integrating the proceduralist vision with the substan-tialist one, and vice versa—the substantialist with the proceduralist one.

We need a 'planning' that starts from a methodology previously integrated between procedure and substance in a kind of advanced progress.

When we face a problem of substance, we will already know which procedural methods must be adopted; these are methods to conceive as limits, bounds (or other) for a procedure of substance. And when we faced with a problem of procedure, we will already know how many substantive cases that planner must face in order to apply the most appropriate procedure to achieve the better solution.

Of course, the construction of a planning methodology of this kind we can pretend to be the task of a sole, even enlightened, colleague, yet best oriented in the research of the true, authentic, methodological integration of disciplines. This would be like pretending *a priori* that Faludi could become a Pico della Mirandola.

3.4.1 The Main Requirements of a New Planning Methodology

For the construction of a planning methodology we would need the cooperative contribution of an entire organised scholarly community of planners of different operational sectors and fields. And the result of this cooperation would be to reflect upon their current work experiences, using environmental re-adaptation to be applied to different and new knowhow outside their usual habit of work, making these similar but different.

It is necessary, indeed, for an elaboration of planning methodology, to start from a comparison of problems and problem analysis between different professional areas.[48]

And the result expected from these initiatives should be the elaboration of a vast 'casuistics' of situations to compare, in order to select those which could have a common vision for a renewed substantive field of action. This would be a common laboratory aimed at creating some constructive and operational factors of sharing approaches and methods deriving from different decisional situations.

All this implies spontaneous coordination by some planning communities to escape from the limits of our own planning experience, and compare it with other experiences, not for pure criticism of other visions or methods of interlocutors (which seems to be the preferred sport of the planning theorists) but for hiding a possible substantive interdisciplinary relational gaps and plugging the need for a vademecum or textbook for planners and students to discover new possibilities of social behaviours under different decisional situations and substantive aspects.

Only after having obtained some collective results in that direction would it be possible to begin speaking of a real (integrated) planning methodology.

Moreover, it is only after doing this that we will have attained a good level of interchange of information to be used towards achieving identical planning objectives, amongst the great disciplinary different areas (economics, sociology, operational systemic engineering, psychology political and managerial science, and so on, all having their own programming experience in respect to their traditional positivistic role). We will then be able to say that we have put into operation a real qualitative leap in the planning method—and to say legitimately to have escaped from the modest application of single methods to single cases of a discipline, in the 'armoured' field of another.

Lastly, it is only after the kind of cooperation and neo-disciplinary fusion here suggested (called 'planology') has been manifested and tested could we feel that we are the owners of a new planning methodology.

For instance, until economists know and are familiar with the best literature of the 'planning theorists' based mostly on the vision of territorial problems, and in general on the cultural area of planners and social engineers, and until within the area of planning studies, conversely, a serious familiarity in respect to the most relevant economical, sociological, and political scientific literature has been developed, especially that oriented toward planning problems,[49] it will be very difficult to speak about planning, and about a unitary planning methodology more precisely.[50]

This does not mean that parts of the various and useful considerations of Faludi aimed at defining the character of a 'planning methodology', and also attentive to the methodological visions of scientific research in general (the object of Popper, for instance, and others scholars of philosophy of the science), are very useful for future elaboration (and I would hope also of implementation in the same time) of an effective planning methodology.

The Faludi book on the relationship between what he calls 'critical rationalism' and a possible 'planning methodology' tends to configure positively a possible methodology of planning as a happy outcome of these relations precisely as a policy of rational planning, which could be no other than the result of the fusion of what he calls 'critical rationalism on one side and the methodology of planning' on the other.

I would like to specify, at this point, that this Faludi's book, published in 1986, over 30 years ago now, is still valid, topical and fresh, regarding its main theme, the construction of such a methodology; it constitutes the best starting point for a revamping of the scientific community under this methodology. However, the 'newness' of the book, unfortunately, is a symptom but also proof of the fact that in 30 years we have not made much progress towards Faludi's vision. We have not progressed in realising the interdisciplinary methodology oriented toward the programming approach that we aim at.[51]

I tried to explore this in this Chapter—even acknowledging the greater and unexpected general contribution offered by the communities of planning theorists, in representing the literature effectively intervened on the programming approach (that is, the pivot of this book)—but it may be best to extract from Faludi's book on the problem of a 'a methodology critical-rationalist of planning' a number of long quotations, and related comments, in the hope to facilitate a kind of re-starting of the argument.[52] In fact, I get the impression that the main argument of Faludi's work (that of a methodology of critical-rationalist of planning) has been mostly ignored.[53]

My own interests involve a weak and solitary attempt to attract the attention of some of those colleagues most motivated about my own interests in this sector; they have induced me to desist from the whole of this argument near planning theorists, without wishing to enlarge the audience of other scholars of social sciences on the issue of their unification and integration from the viewpoint of method.

My wish is that, in subsequent years, younger experts will end up following in the footsteps of Faludi's book, carefully examined, supported by more general works of new scholars from a general approach (of the kind of this work on the programming approach, and other unified experiences), who would try to 'restart' the discourse of building of a new (critical-rationalist) planning methodology, and would enlarge their information and awareness bases in respect of some economic literature. This is with the hope the other young scholars not from the traditional studies could—again in the footsteps of the Faludi book—could receive even more general works (of the kind that this trilogy the programming approach exemplifies) and other multidisciplinary experiences.

I hope that other young scholars will try to work with a comprehensive methodology of planning, often outlined yet never indeed really implemented, in every segment of the programme structure of the system of society, transformed as a truly active 'planning' (and not 'planned') of the same society system.

3.4.2 A Plain Memory again of Some Critical Points and Postulates of the Programming Approach

From what I have said so far, we could summarise the basic character of the programming approach based on the Frischian version in the following points, which could constitute a justification for some distinctive postulates and corollaries in the new planning methodology.

Let us begin from their description, before their formulation.

1. In the social sciences the knowledge basis is given not by the analysis of the phenomena observed, because their repeatability is not certified *a priori*, but only by the analysis of the 'feasibility' of the phenomena programmed (Leontief). This consequently requires the relationship between the ends and the means available for making the ends achievable; it is only in respect to this that it makes sense to develop the analysis.[54]
2. Therefore, with the programming approach, the analysis itself of phenomena must be influenced only by the problem (or problems) to be solved: how to implement an analysis of the means, by their natural scarcity, with that of many objectives to be selected. This aims at the best welfare of communities that enter into reciprocal contact, in order to research and find an optimal solution (or at least one considered as such) between many objectives and the few means and capacities available.

3. In the programming approach, it is only after having operated such a trade-off and built the reference framework (or scenario, or configuration)—which the governmental allows to determine the best possible combination—is it possible to consider the consequential plan's objectives and programmatic actions and programs and projects, allowing for the reference framework to become a plan.

4. However, in order to introduce some preference functions (especially on a political governmental scale) it is necessary for the reference framework to be built in a very different way, with respect to how it has been made until now, under the influence of the 'positivistic' prejudice or preconception (that is, like phenomena that would have objectivity like experimental or natural phenomena, independently from the vision and will of social actors, and of the free sharing and consensus of the people acting).

5. In social phenomena or social policy, the reference framework needs to be a result of a structural and organic, and also 'systemic' compatibility, according to which the model of variables and parameters responds *a priori* to the problems and intentions of the plan and of its participants. (We would say according to the general objectives 'non-quantified' of the plan, if it would not lead to the confusion between them and the objectives/targets of the plan, those which—on the contrary—cannot be formulated if not after the optimisation process of the plan itself as a decision taken through optimisation.)

6. The optimisation process, instead, can be applied only when the model is available and built, with all its data available, sensitive to the possible issues of the process, and when people can 'turn' the model in various scenarios, so that experiments can be practised for a series of technical study cases, or other experimental proofs (by independent or partisan experts) under the standard agreement on technical rules and instrumentation.

7. The programming approach means introducing full cognition of the limits in the effectiveness of public decisions (also with optimisation processes in other multiple optimisation processes) that can give decision-makers of the political authorities full awareness of the effects of alternative choices those working on the reference framework with proofs, never previously seen for the policies of the ruling class and governments of any kind of modern democratic society of the twenty-first century.

8. The programming approach in fact consists in the introduction into the governmental decisions of communities of respectable size a system of permanent control and monitoring of the effects of different alternative policies, acquired through an information level operating, when models have been built and implemented and adequately 'spun', to arrive at supplying a suitable combination; it is to be used for making the major decisions of each single community situation, defined or coordinated on a superior cooperative scale.

The transformation of these eight methodological points into true indicative 'norms' and postulates of action and research can be used, with the help of trustworthy and reliable experts, in the case of contestation in collective negotiations as well (currently outside of any experimental reality) and in operational postulates, requiring long-term cooperation between a remarkable number of scholars, ready to work together in a new field of research in the future.

Will the scientific and professional organisations of planning theorists be interested in implementing such objectives and other closer competences, and call it a 'critical-rationalist' methodology of planning, integrated in the defined way?

3.4.3 A Basic Postulate in the Restarting: The Programming Approach as an Action-Oriented Analysis

I thought for the new planning methodology, it could be possible to formulate a postulate which remains as a general condition of an epistemological reform of every proposition of method to formulate in future.

The *postulate* can be expressed in this way:

1. PLANNING CONSISTS ESSENTIALLY IN AN *ACTION-ORIENTED ANALYSIS* OR TO THE 'DOING', AND NOT IN AN *OBSERVATION-ORIENTED ANALYSIS* OR TO THE 'BEING'

For 'analysis', people understand any kind of reflection or reasoning aimed at improving or rendering knowledge more efficient.

In this case, the knowledge that we would research is that useful to the action, to what we have to do or what we should have to do, rather to what it is.

This distinction, in philosophy, is as old as philosophy itself; it is the distinction between being and ought to be; between the truth and the good, or the useful; between science and ethics. And in economics, from the very beginning, it is between science and art, between theory and policy, between political economy and economic policy.

This juxtaposition is that commonly made between positive and normative analysis.[55]

At the home of IIASA,[56] some time ago, specialists in operational research debated—among philosophers and scholars of other social sciences—the 'scientific' basis itself of the operational research: within the boundaries of which some time ago was reproduced the same 'positivist' ad epistemological dilemma, between 'positivistic' and 'normativistic' approach.

On that occasion a consensus was reached on the need for an operational research approach (that, from the methodological point of view, I consider similar to that of the 'strategic planning', and that in this book I prefer to call the 'programming or planological approach'); it should be freed from the illusion of being founded on any previous positivistic approach, or of being founded on the findings (unimportant if on an empirical or theoretical basis) of constant 'regularities' or on behavioural 'norms'.[57]

3.4.4 The Operational Requirement of Planning: Quantification

The programming approach includes in itself the requirement for the operational research—assessable and measurable in operative and numerical terms, a requirement of the operational planning in its calculability and feasibility.

It is no surprise, therefore, if in its methodology, it comes to include postulates tied to calculability and measurability, as indispensable for any possible feasibility. A general constraint of any product of planning (decision, project, plan, etc.) is sufficient if it is intended as a postulate:

2. The programming approach should be always defined—where possible—in quantitative terms.

The quantitative terms, in fact, are better suited for setting quantitative relations (equally quantitative) with the evaluation of the means, as necessary requisites to achieve the objectives.

The conventional approach, of all the operational sciences (that is, those—such as planning—oriented towards decisions and actions and connected to practical activity in any way) has been that knowledge, derived from positive analysis, is essential in order to orient normative analysis.[58] However, it is not an analysis which supplies certainties.

The latter—not to violate reality—should be based on positive analysis, which should be the indispensable premise for the former. The knowledge is considered as a basis for the feasibility of plans and programs of action.

But the action- (or decision-) oriented analysis introduces a new element (if we prefer, of an 'epistemological' kind): the nature-oriented positive analysis was influenced (or even better, conditioned) by the (normative) action-oriented one.

It is well-known that 'problem-solving' facilitates the ability to choose among variables (and relations among variables) to submit to some feasible analysis regarding hypothetical human and social behaviours, which are not axiomatically positive. This is the conclusion which implies the need for the re-thinking of the epistemology of the operational research (referred to in footnote 1).

It is not the case, however, that we should look deeper into the character of the normative approach in planning, in respect to what is usually defined in planning for the natural sciences.[59]

It is sufficient to assert this argument as a postulate of the planning theory, and of any other type of analysis and evaluation of planning itself.

Whilst in other traditional social sciences (political science, economic science) the presumption that a 'positive' nothing exists does not render planning possible. Nothing can be positive; every analysis is only 'normative'.[60]

I admit that the normative effect has been used in the past as a necessary complement of the 'positive' effect and this can produce a misunderstanding when we affirm that planning is only normative.

Perhaps it would be more convenient to change the word use, and to affirm that all be 'programmatic' (or 'programming'); this means that nothing should be based on the past experiences registered as a source of established 'scientific' natural law; that—on the contrary—in planning, every decision or action should be taken only as actual combination of preferences—more or less negotiated—by stakeholders, between different alternatives of decisional packages. And any decision/action in planning should be studied to understand its feasibility and consistence with the resources and instruments available.

Therefore, there should be the presumption that the behaviour of all subjects participating as decision-takers must be 'organised', as according the political-democratic constitution and the institutions of each community in question, satisfying first what is established by the constitution and institutions, and, in the second place, conforming to the procedural and substantial agreements in planning.

In this way, the presumption should exist that phenomena can be derived and depend only on the decisions (or actions) taken by the authorities, which is illogical (Ragnar Frisch defined this as 'half logic') if thinking the contrary.[61]

3.4.5 Evaluation Ex Ante and Evaluation Ex Post in Planning Methodology

A key factor of the operativity of any conceivable programme in the planning method is the constant relation between intentions and facts, between what is proposed and what is done. This gives the terms of an essential postulate concerning the continued comparison between the objectives and the results of an action.

From the postulate affirmed above, we can derive some corollaries, amongst those, the following[62]:

3. THE PLANNING METHODOLOGY PRESUPPOSES AN EVALUATION OF ANY DECISION/ACTION BASED ON THE COMPARISON BETWEEN EX ANTE ANALYSIS (PROGRAMMED) AND EX POST ANALYSIS (IMPLEMENTED).

The Programming Approach in the Collective Decision... **113**

This corollary seems to exclude, as if not useful, many of the digressions that the 'planning theory' often indulges in on past experience.

They are always interesting and useful to know, implying, however, the risk (not to be under-evaluated) of assuming as data (from the decisional process), which are surely inappropriate to construct reality ex ante, in which every decisional process applies, and to consequently attenuate the engagement on data analysis to those inherent to the complexity of decision-making and to newly arising problems (to be solved).

In other terms, the risk is to weaken the engagement for major research on date of input and the updating of the re-engineering action of the productive processes.

In no other field is it so dangerous to look to the past as it is for planning.

At the same time, this corollary poses as an imperative that every plan is entirely constructed on the interface of ex post analysis of its own resolutions that otherwise would go in at every analysis of results.

The planning presupposes, in fact, a permanent dialogue between the moment of selection and the moment of implementation. Without such a circular process between the two moments, it would be impossible to speak of real planning or of real evaluation.[63]

For example, one of the first postulates or principles of planning should be that every proposition of action or of decisions of any plan must demonstrate its coherency and compatibility with a plan of action and decisions (if they exist) concerning the propositions of a higher, sectorial category of the plan in question. At the same time, they must demonstrate that they are coherent and compatible with the plan of actions and decisions concerning the higher, territorial category of the plan in question.

This example can be used to specify that which could be the corollary in the case that a framework for actions and decisions of a sectorial or territorial category does not exist. Even in this case, a principle of affirmation would be that the plan in question should initiate a virtual coherence at a higher level. In fact, since the higher-level plan normally introduces a larger point of view than that immediately in question, wider interests and visions would be stimulated, and it would be favourable to simulate

114   Volume II. Selected Testimonies on the Epistemological…

these points of view as well in order to find a compromise among these actions and decisions to easily complete a coherent territorial and sectorial framework in the future.

In such a way, the formulation of a methodological document would constitute the acquisition of a level of planning of higher technical quality.

In any case, the most hopeful scenario would be that every society becomes a society that plans (and not only a planned society)[64] and therefore becomes more coherent amongst its different sectors of planning actions; it would also be different on a territorial scale of planning—the principle and the corollary that should be introduced into the vademecum hypothesis of methodology.

It would be desirable to have a marked convergence of schools of thought—economic, social, operative research, analytical and engineering, administrative science, and so on—in consonance with many other schools of thought, arising under different points of views (or so-called 'specialisation') without serving to help a unified planning approach.[65]

If fact, without consciously preparing for this new unified management, technically and politically oriented, the planning theorists risk contributing mostly to—as mentioned—the absence of coordination in the world and that of political and administrative action, eventually stripping itself of any resemblance to the (Myrdalian-style) coordination of planning.[66]

Notes to Chapter 3 (Vol. II)

1. If not in (Hegel's) terms of the well-known 'dialectical cognitive process', for further reference I suggest the work of an important Italian philosopher, Benedetto Croce (1866–1952) (unfortunately not well known outside Italy): *La storia come pensiero e come azione*, ('History as thought and action') (Croce 1938) (translated into English by Sylvia Sprigge as *History as the Story of Liberty* in 1941 in London and published by George Allen & Unwin and in USA by W.W. Norton. The most recent edited translation, based on that of Sprigge's, is *Liberty Fund Inc.* (2000). The 1941 English translation is accessible online through *Questia*).

The Programming Approach in the Collective Decision... **115**

2. John Dewey in 1929 wrote a booklet, *The Quest for Certainty: A Study of the Relations of Knowledge and Action*, in which the relationship between knowledge and action is examined in depth. On pragmatism and its relationship with the objectivity of doing, I recommend a recent work of Richard J. Bernstein, *The Pragmatic Turn* (2010), especially Chap. 5: 'Pragmatism, Objectivity and Truth'. For a useful exposition of the American pragmatists' thinking on relations with the European philosophy and sociology, a work by Hans Joas, *Pragmatism and Social Theory* (1993), is useful.

3. See the reference already noted in **Vol. I**, Chap. 2 (Sect. 2.8.2).

4. This debate has been mentioned in **Vol. I**, Chap. 2 (Sect. 2.8.3), in which I explain how I took it upon myself to read (and in some cases re-read) the most representative authors of the Frankfurt School, with the aim of ensuring that their main works did not contain any relevant anticipation of the epistemological overturning on which the programming approach described in this book is based.

5. I abstain from including in this book the philosophical questions of the authors cited (who have divergent views in many respects), for two reasons:

    (a) Since the early 1950s, and based on the conclusion of my university studies on historicism, such controversy seems out-of-date with respect to the epistemological setting which induced me to put aside my philosophical studies, and, at the same time, my reliance on (positivistic and deterministic) economics, both fields of studies which I found critically unsatisfying. This led me to the role and the approach of planning (that is the basis of this trilogy).

    (b) Philosophical questions would lead us very far from the purpose of this book to develop a new '-ology' (and, if I can allow myself, even a new 'ethic') of the social scientist, having for a long time achieved the understanding that those 'questions' were unproductive and poor in terms of social effectiveness.

6. See my book (already quoted): Archibugi, *Introduzione alla pianificazione strategica in ambito pubblico*, Alinea, Florence, 1999. Some introductory considerations on this argument will be developed in this trilogy in Chap. 8 in **Vol. II**.

7. Which often tries to ape the natural sciences, as Myrdal observed (see cit. in **Vol. I**, Chaps. 1 and 2).

8. In the Chap. 6 of **Vol. II**, we will illustrate the phenomenon of 'reflexivity' introduced by George Soros in the field of the predictability of social and human phenomena.

9. On this point, see Chap. 4 of **Vol. II** on the paradoxical consequences of the reasoning developed more towards 'realism' from the general neo-classical economic theory based on the inclusion of non-economic goods (or 'commodities').

10. This is the exhaustion that has driven away many scholars (among them myself) from the current debate on economic policy because it is based on naive logical premises and oversimplification, and is, therefore, apodictic.

11. Which, we have already said, people try, consciously or not, to ape.

12. I refer to a not marginal part of modern philosophical and epistemological literature, which has used much of this dichotomy in order to characterise a well-defined stream of contemporary thought: the thought that defines itself as postmodern. I would not wish be caught up in a simple reflection on this argument, which is, by its nature, quite alluring, as it risks diverting us from the main path of our argument.

13. This word 'planner' in English, when used without an adjective, is intended almost solely as the city-and-land planner or designer. For the programming of economic activities, other words are used in English, for instance, 'project manager'.

14. A sociological DNA, if people prefer anthropological-cultural and not biological like that discovered only some years ago.

15. This has not impeded, however, a persistent positivism remaining in the programmes of some urban planning schools, where, for instance, the teaching of the analysis of the economy of urban systems in general, takes priority over urban design or planning, just because the positivist argument that the knowledge of the 'natural way' (if not the 'laws') of growing the cities, regions and territories constitutes a preliminary condition in order to suggest a proposal of change for the improvement of urban welfare.

16. Even indeed though in the positivistic approach a breach has opened in this area of socio-economic and geographical research, seeking intrinsic rules for the formation of human settlements and into spatial and regional economics, through interdisciplinary approaches called regional science.

17. Here can be found the methodological ridge between the programming and the positivistic approaches.

18. Faludi is an interesting author, with Viennese cultural roots, a *sui generis* architect or engineer, perhaps influenced in some ways by the remnants of the atmosphere of the Wiener Circle, which was involved in urban issues. He taught on the environment, city planning in the UK, and finally, landed in the Low Countries, a region already largely more open than other countries, even on national scale, to 'comprehensive' spatial planning. Faludi was also inclined to express his own intellectual journey in autobiographical terms (through the concurrence of favourable circumstances—and a scientific meta-disciplinary curiosity). This quality is present in all of his books, from his first work, *Planning Theory* (1973), an expression since his graduate thesis, found itself at the centre— amongst various other factors—of a vast methodological debate, giving a name to a conspicuous chorus called 'planning theorists', about whom we have already spoken.

19. The authors selected by Faludi were almost all Americans, because the critical ferment of the indicated origin's disciplines occurred mainly in the USA and—if I am not mistaken—its epicentre was in the old American Planning Association—which in 1968 was in its 50th year and was keen to extend its scope.

20. Such authors were (in the 1960s, and later): Paul Davidoff (1962, 1965), Donald L. Foley (1964), John Friedmann (1964, 1965), Martin Meyerson (1955, 1956), Ira W Robinson (1972), Melvin M. Webber (1964b, 1968), and others such as Harvey Perloff (1957, 1969a, b); and some—from the British side—as George Chadwick (1971) and J.B. McLoughlin (1969), and so on.

21. Such as Alan Altshuler (1965a, b), Edward C. Banfield (1961, 1968), Yehezkel Dror (1963a, b, 1967, 1971), John W. Dyckman (1964, 1970), Charles E. Lindblom, (1963, 1965, 1968) and (in addition to the Faludi reader), Herbert Simon (1962, 1969), James G. March (1958, 1984, 1988, 1989, 1999, 2008), and Bertram M. Gross (see in the bibliographic references an extensive list of works by him).

22. Such as Amitai Etzioni (1961, 1964, 1968, 1969, 1983, 1988, 1991), Warren Bennis et al. (1961), Bennis, W. (1966), K.D. Benne (1985), Richard S. Bolan (1973).

23. Like William J. Baumol (1968, 1969), Albert O. Hirschman (1977, 1986, 1991), E.J. Mishan (1976, 1981), Nathaniel Lichfield (1975,

118   Volume II. Selected Testimonies on the Epistemological...

1990, 1996), Nathaniel Lichfield et al. (1975, 1998), Lichfield, N. and Darin-Drabkin, H. (1980), James E. Meade (1968, 1989, 1993).

24. Such as C.W. Churchman (1961, 1968), Churchman and Emery (1966), R.L. Ackoff (1960, 1972, 1974, 1986, 1992), Harold Chestnut (1965, 1967), John N. Warfield (1976) and the founders of cybernetics as applied to strategic programming, Anthony Stafford Beer (1966, 1974) and John Friend and Jessop W.M. (1969), Friend and Hickling 1987), Friend et al. (1974) the group of the Institute of Operational Research.

25. We have collected (in Appendix 1 of **Vol. II**) some documents of the important initiative taken by the United Nations (with deliberations and recommendations from the Assembly General and ECOSOC) in the 1950s and in the launch of two decades of development on behalf of the UN on the theme of a 'united' approach on the analysis and planning of development. Towards such an objective, the United Nations relied upon a special (small but active) research institute promoted to Geneva, the United Nations Research Institute for Social Development, which carried out many good studies aiming to establish a form of 'unified' planning. All fell, however, with the crisis of the United Nations itself and the 'realism' that arises in conservatives towards the innovative initiatives that are shown to be right. I gathered the majority of information and the useful bibliography on the politics of the UN regarding the 'unified planning' since the 1950s, which I used in a presentation at the first Scientific Congress of Planning organised in Palermo, Sicily in 1992 (included in Appendix 2 of **Vol. II**). I also felt it was important to include in *Appendix n. 1* in Part II of this trilogy a summary of UN research and on the work carried out by United Nations Research Institute for Social Development in Geneva on the material, which was completely forgotten about later on by the organs that had originally requested it, and as material that even suits the methodology of the programming approach.

26. A now classic book about the multiplicity of 'roots' and 'sources' is John Friedmann's work (1987a, b), an author who even previously (1960) had contributed deeply to the progress of planning theory. I have considered however to criticise the excessive dispersion (I have summarised this in my book, already quoted, *Planning Theory*, from the political debate to the methodological reconstruction; Archibugi 2008a). Of Friedmann's work we can admire the cultural depth, but we cannot avoid noting the strong risk of dispersion of the 'roots', so much so as it loses the sense of

the research itself of those roots. And it is impossible also not to note the risk to the 'origins' of failing to acknowledge some influential figures, which it would be scandalous to ignore.

27. I refer to some well-known to me: that of the Australian Chris Paris ed. (1982), *Critical Readings in planning theory*; Healey P., G. McDougall and M.J. Thomas, eds, (1982), *Planning Theory: Prospects for the 1980s*; and Mandelbaum S.J., L. Mazza and R.W. Burchell, eds (1996), *Exploration in Planning Theory*.

28. E.R. Alexander, *Approaches to Planning: Introducing Current Planning Theories, Concepts and Issues* (1986).

29. I consider the material available to Alexander in that decade perhaps of worse quality for criticism than that available to Faludi; in my opinion, the genre adopted in the text of Alexander allows us to get a better and more up-to-date picture of the limits of the movement of planning theorists.

30. What it could have recovered—in my opinion—is its true 'scientificity' and real social utility, and could have made efficient, that is, producing real result, a large part of the energies expended in the field of the economic theory and in the field of socio-administrative theory, and also in the field of that planning society, which has often been an aspiration declared by many voices of the research (for instance, by Faludi himself, in the last chapter of his first book of 1973).

31. References to this theme have been made in **Vol. I**, Chap. 2 of this trilogy. It would have been sufficient extensive cross-reading of the authors of the scientific community of the spatial planners and these of non-determinist sociologist planners or that of institutionalist, evolutionalist and structuralist economists.

32. See Note n. 26 and Appendix 1 to **Vol. III** of the trilogy.

33. In Appendix n. 2 to **Vol. III** of this publication some documents are collected regarding the Conference of Palermo, which due to the age of the honorary chairmen and other participants, and the financial and organisational failings of some of promoters' institutions, has had to be suspended.

34. In Faludi's book may be less well-known and less read than others of his books (published by Pion, London), the author states that the book is the result of revisiting works of Karl Popper, designated by many as 'critical rationalism'. In my opinion, Faludi's book constitutes a beneficial tool for an attempt to push 'planning theory' out from the confusion of

120 Volume II. Selected Testimonies on the Epistemological...

the debate (partly provoked by himself) that arose during the 1960s and 1970s. And it deserves to be recalled as an initial starting point for a community and work to build a complete methodology of planning.

35. Of a philosophical type, developed by authors who do not show much familiarity with either philosophy or sociology.

36. In fact, here we should begin an open field of observations on the numerous, well-noted and widely discussed misunderstandings that Popper's position generated among his readers (and from Popper himself in the course of his prolific intellectual life, one not devoid of acknowledged and recurrent fine-tuning and revisions). I also believe that overall the 'liberalism' of Popper is anything but incompatible with the rational planning founded on the anti-positivist programming approach. I also think that there is little 'positivism' in his philosophy of knowledge (as, on the other hand, he himself wanted to specify in relation to the misunderstandings on this point of many of his readers). But this discourse would lead us far from the more precise themes of this book. The work of Popper, in fact, notwithstanding its importance and use for the development of the theories of this book, I believe developed theories of philosophy in general beyond the themes studied on the subject of the programming approach. And there are points of contact—these are already sufficiently illustrated in the new work by Faludi cited here. In truth, had I not been interested in what led Faludi to refer to Popper in his work, I would have decided to set Popper to one side in the field relevant to the programming approach, as I have put to one side the problems of the champions of the Frankfurt School (for reasons already explained in **Vol. I**, Chap. 2, Sect. 2.8.3). The great adventure of planning theorists, on the contrary, that I showcased in this chapter, constitutes a potential reservoir of great innovations that should be presented and criticised in the attempt to identify a method for planning.

37. I already developed these critical considerations in my book dedicated essentially to 'planning theorists' (Archibugi 2008a, p. 2)—those known for their vast production—where I used a logical distinction from Faludi's first work (1973a, pp. 4 and 21) on written theories that develop (1) a 'theory of planning' and (2) a 'theory in planning; I added a third category—(3) those that develop a 'theory on planning'. I wanted to evidence that the debate recalled by Faludi had mostly given space to this third category—comments on trouble, hope, failure, objections and all kinds of gossip on planning, not sufficiently written to constitute true

The Programming Approach in the Collective Decision...   121

'lessons for professional guidance' and proposals on organic and systematic methodology; but—on the contrary—capable of misleading the reader on the construction of a useful operative method on decisions for planning.

38. I think that Faludi himself would share this opinion. In fact, it seems to me that he himself tried to answer the numerous comments made, correcting many wrong interpretations, and clarifying both intentions and perspectives from his evaluations.

39. Perhaps, doing so, that is not putting aside a good deal of the debate that his book had suddenly created, Faludi himself continued to increasingly develop a 'discourse' on planning, entering in the misleading factor.

40. Effectively we are discussing a 'framework' or 'structure' planned and requested by dozens of scholars and economists, as mentioned in the first and second parts of this book.

41. The idea that we are speaking of two different arguments is wrong. The difference lies only in the different cultural background of the writers. There are those who try to flee their experience and background and invade something of which they have inadequate knowledge. But that is a very good reason to conceive of other backgrounds and be open to other backgrounds. Or better, to be open to new backgrounds because a large part of the backgrounds have become superfluous and useless for the new approach that we must construct if we wish to depart from a new vision of the function of planning (which goes beyond the scope of this book to that of a 'society that plans' or a planning society).

42. Disciplines developed in the last decades in a singular and integrated way, such as a vacuum packaging, with resounding effects of reciprocal misinformation.

43. The new discipline was projected in response to the needs of the United Nations work and its sectoral and regional agencies, with many 'deliberations' of the General Assembly and ECOSOC in the 1960s and 1970s under the Unified Approach to Development Analysis and Planning. A short summary can be found in note 25 of this chapter. Here I will add that a specific research institute of the UN in Geneva, the United Nations Research Institute for Social Development, has the duty of developing a planning methodology with the scope of unifying the approaches, with a number of good reports that were eventually forgotten. The political, institutional and financial crisis of the UN had the effect of reducing and minimising the activity of the United Nations Research Institute for

Social Development. At that time, together with a few researchers of the institute, a name was given to the new discipline: a science of planning or planology. However, the absence of a real commitment and study of the idea together with the opposition of a few conservatives resistant to anything new, extinguished all life from the idea. More information of the activity of United Nations Research Institute for Social Development and the other positions of the UN on the argument, from the 1950s and 1960s, can be found in Appendix 2, where I elaborated on the argument in **Vol. I**.

44. Facilitated by Faludi himself, who in the Chap. 10 of his book gives a summary of 'critical-rationalist methodology' planning.

45. Faludi's book, which we discussed at length in this chapter, is a mine of interpretations and considerations on the work of Popper, which would be worthy of being included in the studies of all scholars of philosophy. The most interesting parts are: (1) a personal—and very subjective—vision of Popper as a reader and interpreter of philosophy; (2) a careful examination of Popper's philosophy on planning (and on the state); (3) an in-depth analysis of all the 'problems'—and therefore—of Popperian 'problem-solving' connected to the necessary understanding of the 'chains of analysis' and of 'consequentiality' (founded on the 'politics of rational planning' and on its methodology). These arguments are acutely treated but are still not central to the understanding and management of the programming approach and of the programmatic framework. Though not necessary and indispensable arguments for planning, familiarity with and the reading of them is strongly recommended for widening one's understanding of planning.

46. The Institute of Operational Research in London is well-known for its technical contribution to the construction of 'structure plans', so called of many English counties, and was the centre for the application of the operational research for numerous public and private entities. The authorities most representative of the institute are J.K. Friend, W.M. Jessop and A. Hickling.

47. Frankly, I do not know how many of the new things in the field of planning methodology followed in the ten years to follow. I was impelled due to personal circumstances which shifted my area of interest. However, all of the arguments cited and commented in the Sect. 3.3 of this chapter for defining a passage from the theory of planning to the methodology

The Programming Approach in the Collective Decision... 123

of planning. Being transferred from the University of Naples to the Superior School of Public Administration in Rome, I undertook the responsibility with the Italian government for special programs of the government for the formation of public officials in the field of the introduction of strategic planning in the services of all kind of kind of service. (For anyone interested in knowing more about my personal and intellectual experience, please visit my site: www.francoarchibugi.it.) I will return to this type of rational planning in this chapter as a fundamental factor in advancing the efficiency of the programming approach and of the imagined 'planning society'. Unfortunately, in my latest research work and teaching, I did not follow the literature on territorial planning and I lost contact with Faludi.

48. That elsewhere I have ventured to call planology, but in this book I insisted on calling 'programming approach' in the name of Frisch's work. I will again prioritise the creation of academic reforms or transformations in line with the substantial approach of differing concepts of planning.

49. There are also consolidated, mental habits to shed, and we are uncertain whether abandoning such 'paradigms' of thought, even when individualy we have arrived at convictions that are totally obsolete. And there is the most comfortable position of believing that out of the ordinary, the commonplace, one can act with less force and more success. The cynical way out of lazy intellectualism (other than obviously opportunistic politics) is to be able to obtain honours which are substantially unmerited. And more time is lost and resources for advances that could be made rapidly, ones certainly more profitable for the community, the nation and humankind.

50. And not even a glimpse of signs of desire to extend the construction of working groups in both academic research and professional occasions, and to integrate them into a melting pot—a different approach and basic mentality.

51. If this is not true, I would ask colleagues of Faludi himself to indicate bibliographically where any information gaps in my text may be by email [francoarchibugi@gmail.it].

52. I refer to the numerous and crowded international meetings of planning schools of the AESOP, for instance, which I have attended in the past, opened to other backgrounds, not yet familiarise with the programming approach.

124 Volume II. Selected Testimonies on the Epistemological...

53. I would like to know why if this book, among all of Faludi's books has received less attention than others, which have had a great influential role.

54. Perhaps it would be worth acknowledging that the first critical manifestations of criticism of the 'positivistic approach' was not in the field of economics, but in that of sociology.

55. A modern treatment of the problem has been developed by some theorists of operational research; among the best of these treatments are those by C. West Churchman (1971) and by P.B. Checkland (1981).

56. International Institute of Applied System Analysis (Laxemburg, Vienna).

57. See the contributions gathered of the meeting called by the IIASA in the work of Rolfe Tomlison and Istvan Kiss (1984); and the introductive thesis of Kindler and Kiss (1984) and Checkland (1984), as well as the work of Farkas (1984) and finally that of Rolf Tomlinson (1984).

58. For a general understanding of the traditional distinction between positive and normative in the evolution of the economic thought, see Chap. 1 of the work of Hutchinson (1964), which is considered a 'classic' on the matter.

59. On this point, see the essay of Myrdal (1973), which was amply cited in **Vol. I**, Chap. 1.

60. For specification, I asked E.R. Alexander, whom I acknowledge on the matter.

61. I like repeat also here the periphrasis with which Frisch commented on this logic: 'It would be as the decision-taker would say to the expert: "Now you, export, will try to guess what I will do, and you will elaborate your estimations consequently. On the basis of the real information that I will receive, I will decide what I will do"' (Frisch 1976, pp. 91–92).

62. It is obvious, then, why in my didactics at the university, I would call this postulate 'stupid'. But sometimes teachers forget or neglect the stupidity that is generated in this way by inserting it as a theoretical possibility.

63. For the misleading forms of planning that are generated from this corollary of planning methodology, see Chap. 7.

64. As many would consider desirable (see Leontief and Faludi himself) in the last Chap. 1 on critical rationalism.

65. A unified approach to planning and analysis: subject of the 1960s and 1970s for many of the resolutions and recommendations of the UNO (see Appendix 1).

66. I gave the title *Planning Theory* (2003) to my book because it directed me to the category of the 'theories of planning' that is immersed in the tradition of urban and territorial planning. My intention was to gather practical evidence to give a different perspective on the debate surrounding the theory of planning; this prevents me from offering a more critical interpretation of the words and concepts used.

Bibliographical References to Chapter 3 (Vol. II)

Ackoff, R.L. (1960). "Systems, Organizations and Interdisciplinary Research." In *General Systems Yearbook*, Society for General Systems Research 5: 1–18.

Ackoff, R.L. (1974). *Redesigning the Future: A Systems Approach to Societal Problems*. New York: Wiley.

Ackoff, R.L. (1992). *Scientific Method: Optimizing Applied Research Decision*. New York: Wiley.

Altshuler, A. (1965a). 'The Goals of Comprehensive Planning'. *Journal of the American Institute of Planners*, 31 (1965).

Altshuler, A. (1965b). *The City Planning Process: A Political Analysis*. Ithaca, NY: Cornell University Press, 1965.

Archibugi, Franco. (2008a). *Planning Theory. From the Political Debate to the Methodological Reconstruction,* Springer.

Archibugi, Franco. (2008b). *Da burocrate a manager: La programmazione strategica in Italia: passato, presente e futuro* [From burocrate to manager. The strategic programming in Italy: past, present and future], Rubbettino, Soveria Mannelli.

Banfield, Edward C. (1961). *Political Influence,* The Free Press of Glencoe, New York.

Banfield, Edward C. (1968). *The Unheavenly City*. Boston: Little Brown.

Baumol, J. William. (1968). *Economic Theory and Operations Analysis*. Englewood Cliffs, NJ: Prentice-Hall.

Baumol, J. William. (1969). *Welfare Economics and the Theory of the State*. Second ed. Welfare and the State Revisited. Cambridge: Harvard University Press.

Beer, A. Stafford. (1966). *Decision and Control: The Meaning of Operational Research and Management Cybernetics*. London: Wiley.

Beer, A. Stafford. (1974). *Designing Freedom*. London: Wiley.

Benne, K.D. (1985). 'The Current State of Planned Changing in Persons, Groups, Communities and Societies' In: Bennis. W. G. e. alii. *The Planning Change*. New York, College Publishing: 68–82.

Bennis, W.G., Kenneth, D. Benne, and Robert, Chin, eds. (1961). The Planning of Change. New York: Holt, Rinehart and Winston.

Bennis, W.G. (1966). 'Theory and Method in Applying Behavioural Science to Planned Organizational Change'. In: *Operational Research and the Societal Sciences*, edited by J. R. Lawrence, London: Tavistock Publications.

Bolan, R. (1973). 'Community Decision Behaviour: The Culture of Planning'. In *A Reader in Planning theory*. Oxford, Pergamon.

Chadwick, George. (1971). *A Systems View of Planning: Towards a Theory of the Urban and Regional Planning Process*. Oxford: Pergamon Press. Including chapters: (a) 'Plan or Programme?' (b) 'Planning as a Conceptual System.' [Reprint, PSC, 1971] (c) 'A Mixed-Programming Strategy.' [Reprint PSC, 1971].

Checkland, P.B. (1981). *Systems Thinking, Systems Practice*. New York, Wiley.

Chestnut, Harold. (1965). *Systems Engineering Tools*. New York: Wiley.

Chestnut, Harold. (1967). *Systems Engineering Methods*. New York: Wiley.

Churchman, C. W. (1961). *Prediction and Optimal Decision*. Englewood Cliffs, NJ: Prentice-Hall.

Churchman, C. W., and Emery, F. E. (1966). 'On Various Approaches to the Study of Organizations'. In: J. R. Lawrence ed., *Operational Research and the Social Sciences*. London: Tavistock.

Churchman, C. West. (1968). *The Systems Approach*. New York, Delta.

Croce, Benedetto. (1938). History as Thought and Action.

Davidoff, P. (1965). 'Advocacy and Pluralism in Planning.' In *Journal of the American Institute of Planners* Vol. 31 (1965).

Dror, Y. 'A Choice Theory of Planning' In: *International Review of Administrative Sciences*, No. 29 (1963a): 46–58.

Dror, Y. "The Planning Process: A Facet Design." In: *International Review of Administrative Sciences* 29 (1963b).

Dror, Y. (1967). 'Comprehensive Planning: Common Fallacies Versus Preferred Features' In *Essays in Honour of Professor Jac. P. Thijsse*, edited by Van Schlagen F., 85–89. The Hague: Mouton.

Dror, Y. (1971). *Design for Policy Sciences*. Amsterdam: Elsevier.

Dyckman, J.W. (1964). 'State Development Planning: The California Case.' *Journal of the American Institute of Planners* XXX, No. 2 (1964): 144–152.

Dyckman, J.W. (1970). Social Planning in the American Democracy. *Urban Planning in Transition*. E. E. New York, Grossman.

Etzioni, Amitai. (1961). *A Comparative Analysis of Complex Organizations*. New York, Free Press.

Etzioni, Amitai. (1964). *Modern Organizations*. Englewood Cliffs, NJ, Prentice Hall.

The Programming Approach in the Collective Decision... 127

Etzioni, Amitai. (1968). *The Active Society: A Theory on Societal and Political Process*. New York, Free Press.

Etzioni, Amitai. (1969). *Indicators of the Capacities for Societal Guidance*. New York.

Etzioni, Amitai. (1983). *Bureaucracy and Democracy: A Political Dilemma*. Boston, Routledge and Kegan.

Etzioni, Amitai. (1988). *The Moral Dimension: Toward a New Economics*. New York, The Free Press.

Etzioni, Amitai. (1991). Beyond Self-Interest. *Policy Analysis and Economics: Developments, Tensions, Prospects*. D. Weimer. London, Kluwer.

Faludi, A. (1973a). *Planning Theory*. Oxford, Pergamon.

Faludi, A., ed. (1973b). *A Reader in Planning Theory*. Oxford: Pergamon Press.

Faludi, A. (1985). 'A decision-centred view of environmental planning', in *Landscape Planning*, Vol. 12.

Faludi, A. (1986a). *Critical Rationalism and Planning Methodology*. London, Pion Press.

Faludi, A. (1986b). 'The Philosophy of Sir Karl Popper and Its Relevance to Planning Methodology'. In *Critical Rationalism and Planning Methodology*, by A. Faludi, Part II. London: Pion.

Faludi, A., and Waterhout, B. (2002). *The making of the European spatial development perspective: No Masterplan*. London, New York, Routledge.

Farkas, J. (1984). 'Change in the Paradigms of Systems Analysis'. In: Tomlison and Kiss, eds. *Rethinking the Process of Operational Research and Systems analysis*. Oxford, Pergamon.

Foley, D. L. (1964). 'An Approach to Metropolitan Spatial In: M. M. Webber, ed. *Explorations into Urban Structure*. Philadelphia, University of Pennsylvania Press.

Friedmann, John. (1964). 'Regional Development in Post-Industrial Society', *Journal of the American Institute of Planners* XXX, No. 2 (1964): 90–100.

Friedmann, John. (1965). 'A response to Althusser: Comprehensive Planning as a Process.' *Journal of American Institute of Planners* 31 (1965).

Friedmann, John. (1987a). *Planning in the Public Domain: From Knowledge to Action*. Princeton, NJ: Princeton University Press.

Friedmann, John. (1987b). 'The Terrain of Planning Theory." In *Planning in the Public Domain: From Knowledge to Action*. [Reprint-PSC, 1987].

Friend, John K., and Jessop, W. N. (1969). *Local Government and Strategic Choice: An Operational Research Approach to the Process of Public Planning*. London: Tavistock.

Friend, John K. et al. (1974). *Public Planning: The Inter-Corporate Dimension*. London, Tavistock Publication.

Friend, John, and Allen Hickling. (1987). *Planning Under Pressure: The Strategic Choice Approach*. 2nd ed. Boston: Butterworth-Heinemann.

Frisch, Ragnar. (1976). *Economic Planning Studies*. A Collection of Essays edited posthumous, by Frank Long, D. Reidel Publishing Company.

Hirschman, Albert O. (1977). *The Passion and the Interests*. Princeton, NJ: Princeton University Press.

Hirschman, Albert O. (1986). *Rival Views of Market Society and Other Recent Essays*. New York: Viking.

Hirschman, Albert O. (1991). *The Rhetoric of Reaction: Perversity, Futility, Jeopardy*. Cambridge, MA: Belknap Press.

Hutchison, T.W. (1964). *'Positive' Economics and Policy Objectives*. London, George Allen & Unwin Ltd.

Kindler J. and Kiss I. (1984). Future Methodology Based on Post Assumption. *Rethinking the Process of Operational Research and Systems Analysis*. R. Tomlinson and I. Kiss. Oxford, Pergamon.

Lichfield N. et al., (1975). *Evaluation in the Planning Process*. Oxford: Pergamon Press.

Lichfield N. (1975). "A Comparison of the Planning Balance Sheet with the Goals Achievement Matrix Method of Evaluation." In: *Evaluation in the Planning Process*, edited by Lichfield N. et alii, Kettle P. and Whitebread M. Oxford: Pergamon Press.

Lichfield N. and Darin-Drabkin H. (1980). *Land Policy in Planning*. London: Allen & Unwin.

Lichfield N. (1990). 'Plan Evaluation Methodology: Comprehending the Conclusions' In: *Evaluation Methods for Urban and Regional Plans*, edited by D. Shefer and H. Voogd. London: Pion.

Lichfield N. (1996). *Community Impact Evaluation*. London: University College of London Press.

Lichfield N. et al., Ed. (1998). *Evaluation in Planning: Facing the Challenge of Complexity*. Dordrecht, Holland: Kluwer Academic Press.

Lindblom Charles E. (1965). *The Intelligence of Democracy*. New York: Free Press.

Lindblom Charles E. (1968). *The Policy Making Process*. Englewood Cliffs, NJ: Prentice Hall.

March J.G. (1988). *Decisions and Organizations*. Oxford: Basil Blackwell.

March J.G. (1999). *The Pursuit of Organizational Intelligence*. Oxford, Blackwell.

McLoughlin J.B. (1969). *Urban and Regional Planning: A System Approach*. London: Faber and Faber.

Meade James E. (1968). *The Theory of Indicative Planning*. Manchester: Manchester University Press.

Meade James E. Agathopia: *The Economics of Partnership*. Aberdeen: Aberdeen University Press, 1989.

Meade James, E. Liberty, *Equality and Efficiency*. London: Macmillan, 1993.

Meyerson, Martin. (1956). 'Building the Middle-Range Bridge to Comprehensive Planning', *Journal of the American Institute of Planners* XXII (1956).

Mishan Edward J. (1976). *Cost-Benefit Analysis: An Introduction*. New York: Praeger.

Mishan Edward J. (1981). *Introduction to Normative Economics*. New York: Oxford University Press.

Myrdal, Gunnar (1973). *Against the Stream: Critical Essays on Economics*. New York, Pantheon Books.

Perloff Harvey S. (1957). *Education for Planning: City, State, and Regional*. Baltimore: John Hopkins University Press.

Perloff Harvey S. (1969a). *The Quality of the Urban Environment: Essays on "New Resources" in an Urban Age*. Baltimore, John Hopkins Press.

Perloff Harvey S. (1969b). A Framework for Dealing with Urban Environment. *The Quality of the Urban Environment. Essay on "New Resources" in an Urban Age*. H. S. Perloff. Washington, DC, Resources for the Future Inc.

Robinson Ira M. (1972). *Decision-making in Urban Planning: An Introduction to New Methodologies,* Beverly Hill, CA, Sage.

Simon Herbert. A. (1962). 'The Architecture of Complexity.' In: *Proceedings of the American Philosophical Society* (106).

Simon Herbert. A. (1969). *The Sciences of the Artificial*. Cambridge, MA, MIT Press.

Thomas, Huw, and Healey, Patsy. (1991). *Dilemmas of Planning Practice*. Avebury Technical, Aldershot.

Tomlinson, Rolfe and Kiss Istvàn, Ed. (1984). *Rethinking the Process of Operational Research and Systems Analysis*. Oxford, Pergamon.

Warfield J. N. (1976). *Societal Systems: Planning, Policy and Complexity*. New York: Wiley.

Webber, M. M. et alii, ed. (1964a). *Explorations into Urban Structure*. Philadelphia: University of Pennsylvania Press.

Webber M. M. (1964b). 'The Urban Place and the Non-Place Urban Realm.' In: *Explorations into Urban Structure, etc*. edited by M.M. Webber et alii. Philadelphia, University of Pennsylvania Press.

Webber M. M. (1968). 'The Post-City Age.' In *Daedalus*, Fall: 1091–1110.

4

The Programming Approach and the Mainstream Economic General Theory (*from the Isard's 'General Theory'*)

4.1 Some Needs of 'Realism' in the Economic 'Neo-Classical School' of Thought

In the evolutions of economic analysis, pretentiously named 'economic science' by some, there has been no absence of doubt or perplexity concerning the scientific basis and cognitive capacity of the discipline. In Chaps. 1 and 2 of this book, we have discussed the substantial objections made by Gunnar Myrdal and others, and in **Vol. I**, Chap. 8 the approach of Wassily Leontief.

However, the chapters collected here aim only at underlining how the programming approach (as we have called it, following Frisch) has brought into question a good deal of traditional approaches of economics, or at least those directed towards constructing the cognitive base of 'normative' rules of political and decisional behaviour. All this should be carried out by engaging with various fields of analysis and economic policy, which have given rise to their further development into the sub-classes of economic disciplines such as technological development economics, regional and urban economics, environmental economics, labour economics, and so on.

© The Author(s) 2019
F. Archibugi, *The Programming Approach and the Demise of Economics*,
https://doi.org/10.1007/978-3-319-78060-3_4

'Mainstream' economic doctrine, conventionally called 'neo-classical', has not failed to expand the analysis on the validity conditions of its theorems, specifically those considered with respect to their 'realism', given that the most intense criticism, deriving from the less 'orthodox' sectors of economics itself, has centred around the lack of realism.

More than a few scholars—largely accepting these critics' arguments—have attempted to create a less limited basis to economic theory without compromising its analytical foundations too far.

Among these last scholars, I consider Walter Isard one of the most interesting, for the vastness of his approach and the systematisation of his visions.[1] He has attempted—in cooperation with his colleagues—to reconstruct a 'general theory' of behaviour, economic, social or political, even including a 'regional' dimension.[2] Thus he published, in 1960, a 'general theory' through which he responds to the acknowledged lacks of the 'neoclassical theory', nevertheless defending and maintaining the general subjectivist approach.

4.2   Isard's 'General Theory'

The work of Walter Isard in this direction is impressive; at the same time, it is very poorly known, certainly less than other books that led him to be considered the 'father' of 'regional science'. This work deserves the greatest attention, which it has not had to date among the economists of the neoclassical school, nor among the others not of neoclassical school.[3]

4.2.1 In Search of the 'Concept of More Realism'

With his reconstruction of a 'general theory', Isard can be considered to have recovered that 'realism' which had been lost due to the strict economic explanation of human behaviour as located in the crux of the utilitarian tradition:

> It has become increasingly evident to those of us in economics, regional science, and other social sciences that our applied research relating to both planning and policy-making suffers greatly *from our inadequate ability to*

The Programming Approach and the Mainstream Economic...

project behaviour. True, we have developed some relatively strong analyses such as the marginal approach in economic and location theory, and strong operational techniques such as comparative cost, industrial complex, and interregional linear programming. But these have been based on such postulates as a *one-state-of-the-environment world*[4] and profit maximisation. Unfortunately, these postulates, and others associated with them, lead to theoretical results and projections that cannot be said to correspond closely to observed behaviour, at least insofar as we are able to describe and measure such behaviour. (Isard et al. 1969, p. 116)

Isard draws upon reasoning to examine the nature and characteristics of 'some new sets of postulates' that are hopefully more realistic and useful for the projection of behaviour. He thus joins forces with a group of scholars who, after having ingested theories and theorems founded on 'maximisation', recognise the lack of a practical foundation here and hence propose ways to overcome this limitation.

Isard himself states with a certain sadness that:

Most of the social sciences have been concerned with one or more aspects or types of rational and optimising behaviour. Much of economics concerns behaviour designed to minimize cost and effort or to maximize profits, utility, and the economic welfare of the social body. Much of political science, especially the new behaviouristic political science, emphasizes processes whereby individuals and groups act to maximize, for example, their vote, their power, their control over influence networks, or the probability of their retaining a position or status already achieved. Administrative theory also deals with optimisation, for example in its emphasis upon efficiency and cost minimization in the performance of functions or attainment of specific goals. Public policy formation (inclusive of political economy) is easily interpreted as involving for each issue the selection of that alternative which either minimizes or maximizes some measure or function within the setting of numerous institutional constraints. A good part of psychology pertains to the individual attempting to maximize satisfaction within a complex political-social-economic (stimulus) environment which provokes responses and fosters, inhibits, and otherwise influences drives, learning, and adaptation. Sociology investigates the structure and function of social groups and institutions, many of which may be viewed as optimising certain objectives subject to restraining elements: for example, maximizing friendship, morale, and pattern stability subject to spatial, economic, and other prescribed constraints. (Isard et al. 1969, p. 117)

Then Isard seeks to overcome the shortcomings of the traditional approach, with the intention of finding 'new' sets of assumptions, hopefully to achieve a more effective base for understanding and projecting behaviour.

Where and how does Isard hope to find such 'new' sets of assumptions?

It is here that Isard's vast research, ranging over a good part of theories on social structure, is admirable for the architecture of his new 'general theory', whilst it is complicated in terms of his belief in actually grasping that set of 'more realistic' assumptions that could constitute the projections for a more reliable operational approach to planning and policy.

4.2.2 The 'Relaxation' of Assumptions and the Multiplication of 'Casuistics'

In fact, one might wonder (and, he himself does wonder to the same question—but, as we will see, only at the end) whether with the 'complication' of cases, by means of the relaxation of the simplifying assumptions, good service is being done to the sought-after cause of the operational projection of behaviour. Certainly, each case becomes per se—theoretically—more 'realistic', but one may be drawn to ask: how can we identify—in the realities of ex post observations and, even worse, in the realities of ex ante projections—such a detailed correspondence with the theoretical case (and with its all the more sophisticated system of derived assumptions and the system of behaviour projections that results from it)?

In order to better clarify such complexities, it is necessary to describe first, albeit briefly,[5] Isard's route. In the first part of his investigation, being motivated by the collapse of the meaningfulness of the assumptions regarding traditional theories, he begins to explore all the possibilities of 'extending' the usual decision-making models that classical theory provides.

Firstly, remaining within the ambit of classical economic and location theory, insofar as it refers to individual behaviour, Isard thus proposes to re-define it by means of establishing the following components:

The Programming Approach and the Mainstream Economic...   135

1. *Relaxing the 'one state-of-the-environment-world' assumption relaxing, via the introduction of the 'possibility of many states'.*

Thus, Isard considers necessary 'a complete re-examination of the meaning of optimising behaviour and the building from the ground up of a more satisfactory structure for decision-making' (pp. 17–18). This relaxing of assumptions, which, as mentioned, fits into the scheme of traditional economic theory, allows for cases that—whilst being reduced to the bare essentials by Isard himself—already proliferate with reasonably important variations, both found in the assumptions system on the one hand and in the projected behaviour on the other.

2. *The introduction of the variable 'attitudes'.*

Isard writes:

> So long as only one defined state of the environment could exist, economic and location theorists were not compelled to consider the attitude of a profit-maximizing individual.
> However, whether he was a pessimist, an optimist, a conservative decision-maker, or some other type, it was appropriate for him to scan the entire single column of his profit (outcome) matrix and to find the highest element in it. Since by definition the environment could take on only one state, he could be sure that the highest profit would be realised if he selected the corresponding action. This certainty existed whether he chose from an action space containing an infinite number of points (such as in the two cases above) or whether he faced an action space containing a finite number of points. As a consequence, when in the following section we wish to increase the realism of the analysis by admitting several possible states of the environment, we find that we have to consider the individual's attitude as another basic variable.[6]

What are these 'attitudes'?
In regard to attitudes and personality characteristics, Isard refers to already established literature (Churchman 1961; Simon 1957; Edwards 1961, 1972; and others), the axioms of which he further enriches and renders more sophisticated by means of his interpretation of the effects of

'personal style', 'taste', 'capacity of choice', and so on. The main 'types' of attitude that Isard considers are the following:

— 'The 100 per cent conservative', who 'is willing only to consider sure things' (Isard 1969, p. 138);
— 'The expected payoff calculator', whose 'objective is to maximize expected payoff' (ibidem, pp. 133–134);
— 'The 100 per cent conservative regretter', whose 'objective is to minimize the level of regret which certainly cannot be exceeded' (ibidem, p. 134);
— 'The expected regret calculator', whose 'objective is to minimize expected regret' (ibidem, p. 135).

Furthermore, the crossing of these 'types' with 'attitudes' generates the description of further cases. According to Isard's description, the following are results of such proliferation:

— 'The 100 percent optimist': this is the extreme case of the person who is 'certain that for any given action he will receive the highest possible payoff' (Isard 1969, ibidem, p. 136);
— 'The 100 percent pessimist': the other extreme is the person who is 'certain that whatever action he takes, the worst will occur, i.e. he will be left with the least possible payoff' (ibidem, p. 137);
— 'The 100 percent conservative': who, as already mentioned, 'is willing only to consider sure things' (ibidem, p. 138);
— 'The Hurwicz individual': who is characterised by traits of both optimism and pessimism and 'looks at the best and worst outcomes that can be associated with any action, and assigns a weight (probability) to each of these outcomes' (ibidem, pp. 138–139);
— 'The equiprobable expected payoff calculator': this type 'is motivated to maximize expected payoff and who knows that each state of the environment has an equal chance of occurring. Alternatively, he may have no information about the occurrence of the several states of the environment and may simply assume that they will occur with equal probability' (ibidem, p. 140);
— 'The 100 percent pessimistic regretter', who 'is certain that whatever the action he takes he will be left with the highest possible regret' (ibidem. p. 141);

- 'The 100 percent conservative regretter', whose 'objective is to minimize the level of regret which certainly cannot be exceeded' (ibidem, p. 134);
- 'The equiprobable expected regret calculator' (ibidem, p. 141).

The total number of cases introduced by Isard as variations on the system of traditional assumptions is 20, including those indicated above, each with its own system of assumptions and system of projected behaviour.

4.2.3 The Extension of the Objective Function to 'Non-Economic Commodities'

However, Isard's research into new, 'more realistic' situations with the introduction of 'new sets of variables' does not conclude here.

Instead, there is iconoclastic fury directed against the inexpressive and unrealistic sanctuaries of the (neo)classical approach to 'economic' behaviour, but—at the same time—the wish to maintain the bases of neoclassical theory from the critical attacks of heterodox economists; this leads Isard to extend the analysis of factors determining behaviour (of individuals, groups and institutions) to non-economic factors and objectives. He achieve this goal by means of incorporating into the classical 'objective-function' (the would-be expression of a function of social well-being in its general version) the 'non-tangible' goods variables (which Isard calls 'commodities' in order to characterise their 'merchant' nature, and the nature of objects of 'exchange' between individuals, groups and institutions,[7] even if it is an exchange that does not take place through the traditional market, and much less so, through the monetary market).[8]

4.3 'Non-Economic Commodities' (*from Walter Isard*)

Isard provides an interesting classification of so-called non-economic commodities, which merit being briefly recounted here.

First of all, we should recall that before the list of 13 non-economic commodities, which Isard proposes as an instrument for making the

138 Volume II. Selected Testimonies on the Epistemological...

decision-making system 'operational' and for which the 'general theory' should be the instrument, he had designed a structure for the social system.

4.3.1 Borrowing the 'Social Acts'

Isard borrowed this structure from the well-known works of the American sociologist Talcott Parsons (whom in the decades following the Second World War had a particularly strong influence in the American scientific community). Inheriting the tradition of pragmatism (from Peirce, James, Dewey, and others), Parsons developed from 1951 onwards a 'General Theory of Action', which he gradually perfected, in collaboration with colleagues and students,[9] publishing the two volumes of the *Theories of Society* in 1961.[10]

The 'social act', for Parsons, is always a combination of unequal weights of four essentially extreme or 'pure' acts that give rise to four sub-systems of the general social system:

1. '*The adaptive or economy subsystem*, wherein behaviour involves, primarily, the overcoming of environmental constraints and the active manipulation of the scarce resources of both the environment and the social system in order to acquire commodities (or facilities) meaningful for a variety of system goals. Within this subsystem, fall the economic organizations which have typically been designated as firms';
2. *The goal-attainment or polity subsystem*, wherein behaviour primarily involves the setting of priorities or valuations of the diverse, heterogeneous goals of a complex social system, taking into account the needs and directions of both the whole society (or community) and individuals and groups. In this subsystem, fall 'political man' and 'political policy-forming organizations';
3. '*The integrative subsystem*, wherein behaviour primarily involves, within a restricted set of groups or individuals or both, the control of conflict and disruptive tendencies towards deviant behaviour and the promotion of harmony and cooperation. In this subsystem, fall 'integrative' organizations (social groups and institutions and certain legal institutions)';

4. '*The pattern-maintenance subsystem*, wherein behaviour involves primarily the attainment of stability of institutional and interaction patterns and values and,—in a more comprehensive sense than in the integrative subsystem—the management of forces creating tensions among social, economic, and political organizations and individuals with diverse internalised motivational commitments. In this subsystem, fall organizations such as religious and educational institutions'. (Isard et al. 1969, pp. 495–497)

Deriving from the structure of the 'social acts' framed in these four subsystems, and by virtue of inspiration from other very similar important works by other scholars (such as the sociologist Bertram Gross and the philosopher Thomas Kuhn).[11]

Isard deduces a list of 13 'non-economic commodities' that serve to make up the conventional lists of 'economic' commodities.

Although we shall not digress into the general theory of the social system adopted by Isard, I intend only to note the quantity and quality of the 'variables' which he intends to introduce in order to represent the behaviour of groups, organisations, institutions and individuals as 'more realistic', and not as merely more 'economic'. This behaviour cannot be disassociated and disintegrated by a variety of components or factors, which as much as they exist and have an influence on the given behaviour, can never be disassociated from other factors.

4.3.2 From Social Acts to 'Non-Economic Commodities'

The 'non-economic' commodities that Isard intends to include in the general system of social transactions and as a motivational base of behaviour (of organisations, groups and individuals) are as follows:

1. *The 'solidarity' commodity*: it is the 'integration of diversified perspectives within an organization (community, or group). It is a commodity, which has reference to an organization only, and is produced by interaction of individuals within the organization, or by the interaction of the organization with other behaving units. It is not a commodity

which is capable of being possessed by an individual. It embraces cohesiveness (the strength of attraction of individuals to the organization) as well as loyalty (faithfulness of individuals to the values and standards of the organization). One hundred percent solidarity implies joint preference ordering'.[12]

2. The *'power' commodity*: it is the 'ability to influence decisions of an individual or organization. It may be both an individual and organization, through delegation or otherwise. By this definition power embraces the ability to exercise authority, to compel obedience, the exercise of authority implying an asymmetrical relation between two behaving units'.[13]

3. The *'respect' commodity*: it is the 'weighted combination of status, honour, recognition, prestige, esteem, and expressive social approval, which an individual or organization receives. The weights may be objectively specified or simply subjective'.

4. The *'rectitude' commodity*: it is a 'weighted average of religious and moral values such as virtue, goodness, righteousness, responsibility, honesty, and integrity. The weights may be objectively specified, or simply subjective. Its possession by an individual is recognized by the individual, other individuals, and organizations'.

5. The *'affection' commodity*: it is the 'kindnesses, friendliness, love and goodwill bestowed upon an individual or organization, by other individuals and organizations. It embraces popularity'.

6. The *'sociality' commodity*: it is the 'pleasant feeling generated by interaction of individuals in an organization or circle. It is a commodity, which can be produced by a community only, and not by an individual. As a member of the organization, each individual receives a share of this commodity in return (anticipated or unanticipated)'.

7. The *'participation' commodity*: it is the 'involvement in the decision-making and other activities of an organization, involvement that is associated with the active 'belonging to' an organization'.[14]

8. The *'well-being' commodity*: it is the 'health and safety of the individual'.

9. The *'skill' commodity*: it is 'proficiency in practice, whether in arts, crafts, trade or profession; it also embraces the ability to be inventive and creative'.

10. *The 'enlightenment' commodity*: it is the 'knowledge and insight concerning the physical environment and personal, social, and cultural relations'.
11. *The 'achievement' commodity*: it is the 'accomplishment of an individual as evaluated by that individual. It is a commodity that can be consumed by an individual only, and its consumption may be associated with the removal of the tension associated with an achievement (need for achievement)' (Isard et al. 1969, pp. 565–567).

In addition to the 11 'non-economic' commodities listed above, Isard offers another two whose definitions are principally orientated towards the requirements of the general theory that he will develop:

1. *The 'love-tendered' commodity*, a 'commodity which is produced only when an individual—out of pure love—gives a family member, friend, or any other individual some commodity of value (e.g. corn, happiness (utility) of the recipient and without expectation of a quid pro flowers, the 'affection' commodity), with the intention of increasing the quo. The positive outcome of the *'love-tendered' commodity* balances the negative inputs of the commodities involved in unilateral giving, its consumption accounting for inner satisfaction (utility), which the individual achieves from his unilateral giving. Since the 'love-tendered' commodity has utility to the individual, and since utility is defined only over a commodity space, we treat the commodity—love-tendered—as a real commodity. However it is one, which is not marketable. That is, whatever amount of this commodity is produced by an individual, it is directly consumed by him';
2. *the 'sanctions' commodity*, which 'differs from most other commodities in that it cannot be produced by organisations or individuals. It is a commodity which accrues to a participant (an individual or organisation) in his interactions with society. With each *input-outcome plan* (consisting of all commodities other than the commodity-sanctions) that the participant may choose is associated a well-defined amount of the commodity-sanctions, the magnitude of *which is taken to reflect society's net approval or disapproval of that plan*. In this sense, the commodity-sanctions are an a-typical commodity; yet, we conceive it

to have significance (utility) for the individual and to enter into the profit decisions of organisations. In this latter sense, it is a real commodity; so we treat it as such' (Isard et al. 1969, p. 568).

Finally, Isard introduces—as a non-economic commodity—the 'vote', as a

resource that is frequently perishable. It is an input in a situation where the output is a decision (the decision being one of the several—at least two—alternatives available for selection). It is an explicit unit expression of support or opposition to alternatives available for selection'. (Isard 1969, pp. 568–569)

4.4 The Isard 'General Theory' and the Planning Accounting Frame

Thus, having widened the field of 'commodities' exchanged and the motivations for such 'social acts', as well as the decisions and the choices inherent in them, Isard continues to expand a 'general, social, political, and economic theory for a system of regions'. It seems that he here openly applies the same theorems of the general theory of economic equilibrium (of Walrasian origin) as in the more recent version of Arrow and Debreu (1954) and of Isard's own work with Ostroff (1958).

But let us reconsider here the concerns previously mentioned, which arise out of the theory in question. May a complex system, such as the one provided by Isard, be a source for the protection of more realistic behaviour, and consequently more advantageous for the construction of 'decision-making models'—those models with which decision-makers (individuals, groups and organisations, but above all the public decision-makers of a planning policy) may make decisions about the future?

In order to make the decision-making procedures more 'realistic,' moving from the schemes already seen with a single participant to those with two participants and finally to those with n-participants, Isard lists as many as 77 different cases of decision situations with just as many assumption systems and behavioural projections (these are exceptionally theoretical and so have only academic value). Moreover, all the above builds this so called 'realistic' approach by virtue of the condition which excludes another entire series of 'cases', which would be implied if one were to omit the overwhelming number of 'implicit' assumptions' (as Leontief would call them, see **Vol. I**, Chap. 8).

Furthermore, many other cases would arise if we could introduce the presence of decision factors coming from the 'market' of 'non-economic commodities'. These commodities are those which have not yet been brought into play by means of the analysis of decision processes, but only in the still very roughly estimated architecture of a general accounting system (which even Isard called 'the multi-regional, social and political economic accounting frame').

Isard himself overlooks the reason for concern regarding the 'decision analysis' so far carried forward by him in his relentless quest for greater 'realism'.

At the conclusion of his colossal work, he dedicates his last chapter to a retrospect and prospect on some critical areas for future research, writing:

> True the logical structure of the analysis of these chapters, with the associated mathematical statements in the Appendix chapters, may appear impressive to some scholars. To others, however, the list of unrealistic assumptions, explicit and implicit, may appear still more impressive—and may lead them to view the derived logical structures as refinements concerned with the consistency of a system, and which in successive rounds of reformulation and restatement increasingly turn in upon themselves and grow more and more remote from reality. (Isard et al. 1969, p. 823)

I admit that I belong to this latter category of readers. I am under the impression that in the quest for 'realism', one finds oneself in hypothetical situations that become only more unrealistic.

But this tendency away from 'realism' occurs—and this marks my point of concern—as a result of the application of an unsuitable approach: that is that of 'positivist' analysis.

In the programming approach—that is, linked to hypotheses of future behaviour, mainly of groups and governments—there is no more need for this 'extreme' realism, which seems to distance itself so far from reality as to take on an aspect of extreme chance.

In the programming approach—which is totally aimed at an ex ante decision-making—the classification of possible types of decisional behaviour must be addressed according to the notion of 'reasonableness', to the theoretical probability of certainty, which may render coherent and acceptable a complex set of attitudes, motivations and decisions; these are all made coherent by their explicit policy-making, by their negotiation, by the adoption of co-operation procedures, and by the spread of information.

Isard himself, on the other hand, shows he is aware, on more than one occasion, of these aspects—for example, when he realises that his own analysis of 'interdependent decision situations in political space' is defective; he feels that there should have been 'introduced the judicial and regulatory processes of government units explicitly through restricting action spaces, etc., and perhaps through imposing certain co-operative procedures' (Isard 1969, p. 833).

But we are—as always—in the logic of 'explaining' behaviours and not 'hypothesising them'—a subtle but strategically different logic.

If Isard's multi-functional, multi-sectorial and multi-regional model was initiated only by means of the construction and elaboration of an accounting frame (which Isard himself considers the most important outcome of his elaborate general theory), I would have nothing to say: a sufficiently taxonomic scheme would have to construct a system of economic and non-economic accounts, perhaps thereafter encountering frightening problems of data collection, interpretation and acceptance of statistical approximations, but nevertheless serving as a useful platform for possible decisions programming.[15]

4.5 Isard's 'General Theory' Between a 'Positivist' Methodology and the Programming Approach (*An other Interesting Proposal by Isard for an Even More General Theory*)

Thus, it would not be inappropriate to say that Isard has provided a very important contribution to planology with his general theory by means of the construction of a general accounting framework in the social system.

Isard's attempt aims, as discussed throughout the chapter, to extend 'the competitive-equilibrium frameworks of Arrow and Debreu to a broader system wherein we consider social and political commodities in addition to economic goods' (p. 599). Isard acknowledges, moreover—at the end of his impressive exposition—that there is a 'need for a more adequate accounting framework in the political (polity or goal-setting) subsystem' (p. 836) and that his emphasis was placed more on theoretical aspects than on the construction of the framework. Despite this shortcoming, Isard's scheme represents a very important contribution, in addition to others (Gross 1966a; Fox 1985; Drewnowski 1974; Archibugi 1971, 1974) to the schematisation of accounting reference frames for planning, founded on extended or integrated accounts, which include not only economic accounts but also social, environmental and political ones.

However, the operationality of the Isardian accounting framework still seems founded on the selection, analysis and projection of behavioural relations, as well as on the quantification of parameters extracted from reality ex post, and in this way projected onto the future.

Then, what the Isardian framework projects onto the future are also the objectives which are still those on which have been based the choice processes in the past, in their turn based on the past conditions, which are also often altered. Thus, even the 'parameters' that are measured on the basis of those choices are those that express a relation with means, which take into account only conditions, capacities and knowledges of the past, which often no longer exist in the present, and least of all in the future. In short, the data with which the planning accounting framework is built, on which choices, decisions and compromises should be made, in the present for the future action, become greatly influenced and made obsolete by the parameters of the past, and also become conservative paradigms.

In this case, adopting this viewpoint, one has the impression that the very criticism that Isard himself fears, that of 'sophistication'—'which in successive rounds of reformulation and restatement increasingly turns in upon themselves and grow more and more remote from reality'—seems more plausible. The behavioural relationships become, in such a way, the object of decisional analyses, and not just of descriptive ones.

They are analysed, in other terms, for their supposed or verified validity, not only for the past but also for the decisions that relate to the future. This, in fact, would represent an error in method, risky for the false assumptions on which it would be based, that is, the idea of being able to achieve 'realistic' behaviour that may be projected onto the future. It would be an error called by Frisch 'decision use' of 'descriptive models'. It is a question of error shared by all kinds of 'growth model', the heart of any kind of econometrics, as sharply criticised by Frisch as an epistemological mistake. It is a mistake that is, nevertheless, still almost universally practiced by the mainstream economics, of neo-classical setting, but on which any other positivistic economics tend to shift.

In regards to this matter, we could extend the analysis of the relationships between planology and regional science (with reference also to the evaluation developed by the theorists of decision-making processes, as we have seen more clearly in **Vol. II**, Chap. 3). I will leave this aspect to the impact evaluations on specific fields of economic analysis (excluded from this book).

Furthermore, the analysis of general equilibrium (as understood in Isard's general theory) is founded on such a vast set of explicit or implicit conditions that its usefulness for planning is, in turn, nullified. It postulates a harmony ex ante of any spontaneous combination of factors, conditions, negotiating forces, decision processes and desires or choices, and so on; this corresponds more or less to the same accord that any analysis ex post is able to model—in the search for realism—on the basis of the events observed.

Thus, from the point of view of general equilibrium, the decision problem (aimed at the future) is constituted not only by virtue of the 'projection' of 'realistic' behaviour, but also by that of postulating 'reasonable' behaviour (as Isard refers to it on more than one occasion).[16] These are behaviours elaborated and decided with reference to: (1) decisional situations involving of the majority of social subjects (individuals, but also organisations, interest groups and governments of all shapes and sizes); and (2) existing or easily hypothetically practicable decision systems.

However, on this matter, I should refer to our more detailed discussion of the relationship between the programming approach and decisional approach in **Vol. I**, Chaps. 6 and 7.

The Programming Approach and the Mainstream Economic...   **147**

Notes to Chapter 4 (Vol. II)

1. Walter Isard, et al. *General Theory; Social, Political, Economic and Regional, with Particular Reference to Decision-Making Analysis*, MIT Press, Cambridge, 1969.
2. Perhaps due to the fact that Isard himself owed his main notoriety as one of the major exponent of the so called regional science.
3. I think that it would be very useful if a historian of economic thinking would do a critical survey of the acceptance obtained by Isard in the scientific community, with the book in question, and of the reason for its missed lack of appeal. His general theoretical vigour was not bread for many followers of regional economics, among which—on the contrary—he has had with other works (Isard 1956, 1960) much consensus and celebration. But it is strange that when Isard left the schemes of regional science, to which his name and reputation are connected, and he entered a more general discussion, one more theoretical and more comprehensive, and less based on conventional premises, he did not receive more attention, with responses and resonance of consent and dissent, appropriate—in my view—to his worth.
4. I would have preferred to use the expression 'state of context', because of the ambiguity in 'environment' in recent times, in many cases and in many languages.
5. However, direct acquaintance with Isard's work is recommended.
6. Isard et al. 1969, p. 130.
7. We will use anyhow the word 'goods' and not 'commodities' for reasons of style.
8. See **Vol. II**, Chap. 8 on the measuring of the real objectives, and **Vol. III**, Chap. 4, concerning the quantification of the planning accounting frame.
9. See Parsons, T. and Shils, E.A. (1951), Parsons T. et al. (1953), Parsons, T. and Smelser, N.J (1957).
10. See T. Parsons (ed). 1961. See also Black, M. (1961) *An anthology on Talcott Parsons.*
11. B.M. Gross (1966a) and Thomas Kuhn (1963).
12. Personally, I have studied this commodity ('solidarity') from a different point of view—as a factor in changing the patterns of the 'capitalistic' economy (and 'society') and moving it towards a new 'associative economy' or 'post-capitalist society'. (See Archibugi 2000.)

13. Ideas and specifications may be found on this 'non-economic' commodity in the vast literature on policy science, which Isard has referred to via authors such as Banfield (1961), Harsanyi (1962), Gross (1964) and Dahl (1957).
14. On this, see in particular the works by McClelland (1953, 1961) and Gross (1964).
15. See in Isard, the treatment of his 'General Accounting Framework in the Social System' (see **Vol. II**, this chapter).
16. However, on this matter, Isard states: 'It is difficult to define exactly what is meant by 'reasonable' in this context. For our purposes, we choose to adopt the approach suggested by Luce and Raiffa' (Isard et al., ibidem, p. 842). Isard refers to Luce and Raiffa, 1958, p. 332. The guiding principles evoked here are briefly: 'Efficiency, Simplicity, Normality, Strategy, Pre-indeterminacy'. (For further elaboration, see Isard et al., ibidem, p. 842.)

Bibliographical References to Chapter 4 (Vol. II)

Archibugi, Franco. (1971). *Un Quadro contabile per la pianificazione nazionale*, [An accounting frame for the national planning] in: V. Cao-Pinna, ed., Econometria e Pianificazione [Econometrics and Planning], Etas-Kompass, Milano.

Archibugi, Franco. (1974). A System of Models for the National Long-Term Planning Process, UN-ECE Seminar on *The Use of Systems of Models in Planning*, UNECE Conference, Moscow, 2–11 Dec 1974 (Revised version: *The Configuration of a System of Models as an Instrument for the Comprehensive Management of the Economy*, Paper for the 'XII International Input-Output Conference', Seville, 1993.

Archibugi, Franco. (2000). *The Associative Economy: Insights beyond Welfare State and into Post-capitalism*, London, Macmillan, 2000.

Arrow, J. Kenneth and Debreu G. (1954). 'Existence of an Equilibrium for a Competitive Economy' *Econometrica* 22(3): 265–290.

Banfield, Edward C. (1961). *Political Influence,* The Free Press of Glencoe, New York.

Churchman, C. W. (1961). *Prediction and Optimal Decision*. Englewood Cliffs, NJ: Prentice-Hall.

Drewnowski, J. (1974). *On Measuring and Planning the Quality of Life*, Mouton, The Hague, 1974.

Edwards, W. (1961). 'Behavioural Decision Theory', *Annual Review of Psychology*, No. 12, pp. 473–498.

Edwards, W. (1972). 'Social Utilities' *The Engineering Economist Sumner Symposium*, IV: 119–129.

Fox, K.A. (1985). *Social System Accounts: Linking Social and Economic Indicators Through Tangible behaviour Settings*. Dordrecht, Reidel Publishing Company. Included chapters: (a) 'The Classification of Stocks of Physical Capital and Consumer Durables 'Linking Social and Economic Indicators through Tangible Behavior. (b) 'The Classification of Roles in Social System Accounts'. (c) 'Social System Accounts Based on Behavior Settings: Some Next Steps'. (d) 'The Classification and Delineation of Communities and Regions in Social System Accounts'

Gross, B.M. (1966a). 'Activating National Plans.' In: *Operational Research and the Social Sciences*, edited by J. R. Lawrence. London: Tavistock.

Gross, B.M. (1966b). 'The State of the Nation: Social Systems Accounting.' In: *Social Indicators*, edited by R. A Bauer. Cambridge: MIT Press.

Harsanyi, J.C. (1962). 'Measurement of Social Power, Opportunity Costs and the Theory of Two Persons Bargaining Games', *Behavioural Science*, 7 (67–80).

Isard, W. et al. (1969). *General Theory: Social, Political, Economic, and Regional with Particular Reference to Decision-Making Analysis*. Cambridge, MA, MIT Press.

Kuhn, A. (1963). The study of society-A unified approach, Richard D. Irwin, Inc., The Dorsey Press, Inc.

McClelland, D. C. et alii (1953). *The Achievement Motive*. New York, Appleton-Century-Crofts.

McClelland D.C. (1961). *The Achieving Society*. Princeton, NJ, Van Nostrand.

Parsons T. & Shils E. A. (1951). *Toward a General Theory of Action*. Cambridge, MA, Harvard University Press.

Parsons T., R. F. Bales & E. A. Shils, (1953). *Working Papers in the Theory of Action*. Glencoe, IL, The Free Press.

Parsons T. & N. J. Smelser (1957). *Economy and Society, A Study in Integration of Economic and Social Theory*. Routledge and Kegan Paul, London.

Simon, Herbert. A. (1957). *Models of Man. Social and Rational*. New York, Wiley & Sons Inc.

5

The Programming Approach and the Management Sciences

5.1 The Programming Approach and the Administrative Sciences: Neglected Interrelations

The programming approach changes the logical basis of an important part of the political and administrative sciences which are most closely related to it.

In this chapter, after having examined the ways in which the administrative sciences could themselves be considered versions of the programming approach itself, even if integrated with all the other social scientific disciplines, as purged of their determinist approach, we will examine and argue why the principle of bounded rationality (now a central argument in the administrative sciences and also in the epistemology of economics) has become, in the planning sciences, absolutely inappropriate.

5.1.1 Management Sciences as Context

The economic analysis of public programmes and the control of the effectiveness of public expenditure has, for many years, been the focus of

© The Author(s) 2019
F. Archibugi, *The Programming Approach and the Demise of Economics*,
https://doi.org/10.1007/978-3-319-78060-3_5

151

scholarly attention, but also of interest to political operators and general public opinion. All this was developed alongside 'management science'.

In fact, this science was created when people began dismissing the notion of being able to know and 'explain' the secrets of economic life, or 'the wealth of nations', as based on the behaviour of the 'economic individual' within his socio-legal context, in his universal meaning ('rules' or 'laws') and predicated upon the principle *homo oeconomicus*, seen as a 'producer' or 'entrepreneur' (rather than as a 'consumer' or 'customer').[1]

Furthermore, this management science improved subsequently once effectiveness in the production of goods and services was ascertained; in the enterprise of production (especially of a large scale), it is not due to the 'shrewdness' and personal capacity of an entrepreneur/manager (operating legally with his own, or other, capital means; or also operator in 'public' or in 'private' business), but to the organisation, and to the more or less 'scientific' methods which production activity itself induces and develops, and to which (and through which), it can be applied.

Therefore, everything was developed alongside so-called 'managerialism'—the assumption of an autonomous profession, with respect to historical 'entrepreneurialism'—at the basis of which lies the theory of a standard behaviour of entrepreneurs first and of organisations later. Thus originated, all that became management and the control of business matters through a managerial capacity that one can learn, not only through experience, but also through education.[2]

Obviously, everything originated in parallel with the increasing average dimension of enterprises, by means of concentration: a historical phenomenon considered ineluctable by all (from Stuart Mill to Marx, from Marshall to Pigou, from Schumpeter to Keynes), and—at least until some years ago—confirmed by historical developments; this developing alongside big business projected towards multi-sectoriality and multi-nationality.[3]

All this, however, originated without denying the possible role of the 'personality' and the 'human factor' in the organisation. But we are also dealing with an entirely different role, one subordinated to the working modality of the organisation, which is subject (much more than the traditional and personal small business) to the rules of knowledge (which is learned and learnable) of an objective 'rationality'—of a largely standardised knowhow, the bringer of a new profession, that of the manager: managerialism.[4]

An aspect of the 'large dimensions' which is parallel to the profession of managerialism, and to the rise of organisational 'science', is the incredible increase in the size of the public sector of the economy. This is an increase not only absolute, arising from total growth in population, employment and incomes, but also 'relative', that is, proportional to the increase in employment and of national product. The big business of the private sector has been flanked by the large organisations of the public sector and together they have contributed to laying the foundations of a society based on a large scale.[5]

Therefore, everything originated from the necessity of assuring management on a scale to match these large dimensions, and on the creation of a 'discipline' suitable to forming this management: management science.

Arising in conjunction with the professionalisation of managerial skill, managerial or organisational science has been practised at all times and in all places.[6] However, it was only after the Second World War—and probably in connection with the technological and organisational tensions arising from that war—that management and organisational technologies have been emphasised on a large scale.

With management science and organisational science, management and organisation themselves become the object of knowledge and of analysis. How does one manage? How does one organise?

But in this sense, management 'science' was not born as a 'positivist' science—as a science aiming at the analysis and discovery of 'objective' rules and laws of work, concerning something that is natural and independent of the will of the subjects, managers and organisers. In this case, one deals with a science of doing and not of being—a science of action.

However, even if the distinction between the two scientific approaches has been largely accepted, it has been more difficult to arrive at the logical consequences of such a distinction (a point which, moreover, applies to most of the concepts of political science).

In fact, organisation and organisational problems have not been the objects of study on the part of sociologists or—for the most part—political scientists, because their disciplines were, and still are, oriented towards *what is* and not towards *what to do* (what ought to be done). Therefore, such disciplines have not been concerned with the comprehensive framework of the sciences of being, the positivist sciences, not unlike what happened with juridical or economic sciences.

One could argue that for these latter sciences—as is quite evident for the juridical and political sciences, but also more obvious for economic sciences (which incorporates in its etymon the Greek concept of *nomos*, that is, of norm or of principle of action)—they have strayed beyond the borders of a traditional scientific concept, as approached upon an epistemological plane.

Organisation, in fact, is actually posed on an alternate plane—the pragmatic or action plane—incompatible with that of the common concept of science. Its 'science' (if it is still legitimate to use this word: it depends on how much we are disposed to change its meaning) attempts to answer to the epistemological question how we should act rather than what we should understand it as being.

Therefore, the true foundation of organisational science concerns the particular and distinct nature of a science of doing or of action.

5.1.2 Organisational Science as a 'Results-Based' Discipline

Organisations are institutions that act, and as such, are based on and evaluated according to the results of what they achieve.

Thus, the results must be evaluated with reference to the organisation's aim, mission, objectives and targets.

If we keep clear the nature and function of the organisation with respect to other societal institutions, we are obliged to limit the science of organisation in terms of a 'science of results', a science of performance to achieve a result.

This is the reason why a correct vision of organisational science concerns the nature of a results-based science.

The result, in an organisation, is always oriented towards the outside. A society, community or family is a self-referential institution and is an end in itself, and in a certain way is self-sufficient. But all organisations exist only if and for as long as they achieve results to provide and deliver. Otherwise their existence makes no sense.

Internally, an organisation has costs. It exists, however, only if it produces benefits and utilities. But these will exist only if the results are acknowledged from the outside.

The results of a hospital, or of any kind of healthcare organisation, are recoveries by patients. The results of a school or university are the graduates, who introduce what they have learned into their future job and lives. It is not unlike a business enterprise, which is judged useful if (and only if) there are customers who purchase its products or its services; therefore, the customers and sales are the results of their business.

Therefore, the costs, in every public organisation, must always refer to the results obtained. The principle of any organisation is not to exist in itself, like the family, or a religious or ethnic community, but to exist as a function of the results it produces and the tasks it performs through its actions.

Thus, public organisational 'science' essentially becomes nothing more than a science of how to achieve results, a science of effectiveness, understood as the optimal relation between costs and results, between means and ends.[7]

Results, in effect, are also the benefits, the outcome of a public organisation. When the organisation is aimed at results of individual or private interest, they are private gains or profits; when it is aimed at results of collective or social interests, they are collective or social benefits or profits.

Whilst we are dealing with utilities and profits, in any case, we are still dealing with results (appropriate to the particular context) for every organisation. Organisational science, therefore, is identified by its effort to evaluate the expected results for each organisation as a function of its institutional nature and, overall, of its 'mission'.[8]

Result evaluation thus becomes the core of organisational science. It becomes what is currently called 'results-based management'.[9]

5.2 The 'Cultural' Origins of Managerial Planning in the Public Sector

Systems analysis and systems engineering have noticeably influenced management and organisational sciences, and are at the roots of the programming approach. But, also with respect to these two important strands, we are obliged to acknowledge the influence of a misleading 'positivist'

156   Volume II. Selected Testimonies on the Epistemological…

approach and, in opposition to this, a 'true' programming approach (in the Frisch sense). We must develop a useful digression on this point.

John Friedmann, an influential American author with experience in the field of urban regional planning, produced a book in the 1987, *Planning in the Public Domain*,[10] stating that the main strand of policy analysis, which has played a central role in the political science in the last decades, has resulted from three different strands of intellectual research: (1) systems engineering, with a strong preference for quantitative models and closed systems[11]; (2) management sciences, with an inclination towards a 'general system theory' approach, emphasising the cybernetics of 'open systems'[12]; and (3) policy sciences, oriented towards 'behaviouralism', with a particular focus on political institutions and the acknowledgement—greater than in the other two strands—of the role of non-rational behaviour in human matters.[13]

I would not be able to give proper weight to each of the strands contributing to policy analysis and their application to public policy.[14] Undoubtedly, as management science, the sociological strand and that closest to traditional political science has an important role. But also, systems analysis and systems engineering contribute to an important change of approach ('the systemic approach').[15] On each of these three strands mentioned above, we have to critically comment on their position with respect to the role they have had in strategic planning, but also on the demarcation that the latter represent.

5.2.1 The Role of the 'Systemic' Approach

There is some truth in the claim (see, for instance, Friedmann, cit.) that the systemic approach has noticeably changed the mode of studying social phenomena. Therefore, we will start from the five points with which Friedmann tries to summarise (on the basis of expositors and critics of systems theory) the negative influence of the systemic approach by contemporary culture of planning.

These points—it seems —are the following[16]:

1. System theory has changed our views about causality. We no longer think in terms of linear relations of the form (A→B), but instead we take

The Programming Approach and the Management Sciences   157

into account the possibility of feedback: (A← →B). Causality, we now know, is complex and circular. This knowledge relieves us of Weber's burden of responsibility, since actions are seldom efficient, setting in motion a complex web of actions and reactions whose ultimate outcome is unforeseeable.

2. System theory has introduced us to the notion that every 'open' system is surrounded by an 'environment' with which it is in constant interchange, gathering or dissipating energies or achieving a 'steady state.' Systems must consequently adapt to their environment by introjecting parts of it (enlarging system boundaries), controlling other parts (which requires energy), or conforming to external conditions in ways that will maintain a condition of steady state within'.

3. System theory is based on the implicit assumption that all systemic relations are fundamentally harmonious, so long as the system itself remains in a state of equilibrium with its environment. Fundamental conflict is not a system concept. This assumption allows us to think of systems as inherently benign and manageable'.

4. All systems, it is said, conform to the principle of hierarchy, which is perceived as the 'deep structure' of the world. This assumption makes it easy to accept the notion of 'controlling over layers' and socio-political 'elites' (Etzioni). Hierarchies are derived from natural laws (the conservation of energy, the capacity of information channels, distance-decay relationship) and are therefore unavoidable.

5. System theory tends to be reductionist (in the sense that all things are systems by virtue of ignoring the 'specific, the concrete, the substantive', and in the sense that such assertions are confirmed by the 'reluctance of policy analysts to declare their substantive, sectorial interests').[17] (Friedmann 1987a, pp. 143–144)

Subsequently, we will use the five points to express some countercomments and objections to them.

The very general observations, which I believe are necessary to make on the contribution of systems theory, are the following:

Point 1 It could be true that, from a certain point of view, systems theory 'has changed our views about causality'. But this is true only from the point of view of the generic effect it could have on the average level of understanding (one admittedly increasing) of a public unfamiliar with a serious

158   Volume II. Selected Testimonies on the Epistemological...

culture, whether this is philosophical or scientific. If 'causal complexity' had to wait for systems theory to emerge before entering into the philosophical and epistemological heritage of mankind,[18] we would not have had any serious scientific progress of the type represented by Bacon, Galileo, Copernicus, Lavoisier, and so on, leading up to all the physical, chemical and biological sciences of the nineteenth century. If, indeed, what the authors and the supporters of systems theory thought was true, it would be ingenuity deserving of the criticism that Friedmann evokes. Thus, with respect to the first point, we can more modestly assert that systems theory has been largely popularised and has achieved the aim of rendering more 'critical' the approach and certain visions of the administrative sciences, as well as of public policy, than in the past.

It would be even more ingenuous to assert the fact that knowing that actions—in a circular systemic framework—'are seldom efficient, setting in motion a complex web of actions and reactions whose ultimate outcome is unforeseeable and relieves us of Weber's burden of responsibility'.

Beside the fact that it does not seem right for me to involve Weber in so simple an assertion (himself the defender and sponsor of the inherent 'rationality' of modern social action), who else could affirm that the contribution of systems theory is that of asserting the unpredictability of the results of human action, when an improved knowledge of the complexity of interactions has been recommended by all systems theorists precisely not to make ingenuous mistakes in the prediction of direct effects without the perception of complex impacts? And, furthermore, who could bring predictability, but above all planning itself, to a higher level of 'rationality'?[19] I have never met a serious systems theorist who would align himself with the thesis of planner irresponsibility, even if this could be the basis of a very superficial critique of systems theory.

Point 2 There is no greater element of truth in the assertion (again reported by Friedmann) that 'systems must consequently adapt to their environment'.

All this refers to the interrelations between different phenomena that a systemic view allows us to better understand. This is valuable for the

The Programming Approach and the Management Sciences 159

natural sciences (where the systemic approach poses itself as a simple improvement of the causal relationship between different objective phenomena); it is equally valuable for the social sciences (intended in the pragmatic sense, that is action-oriented) where the relation between phenomena should be translated into the relation between decisions and actions, and the 'interaction' between their effects. The described 'adaptation' of a system to its environment, presented as an 'extension' of the same through the interjection of external parts, has no other meaning (in the social context) other than the assumption of systemic relations on a higher scale than the one in question. Therefore, it is a process inherent to the systemic conception, and it is an integral part of the logical and epistemological progress of planning science (or of 'planology').

Regarding the maintenance of a steady state (from confusion to that of equilibrium), the possibility is not excluded that disequilibria are developed within the state itself; further, it is presupposed because, if not, how could it be 'steady' except with respect to a hypothetical 'non-steady' state, which is moving from one equilibrium to another (through disequilibria of different kinds) bringing things back to stability? But this process of returning to stability, or alternatively the steadiness itself, can be seen from two points of view: (1) from that of the (formal) nature of steadiness, in which it remains always the same, immobile and in force; (2) from that of the (substantial) nature of a dynamic (dialectic) relation with instability, in which it changes; it is never the same because it is the result of equilibria which are always compromised by disequilibria; therefore, it is steady in movement and in change and always shows new and more advanced aspects.

Words must be used with explicit reference to the concept they wish to express, but also to their possible double sense, otherwise communication between interlocutors does not occur, and reasoning becomes loaded with misunderstanding, equivocations, false problems and, in sum, counterproductive within a working environment.

In the second aspect, the stability, together with the equilibrium which should represent and express it, is never completely achieved; it is a potentiality which never becomes an actuality; it is a continual effort towards ends that never attain a rationality which steers actions, but which never become totally rational.[20]

160   Volume II. Selected Testimonies on the Epistemological...

Point 3 Even the third assertion presented by Friedmann as a contribution to systems theory, which is based 'on the implicit assumption that all systemic relations are fundamentally harmonious, so long as the system itself remains in a state of equilibrium with its environment', does not seem to me to be an incorrect assumption,[21] but an obvious assertion that is hard to refute and, therefore, of no particular critical use. It would seem rather that the next affirmation (which is not clear whether Friedmann attributes to himself or to systems theorists), 'that the fundamental conflict is not a systemic concept', has no nexus with the assumptions above. Furthermore, it had no nexus with the conclusion that 'this assumption allows us to think of systems as inherently benign and manageable'. Even in this case it seems to me that there is confusion between concepts and words. Already, it is implicit that harmony exists as long as equilibrium exists between a system and its environment, and after that ceases.[22] Why should this conflict, admittedly fundamental, not be a systemic concept? If any system is challenged by disequilibria, in order to restore stability, any conflict is a necessary moment of the equilibrium (the harmony). Equilibrium and disequilibrium, conflict and harmony, all exist as concepts that are 'inherently systemic' as long as they are used in a systemic way. Furthermore, why should we think that only because we insert disequilibria and disharmony into the systemic logic that we should have to exclude the possibility that the system could be benign and manageable? Should we, on the contrary, consider them malign and unmanageable? It is not at all clear.

Point 4 The fourth point concerning systems theory is that which would 'conform to the principle of hierarchy, which is perceived as the "deep structure" of the world.' Aside from the fact that I have never encountered any systems theorists who have placed such a strong emphasis, either positive or negative, on the hierarchical principle, the question arises: could one contend (systems theorist or not) that the principle is not in fact logical, that it is inherent—with many others—to any type of natural phenomenon and that it is not intrinsic to our capacity or reasoning itself (a 'category of the reason' as one associates with Aristotle or Kant)? Moreover, would it be valid to transfer the obviousness of this logical principle even to the field of political and social conception, which is more or less in favour of a system of 'hierarchical' and authoritative control of political regimes? (This is what Friedmann seems to be doing when he asserts that this assumption makes it easy to accept the notion of 'controlling over-layers' and 'socio-political elites'.)

Point 5 Here we are concerned with a more explicit criticism. First of all, the use of the concept of 'reductionism' to characterise the prevalence of a formal—procedural—approach with respect to the substantial one, does not seem to me the most appropriate: all this not only regards the systems theory (discussed here) but also the other disciplines and fields of knowledge, where it is always advisable to recommend a proper balance between formalisation and the description of facts, between process analysis and substantive analysis. What has sometimes been translated, suddenly and very often, into minor antagonisms (if not motivated by more substantial reasons such as like deduction and induction, rationality and reality, reason and practice, and so on).

In our case, the criticism (reported in Friedmann's fifth point) comes to assert: 'The search for a General System Theory, with its alluring prospect, has so far failed to yield significant meta-theories capable of integrating all knowledge. Still, from time to time, world-shattering conclusions are announced which, because they are unverifiable, substitute for the more empirically grounded knowledge of separate disciplines or specific interdisciplinary work.'

However, here it seems that one forgets that any study to clarify—and to render more intelligible—the 'complexity' (and this is a characteristic of systems theory, as stated in the first point) passes inevitably (as with all things related to complexity) through a reduced model of itself. And it does not seem to me that for this reason we should reproach systems theory in any specific way in comparison to other, more diffused approaches. We may also agree that the temptation to simplify any other knowledge of reality with a model of systemic relations pulls very strongly on systems theorists, who often embark on the pursuit of solving substantive problems with a scarce familiarity and experience of the problems themselves.

But this does not say anything against the operational use of modelling for any system, which allows (when useful and feasible) for better control of the effect of a set of co-ordinated actions, and thus, more generally, higher consistency between suggestions arising from any type of programming, and a better capacity to evaluate, access and control its effects.

To conclude, it is my opinion that the brief survey by Friedmann on the contribution of systems theory to planning and to policy analysis succeeds in painting a more negative than positive picture, and this seems to me unfair. Though I am conscious of the limited meaning that systems theory has had with respect to the entire philosophical and epistemological tradition, the introduction in various operational planning processes of a consciousness of the inter-relationship between different and concomitant events, and the implicit request to evaluate the effects from multiple points of view, or to evaluate the lateral effects, or counter-effects, seems to me to constitute a wide and positive contribution to the traditional way of projecting and planning; and, therefore, a significant contribution to the path towards what we call integrated, unified, comprehensive, or, more precisely, 'systemic planning'.[23]

On the other hand, criticism directed at systems theory and at its application to planning (which Friedman echoes, but with what amount of personal agreement it remains unclear) does not seem to be adequate in terms of its intrinsic logical sufficiency.

5.2.2 Management Sciences: Between Rationality and Romanticism

The other strand of research indicated by Friedmann is that of 'management science'. Its nature, origins and developments are indeed very confused. From one side, we cannot ignore the direct influence which systems analysis and system engineering have had not only on the renewal of the concept of 'scientific' management, already developed above all in connection with the managerial revolution of the first half of the twentieth century (before the Second World War, the most representative writers being Frederick W. Taylor and Harlow S. Person, champions of the simultaneously acclaimed and condemned 'Taylorism'[24]), but also in giving new scientific content to scientific management in the immediate post-war period.

The Programming Approach and the Management Sciences **163**

Rightly, with respect to this strand, Friedmann cites some authors, such as Churchman, Ackoff, Beer, who are, on the other hand, well-known and acknowledged promoters of systems analysis.[25] But there is another strand of management sciences which has been preoccupied with contesting a pretended 'technicism' in the application of new analytical instruments, claiming both a non-technical entitlement in decision-makers (politicians and top managers) and an extraneousness to rational motivation and behaviour, of the kind of which technicians can be the carriers.

More likely, a contribution often counterproductive to the strengthening of policy analysis and of strategic planning has come from that other strand (the third) which Friedman identified as confluent with it—that of the political and administrative sciences. This last strand, in fact, has diminished in its whole, the pushing of planning to study in depth and improve the method and extent of practices coordinated on many various operational scales and levels, through the introduction of an equivocal concept of rationality boundaries in the public decision-maker's behaviour. On this concept—the most well-known proponent is Herbert Simon—a misconstrued distrust of the prescribed 'planning rationality' and a pervasive scepticism about the application capacity of the planning itself, has been diffused.

These equivocations and misunderstandings must be addressed without delay.[26]

5.3 The Political and Administrative Sciences and the Concept of Bounded Rationality

5.3.1 The Imprecision and Relativity of the Concept of Bounded Rationality

The well-known notion (and related concept) of a bounded rationality in decision-making applies especially in the case of public choices and public administration, but is also valuable for private choices, private management and generally for any kind of planning; it is based on a combination of analytical arguments, coming from a mix of disciplinary biases, which—in spite of their persuasive effect that has made them so popular—have made it very confusing and misleading in its nature and definition.

For the most part, the meaning of the concept of bounded rationality arises out of, as is well known, the notion that in any decision there are always limitations or boundaries of time (in which to make decisions), resources, information, intellectual capabilities, and so on. The obvious conclusion is: decision-making is always bounded by something.

However, another implicit belief is also incorporated in this assertion. If there were no limitations, a decision could be 'rational' or 'optimal'. In practice, such a decision could be 'un-bounded'. What would we call it? A 'pure', perfect decision, exempt from limitations?

At this point, however, we must ask ourselves: is there anything in the life of people, in their values, in their actions, in their thinking, that is not 'bounded'? Everywhere, humanity, in any decision, as in any reasoning, will be limited by the striving for rationality. But what does all this tell us other than that humans become permanent 'searchers' or 'bringers', according to their circumstance? And what does this tell us contrary to the other assertion that they should be, in any way, searchers and bearers of such rationality?

Even the purest mathematical theorem is, by definition, subject to the same limitation on knowledge: if in no other respect than to the latter progressions of knowledge of mathematics which it itself has spread.

Imagine if we did not take for granted that much of the modelling we create in order to understand and manage the reality of things in certain ways, or to give sense to our actions, was the product of a bounded rationality. But if rationality is bounded by itself, there is no need to introduce the bounded rationality as a limitation on itself.

On the other hand, in which way should, or could, our limited knowledge limit the search for knowledge itself? Would this mean, perhaps, that, knowing the limitations of every human action with respect to goodness, we should not try to be good? Or, knowing the limitation of any aesthetic expression, should not pursue beauty?

Here are produced all the equivocations between the propositions concerning *being* (positivism) and those concerning *what should be*, which are based on a foundation different from that of factual observation (ex post),

The Programming Approach and the Management Sciences 165

and, on the contrary, on the formulation of purposes and actions which concern (ex ante) their feasibility.

Therefore, the study of constrained optimums or of constrained maximums (or minimums) includes consciousness of the limitations. And it is helpful to a very small degree to say that these limitations could never be known in their entirety and, therefore, that the optimum will never be a 'true' optimum, an 'absolute' optimum, but always an optimum with respect to the limitations which we are capable of taking into account *pro tempore*. This does not exempt us from the effort or from the intellectual duty of pursuing that optimum, that maximum (or minimum) given the limitations; neither does not exempt us from the utility and the intellectual duty of obtaining a deeper understanding of most of the limitations (which we do not know) in order to render the study of this optimum more valid and significant (that is, more 'rational').

Therefore, rather than emphasise the obvious—that our rationality is limited (which seems to me to have no heuristic value in a programming approach)—we should avoid putting out 'theories' or general behavioural formulae. Instead, we should deepen—I would say, case by case—our knowledge of what in every proposition, proposed to us in the name of an (equally obvious) rationality, is limited by conditions or constraints which have not been included in the calculation; this means that we should limit ourselves to exploring how the outcome of the rational calculation was not at the level of the rationality claimed.

In other terms, it seems to me that rationality in its concrete manifestations or applications can be contested only in the name of a superior rationality. But, consequently, this superior rationality must be demonstrated, by including new limitations to the calculation, ignored by the proposition which we intend to contest, and not in the name of something like a general alternative to rationality, which does not exist, if not in an act of anti-rational faith—that is, in the name of an 'anti-rational' philosophy or irrationalism.[27]

But as it is not possible to deny rationality through rational arguments, at the same time it is also not possible to attribute to the study of rationality the negative results of a bad application of rationality.

It is only in the name of rationality that we can identify and contest its inadequate applications.

5.3.2 The Concept of Bounded Rationality in the Case of the Programming Approach

At this point, we have to ask ourselves: what relationship exists between management science, or result-based science—knowledge oriented towards achieving results—and the programming approach?

Undoubtedly, since the management sciences are results-based or results-oriented sciences, the programming approach is intimately con-natural with them. However, a foolish positivist ambition has been insin-uated even within these sciences to answer queries of this kind: how do decision makers make their decisions? And to these kinds of queries do people think it is possible to give an alternative answer to that which, for a long time, was given by the social and economic sciences, based on the hypothesis of a factual and prescriptive 'rationality' in the decision-makers' decisions, as a reference point for any evaluations or choosing processes on the part of experts and decision-makers themselves?

The alternative answer, which seems common sense, is that decision-makers—especially those in public administrations—are neither search-ing for rationality nor for 'optimal' choices but are happy with reasonable and satisfying choices. This has developed the well-known formulation of a 'theory' concerning behaviour inspired by a non-complete, but rather 'bounded' rationality—that is, the 'theory of bounded rationality'.

The remaining pages of this chapter will be dedicated to the relation-ship, more epistemological than methodological, between the theory mentioned above and the programming approach with which we are dealing.

Let me immediately say that I think the theory of bounded rationality, at least in its most general and popular formulation, has little to do with the methodology of the programming approach. Moreover, I believe that through this theory some equivocal and dangerous elements have been introduced into planning theory and practice; these risk compromising the correct consideration of rationality in planning processes. The ele-ments which have introduced have a pervasive scepticism about the capacity of implementing planning processes themselves, and have intro-duced many misunderstandings about the role and modes of operations

The Programming Approach and the Management Sciences 167

of both plan preparation and plan implementation. All this imposes serious damage on the scientific progress of planning and on the extension of more rational and enlightened—and more technically effective—behaviour on the part of political operators and on the part of governments and their bureaucracies.

This last strand in administrative sciences, in fact, has had the effect of diminishing in its entirety all efforts at planning to deepen and improve its own methods in the sense of achieving greater and greater levels of rationality by means of greater and greater levels of information, elaboration and evaluation, and by extending its practices, co-ordinated on various scales and operational levels.

With the introduction of the concept of limits of rationality in the behaviour of public decision-makers—the most influential author is Herbert Simon here—an unintentional mistrust in the prescribed rationality of planning has been established.

These equivocations and misunderstandings must be dealt with further.[28]

5.3.3 The Optimisation Principle and the Programming Approach

From this vision also comes the surpassing of any principle of 'bounded rationality' and the recovery of the postulate that a future decision- or action-oriented analysis is fundamentally optimality-oriented.

If the analysis is oriented towards action (ex ante) and not towards the nature of observed things, more or less (ex post), any limitations on the decisional objective fail: the analysis cannot do anything other than plan for the best result with respect to the objectives, given the constraints.[29] These limitations are incorporated into optimal planning decisions.

In the ex post reality this 'best result', given the limitations, may not have occurred, or may have occurred only in a limited way; this has no importance for the planning theorist (or methodologist). It might concern the analysis of *temporis acti*, but not the analysis of *temporis agendi*. Therefore, this might interest the 'onlooker'—as Ragnar Frisch asserted, in defining the programming approach; either it might interest the

168   Volume II. Selected Testimonies on the Epistemological...

planning historian, or the kind of planning theorist who is not concerned with creating new, rational methods to improve planning, but only on commenting on the mistakes of the past. But all this does not concern the planner or the political decision-maker.[30]

On the contrary, in a programming approach, what could a bounded rationality mean for the planner (planning theorist or the decision-maker)? That at the time of the decision he should say: 'My preferred solution would be this (A), but I choose, or I suggest this other (B) that is not the best, but of which I am equally satisfied?' And if someone would ask why, what could he answer? 'Don't ask me because I don't know.'[31]

Indeed, if he knew, he would have been obliged to include the reason for this fact in the list of the objectives, and within the trade-offs (optimisation procedures) between different objectives that any decision unavoidably implicates.

Had he not known, who would dare to contest the fact that he was not completely rational, but only rational to a limited extent? And who would dare suggest to him more rational behaviour (given their own limits and considering their behaviour rational), except as an act of faith, in front of an external suggestion to him? Or—if he would search for the most rational possible solution to his problem—who would dare suggest that he be a little 'less rational', to be happy and to live without having defined the concrete possibility of more rational actions?

In conclusion: who dispenses the 'patents of rationality'? And who decides when we are dealing with behaviour of bounded rationality, faced with—for necessary, logical alternatives—possible behaviour of unbounded rationality?

In fact, we can admit that, in practice, decision-makers could be unconscious, or ignorant, of their preferences; that they could be consciously unconscious of them is something that concerns maybe psychiatry, but not behavioural psychology.

How does this concern the planner, who exists precisely to render the most rational, explicit and conscious possibility, in terms of the motivations, goals and choices of the decision-maker, and of himself as planner? How this all concerns the 'planning theorist', who should direct the process through which to organise the decisional system in the best and most effective way, remains an academic puzzle.

5.4 Conclusion: The Political and Administrative Sciences and the Programming Approach

The vision illustrated here allows us to locate the limited role of positive analysis in the programming approach; this reflects, therefore, the essence of the policy sciences such as economic policy, strategic planning, management sciences and so on.

In effect, the reflection and 'science' of administrative and political behaviour can only suggest some kind of limitation to possible rational theorems of administration and political action, from a position of ex post analysis. Indeed, only in an ex post analysis is it possible to evaluate how much an administrative or political action has been limited (or constrained or conditioned), and how far it is pursuing a rational principle of conduct. In fact, it is only by an ex post analysis (say 'historical') that it is possible to identify those 'new' conditions or constraints that have had a negative impact on the implementation and have limited the success of this action.

Here we may introduce more methodical doubt into that which we can call a 'positivist' pretension of an important part of the political sciences; can our principle of conduct for future actions be assumed on the basis of historical, ex post evaluation of examined past behaviour?[32] Are we sure that what has registered as phenomena, or relations among them, in the past, can be extrapolated in the future?

We know, obviously (and with great emphasis from political and administration scientists), that the most rational decisions are always limited by an ignorance co-efficient (or limitation of knowledge and information): what then can we extract from an ex post analysis for an ex ante decision?

The programming approach would intend exactly to overturn the method. It would suggest leaving out ex post analysis—of little significance for the future—and directly elaborating not rules but decisions themselves on the basis of a decisional process that would be the most rational possible. These include (according to our vision above) the maximum possible constraints, conditions and acknowledgeable limitations, given the circumstances, not received in the past but valid for the future.

Would this not be the true programming approach that we have inherited from Frisch and by other founder of the planning methodology?[33]

If we must talk of 'rules' or 'guidelines', would it not be better if these were taken from the decisional process itself, in the attempt to make it as well informed and technically advanced as possible?

Would it not be better, dealing with the future, that the decision and its process (rather than exploring the field of past behaviours of groups, communities, cultures, and so on, and trying to assume a stable 'theory') be based, on the contrary, on an evaluation of possible future behaviours, expressly studied or even only hypothesised?[34]

And would it not be better that the decision and its process, oriented in such a way, be acknowledged as a factor affecting those behaviours?

The programming approach postulate, formulated above, should cut out—as falling outside of the proper field of planning theory—all the endless rigmarole on bounded rationality which has occupied—as we have seen—so much of the political and administrative sciences, and for so long.

Furthermore, admitting that it could be possible (although I personally would be reticent to concede this) to use a 'positive' approach in the human social sciences,[35] the ex post scientific analysis of behaviour could be exempt from errors and the discovery of regular behaviours (according to someone who is directly determined by the 'theory', that is, by the innate 'rationality' of behaviours). All this has absolutely nothing to do with planning theory (as a result of the reasoning laid out in the previous paragraph and from the postulate that we derived).

This approach may concern the (positivist) sciences of being (admitting but not conceding, I repeat, that these sciences be those related to human and social actions) but not the sciences of action (or praxeology),[36] such as planning.[37]

This is also the reason why I have a greater propensity not to confuse strategic planning with the 'sciences' discussed above, and why I would be inclined to consider the programming approach as based mainly on a criticism of the approach of those substantially positivist sciences.

And lastly, this is also the reason why strategic planning has its foundation, in my opinion, in a clear demarcation from a positivist approach, basing itself only on a programming approach,[38] oriented exclusively

The Programming Approach and the Management Sciences 171

towards future action and towards related decision-making; oriented, as said in the previous paragraph, to the total inclusion, in the decisional process itself, of the constraints, conditions and limitations which can derive from values, viewpoints, cultures, concrete aspirations and historical circumstances, and also resources, or other things, which a truly evolutionist concept of society can formulate.

To conclude, I think that according to this vision, strategic planning does not need a 'theory of political and administrative behaviour' but simply (if you will) a 'planning theory': a theory, however, only pragmatic and operational, decision-oriented—that is, oriented towards the improvement of decision rationality and of operational efficiency in any historical, geographical or cultural conditions.[39]

Strategic planning, therefore—as operating in the field of organisations, and more so in the field of public organisations—if understood correctly, represents a pillar, the main pillar perhaps, of that 'planning science' (or planology) which is emerging as a confluence of a series of inter-disciplinary or trans-disciplinary fields of studies, and which, I believe, directs us towards the constitution of a new discipline of basic importance for public management and governance, on any level, geographical or territorial, in the coming decades.[40]

Notes to Chapter 5 (Vol. II)

1. For this reason, I maintain that political economy develops more as a 'theory of production' than as a 'theory of consumption'. See the reference to classical economics made in the brief historical schematic reconstruction of the economic theory by Frisch, already considered in Sect. 3.7 of this book, and also in my book—already mentioned—*The Associative Economy: Insights Beyond Welfare State and Into Post-Capitalism* (Archibugi, Macmillan 2000).

2. The technical and less technical literature on managerialism is endless. This literature emerged from the well-known studies developed in the 1920s and 1930s by Berle and Means (1932), developed also by various involving economists, sociologists, political scientists, and so on, up to the present day. As a summary of the different interpretations of the

structural changes in contemporary society, there is a good essay (unfortunately only in Italian) by Giorgio Ruffolo, on large corporations in modern society (1967). See also a more recent interpretation of managerialism in my book mentioned above.

3. The multi-dimensionality of big enterprises is strongly discussed in the work cited by Giorgio Ruffolo (1967).

4. A modern 'cantor' of managerialism has been Peter Drucker, who in the last 30 years has produced a great quantity of books (mostly bestsellers) on the argument, books that I would recommend for the numerous interesting analyses of the evolution of contemporary society. (See especially Drucker 1954, 1964, 1996.)

5. From the huge growth of the public sector in advanced economies during the last century (with the amount of the outlay increasing from 15% to 50% of gross national product in the average OECD country), a great amount of literature has developed. A synthesis of the subject with adequate bibliographical references can be found in Chap. 9, 'Expansion and Decline of Public Service', in *The Associative Economy*.

6. Drucker says: 'Management has been around for a very long time. I am often asked whom I consider the best or the greatest executive. My answer is always "the man who conceived, designed and built the first Egyptian pyramid more than 4000 years ago—and it still stands". But management as a specific kind of work was not seen until after the First World War—and then by a handful of people only. Management as a discipline only emerged after World War II' (Drucker 1993, p. 39). Something of this sort could also be said of strategic planning.

7. See Drucker, *Managing for Results* (1964).

8. On this point, see an interesting essay by Churchman and Emery (1966).

9. Even on results-based management, the literature is extensive. For an overview, I would suggest the book edited by Kathryn Newcomer (1997). More concepts on organisational science as a science of effectiveness, on the designing of results, and on the rise of strategic planning can be found in one of my books, *Introduction to Strategic Planning*, 2005, especially Chap. 3.

10. J. Friedmann, *Planning in the Public Domain: From Knowledge to Action*, Princeton University Press, 1987, p. 139.

11. For more information: A.D. Hall III (1962, 1969), Quade, ed., (1975), Quade and Boucher (1968), Chestnut (1965, 1967), Warfield (1976, 1990).

The Programming Approach and the Management Sciences 173

12. For more references, see: Churchman (1961, 1966, 1968, 1979), Churchman and Verhulst, eds. (1960), Ackoff (1960, 1961, 1968, 1974, 1981), Ackoff and Emery (1972), Beer (1966, 1974).

13. The major representative, or rather the 'guru', of this strand, at the beginning of the post-war period, was Herbert Simon (1941, 1960, 1983).

14. A book edited by Havemann and Margolis (1970) provides in its numerous essays a very useful and interesting overview of the subject.

15. For a deeper vision of this approach, I suggest a well-known work by Churchman (1968, with many later editions). Based on the debate developed on his work, Churchman himself, more than ten years later, integrated this work with a new contribution (1979).

16. In the list of the five points, it is not clear whether Friedmann intends to share, and up to which point, the critical arguments on the systemic approach. My observations, therefore, are not addressed to the author of the synthesis but to the contents of the text, both descriptive or critical.

17. Here Friedmann refers explicitly to the critical analysis of systems theory developed by Lilienfeld Robert (1978). Another critical analysis of systems theory to which Friedmann refers is that of David Berlinski (1976). See the answers to these criticisms in Churchman (1979).

18. This dates back to the causal principles of Aristotle, largely debated in the whole history of philosophy, and also to the scientific methodology (from Thomism to Liebnitz, from Kant to Schopenauer, and from Newton to Einstein). A pre-modern (and in some ways also 'postmodern') pamphlet on the concept of causality is in the classical early work of Schopenauer, *On the Fourfold Root of the Principle of Sufficient Reason* (1813). Among the many modern treatises I have learned from is the work of Mario Bunge (1962) on the role of the causal principle in modern science, as well as *Causal Explanations* by Piaget and Garcia (1971), which is an entirely different work, but for this context, complementary enough. Some limited observations related to the economics can be found in the well-known pamphlet by John Hicks on 'causality in economics' (Blackwell 1979).

19. In reference—to quote only one author—to the efforts of Churchman in his work *Prediction and Optimal Decision* (1961).

20. See what we say below on rationality and its supposed boundaries.

21. It is not clear if their position is shared by Friedmann, who cites them.

22. Here it seems obvious to me that harmony and equilibrium can be seen as synonymous, as can their opposites, conflict or disharmony and disequilibrium.

23. One of the first attempts at building a theory of planning based on the systemic approach was undoubtedly that of Hasan Ozbekhan, who prepared a background paper, 'Toward a Planning Theory' for the OECD (for a meeting in Bellagio, Italy in 1969), at which for the first time it was investigated how to conjoin systems theory and the programming approach (OECD 1969). (This essay was translated into Italian in the short-lived journal, *Futuribile*, 1971.) In Ozbekhan, see a report of the proceedings of another interesting symposium held in Los Angeles in 1968 at the College of Planning (and distributed through the 'Institute of Management Science' in Providence) (Ozbekhan and Talbert 1969).

24. At the beginning of 1911, Taylor wrote the well-known book on the *Principles of Scientific Management*—the bible of so-called 'Taylorism'—which influenced even Vladimir Lenin and through him became a permanent reference point of Marxist, socialist and unionist literature, but which also fascinated the wider, cultivated public. For instance, see a chapter from Drucker on the 'productivity revolution' (Drucker 1993, pp. 29–36). Person, less well known, had a determining role in consolidating, in the 1930s, 'scientific management' in American industry and in business schools. He was the President of the 'Taylor Society'.

25. Churchman, edited with Verhurlst (1960), a book on the 'sciences of management'. But his most noted contributions concern operational research and the diffusion and application of the systemic approach (Churchman 1957, 1968, 1979). The same can be said of Stafford Beer, a great promoter of operational research (1966), and of Russel Ackoff (Ackoff and Sasieni 1968).

26. There are more arguments in a paper that I prepared (in honour of Nathaniel Lichfield) (*Pitfalls in Planning and Plan-Evaluation*) in E.R. Alexander, ed. 2006.

27. In spite of this, we need to acknowledge that this 'fight against reason' and these 'crepuscular' and obscure moments in the history of ideas are studded in the entire history of human philosophy that we know, and the history of any civilised manifestation of mankind. But it is not my intention here to philosophise beyond a certain limit about the destiny of philosophy.

28. Even if—in my opinion—they do not deserve much more than this rapid treatment.

29. The word 'optimisation' expresses in any language a concept of a maximum constrained under certain conditions, which is the foundation of rationality and which can be expressed also in the words *effectiveness*,

The Programming Approach and the Management Sciences 175

efficiency, productivity, and so on. It is matter of a relation which has had and has different nomenclatures (all equivalent, for our discourse).

30. For further considerations on my part, regarding the double, separate roles of the planner-expert, on the one hand, and the planner-decision-maker, on the other, see Archibugi (1998).

31. How much more exhilarating it would be if he answered: 'Why? Because Professor Simon said that usually decision-makers, like me, think of satisfying and not optimising their preferences.'

32. There is a certain amount of literature on this topic; my preferred references remain Tinbergen (1971a, b), Leontief (1976a, b), Frisch (1965) and Myrdal (1980).

33. On this argument see more detail in Archibugi (2000) and in the **Vol. I**, Chap. 2.

34. This future behaviour of groups, stakeholders and politicians, which could constitute the real limit to the rationality of the process, should be the object of planning negotiations, but on the basis of an advanced systemic knowledge of the optimal decisions.

35. The reasons pervade all the chapters of this book starting from the recalling of the Myrdalian thesis in the introduction to Chap. 1.

36. I The roots of an assertion of this kind may be found in a good deal of American theory of society, especially in Talcott Parsons and Shils E.A (1951); but even in a good deal of the American philosophy of knowledge (or 'pragmatism'), above all in Dewey (1944) or in C.I. Lewis (1946). The foundations of prasseology, as is known, were defined later (Kotarbinski 1965; Kaufmann 1968).

37. Furthermore, any debates on the concept of rationality (Cartesian or non-Cartesian, bounded or non-bounded) should fall outside the proper field of planning theory. These debates, in fact, belong directly to the fields of philosophy and epistemology (disciplines for which—moreover—I do not believe that planners or political scientists are particularly well-equipped).

38. The 'programming approach' as developed from some important planning economists (for instance, Frisch, Tinbergen, Leontief) has been the subject of the previous chapters of this book. For more annotations, see also the cited essay of mine (Archibugi 1999).

39. Naturally, as far as political and administrative sciences abandon the 'objective' behavioural analysis approach (which we have defined as 'positivist') and adopt, on the contrary, a 'programming approach', decision-oriented, or functional to decision, then the roots of strategic planning

176   Volume II. Selected Testimonies on the Epistemological...

on which sciences can be fully recognised and any needs of demarcation of it from them disappear. Moreover, it could be stated that strategic planning can identify itself in the political and administrative sciences. And the last can identify themselves in the first.

40. See Archibugi (1992a, 1996 2nd ed). See also Chap. 9 of the already cited *Introduction to Strategic Planning* (Italian ed. 2005; English: in preparation).

Bibliographical References to Chapter 5 (Vol. II)

Ackoff, R.L. (1960). "Systems, Organizations and Interdisciplinary Research." In *General Systems Yearbook*, Society for General Systems Research 5: 1–18.

Ackoff, R.L. and Sasieni, M.W. (1968). *Fundamentals of Operations Research.* New York: John Wiley and Sons.

Ackoff, R.L. and Emery, F.E. (1972). *On Purposeful Systems.* Chicago: Aldine-Atherton, 1972.

Ackoff, R.L. (1974). *Redesigning the Future: A Systems Approach to Societal Problems.* New York: Wiley.

Archibugi, Franco. (1992a). *Introduction to Planology: A Survey of Developments Toward the Integration of Planning Sciences.* Rome, Planning Studies Centre.

Archibugi, Franco. (1992b). 'The resetting of planning studies', In: A. Kuklinski, ed., Society, Science, Government, Warsaw: KBN.

Archibugi, Franco. (1996). *Towards a New Strategy of Integrations of Cities into their Regional Environments in the Countries of the European Union, (with special Respect to France, Germany, Great Britain and Italy).* [An Ongoing Report of the Study promoted by the European Commission (DGXII) presented to the 'Second United Nations Conference on Human Settlements (Habitat II)', Istanbul, June 3–4 1996]. [Available also in. www.francoarchibugi.it].

Archibugi, Franco. (1998). 'Planning Theory: Reconstruction or Requiem for Planning?' (Presented to the Planning Theory Conference, Oxford 2–4 April 1998). [Available also in. www.francoarchibugi.it].

Archibugi, Franco. (1999). *Introductory lectures of Strategic Planning,* High School of Public Administration, Rome.

Archibugi, Franco. (2000). 'The 'programming approach': Methodological considerations based on the contributions by Frisch, Tinbergen and Leontief', paper presented to the EAEPE Conference 2000 (Berlin 2–5 November 2000). [Available also in. www.francoarchibugi.it].

Beer, A. Stafford. (1966). *Decision and Control: The Meaning of Operational Research and Management Cybernetics.* London: Wiley.

The Programming Approach and the Management Sciences   177

Beer, A. Stafford. (1974). *Designing Freedom.* London: Wiley.

Berle, Adolf A. Jr. and Means, G. (1932). *The Modern Corporation and Private Property*, Harcourt, Brace & World.

Berlinski, D. (1976). *On System Analysis: An Essay Concerning the Limitations of some Mathematical Methods in the Social, Political, and Biological Sciences.* Cambridge, MA: MIT Press.

Bunge, Mario. (1962). *Intuition and Science.* Prentice-Hall.

Chestnut, Harold. (1965). *Systems Engineering Tools.* New York: Wiley.

Chestnut, Harold. (1967). *Systems Engineering Methods.* New York: Wiley.

Churchman, C. W. (1961). *Prediction and Optimal Decision.* Englewood Cliffs, NJ: Prentice-Hall.

Churchman, C. W., and Emery, F. E. (1966). 'On Various Approaches to the Study of Organizations'. In: J. R. Lawrence ed., *Operational Research and the Social Sciences.* London: Tavistock.

Churchman, C. W. (1957). *An Introduction to Operations Research.*

Churchman, C. West. (1968). *The Systems Approach.* New York, Delta.

Churchman, C. West. (1979). The Systems Approach and Its Enemies. New York, Basic Books.

Churchman, C. West and Verhulst, M. (1960). *Management Sciences.* New York, Pergamon Press.

Dewey, John. (1944). Some questions about Value, *The Journal of Philosophy,* Vol. 41 (17).

Drucker, P.F. (1954). *The Practice of Management.* New York, Harper.

Drucker, P.F. (1964). *Managing for Result; Economic Tasks and Risk-Taking Decisions.* New York, Harper.

Drucker, P.F. (1993). *Post-Capitalist Society.* New York, Harper Collins.

Friedmann, John. (1987a). *Planning in the Public Domain: From Knowledge to Action.* Princeton, NJ: Princeton University Press.

Friedmann, John. (1987b). 'The Terrain of Planning Theory." In *Planning in the Public Domain: From Knowledge to Action.* [Reprint-PSC, 1987].

Frisch, R. (1965). 'General Outlook on a method of advanced and democratic macroeconomic planning', (paper presented at CIME Study Week, L'Aquila, 29 Agosto–7 Settembre 1965). In: de Finetti ed., *Mathematical Optimization in Economics*, Roma: Cremonese Edizioni 1966.

Hall, A.D. III (1962). *A Methodology for Systems Engineering.* Princeton, Van Nostrand.

Hall, A.D. III (1969). 'Three-Dimensional Morphology of System Engineering.' IEEE *Trans. Syst. Sci. Cybern.* SSC 5(2): 156–160.

Haveman, Robert H. and Margolis, Julius (1970). Public Expenditures and Policy Analysis. Chicago, Markham Rand McNally.

Hicks, J. (1979). *Causality in economics*. Oxford, Basil Blackwell.

Kaufmann, A. (1968). *Le tecniche decisionali: introduzione alla praxeologia.* [Decisional techniques. Introduction to Praxiology.]. Milano, Il Saggiatore.

Kotarbinski T. (1965). *Praxiology: An Introduction to the Science of Efficient Action.* Oxford, Pergamon Press.

Leontief W. (1976a). 'National Economic Planning: Methods and Problems.' In: Leontief W. and H. Stein (eds) *The Economic System in an Age of Discontinuity: Long-range Planning or Market Reliance*, New York University Press. Republished in Essays in Economics, Vol. 2, *Theories, Facts and Policies*, Blackwell, Oxford, 1977.

Leontief, Wassily (1976b). 'An Information System for Policy Decision in a Modern Economy'. In: *Forging America's Future,* [Strategies for National Growth Development. Washington, DC, Report of 'The Advisory Committee on National Growth Policy Process'. Vols. 3].

Lewis C.I. (1946). An Analysis of Knowledge and Valuation, Open Court.

Lilienfeld R. (1978). *The Rise of Systems Theory: An Ideological Analysis.* New York, Wiley.

Newcomer E. K., Ed. (1997). *Using Performance Measurement to Improve Public and Nonprofit Programs.* San Francisco, Jossey-Bass Publisher.

Ozbekhan H. and G. E. Talbert, Ed. (1969). *Business and Government Long-Range Planning: Impacts Problems Opportunities.* Providence, RI, Institute of management Sciences.

Parsons T. & Shils E. A. (1951). *Toward a General Theory of Action.* Cambridge, MA, Harvard University Press.

Piaget J. and Garcia R. (1971). *Understanding Causality.* New York, Norton, 1974.

Quade E.S. and Boucher, W. I. (1968). *Systems Analysis and Policy Planning, Applications in Defense.* New York, American Elsevier.

Ruffolo G. (1967). *La grande impresa nella società moderna.* [The great corporation in the modern society], Laterza, Bari.

Simon Herbert A. (1941). *Administrative Behavior.* London, Macmillan.

Simon Herbert. A. (1960). *The New Science of Management Decision.* New York, Harper & Row.

Tinbergen, J. (1971a). *Two Approaches to the Future: Planning Vs. Forecasting,* [mimeo].

Tinbergen, J. (1971b). Comment faut-il étudier l'avenir?, pp. 1–2.

Warfield J. N. (1976). *Societal Systems: Planning, Policy and Complexity.* New York: Wiley.

6

The Programming Approach, the Crisis of Traditional Economics and the Unavoidable 'Post-Capitalism', Leading to a 'Global Sovereignty' (*A Peculiar Analysis of George Soros*)

6.1 'Crisis'? For Who and About What?

So far, the aim of this book has been to discuss the logical (or epistemological) basis of 'economics' and its historical evolution from its origins to today. The implicit question on every page in this book has been: have we achieved in modern economic science some certainty about its use, in order to arrive at results in managing targeted objectives in the development of human communities? More specifically, have we achieved enough certainty to overcome the welfare crises that emerge, from time to time, in these communities, and therefore in avoiding a decline in the welfare level of the communities in question?

Therefore, we have focused so far on the 'crisis' of economics, in the sense of economic theory, and not of the 'crises of real economies', of 'recessions', which are increasingly more influential, and of 'decisions/actions' that take place at national or multinational decisions levels (at institutional and corporative level) in order to avoid such recessions.

All this is due to the unavoidable and ever-growing interdependence in the commercial and capital exchanges within every national community with the economies of other countries, as parts of a unique system to be improved at a global scale.

© The Author(s) 2019
F. Archibugi, *The Programming Approach and the Demise of Economics*,
https://doi.org/10.1007/978-3-319-78060-3_6

Dealing with the crisis of economic theory, and its inability to respond to the requirements of analysis and a treatment of its ills, we also consider the question whether the crisis in the global economy, in its single and multiple focus, should not be attributed to the economic theory in question, to its abstract and erroneous assumptions and its inability to evaluate and repair damage. Alternatively, should it be attributed to the specific nature of the global system, of a 'capitalist' nature, which is particularly susceptible to crises due to its innate instability and the prevailing level of uncontrolled speculation that it both inspires and to which it is subject?

An ancient thesis, generally of a 'socialist' mark suggests that economic crises are always the fault of capitalism, its defects and its contradictions, which will lead inevitably to its collapse. Even Joseph Schumpeter said this, though simultaneously confessing a sense of uncertainty surrounding his own words.

In the prologue of his last book *Capitalism, Socialism and Democracy* (1942), Schumpeter develops the reasons—pros and cons—for his answer, over roughly 150 pages.

> Can capitalism survive? No. I do not think it can. But this opinion of mine, like that of every other economist who pronounced upon the subject, is in itself completely uninteresting. What counts in any attempt at social prognosis is not the Yes or No that sums up the facts and arguments which lead up to it but those facts and arguments themselves. They contain all that is scientific in the final result. Everything else is not science but prophecy. (Schumpeter, *Capitalism, Socialism and Democracy, Prologue*, Allen & Unwin, 1942)

6.2   The Global System of Capitalism

However, while waiting upon such a 'collapse' of capitalism, many have elaborated on different descriptions of the collapse itself, from the most prudent to the most catastrophic, from the most meditated to the most charlatan. All that flows into a concept of a System-World,[1] and in a theory and methodology of analysis of such a system by Immanuel Wallerstein and associated scholarship who, 'inheriting' the rather 'biased partial', influence of Marxist criticism, contributed to outline a vision of

The Programming Approach, the Crisis of Traditional... 181

the future, one bounded to the extrapolations and deformations of the negative and pessimistic global capitalism.

From that, they produced—in the final years of the century—work aimed at exploring the trends of a capitalist world economy,[2] alongside other works of theory and methodology of analysis of the global system,[3] and (again with Terence K. Hopkins 1996), on the transition towards the 'System-World' from 1945 to 2025.[4]

The study of the global system as a 'system' has been developed by many authors everywhere in the world.[5] I consider the group of Wallerstein and associates one of the best of such groups of thinkers, especially when they begin to be liberated from the Marxist imprinting due from the historical changes that have occurred in the capitalist and post-capitalist system.

They have made many adjustments in the original position;[6] I would like to follow their new reflections, which date to the start of the twenty-first century.[7]

With the new fruitful cooperation with Alfred Kleinknecht and Ernest Mandel, Wallerstein explored the older and classical studies on the cyclical character of crises, participating in the relaunching of such studies on later capitalism, through an updated and interesting collection of writings: *New Findings in Long Wave Research* (London: Macmillan, 1992).

Lastly, Wallerstein dedicated himself to a better 'historicisation' of the discourse on the economic crisis and the survival of capitalism, with an approach a little more aloof and mature (and consequently with better scientific appeal) in respect of the previous works, on the different phases of capitalism, participating with Alfred Kleinknecht and Ernest Mandel on[8]: *Historical Capitalism with Capitalist Civilization* (London: Verso, 1983).[9]

However, the series of these journeys, from the most academic to the most militant, from those more conventional and conformist to the most radical and revolutionary, does not move outside the knowledge approach (which in this book we have called positivist-scientific—that is, it has the ambition of discovering the 'laws' of history, which are at the basis of what will inevitably happen).

This is precisely the contrary of what the programming approach proposes. This trilogy has offered in the first part, an exposition of the first proposers of this line of thought, in the second, various testimonies, and in the third, a discussion, with a practical example, of future research options.

Such a 'system' is—by definition—based on an inter-relationship between territorial, functional (technological), and sectorial phenomena, on the one side, and political, economic, socio-demographic phenomena, on the other.

These phenomena are still very far from our capacity to be known or controlled; to say otherwise is closer to presumptuous ignorance than to knowledge, and therefore more perilous, since it is more inducive to 'driving in the fog', (as Frisch, Leontief and other wiser economists of our approach used to emphasise).

We should overall feel the necessity, if not the duty, to understand these phenomena deeply and systematically, before coming to general conclusions regarding our problems following impressions and truths at first sight, before gaining certainty of their pertinence and ad hoc effectiveness. Rather than be based only on the general assumptions of 'rational', abstract, and 'implicit theorising', as Leontief defined it in 1937 (see **Vol. I**, Chap. 8 for more on this subject).

These phenomena are those on which we will return to in this book (in terms of applied programming approach in the form of Programming Accounting Framework (PAF), in all chapters of **Vol. III**).

In short, the readers of this work should already be aware that nothing should be said and acted upon before putting in place, in an active and operational way, the process (politically described in **Vol. III**, Chap. 4 of construction of the PAF) that should be followed—as a priority—for every serious governmental decision. Without the effectiveness of the PAF, nothing is credible, secure or acceptable. Nothing could be also ascertainable, as a commitment by social actors, after their engagement in the planning process.

Consequently, the first absolute task of any government should be to create a suitable institution to construct a PAF, starting from the guidelines, as described by scholars 40 years ago in the Western countries, for a PAF (and reintroduced in this book) that is technically revised and updated by special technical bodies.

6.3 Can Economics Manage Economic Crises? (*According to the Vision of I. Wallerstein and Associated*)

Last but not least, it does not seem right to not take a look at the crisis of economics, which we have treated as the overturning in the methodological approach, from the positivistic to the programming one, and at its implications for the validity of economics itself. It does not seem right not to take a look—I insist –at the work of some scholars that have studied the problem under the profile of the economic crises of the capitalist economic system as well, which is of interest for **Vol. III** of this book.

George Soros is one of these scholars, as well as being one of the most significant.

The fact that the concept of a 'crisis' of economics could be put in relation to the critical economic events, called conventionally 'economic crisis' in real modern economies, could not and should not surprise anyone. It is a connection so obvious that it is almost trivial. If economics (the 'economic science or doctrine'), through its analysis and its suggested policies is not capable (as it has not been) of avoiding crises or of governing them, this means that the economics of today (as in the past, when countries and nations had to face multiple crises throughout history) was not, and still is not, working.

To ascertain this fact, in the state of things, is somewhat superficial.[10] This is the reason why I avoid referring to and commenting on all kinds of statements based on the relationship between economic crisis and the crisis of economics.

I also intend to omit commenting on those people whom have considered—and still consider—that economic and financial crises in general are an *outcome* of capitalism and that, consequently, the way out from the crises can only happen through getting out of capitalism. As already said, this was one of the main issues of nineteenth-century 'socialism', revisited in the twenty and twenty-first centuries, with a certain approximation and schematism, and sometimes, ideological ingenuousness, without a sufficient in-depth focus on its mutations, in the meantime, of capitalist society. (Many important scholars have succumbed to this perspective, such as Joseph Schumpeter,[11] and many others.)

The persistence of the called 'economic crisis' today drives us to expect—in the critical line of the positivist approach—the demise of economic theory, and to achieve a greater and more aware 'planological' knowledge of the programming approach.

If we leave aside this argument, I would not like to neglect in any way some subordinate version of it, which I consider less superficial and would prefer to summarise in the form of questions.

Can today's economics propose a strategy capable of addressing the recurrent crises of tomorrow? And in what direction? And under what conditions?

And, again, should the transformations of the economic system today in relation to those of the past not lead us to say that nothing in past crises, compared to that which we often induced in the illusion of discovering from actions executed and from results obtained, measured ex post, those actions for facing the results to be obtained in the future, given the new objectives and the actions (supposed adequate) for a possible future?

After all, can the economic analysis of events and past policies provide valuable lessons for us in the management, with the same criteria, of an unknown future?

In other words, are we sure that our conceptual and methodological instruments, as economists, can enable us to recommend an economic policy capable of obtaining determined results, expected and/or preferred, given the existing constraints and limitations (the 'situational' constraints, as some call them)?

Are we sure that 'cause-effect' relational propositions derived from research and economic analysis are adequate instruments for implementing and achieving desired goals in the future?

It seems to me that so far, this book has been inspired by the establishment and conviction that the answer to these questions is negative.

6.4 A New *Tabula Rasa*?

Since the answer is no, the approach that has always been used by economics—defined as 'positivist' or 'determinist'—was not, in the past, and it would will not be in the future, able to find the right way to obtain positive answers to these questions.

And we should wonder if the right approach, on the contrary, should not be that of completely overturning the 'positivist' approach, which is based on formulating *a priori* the principles or rules of behaviour of people, assumed as 'needed', 'rational', or 'natural' and hence 'universal' (but which are not useful to explain and forecast facts ex post in the future presuming trends in the same way as we did in the past). In fact, this approach has failed in the past and we should assume that it will also fail in the future.

It raises overbearingly the question whether it would not be better to start from the analysis of the present and of a possible future, without scientific 'prejudices', and if the right approach would be to create a *tabula rasa* for any new 'theory', beginning with present problems—for which from Frisch onward we have referred to as the programming approach, overturning the positivist one, and studying—case-by-case—how relations can be configured in the historical situation or for the case in question in respect of the possible solutions for the problems to be faced.

Formulated in such a way, the 'right method' is that which emerges by itself from the examination of individual cases—cases that are not generalisable, and whose solutions come from the feasibility analysis of single actions, in the given situations, adequately studied and hypothesised in relation to the problems to solve, according to a strategic and systemic approach.

Surrounding this aspect of the indeterminateness of historical phenomena, which derives from the 'logic of scientific research', as Karl Popper's works stressed, along with other authors of the schools dedicated to 'logical positivism'. And myself, in this second part of this book, I dedicated to possible forerunners of the programming approach, I have explored some interesting quotations in respect of the main theme of this work.[12]

Among the numerous critics of capitalist society, oriented towards a historicist vision, one in which I found the greatest conceptual proximity to the overturning from the positivist approach to the programmatic approach (which is the core of the epistemological analysis of this book) is the work of a unique economist, George Soros,[13] who, during his life, has coordinated and 'theorised' different personal experiences of research and action: from that of a financial operator (of renowned success) in the financial markets,[14] to that, less acknowledged in the milieu of 'academia',

186 Volume II. Selected Testimonies on the Epistemological...

but equally deserving of respect as a radically critical economist, characterised by a kind of philosophical approach, that of Popper's 'logical positivism', of which he was an intelligent and cultivated student,[15] and finally that of a political scientist, a tenacious and combative—just like Popper—promoter of the concept of an 'open society',[16] to which he has dedicated an important part of his more recent philanthropic activity.[17]

His opus deserves attention in this book, because his theory of reflexivity is consistent and compatible with the epistemological overturning on which the Frischian and programming approach are based, and to which we will dedicate special attention. I will quote other passages of Soros's work as well, which seem to me to be on the same wavelength of a new methodology of planning.

6.5 From *Logical Positivism* to a *Theory of Reflexivity*

6.5.1 Social Phenomena and Natural Phenomena

Soros is quite explicit on this point. In the Preface to his most important book on the methodological point of view, he states categorically, almost as *incipit* of his book:

> I was greatly influenced by Karl Popper, the philosopher of science [...]. I absorbed Popper's ideas about critical thinking and scientific method. I did it critically and I came to differ with him on an important point. Popper claimed that the same methods and criteria apply to both natural and social sciences. I was struck by a vital difference: In the social sciences, thinking forms part of the subject matter whereas the natural sciences deal with phenomena that occur independently of what anybody thinks. This makes natural phenomena amenable to Popper's model of scientific method, but not social phenomena. (Soros 1998, p. ix)

> [...] Partly as a result of that experience and partly on the basis of my experience of the capitalist system, I came to the conclusion that the conceptual framework I had been working with was no longer valid. I sought to reformulate the concept of open society. In Popper's formulation, it stood in

The Programming Approach, the Crisis of Traditional... **187**

contrast with closed societies based on totalitarian ideologies, but recent experience taught me that it could be threatened from the opposite direction as well: from the lack of social cohesion and the absence of government. (Soros 1998, p. x)

Leaving aside the political implications hinted at in the final part of this declaration (which will be examined and explained through the sequence of Soros's work), I will limit at the outset—despite completely sharing these implications—my own attempt to deepen and emphasise the epistemological aspects of the declaration (concerning the separation between his method and that of Popper).[18] Then I will consider from the outset that this *incipit* could emerge from my own prose in this work as well.

The interesting point is what we have called (see Introduction) the epistemological overturning, and it is that to which Soros refers to in his work as the 'theory of reflexivity'.

This theory is based on a reflection related to something that has represented, ever since, a universal and permanent question of philosophical reflection: the issue of the relationship between knowledge and reality, or in other words, between thinking and reality.

6.5.2 Thinking and Reality

Soros himself says:

I must start, at the beginning, with an old philosophical question that seems to lie at the root of many other problems. What is the relationship between thinking and reality? This is, I admit, a very roundabout way of approaching the world of affairs but it cannot be avoided. Fallibility means that our understanding of the world in which we live is inherently imperfect. Reflexivity means that our thinking actively influences the events in which we participate and between reality and our understanding of it, the gap between the two, which I call the 'participants' bias, is an important element in shaping the course of history. The concept of open society is based on the recognition of our fallibility. Nobody is in possession of the ultimate truth. This may seem obvious enough to ordinary readers, but it is a fact that political and economic decision makers, and even academic thinkers, are often unwilling to accept. This refusal to accept the inherent gap between reality and our thinking has had a far-reaching, and historically very dangerous, impact.

188   Volume II. Selected Testimonies on the Epistemological...

The relationship between thinking and reality has been, in one form or another, at the center of philosophical discourse ever since people became aware of themselves as thinking beings. The discussion proved to be very fertile. It has allowed the formulation of basic concepts such as truth and knowledge and it has provided the foundations of scientific method. (Soros 1998, p. 4)

In effect, throughout the known history of mankind, no philosophy, religion, 'principle of action' and/or work, exists, which does not have, as its appropriate starting point, that issue—the relation between thinking and reality, although, however, that such issue has rarely found a decisive epistemological definition.

The theory of reflexivity is introduced in Soros's book beginning from this ancient issue:

It is no exaggeration to say that the distinction between *thinking* and *reality* is necessary for rational thought. But beyond a certain point, the separation of thought and reality into independent categories runs into difficulties. Although it is desirable to separate statements and facts, it is not always possible. In situations that have thinking participants, the thoughts of these participants are part of the reality about which they have to think. It would be foolish not to distinguish between thinking and reality and to treat our view of the world as if it were the same as the world itself; but it is just as wrong to treat thinking and reality as if they were totally separated and independent. People's thinking plays a dual role: It is both a passive reflection of the reality they seek to understand and an active ingredient in shaping the events in which they participate. (Soros 1998, pp. 4–5)

Further, he affirms:

There are, of course, events that occur independently of what anybody thinks; these phenomena, such as the movement of planets, form the subject matter of natural science. Here thinking plays a purely passive role. Scientific statements may or may not correspond to the facts of the physical world, but in either case the facts are separate and independent of the statements that refer to them.[19] Social events, however, have thinking participants. Here the relationship between thinking and reality is more complicated. Our thinking is part of reality; it guides us in our actions and our actions have an impact on what happens. The situation is contingent on what we (and others) think and how we act. The events in which we participate do not constitute some sort of independent criterion by which the truth or falsehood of our thoughts could be judged. According to the rules of logic, statements are true if, and only if, they correspond to the facts. But in situations that have thinking participants, the facts do not occur independently of what the participants think; they reflect the impact of the participants' decisions. As a result, they may not qualify as an independent criterion for determining the truth of statements. That is the reason why our understanding is inherently imperfect. This is not an abstruse philosophical debating point, comparable to Berkeley's question about whether the cow in front of him ceases to exist when he turns his back. When it comes to decision making, there is an inherent lack of correspondence between thinking and reality because the facts lie somewhere in the future and are contingent on the participants' decisions. (Soros 1998, p. 5)

However, Soros specifies:

The lack of correspondence is an important factor in making the world the way it is. It has far-reaching implications both for our thinking and for the situations in which we participate,—implications that are deliberately ignored in standard economic theory [...] The point I want to make here is that participants in social events cannot base their decisions on knowledge for the simple reason that such knowledge does not exist at the time they make their decisions. Of course people are not bereft of *all* knowledge; they have the whole body of science (including social science, for what it is worth) at their disposal as well as the ledge is not enough to reach decisions. Let me cite an obvious example from the world of finance. If people could act on the basis of scientifically valid knowledge, then different investors would not be buying and selling the same stocks at the same time. Participants cannot predict the outcome of their decisions in the way scientists can predict the movement of celestial bodies. The outcome is liable to diverge from their expectations, introducing an element of indeterminacy that is peculiar to social events. (Soros 1998, p. 6)

6.6 The 'Theory of Reflexivity' (*According to George Soros*)

Concerning Soros's theory of reflexivity, I prefer to leave the exposition to the prose of the author, in acknowledgement of its conciseness.[20]

> The best way to approach the relationship between the participants' thinking and the social events in which they participate is to examine first the relationship between scientists and the phenomena they study.
>
> In the case of scientists [of the nature] there is only a one-way connection between statements and facts. The facts about the natural world are independent of the statements that scientists make about them. That is a key characteristic that renders the facts suitable to serve as the criterion by which the truth or validity of statements can be judged. If a statement corresponds to the facts, it is true; if not, it is false. Not so in the case of thinking participants. There is a two-way connection. On the one hand, participants seek to understand the situation in which they participate. They seek to form a picture that corresponds to reality. I call this the *passive* or *cognitive* function. On the other hand, they seek to make an impact, to mold reality to their desires. I call this the *active* or *participating* function. When both functions are at work at the same time, I call the situation *reflexive*. (Soros 1998, pp. 6–7)

And he adds:

> When both functions are at work at the same time, they may interfere with each other. Through the participating function, people may influence the situation that is supposed to serve as an independent variable for the cognitive function. Consequently, the participants' understanding cannot qualify as objective knowledge. And because their decisions are not based on objective knowledge, the outcome is liable to diverge from their expectations. (Soros 1998, pp. 6–7)

Soros acknowledges also that there are 'vast areas where our thoughts and reality are independent of each other and keeping them separate poses no problem. But there is an area of overlap where the cognitive and participating functions can interfere with each other and when they do our understanding is rendered imperfect and the outcome uncertain.'

He adds:

> When we think about events in the outside world, the passage of time can provide some degree of insulation between thought and reality. Our present thoughts can influence future events, but future events cannot influence our present thinking; only at a future date will those events be converted into an experience that may change the participants' thinking.[21] But this insulation is not fool proof, because of the role of expectations. Our expectations about future events do not wait for the events themselves; they may change at any time, altering the outcome. That is what happens in financial markets all the time. The essence of investment is to anticipate or 'discount' the future. But the price investors are willing to pay for a stock (or currency or commodity) today may influence the fortunes of the company (or currency or commodity) concerned in a variety of ways. Thus changes in current expectations affect the future they discount. This reflexive relationship in financial markets is so important that I deal with it later at much greater length. But reflexivity is not confined to financial markets; it is present in every historical process. Indeed, it is reflexivity that makes a process truly historical. (Soros 1998, pp. 7–8)

6.6.1 The Sense of History

Soros aims to clarify the sense of history:

> Not all social actions qualify as reflexive. We may distinguish between humdrum, everyday events and historical occasions. In everyday events, only one of the two reflexive functions is at work; either the cognitive or the participating function remains idle [...] But there are occasions when the cognitive and participating functions operate simultaneously so that neither the participants' views nor the situation to which they relate remain the same as before. That is what justifies describing such developments as historic.
>
> A truly historic event does not just change the world; it changes our understanding of the world—and that new understanding, in turn, has a new and unpredictable impact on how the world works.[22]
>
> Of course, people think not only about the outside world but also about themselves and about other people. Here the cognitive and participation functions may interfere with each other without any lapse of time.[23]
>
> If the passage of time can insulate the cognitive and participating functions, reflexivity can be envisaged as a kind of short circuit between thinking

192   Volume II. Selected Testimonies on the Epistemological...

and its subject matter. When it occurs, it affects the participants' thinking directly, but the outside world only indirectly.

The effect of reflexivity in shaping the participants' self-images, their values, and their expectations is much more pervasive and instantaneous than its effect on the course of events. It is only intermittently, in special case, that a reflexive interaction significantly affects not only the participants' views but also the outside world. These occasions take on special significance because they demonstrate the importance of reflexivity as a real-world phenomenon. By contrast, the endemic uncertainty in people's values and self-images is primarily subjective. (Soros 1998, pp. 8–9)

I wanted to reproduce in its entirely (omitting only examples and explanatory metaphors) the thoughts of Soros on what he calls 'reflexivity', on the relation between thought and facts, between the 'cognitive' function and that of 'participant', which I see as between 'projecting' or a 'programming' function and a 'decision' (or action) function, precisely in the cases where they interact and reciprocally impact the reflexivity, which many others identify as the knowledge/action process.[24]

This is a crucial point linking the epistemology of Soros which, even though deriving from different branches, seems to provide a serious contribution to an economic epistemology based on decisions, as developed in this book.

Firstly, I would like to note that Soros eliminates the idea (of a positivistic type) that, in the case where there are 'thinking' participants who cannot be expected to derive rational and thinking solutions different from the 'facts', and those inexhaustibly determined by natural laws, we cannot search for solutions 'open' to change, conscious and motivated by ourselves, with respect to our own visions or values, or preferences.

6.6.2   Does Reflexivity Oblige Us to Accept 'Indeterminacy'

Firstly, the reflexivity effect, as described by Soros, serves unfortunately to highlight simply the indeterminacy:

The next step in analysing the impact of reflexivity on social and economic phenomena is to point out that the element of indeterminacy I speak about is not produced by reflexivity on its own; reflexivity must be accompanied by imperfect understanding on the part of the participants. If by some fluke people were endowed with perfect knowledge, the two-way interaction between their thoughts and the outside world could be ignored. Because the true state of the world was perfectly reflected in their views, the outcome of their actions would perfectly correspond to their expectations. Indeterminacy would be eliminated, as it derives from the feedback between inaccurate expectations and the unintended consequences of people's expectations (perhaps changing but always biased). (Soros 1998, pp. 9–10)

From another point of view, Soros observes:

[T]he contention that situations that have 'thinking' participants contain an element of indeterminacy is amply supported by everyday observation. Yet it is not a conclusion that has been generally accepted in economics or social science. Indeed, it has rarely even been proposed in the direct form in which I have put it here. On the contrary, the idea of indeterminacy has been vehemently denied by social scientists who assert their ability to explain events by scientific method. Marx and Freud are prominent examples, but the founders of classical economic theory have also gone out of their way to exclude reflexivity from their field of study, despite its importance for financial markets. It is easy to see why. Indeterminacy, the lack of firm predictions and satisfactory explanations can be threatening to the professional status of a science. (Soros 1998, p. 10)

My conviction is that the programming approach and the epistemological overturning of the method pose the problem of indeterminacy (or determination) in a completely new way. Economists should not search for the determinateness (in other words, the reality) in the things they study, such as natural scientists, but should search for it in the decisions they make. The determinateness can be found (or, better, can be 'determined') in the methods and from the factors that are used in searching for it.

In the field of human and social relations, which are not subject to any natural law but are 'open' to thought-heavy solutions desired by subjects, the problem of change is to establish the feasibility of ideas and programmes.

And, therefore, we should not wait for things to take their natural course because this course does not exist, as that of the 'invisible hand' of Adam

Smith, which is often the case and contributes to the creation of a number of obstacles, equivalent and surprised by the actions and decisions aimed at change and improvement of things, in the right way, when it is supposed that it can work on its own without any active contribution by the participants.[25]

6.6.3 Does 'Reflexivity' Oblige Us to Revise Our Confidence in a Continuous Capacity and Effectiveness of Public Planning?

Soros's pessimism, indeed, sounds limited and a little malicious. But it is roughly the same answer that I myself would give in its substance, attributing this indifference to the 'reflexivity', only if conditioned by the positivist approach, as applied in the normal scientific approach used throughout all the natural sciences.

The question is about the missing distinction between the social sciences and the natural sciences, because the reflexivity can be produced only in the case of the human and social cases. And the lack of determination comes from reflexivity because it is not accepted by free human thought, which can alter and modify positivistic logics.

In any case, in spite of the emphasis on the 'financial markets', neoclassical economics (I would include also classical economics), goes wrong when it underestimates the importance of 'reflexivity' or denies its existence.

It is faulty also because, in this way, it tends to deny the epistemological justification of its own theoretical validity (in the name of an asserted, but powerless, pretence in respect to reality).

Doing so, mainstream economics fixes this kind of methodological 'absolutism' and cannot perceive—in light of historical accounts—the possibility of in a way taking into account the anomalies in the relation between cognition (projecting) and participation (implementation).

6.7 Design and Political Participation

After having brought to our attention the ways in which the reflexivity theory has appeared in some periods in the history of ideas, Soros tell us how he arrived at applying the reflexivity concept to the understanding of finance, policy and economics, at the beginning of the 1960s, before the birth of the 'theory of the evolutionistic systems'. It does not seem to me that he has ever stated precisely what he intended with such theory; however, he mentions that he was helped by Karl Popper's writings concerning the concept of self-reference. Soros states:

> What reflexivity and self-reference have in common is the element of indeterminacy. Logical positivism outlawed self-referent statements as meaningless, but by introducing the concept of reflexivity I am setting logical positivism on its head. Far from being meaning- less, I claim that statements whose truth value is indeterminate are *even more* significant than statements whose truth value is known. The latter constitute knowledge: They help us understand the world as it is. But the former, expressions of our inherently imperfect under- standing, help to shape the world in which we live.
>
> At the time I reached this conclusion, I considered it a great insight. Now that natural science no longer insists on a deterministic interpretation of all phenomena and logical positivism has faded into the background, I feel as if I were beating a dead horse. Indeed, intellectual fashion has turned to the opposite extreme: The deconstruction of reality into the subjective views and prejudices of the participants has become all the rage. The very basis on which differing views can be judged, namely the truth, is being questioned. I consider this other extreme equally misguided. Reflexivity should lead to a reassessment, not a total rejection, of our concept of truth. (Soros 1998, p. 13)

And he maintains that 'the two concepts—cognition and participation—are [...] strictly bound, but they should not be confused'.

That creates a positivity crisis with respect to the phenomenon and presumed economic facts and forces a credible application of the relationship between cognition and participation, as an instrument for a political-economic efficiency and performance, one simultaneously strategic (multi-dimensional) and systemic (that which takes lateral effects into account).

Therefore, an imperative of an operational type is needed to find a way to bring together the 'effects' of a cognitive function with the 'results' of the participating function, the 'method' by which Frisch recommended constant collaboration between the political authorities and experts in the whole process of programming, so that the political and technical responsibilities would not be disjointed.

I will return later to the indispensable collaboration for applying the programming approach to the social and economic choices that are not only an academic exercise, but really an exercise that looks at the political decisions in the process (which is often called planning).

In fact, only those choices can legitimate that process with the conditions and limits that we illustrated in the first two volumes of this trilogy.

In fact, it deals with not ignoring the 'reflexive' connection in the behaviour of participants on each possible solution on proposed optimality; but this deals, further, with making subjects committed and active in the choices to be taken in the communal research of feasible management, feasibility that should be demonstrated and measured in the process of programming towards its conclusion, with the necessary compromises accepted across the negotiation of parts—that is, the participants and the successive re-elaboration of the new temporal phase.

And Soros concludes: 'The reflexiveness should guide towards a new reassessment, not to a total rejection of our concept of reality.'

A wise conclusion.

6.8   Reflexive Concept of Truth (*According to George Soros*)

6.8.1   An Interactive Vision of Reality

Not truly abandoning the approach that we have called 'deterministic' (that is, the faulty current 'economic theory'), without founding this 'economic theory' on the institutional policy decisions themselves that are controlling the implementation (so without allowing them to come from those very same decisions, making feasible the programming process itself) would be like growing old in a sort of 'reserved' club of universal economists that forever discusses a series of abstract, theoretic and logical connections among aggregate phenomenon (so-called 'scientific debating or reflection').

It would be like impossible to suggest coordinated forms of intervention tied to a sort of programming (which is never understood in the political decision-making of governments, and therefore very far from any realistic possibility of implementing any good idea, by means of reflective, chaotic and casual action).

It should be necessary to find a way for institutional (or political) decision-makers to succumb to the infinite sum of humanitarian, political and practical decisions and actions (of a reflexive type) in channelling all of these practical decisions, including the internal dynamics of the decisional process at large, with more patient negotiation, and virtually aware of the pros and cons from the viewpoints of the participating in the decision-making, which would be part of a programming process, one based on the PAF and aware of the complex future advantages of public management.

Therefore, we could progressively proceed to an even better and more advanced level of knowledge on the problems and solutions to be studied by the participants.

It is necessary, on the contrary, to avoid that the political economy as such since without effective programming to meet that lack of determination which, unfortunately, the reflexivity tends undoubtedly to confirm. It is further condemned on behalf of the researchers and economic theorists of 'determining', subjectively, the future, integrating it with the political decisions and not only with those facts but also those 'thoughts of the thinkers', if seen in terms of groups, classes, ethnic groups, regional and national communities that are ready to combat. These, however, would probably prefer more wisely to find compromises, which are usually more advantageous than conflicts, through negotiation and collective bargaining.

I believe that, in such a way, it is possible to give to social sciences, as Soros suggested, the ability to influence facts by means of the theory and mechanisms of 'reflexivity'. And this can be made on the basis of dialogue between the cognition and participation functions (to use the words of Soros) at a level that is more efficient in respect of reality and its implementation.

198 Volume II. Selected Testimonies on the Epistemological...

Therefore, it seems legitimate that we ask ourselves: the cognition and the participation upon which reflexivity is founded are not found in 'realised thought' of a systemic process that I would call programming? Is this a process that constitutes at every moment the only way of giving a feasibly operative content for decisions and preferences of participants? On the other hand, is this not the very leitmotiv of this book regarding the programming approach?

The programming approach is an operational variant of the praxeo-logic approach,[26] which belongs to a 'pragmatic' vision of life and truth, corresponds to that part of the 'theory of reflexivity' that concerns the concept itself of truth, and springs from the vision of Soros, who distanced himself from the logical positivist approach of Popper.

The programming approach is at the core of our attempt to explore if there have been testimonies that have anticipated the importance—for any future social science—of an epistemological overturning, on which the programming approach itself is aimed (this is essential to **Vol. III** of this book).

This justifies the reason why we stop a little short of documenting the entirety of Soros's vision, in this chapter, specifically his affirmation (as cited above) that 'the reflexivity should guide towards a new evaluation, not a total refusal of our concept of truth'.

Soros, developing further the reflexive concept of truth, distances himself from logical positivism in such way:

> *Logical positivism* 'classified the statements (in other terms, the truth) as true, false, or meaningless'. After dismissing meaningless statements, remain those true or false.
>
> The scheme is eminently suitable to a universe that is separate and independent of the statements that refer to it, but it is quite inadequate for understanding the world of thinking agents. Here we need to recognize an additional category: reflexive statements whose truth value is contingent on the impact they make. […]
>
> We cannot live without reflexive statements because we cannot avoid decisions that have a bearing on our fate; and we cannot reach decisions without relying on ideas and theories that can affect the subject matter to which they refer. To ignore such statements or to Force them into the

The Programming Approach, the Crisis of Traditional...   199

categories of 'true' and 'false' pushes the dis- course in a misleading direction and places our interpretation of human relations and history in the wrong framework. (Soros 1998, pp. 13–14)

And, after some metaphorical examples (that could be, however, more pertinent in order to be more effective) he corrects:

I am not claiming that a third category of truth is indispensable for dealing with reflexivity phenomena. The crucial point is that in reflexive situations *the facts do not necessarily provide an independent criterion of truth,* we have come to treat correspondence as the *hall- mark of truth.* But correspondence can be brought about in two ways: either by making true statements or by making an impact on the facts themselves. Correspondence is not the *guarantor of truth.* This caveat applies to most political pronouncements and economic forecasts.

I hardly need to emphasize the profound significance of this proposition. Nothing is more fundamental to our thinking than our concept of truth. We are accustomed to thinking about situations that have thinking participants in the same way as we do about natural phenomena. But if there is a third category of truth, we must thoroughly revise the way we think about the world of human and social affairs. (Soros 1998, pp. 14–15)

The interactive vision of reality is introduced by Soros with some general considerations, which should not be neglected, for a general understanding of the process. Yet, tracing a distinction between statements and facts, between our thoughts and reality, Soros reminds us that:

We may be justified in drawing a distinction between *statements* and *facts,* our *thoughts* and *reality,* but we must recognize that this distinction has been introduced *by us* in an attempt to make sense of the world in which we live. Our thinking belongs in the same universe that we are thinking about. This makes the task of making sense of reality (i.e., reason) much more complicated than it would be if thinking and reality could be neatly separated into watertight compartments (as they can be in natural science). Instead of separate categories, we must treat thinking as part of reality. This gives rise to innumerable difficulties, of which I should like to discuss only one. (Soros 1998, pp. 15–16)

200   Volume II. Selected Testimonies on the Epistemological...

Soros is thus led to allude to a framework that is much more 'critical-realistic' of the situation (born from the discovery of 'reflexivity'): the framework of an '*interactive vision of reality*'[27]:

The last of Soros's expressions, it seems is very effective in representing the interaction between reality and thinking: 'The reality has the power to surprise the thinking and the thinking has the power to create the reality.'[28]

Then it seems Soros draw an important conclusion from this long consideration:

> That said, I have little sympathy with those who seek to deconstruct reality. Reality is unique and uniquely important. It cannot be reduced or broken down to the views and beliefs of the participants because there is a *lack of correspondence* between what people think and what actually happens. This *lack of correspondence* stands in the way of reducing events to the participants' views just as it thwarts the prediction of events on the basis of universally valid generalizations. *There is* a reality, even if it is unpredictable and unexplainable. This may be difficult to accept, but it is futile or downright dangerous to deny it [...] Reality exists. But the fact that reality incorporates inherently imperfect human thinking makes it logically impossible to explain and predict. (Soros 1998, p. 17, *my italics*)

This conclusion is very important, because it sounds like an invitation to start from the presupposition that—though reflexivity pulls in favour of uncertainty—there is always the chance to incorporate in decisions themselves, both the moment of rationality and of better knowledge of the reality, together with the moment of the different preferences of the various thinking and autonomous participants. Then, in doing so, it should be not impossible to make decisions that could be less contingent and wiser than those drawn from a simple clash of interests that are the result of purely negative and short-term interactive relations. And it should not be impossible to make decisions in the medium and long term that include a sort of political conscience of a common good; these that may be imperfect, offering the best outcome of a technology of planning and/or technology of negotiating, delivering a PAF with the best strategic and systemic scientific global cooperation (see **Vol. III**).

6.9 *Fallibility* and Recognised *Reflexivity*

Here Soros offers a revision of the Popperian concept of fallibility in order to fit it to the effects of fallibility arising from the methodological acceptance of reflexivity. This is the vision of the world in which the thinking of participants which must be compared and controlled. The thinking participants must impose some interpretative model on what they are observing. Soros affirms that:

> the reflexive process would never end if they did not end it deliberately. The most effective way to bring closure is to settle on a pattern and emphasize it until the actual picture recedes into the background. The pattern that emerges may be far removed from the underlying sensory perception but it has the great attraction of being understandable and clear. That is why religions and dogmatic political ideologies have so much appeal. (Soros 1998, pp. 17–18)

It is in the success of the group evaluation in the field of the socio-economic programmes that it is especially convenient to conserve and strengthen the interaction between reality and thinking, to give meaning to a programming and political approach determined by the political will.

Soros offers two types of fallibility:

1. one 'more moderate, more substantiated by an official version which take the concept of reflexivity and justify a critical way to think to an open society';
2. and another, more radical, an idiosyncratic version that guided me effectively in life.

> The public, moderate, version has already been discussed. Fallibility means that there is a *lack of correspondence between the participants thinking* and the *actual state of affairs*; as a result actions have unintended consequences. Events do not necessarily diverge from expectations, but they are liable to do so. There are many humdrum, everyday events that play out exactly as expected, but those events that show a divergence are more interesting. They may alter people's view of the world and set in motion a reflexive process as a result of which neither the participants' views nor the actual state of affairs remains unaffected. (Soros 1998, pp. 18–19, emphases added)

6.10 The 'Feasibility of the Plans'

6.10.1 The 'Feasibility of Plans' as a Pivot Around Which to Rebuild the Programming Approach and the Methodology of Planning

This creates a crisis of 'positiveness' about presumed economic phenomena and facts underway, and prevents the credible application of that relation between cognition and participation as an instrument of an effective economic policy, at the same time strategic (with multiple objectives) and systemic (taking account of the 'lateral effects'), be drawn from the analysis itself of the feasibility of the decisions and actions to be taken for possible improvements without dangerous and useless splits, or situations in the hands of chaos or of a stochastic process.

In other terms, traditional economic theory is wrong, because it fails to introduce a practice of advanced economic policy—advanced and also 'scientific'—that is appropriately provided and supported by the PAF, and of knowledge instruments on situations of interdependence of the economic phenomena,[29] whether of a strategic or systemic character.

Today we are still quite far, at a global level, from having such knowledge at our disposal.[30] This would require that we have the imperative to guarantee the construction of such knowledge,[31] in a planetary project not inferior, in dimension and importance, to those which have already been implemented in other sectors of international scientific policy.

Instead, to declare it inevitable to give way to an indefinite sum of human and political practical decisions and actions, of a 'reflexive' type, we should programme the absorption of all of these practical decisions, individually taken, including those within a larger decisional process; this is painstaking work, and more contractual and virtually analytical of the pros and cons of different solutions, if we measure the multiple advantages of different solutions under different conditions.

And increasingly close to rational awareness of the set of 'problems', and their practical, negotiated solutions,[32] are their intention—this becomes an 'exclusive' field of a kind of university club of economists, which discuss a series of supposed abstract, theoretical, logical, aggregate connections, between phenomena more and more far and misunderstood by governmental decision-makers, very distant from the real possibilities of implementation of any 'fine idea', through the chaotic and casual action of reflexivity theory.

So settled, the lack of determination, which unfortunately the reflexivity tends without doubt to confirm, reduces itself, by the research and the economic policy, to affect not only on the facts, but also the thinking of the thinkers, especially if seen in terms of groups, classes, ethnical and religious communities that are ready to fight, but—probably more judiciously—prefer to find 'compromise', usually more advantageous than fighting, through negotiation or collective bargaining.

I believe that we can equip the social sciences (as also Soros would wish to suggest) in order to impact on the facts throughout the theory of 'reflexivity' with specific instruments (such as the PAF outlined in this book, in the footsteps of Frisch's Oslo model) or other systems suitable for dialogue and common cooperation with the two functions of cognition and participation (using Soros vocabulary) at a greater level of effectiveness in terms of reality and implementation.

In other terms, we should determine that the reflexivity would find itself exercising its reaction to planning inside the planning system and procedural management itself, with new experiences of multi-objective methods of computation, involving special engagement of reciprocal responsibilities in terms of the results.

Therefore, it seems legitimate to ask: is it not the case that the best way to transform cognition and participation, which are the basis of reflexivity into 'achieved thought', would be through a strategic and systemic process that is best described as 'planning'? A process that constitutes in any moment the only opportunity to provide the content of operative feasibility to the choices and preferences of the participants?

Is this not the leitmotiv of this trilogy?

6.10.2 A Reflexive Concept of the Truth, but with an Interactive Vision of Reality

In natural science, scientific statements can or cannot correspond to the facts of the physical world, but in all cases the facts are separated and independent from the statements referring to them. In social events, however, the scientific statements involve some 'thinking participants';

this constitutes both their strength and their weakness. Here, in fact, the relationship between thought and reality is more complicated.

Our thoughts are part of the very reality that we think of and design; they guide us towards our actions, and our actions always have an impact on what happens. The situation is contingent on what we (and others) think and on how we act. The events in which we participate do not constitute a sort of independent criterion through which the truth or the falseness of our thoughts could be assessed.

According the rules of the 'logic of scientific research' (for instance, from Popper), the statements are true only if they correspond to the facts. But in situations where there are participants that think, the facts do not occur independently from what the participants are thinking about them; they are a reflection of the impact of the participants' decisions or preferences.

As a result, they cannot qualify as an independent criterion for the determination of their truth.

This is the reason for which our understanding is inherently imperfect. Soros insists on this point (see quotation already reported above in Sect. 6.5.1).

Soros provides an ('obvious') example drawn from the financial world. But Frisch, on the identical argument, draws his criticism (of epistemological validity) inside the world of econometric models, against the so called 'growth models', which in his time were raging in the current econometric models, opposing the logic of the 'decisional models'.

Frisch defined, in effect, the 'growth model' simply as a 'half logic' if and when used as a tool of economic policy;[33] their 'stupidity' came from the evidence that the illogical use that their builder was failing in the results, which included governmental decisions that the model themselves were involved in.[34]

The results of the analysis, not only the results of 'cognitive' analysis and reciprocally influenced by those of 'participative' analysis (Soros)—or also 'programmatic' (Frisch, Tinbergen, etc.)—are no longer reliable or certain from a 'scientific' point of view, as those deriving from the analysis of objects in 'nature' or natural sciences.

In a few lines, Soros actually puts his finger on what I call the overturning of the positivistic approach, basing it on the 'bi-uniqueness' of the thought–action relationship. This happens, according to Soros, only when we are in the presence of 'objects that think' (as objects of analysis),

The Programming Approach, the Crisis of Traditional...   205

that is, also participants that 'reflect' on themselves and their actions, demonstrating unexpected influence in a one-to-one way on their separate functions.

In this way, Soros repeats with a clear and complete consciousness what many philosophers and a few sociologists over the years, (but.... unfortunately, not many economists) have said, that

> through the participating function, people may influence the situation that is supposed to serve as an independent variable for the cognitive function, and consequently, the participants' understanding cannot qualify as objective knowledge. And because their decisions are not based on objective knowledge, the outcome is liable to diverge from their expectations. (Soros 1998, p. 7)

6.10.3 The Program's *Feasibility* and Its Relationship with the Logical Positivism

Soros does not say that there is a third category of truth for treating reflexive phenomenon. He intends only to say—as his crucial point— that in reflexive situations 'facts do not necessarily supply independent criteria of reality.' One could also consider the correspondence between intentions and facts as a hallmark of truth. 'But the correspondence can be obtained in two ways: or pronouncing truthful affirmations, or having an impact on the facts themselves. The correspondence is not a guarantee of truth.' This caveat—says Soros—is applied to most political statements and economic predictions.

Nothing is more important than our thought of the concept of reality. Unfortunately, if we are used to thinking that in situations in which there are 'thinking participants' (as Soros call them) in the same way that we do towards the reality of natural phenomenon without taking into consideration their alternative role (or 'reflexive' one as Soros would say), then we should radically change our direction of research in the humanitarian and social sciences.[35]

For the magnitude of uncountable difficulties regarding thought and fact, they interconnect in the process called 'reflexivity'; despite being 'complicated', I do not believe that there are any other paths for working and collaborating together, in some way, to improve and simplify it. If the objectives or instruments used to achieve these goals are not agreed upon by all interested parties, I do not believe that there is any other way except operating for an improved level of participation and consensus tied to the real feasibility of the programmes, pushing all participants to negotiate among themselves on the rules of decision-making and the decisional system. If 'the reality has the power to surprise the thought' (and that which pushed us to accept our own 'fallibility'), there is also a 'thought that has the power to create reality', which pushes us even closer to a 'scientific' utopia, where we can model the future through appropriate instruments of consciousness.

Yet it is very important to ascertain, thanks to the argument based upon the 'reflexivity' of thought among participants, which has its own role in influencing the facts and urging us to let go ourselves to our impotent and unavoidable destiny, which renders us so passive and 'dependent' with respect to natural 'laws'.

Overlooking natural laws (which we, as human beings, have very small ability to impact, beyond that of knowing how to utilise them for achieving our goals), in regards to human behaviour, on the other hand, where laws do not exist, beyond those which we 'prefer' and are established by human beings, it is necessary for us to divide and produce systems of convenience, in which preferences are in some way politically managed, without being overpowered by stronger and more prepared social groups and classes, ones more richer in resources and privileges. These can safeguard the role and freedom of single individuals, without profit for social position, and to be acknowledged only for own individual 'merits', avoiding the possibility that these personal merits could constitute a privilege for the social groups and classes of belonging, but remaining only personal, at the limits of what the society, as a whole, considers justified.

Hence, we are speaking of a simple vision of an integrated society, one open to new visions and new 'realities' (not threatening—as seen in the past until today—its own destruction); this is an open vision towards all, all except its destruction. The only 'true' problem is that of measuring its ability to manage, without conflict, class struggles, and conflicts among groups for power and interests, and who to trust in using this uncontrolled instrument of human evolution, in imitating what positivism hypothesised and formulated, without ever demonstrating this, as a 'natural law' of selection and survival.

The Programming Approach, the Crisis of Traditional... 207

From this position, Soros derives from his own experience and generalises upon what happens on a more general historical plane, with very interesting observations that deserve more attention. He had already warned us of this (see quotation; Soros 1998, p. 13).

A truly historic event does not actually change the world; it changes our comprehension of the world and this new comprehension, in turn, has a new and unpredictable impact on the way that the world works.

Another interesting point that Soros makes on reflexivity is that the passage of time can 'insulate' the 'cognitive' and 'participative' functions from each other (see Soros 1998, p. 9).

6.11 From the *'Fallibility'* to the *'Feasibility'*

Despite adhering to the Popperian form of scientific research founded on 'fallibility' (as a consequence of the 'falsification' necessary for 'scientific' propositions), in the case of social research, where there are 'heavy' subjects involved that participate in an active way in the same research, the Popperian fallibility takes on an aspect that is completely overturned epistemologically.

In fact, Soros ended up proposing two different versions of fallibility, creating some further problems:

I offer two versions of fallibility: first, a more moderate, better substantiated 'official' version that accompanies the concept of reflexivity and justifies a critical mode of thinking and an open society; and, second, a more radical, idiosyncratic version that has actually guided me through life.

The public, moderate version has already been discussed. Fallibility means that there is a lack of correspondence between the participants' thinking and the actual state of affairs; as a result actions have unintended consequences. Events do not necessarily diverge from expectations, but they are liable to do so. There are many humdrum, everyday events that play out exactly as expected, but those events that show a divergence are more interesting. They may alter people's view of the world and set in motion a reflexive process as a result of which neither the participants' views nor the actual state of affairs remains unaffected. (Soros, ibidem, 1998, pp. 18–19)

Fallibility has a negative sound, but it has a positive aspect that can be very inspiring. What is imperfect can be improved. The fact that our understanding is inherently imperfect makes it possible to learn and to improve our understanding. All that is needed is to recognize our fallibility. That opens the way to critical thinking and there is no limit to how far our understanding of reality may go. There is infinite scope for improvement not only in our thinking but also in our society. Perfection eludes us; whatever design we choose, it is bound to be defective. We must therefore content ourselves with the 'next best thing', a form of social organization that falls short of perfection but is open to improvement. That is the concept of the open society: a society open to improvement. The concept rests on the recognition of our fallibility. I explore it further later on, but first I want to introduce a more radical, idiosyncratic version of fallibility.

Soros goes on to describe the second version of fallibility, the radical one, describing it and noting its differences from the former. He changes tack, speaking from his own personal experience.

At this point, I shall change my tack. Instead of discussing fallibility in general terms, I shall try to explain what it means to me personally. It is the cornerstone not only of my view of the world but also of my behavior. It is the foundation of my theory of history and it has guided me in my actions both as a participant in the financial markets and as a philanthropist. If there is anything original in my thinking, it is my radical version of fallibility. (Soros 1998, p. 19)

Nevertheless, it is this dichotomy of versions of fallibility (and the practice that derives from it) that are unclear to me. Both the 'moderate' version and the 'radical' (to use Soros's expression) are founded on the concept of 'reflexivity' and its application to history. But can this concept be divided into moderate or radical? Both the versions are founded on the determining factor of the presence of human thinking in its comparison with reality, which allows it to influence reality, increasing its fallibility.

Therefore, I find it difficult to see the difference between the two versions, not only in the presentation (the different 'tack'), which leads to the suspicion that the radical version better suits personal (and/or individual) historical-political-social experience. But is this suspicion legitimate? This point deserves some clarification by Soros.

The personal experience of the 'radical' fallibility, which is definitely less relevant in terms of general logical problems for all those that operate in the field of political and social decisions (on any level). Here, in this field, Soros talks only of 'moderate fallibility' as an instrument inspired by the management of imperfection when this inevitably appears on the scene of history.

In what then does the construct of the human mind, which translates into a vision of realisation or of a programmed intention, described for the radical vision of fallibility, have less quality and less chance of constructing the basis of a useful explanation for a generalised behaviour for the construction of an 'open society'? And therefore, could it and should it be a less useful discourse in the field of decisions and public choices, in increasing the need for coherence, rationality, coordination, visions in the medium and long term?

This is how Soros expresses himself, speaking of the radical vision of fallibility, from a more stringent perspective, which could be justified though the arguments presented so far:

> I contend that all constructs of the human mind, whether they are confined to the inner recesses of our thinking or find expression in the outside world in the form of disciplines, ideologies, or institutions, are deficient in some way or another. The flaw may manifest itself in the form of internal inconsistencies or inconsistencies with the external world or inconsistencies with the purpose that our ideas were designed to serve. This proposition is, of course, much stronger than the recognition that all our constructs *may* be wrong. I am not speaking of a mere lack of correspondence but of an actual flaw in all human constructs and an actual divergence between outcomes and expectations. As I explained earlier, the divergence really matters only in historic events. That is why the radical version of fallibility can serve as the basis for a theory of history. (Soros 1998, pp. 19–20)

But perhaps, rather than as the basis for a 'theory of history' (just as all the theories are strongly threatened by the same 'theory of fallibility') the 'radical' version of fallibility (not so different from the 'moderate' one) could lead to an effort to reduce the discrepancy between results and expectations, with a less 'extreme' pragmatic logic than that discussed by Soros and described here:

> The contention that all human constructs are flawed sounds very bleak and pessimistic, but it is no cause for despair. Fallibility sounds so negative only because we cherish false hopes. We yearn for perfection, permanence, and the ultimate truth, with immortality thrown in for good measure. Judged by those standards, the human condition is bound to be unsatisfactory. In fact, perfection and immortality elude us and permanence can only be found in death. But life gives us a chance to improve our understanding exactly because it is imperfect and also to improve the world. When all constructs are deficient, the variations become all important. Some constructs are better than others. Perfection is unattainable but what is inherently imperfect is capable of infinite improvement.[36] (Soros 1998, pp. 20–21)

This 'infinite improvement'—and the inherent fallibility of both versions—can be obtained, with the support of 'thinking' participants in the human 'constructions' bringing closer, pragmatically, thinking and reality.

Where can we find the reasons, the energy, analysis, techniques and motivations to make more plausible and more direct the cause–effect relationships, on the one hand, between aspirations/preferences, and consequent decisions/actions, and, on the other, the consequent results? Is it not in these terms that the 'discrepancy between expectations and results' that Soros places at the basis of fallibility and improvement is always manifested?

The human 'constructions', which I would directly call 'programmes', are fallible above all in their feasibility (also due to the different motivations of the subjects involved). It is their missed analysis that makes their formulation misleading, both because it does not ascertain their feasibility and because it makes misleading and dull the concept of programmes, which includes the principle of the demonstration of its feasibility.

In fact, a programme without programming is *not* a programme worthy of the name. Neither is a programme without continuous monitoring of its implementation and its adjustments.

The Programming Approach, the Crisis of Traditional... **211**

Then, could the well-studied, well-demonstrated, well-controlled and updated feasibility permanently adapted to the changing reality not be the 'sufficient reason' of governments of the fallibility of programmes (or constructions) of any type, level or genre?

Could the following affirmation by Soros that returns to the sense of current and common language not be regarded also in the light of these latter considerations of the feasibility of programmes?

It seems that the participative function indicated by Soros—intended not on an individual plan (apart from when manifested in the field of individual choices), but on a political and social level—could be that which in the chapters of this book has been called the programming approach. This is an approach that is just as rigid in its analysis and in the consciousness of limits born from its systemic nature that can be very 'open' to the negotiation of objectives and open to any variability of a territorial, temporal, cultural type. The strong inclusion of reflexivity and the subjectivity of the process of planning make the approach sensitive to the variability of circumstances. Therefore, a condition resulting from an open society does not lose the quality of its decision-making methods, but neither do the quantity of its opportunities and the permanent improvement of that tool of optimisation.

Soros concludes his analysis of this aspect as follows:

Constructs, like actions, have unintended consequences and those consequences cannot be properly anticipated at the time of their creation. Even if the consequences could be anticipated, it might still be appropriate to proceed because those consequences would arise only in the future. So my working hypothesis is not incompatible with the idea that one course of action is better than another, that there is indeed an optimum course of action. It does imply, however, that the optimum applies only to a particular moment of history and what is optimum at one point may cease to be so at the next. This is a difficult concept to work with, particularly for institutions that cannot avoid some degree of inertia. The longer any form of taxation is in effect, the more likely it is that it will be evaded; that may be a good reason for changing the form of taxation after a while, but not a good reason for having no taxation. To take an example from a different field, the Catholic Church has evolved into something quite different from what Jesus intended. (Soros 1998, pp. 22–23)

In other words—continues Soros—theories and policies can be temporarily valid at some moments in history.

> It is to bring this point home that I call them *fertile fallacies*: flawed constructs with initially beneficial effects. How long the beneficial effects last depends on whether the flaws are recognized and corrected. In this way, constructs may become increasingly sophisticated. But no fertile fallacy is likely to last forever; eventually the scope for refining it and developing it will be exhausted and a new fertile fallacy captures people's imagination. What I am about to say may be a fertile fallacy, but I am inclined to interpret the history of ideas as composed of fertile fallacies. Other people may call them paradigms.
>
> The combination of these two ideas-that all mental constructs are flawed but some of them are fertile-lies at the core of my own, radical version of fallibility. I apply it to the outside world and to my own activities with equal vigor and it has served me well both as a fund manager and more recently as a philanthropist. Whether it will also serve me well as a thinker is being tested right now, for this radical version of fallibility serves as the foundation for the theory of history and the interpretation of financial markets that I lay out in the rest of this book. (Soros 1998, ibidem, pp. 22–23)

6.12 A Radical Criticism of the *Economics* as Studied and Practiced

From the 'discovery of 'reflexivity', as a modality in which, in the social sciences—carried out by thinking beings that can 'reflect' on their behaviours and about the studied 'laws'—the subjectivity of the research itself is accepted (as Myrdal was asserting). Thus, for Soros there emerge many important forms of 'assists' against the pseudo-scientific and deterministic-positivistic use of the social sciences, in their attempt to ape, clumsily and in dangerous ways, the natural sciences.

This is the 'methodological argument', which I have tried to outline since the first chapter of this book, referring to the critical-historical role developed in that direction by Myrdal.

At the beginning, I was pressed by the emergency to proceed (once we have fixed this phase of historical-positivistic misunderstanding and underestimation of the whole of economics) to that alternative one of operational and praxeological policy, which (in the footsteps of Frisch and others, ignored and unknown) could recover the future of economic research from its decline and 'demise'.

Soros, the most recent of the contributors to the radical critique of economics, has been presented in this book as the last, but not least, contribution.

I have, therefore, focused on his contribution so far in this chapter, on the epistemological aspect, to support the hypothesis of the overturning of the approach that this book develops.[37]

The deductions that Soros made from his concept of 'reflexivity' for a more organic political vision are also illustrated by other writings by Soros, and also by other authors that focused on the subject. Therefore, the most notable and popularised writings by Soros are on the themes of: (1) the crisis of economic theory; and (2) the character, perspectives and above all, the risks of collapse of the global capitalist system.

I have chosen, therefore, to examine these themes in the two last paragraphs of this chapter, without commenting, although I share the substance and the expression, choosing rather to refer to other works by Soros himself on these themes.

I feel, therefore, also the need to declare from the outset that I strongly share the ideas proposed by Soros. It is precisely for this reason that I invite the reader not to settle for my brief summary in the two sections that follow, but rather to view specific writings that the author has produced in order to determine questions of interpretations of successive events on the subject of the global financial crisis.[38]

6.13 The Criticism to the Global Capitalism Without Public Planning, and Criticism of the 'Market Fundamentalism' Which Supports it

The first question that should be posed is whether a 'global capitalist system' exists or not. This question, however, risks being merely a rhetorical one.

It was certainly not in the contemporary world where the discussion concerning 'capitalist systems' was illustrated. There is an immense literature that deals with this subject from the end of the 1800s onwards (perhaps even before), projecting economic analysis on the functioning of capitalist systems, 'capital' factors, as the basis of traditional economic theory, which manifests itself in a system of standard behavioural relations, on which a system of control is elaborated and public politics are studied.

The declared aim of such controls and politics, independently of the degree of development that capitalism had reached in any national economic reality is that of avoiding abuse and damaging effects, within each and every country and society, and to arrive at a meaningful 'nation-state' identity (independent and autonomous) in each of the respective countries and national societies.

A capitalist, initially multi-national 'system' was produced from multilateral relations that involves a few nations which demonstrate institutional conditions of security and operative guarantee, and are truly 'global', insofar as those conditions are reached in both the sense of cultural communications and that of intensification of commercial relations, on different efficiency levels and dimensions that provide the conditions for scattered nation states to emerge, in the context of a consolidated capitalist and truly 'global' system.

The capitalist system unfortunately is moving further from attending the unpriced goods, or so called nonmarket sector, which are necessary to guarantee the commonwealth of people. This results in the erosion of moral values in the national and international levels. Stability cannot be guaranteed by simple commercial exchanges, which is traditionally considered as the object of economy, leaving excessive liberty to the speculation of capital.

6.14 The Global Capitalist System: An Incomplete Regime

The crux of the matter, is a question of how the theoretical framework, which Soros has elaborated, can give a new view upon the history. To begin with his description of the current situation:

> We live in a global economy that is characterized not only by free trade in goods and services but even more by the free movement of capital. Interest rates, exchange rates, and stock prices in various countries are intimately interrelated and global financial markets exert tremendous influence on

economic conditions. Given the decisive role that international financial capital plays in the fortunes of individual countries, it is not inappropriate to speak of a global capitalist system. (Soros, p. 101)

Therefore Soros sees a danger in such globalisation of a capitalist system, as it is liberal and poorly regulated. The pursuit of the profits cannot guarantee the stability in our society:

My critique of the global capitalist system falls under two main headings. One concerns the defects of the market mechanism. Here I am talking primarily about the instabilities built into international financial markets. The other concerns the deficiencies of what I have to call, for lack of a better name, the nonmarket sector. By this I mean primarily the failure of politics both on the national and on the international level. (Soros, p. 102)

Furtherly, he adds a new perspective to the global capitalist system, calling it a regime, but straightafter describes the shortcomings of this regime:

Although we can describe global capitalism as a regime, it is an *incomplete* regime: It governs only the economic function, even if the economic function has come to take precedence over other functions. The current regime has a history but it is not a well defined one. It is difficult even to identify when the regime came into existence. Was it in 1989 after the collapse of the Soviet empire? Around 1980 when Margaret Thatcher and Ronald Reagan came to power? Or at some earlier date? Perhaps it was in the 1970s when the offshore market in Eurodollars developed. The distinguishing feature of the global capitalist system is the free movement of capital. International trade in goods and services is not enough to create a global economy; the factors of production must also be interchangeable. Land and other natural resources do not move and people move with difficulty; it is the mobility of capital, information, and entrepreneurship that is responsible for economic integration. (Soros, pp. 105–106)

In this way, Soros put stress that globalisation of the economy consists only in the movement of capital. Therefore it has taken the central role in the world and international financial markets play in almost equal position with sovereign states.

Here Soros defines the difference between democracy and capitalism:

There is a widespread belief that capitalism is somehow associated with democracy in politics. It is a historical fact that the countries that constitute the center of the global capitalist system are democratic but the same is not true of all the capitalist countries that lie on the periphery. In fact, many claim that some kind of dictatorship is needed to get economic development going. Economic development requires the accumulation of capital and that, in turn, requires low wages and high savings rates. This is more easily accomplished under an autocratic government that is capable of imposing its will on the people than a democratic one that is responsive to the wishes of the electorate. (Soros, p. 109)

To add more:

Truth be told, the connection between capitalism and democracy is tenuous at best. Capitalism and democracy obey different principles. The stakes are different: In capitalism wealth is the object, in democracy it is political authority. The criteria by which the stake are measured are different: In capitalism the unit of account i money, in democracy it is the citizens' vote. The interests that are sup- posed to be served are different: In capitalism it is private interests, in democracy it is the public interest. In the United States, this tension between capitalism and democracy is symbolized by the proverbial conflicts between Wall Street and Main Street. In Europe, the extension of the political franchise led to the correction of some of the worst excesses of capitalism: the dire predictions of the Communist Manifesto were in fact frustrated by the broadening of democracy. (Soros, p. 111)

6.15 The Future of Global Capitalist System

Soros turns back to the past lessons in order to predict the future of the global capitalist system. First of all, he notices the certainty in which we lived up until the First World War:

What can we say about the future of the global capitalist system. The past may offer some clues. In some ways, the nineteenth-century version of the global capitalist system was more stable than the current one. It had a single

The Programming Approach, the Crisis of Traditional... **217**

currency, gold; today there are three major currencies crashing against each other like continental plates There were imperial powers, Britain foremost among them, that derived enough benefits from being at the center of the global capitalist system to justify dispatching gunboats to faraway places to preserve the peace or collect debts; today the United States refuses to act as the police force of the world. Most important, people were more firmly rooted in fundamental values than they are today Reality was still regarded as something external and thinking was still considered a means of attaining knowledge. Right and wrong true and false were considered objective criteria on which people could depend. Science offered deterministic explanations and pre dictions. There were conflicts between the precepts of religion and science but they both covered the same ground: They offered dependable guide to the world. Together, they created a culture that, in spite of its internal contradictions, dominated the world. (Soros, p. 125)

Unfortunately, contemporary global capitalist system gives much less certainty. It functions as cycles of booms and busts:

I am reluctant to apply the boom/bust model to the global capitalist system because I consider the system too open-ended and incomplete fit the pattern neatly. Yet, almost against my better judgment – I do not want to give the impression that everything should be interpreted as a boom/bust phenomenon – I can identify the makings of a boom/bust pattern: a prevailing trend, namely, international competition for capital, and a prevailing bias, namely, an excessive belief in the market mechanism. In the boom, both bias and trend reinforce each other. In the bust, both of them fall apart. What will bring about the bust? I believe the answer is to be found in the tension between the global scope of the financial markets and the national scope of politics. Earlier I described the global capitalist system as a gigantic circulatory system sucking capital into the center and pushing it out into the periphery. The sovereign states act like valves within the system. While the global financial markets are expanding, the valves open, but if and when the flow of funds is reversed they stand in the way, causing the system to break down. (Soros, p. 126)

He continues:

The global capitalist system is supported by an ideology rooted in the theory of perfect competition. According to this theory, markets tend toward equilibrium and the equilibrium position represents the most efficient allocation of resources. Any constraints on free competition interfere with the efficiency of the market me therefore they should be resisted. In previous discussions, I described this as the laissez faire ideology but market fundamentalism is a better term. This phrase is better because fundamentalism implies a certain kind of belief that is easily carried to extremes. It is a belief in perfection, a belief in absolutes, a belief that every problem must have a solution. It posits an authority that is endowed with perfect knowledge even if that knowledge is not readily accessible to ordinary mortals. God is such an authority and in modem times science has become an acceptable substitute. Marxism claimed to have a scientific basis; so does market fundamentalism. The scientific basis of both ideologies was established in the nineteenth century when science still promised to deliver the ultimate truth. We have learned a great deal since then both about the limitations of scientific method and the imperfections of the market mechanism. Both Marxist and laissez faire ideologies have been thoroughly discredited. The laissez faire ideology was the first to be dismissed, as a consequence of the Great Depression and the rise of Keynesian economics. Marxism lingered on in spite of the excesses of Stalin's rule but, following the collapse of the Soviet system, it is now in almost total eclipse. (Soros, pp. 126–127)

Soros divides with his readers une personal memory which illustrates us how the view we had about the global capitalist system has changed:

In my student days in the early 1950s, laissez faire was even more unacceptable than state intervention in the economy is today. The idea that it would stage a comeback seemed inconceivable. I believe that the revival of market fundamentalism can be explained only by faith in a magic quality ("the invisible hand") that is even more important that the scientific base. Not in vain did President Reagan speak of "the magic of the marketplace." A key feature of fundamentalist beliefs is that they rely on either/or judgments. If a proposition is wrong, its opposite is claimed to be right. This logical incoherence lies at the heart of market fundamentalism. State intervention in the economy has always produced some negative results. This has been true not only of central planning but also of the welfare state and of Keynesian demand management. From this banal observation, market fundamentalists jump to a totally illogical conclusion: If state intervention \is faulty, free markets must be perfect. Therefore the state must not be allowed to intervene in the economy. It hardly needs pointing out that the logic of this argument is faulty. (Soros, pp. 127–128)

The Programming Approach, the Crisis of Traditional... **219**

In this way the fundamental way of thinking, that is the logic either/or has leaded us to leave the leading role to the capitalism instead of the governments.

> Publicly traded companies are increasing in numbers and size and the interests of shareholders loom ever larger. Managers are as much concerned with the market for their shares as with the market for their products. If it comes to a choice, the signals from financial markets take precedence over those from product markets: Managers will readily divest divisions or sell the entire company if this will enhance shareholder value; they maximize profits rather than market share. Managers must either acquire or be acquired in an increasingly integrated global market; either way they need a high price for their stock. Their personal rewards are also increasingly tied to the price of their stock. The change is particularly pronounced in the banking sector, which is undergoing rapid consolidation. Bank shares are selling at several times book value, but managers, mindful of their stock options, continue to repurchase shares, reducing the number of shares outstanding and increasing the market value of the shares. Merger and acquisition activity is reaching unprecedented levels as industries are consolidating on a global basis. Cross-country transactions become ever more common. The establishment of a single currency in Europe has given Europe-wide consolidation a tremendous push. This realignment of companies is occurring faster than one could have imagined. Global monopolies and oligopolies are beginning to emerge. There are only four major auditing firms left in the world; similar but less pronounced concentration is taking place in other financial functions. Microsoft and Intel are on the verge of worldwide monopolies. (Soros, pp. 128–129)

Such triumphant growth of capitalism cannot pass without consequences. It becomes a source of potential instability.

Notes to Chapter 6 (Vol. II)

1. See I. Wallerstein, *The Capitalist World-Economy,* Cambridge Univ. Press, 1979, and other books related to the theory and methodology of analysis of the world-system. See also by Wallerstein, and T.K. Hopkins, and others, *World-Systems Analysis: Theory and Methodology*. Beverly Hills: Sage, 1982, and (also with Terence K. Hopkins), on the ways of transition

toward a world-system since 1945–2025 (Wallerstein and Hopkins, *The Age of Transition: Trajectory of the World-System, 1945–2025*. London: Zed Press, 1996).

2. Wallerstein (1979), *The Capitalist World-Economy.*
3. *World-Systems Analysis: Theory and Methodology.* Beverly Hills: Sage, 1982.
4. Wallerstein and Hopkins (1996), *The Age of Transition: Trajectory of the World-System, 1945–2025.*
5. See for instance Sanderson, S. (1955) *Civilizations and World Systems*; Hout, W. (1993) *Capitalism and the Third World: Development, dependence and the world system*; Shannon, T. (1989) *An introduction to the World System Perspective.*
6. From the first volume on world system theory (Wallerstein, *The Modern World System*, 1974).
7. For example, Wallerstein, I. (2000), *The essential Wallerstein*, New Press. Wallerstein Immanuel (2001); *Unthinking social science: the limits of nineteenth-century paradigms* (new ed. with a new preface), Temple University Press.
8. Ernest Mandel, author of a good analysis of *Der Spaetkapitalismus* (1975) and active militant of the 'Fourth International' (Trotskyist).
9. Let me introduce a brief personal memory of Ernest Mandel, who after his death in 1995, has left me, more than before, the personality of a serious scholar, rather than the tenacious Trotskyist militant. In fact, Ernest Mandel was a good friend of mine when I was younger, between 17 and 19 years old (he was three years older), when he frequently came to visit Rome, my home city (as a guest in my parent's house) between 1945 and 1946, right after the end of the war, for his work as leader of the political movement party 'Fourth International' ('Trotskyist') in a still-clandestine world of 1945, following the German occupation of Rome in 1943–1944, when I was already relatively active in the 'Resistance movement'. I considered myself a member of such.

   My youth was sympathetic of the movement at that time, and we, as movement, called him 'Walter' (because he told us to fear the group of political antagonists of the USRR, and philo-Soviet countries, which were potentially in danger of 'Stalin'-like execution, a few years after the assassination of Trotsky in Mexico). He had informed; most of all assassins in Italian company workers escaped to the USRR, since persecuted by fascists, but contrary to the Stalin policy regime considered in its historical role counter-revolutionary (and only sympathetic to the Trotskyist group). Togliatti was still head of the PCI in the USRR, but

The Programming Approach, the Crisis of Traditional...   **221**

an officer of the Stalin regime, and contributed to the identification and of many communist comrade refugees and Trotskyists, in the USSR, from the fascist persecution, but was sent to die in Siberia by Stalin, because of sympathisers of Trotskyist positions.

At that time, I was both a friend and admirer of Walter, or Ernest, for his great knowledge of Marxist texts (which I still had not yet read, at the time) and for his historical understanding. We shared a dislike for the Communist Party in Italy, tied by its hands and feet to the Russian Stalinian system of power (from Stalin to Gorbachev, without serious interruptions), without good reasoning but purely political opportunism, in its falsity, and whose members should have never thought—after the fall of the war—of being able to call themselves 'socialists' after the damage done thanks to the Soviet Stalinism, to the entire socialist left movements in Europe and across the world. As well as the Italian movement, made with bad conscience and knowledge as well as poor ethical sense, recycled in democratic life (without abandoning, however, the methods and style acquired in its long hibernation in Stalinism and of purely political incentives).

But—at the same time—I held a different attitude towards political ambiguity and unclear politics on behalf of European social-democratic parties towards the creation of a new, international socialist party, in particular on the creation of totalitarian socialist parties in a few countries and nationalist pressures from single countries, and other divergent views on the relationship with emerging countries of the ex-colonial Third World. We were also divided on the political style in general on the interpretation of facts, that which I define as 'sectoral' and non-conforming with the socialist spirit; in this way we occupied different spheres, naturally distanced from the possibility of collaborating together since our thoughts and feelings were so divided.

Nonetheless, I continued to follow his so-called 'scientific' work, which seemed increasingly influenced by his political activism, undermining the principles of study to which I adhere, which should never condition my scholarly awareness, in its facts and reasoning, with partial or personal interests.

10. As happened to Queen Elizabeth some years ago at an official occasion, as already referred to in a note (n. 1) of the first paragraph, as when she wondered, as any good housekeeper would: 'why did so many excellent economists, of which since time we are so proud, fail to predict this global financial crisis, and so many policymakers mishandle it—while some saw it all coming?'

222   Volume II. Selected Testimonies on the Epistemological...

11. In his last book, *Capitalism, Socialism and Democracy* (1942), 2nd ed. London: Allen & Unwin, 1954. Leaving aside Schumpeter, who is the most classic (but totally ignored today) in the argument, we cannot forget other equally important authors who became 'classics' on the matter, such as: Charles Kindleberger (*Manias, Panics and Crashes*, 2000), Hyman Minsky (*Stabilizing an Unstable Economy*, 1986), and even John Kenneth Galbraith (*A Short History of Financial Euphoria*, 1990). More recently, Carmen Reinhart and Ken Rogoff examined eight centuries of financial crises and showed this to be a recurrent pattern in history: *This Time Is Different: Eight Centuries of Financial Folly,* (2008). The recent book by Giorgio Ruffolo is a very amusing 'cult' puzzle of arguments around this theme, imbued with historical shrewd and competence (Giorgio Ruffolo, *Il Capitalismo ha i secoli contati....* Einaudi, 2008). Let me add how Ruffolo's books is one of the Italian authors (although of not many indeed) who does not deserve not to be ignored by the international reader, since he is only available in a language as peripheral as Italian.

12. I did this especially with Frisch's planning approach and the method described in the whole second volume of the book. But I did not find in the logic of the scientific research and in the works of the logical positivism, and also in its critics (Karl Popper, the Frankfurt School, and so on) much of interest with respect to the aim of the epistemological overturning, just because the whole of the debate was oriented too much towards the unification of logical thinking and not oriented enough towards the analysis of the role of human reflection on the veracity of the approaches and their capacity to determine, in positive terms, the implementation of events.

13. George Soros, Hungarian (1930), naturalised American citizen (1961), migrated to London in 1947 (at 17 years), to study at the London School of Economics.

14. As a financial operator, he was responsible for significant, well-known operations from which he made notable profits, even being referred to in the title of one of the most numerous biographies, 'the billionaire who broke the Bank of England' (David Litterick, *The Telegraph*, 13 September 2002).

15. At the London School of Economics, where he received in 1954 a PhD in philosophy at 24 years of age, and after a long and eventful career as a financial magnate in 1998, *The Crisis of Global Capitalism*; his work—in

The Programming Approach, the Crisis of Traditional…   **223**

my opinion—of greatest cultural engagement and on which I will focus in this chapter.

16. With his work in 2001: *Open Society: Reforming Global Capitalism,* and that produced with Mark A. Notturno, *Science and the Open Society: The Future of Karl Popper's Philosophy* (2000)—where some divergences on the role of the reflexivity between Soros and Popper are analysed.

17. The word philanthropy, expressed from a conceptual viewpoint, covers a good part of the numerous actions that Soros had promoted, sustained, theorised, sponsored and funded, with the intent of implementing a more open society than that found in singular circumstances or countries, where, for one reason or other (economic and cultural backwardness, political-religious influence, scarce experience of civil or democratic cohabitation, and so on) a certain deficit of 'democratic guarantee', even in those countries deemed securely democratic, is being manifested.

18. After at least a decade of notable neglect of Soros's writings by academics, writings considered perhaps more the fruit of media notoriety rather than their possible scientific value (a bias developed for quite understandable reasons). It is significant that the *Journal of Economic Methodology*, an esteemed specific journal in English, (JEM, vol. 21, 2014, pp. 309–329) decided to subject his writings to an explicit symposium of professional scholars of economics invited by the journal itself. For the symposium, Soros prepared, as an introduction, a paper selecting the main arguments of his reflexivity theory, entitled: *Fallibility, Flexibility and the Principle of Human Uncertainty.* This paper is recommended for a wider and rapid acquisition of the 'theory of reflexivity' by Soros.

19. But the existence of a material world independent of human observation has been a matter of heated dispute among philosophers since the age of Berkeley.

20. And at the same time, I cannot neglect remembering other arguments on similar subjects and conclusions, among which is one of the last contributions by Gunnar Myrdal: *Objectivity in Social Research*, (1970), a theme that we cannot avoid to consider as central, always under definition and redefinition in the Myrdalian work.

21. Soros specifies also that:

> *Not all social action is qualified as reflexives.* (It continue, p. 8 (ibidem) and citation to p. X of this vol.)

224   Volume II. Selected Testimonies on the Epistemological…

22. Soros cites some examples:

> The French Revolution was such an event. The distinction between humdrum and historic events is, of course, tautological, but tautologies can be illuminating. Party congresses in the Soviet Union were rather humdrum, predictable affairs, but Khrushchev's speech to the Twentieth Congress was a historic occasion. It changed people's immediately, the speech had unpredictable consequences: The outlook of the people who were in the forefront of Gorbachev's glasnost was shaped in their youth by Khrushchev's revelations. (Soros 1998, p. 8)

23. And adds:

> Consider statements like 'I love you' or 'He is my enemy.' They are bound to affect the person to which they refer, depending on how they are communicated. Or look at marriage. It has two thinking participants, but their thinking is not directed at a reality that is separate and independent of what they think and feel. One partner's thoughts and feelings affect the behavior of the other and vice versa. Both feelings and behavior can change out of all recognition as the marriage evolves. (Soros 1998, p. 9)

24. About this we have dealt amply in Chap. 3.

25. In the general introduction (**Vol. I**) of this trilogy, I tried to illustrate the damage created by the approximate and pseudo-scientific approach of economics that emerged at the very beginning of economic research itself, which would have obscured the pathway for improving the sustainability of democratic conditions in the field of economic events. The positivist-economic approach permitted the creation of an ever more divergent (full of social struggles, ego-centricism and even destructive war among the beneficiaries of capital and power) group that was subject to the abuse of power and class struggle along with brutal antagonism and violence, destruction of wealth and social injustice. The capitalism that we celebrate throughout the world today—as rightfully affirmed by Soros—did not eliminate, however, in many parts of the world in a fair and efficient way those extreme social and class conflicts, preventing us from truly claiming the triumph of democracy, despite some legislative-political progress.

26. See Chap. 1 for Ludwig von Mises' position.

The Programming Approach, the Crisis of Traditional... 225

27. Soros provides a metaphor which deserves to be reproduced:

> It is impossible to form a picture of the world in which we live without distortion [...] The world in which we live is extremely complicated. To form a view of the world that can serve as a basis for decisions, we must simplify. Using generalizations, metaphors, analogies, comparisons, dichotomies, and other mental constructs serves to introduce some order into an otherwise confusing universe. But every mental construct distorts to some extent what it represents and every distortion adds something to the world that we need to understand. The more we think, the more we have to think about. This is because reality is not given. It is formed in the same process as the participants' thinking: The more complex the *thinking*, the more complicated *reality* becomes. Thinking can never quite catch up with reality: Reality is always richer than our comprehension. *Reality has the power to surprise thinking, and thinking has the power to create reality*. (Soros 1998, pp. 16–17, emphases added)

28. Another Soros observation is very interesting:

> This point was brought home to me by Kurt Gödel. He proved mathematically that there are always more laws in mathematics than the ones that can be proved mathematically. The technique he used was to denote the laws of mathematics by so-called Gödel numbers. By adding the laws to the universe to which they relate, namely, the laws of mathematics, Gödel has been able to prove not only that the number of laws is infinite but also that it exceeds the number of laws that can be known because there are laws about laws about laws *ad infinitum*, and what is to be known expands in step with our knowledge.
>
> The same line of reasoning could be applied to situations that have thinking participants. To understand such situations, we need to construct a model that contains the views of all the participants. These views also constitute a model that must contain the views of all the participants. So we need a model of model builders and so on, ad infinitum. The more levels the models recognize, the more levels there are to be recognized—and if the models fail to recognize them, as they must sooner or later, they no longer reproduce reality. If I had Gödel's mathematical skills, I ought to be able to prove along these lines that participants' views cannot correspond to reality.

It has been pointed out to me by William Newton-Smith that my interpretation of Gödel numbers differs from Gödel's own. Apparently, Gödel envisaged a platonic universe in which Gödel numbers existed before he discovered them, whereas I think that Gödel numbers were invented by him, thereby enlarging the universe in which he was operating. I think my interpretation makes more sense. It certainly makes Gödel's theorem more relevant to the thinking participant's predicament.

29. With the construction of input-output modelling of Leontiefan type, non-limited, however, to the input-output of commodities (rigorously involving, moreover, monetary/real relationship), but to the input-output of phenomena, of decisions and actions in a wider area of social and human relationships, stimulating the attention and assessment of many traditional disciplines in order to gain awareness in physical and technical accounting on the effects of such relationship, in a grandiose effort of scientific coordination, which until now has been absent, determined as closed within the traditional disciplinary fences, but overall has weight from the limited habits and practices, which had been the most important obstacle to human research and progress.

30. And in order to obtain those, it would be necessary to mobilise a huge international independent operation under the direction of the United Nations and its agencies, well equipped and funded (some interventions of this kind are outlined in **Vol. II** of this trilogy).

31. Not inferior to years of commitment for the think-tanks most qualified and equipped globally, following the work of Frisch (the 'decisional models' of Oslo) recalled throughout this book, and also in the system traced in **Vol. III**, Chaps. 3 and 4.

32. Solutions that, without that reflexivity organised at the higher level of community responsibilities, through the simultaneous functions, where practicable, of the cognition and of participation (two items from Soros's nomenclature), the characteristics in respect to the requirements of one or other functions, it will be very difficult to find these.

33. Models of various forms related to various standard 'thinkings' then in vogue with various schools, but all based on techniques of forecasting without any subjective role of participants, without taking into account—as Soros affirms—that 'participants' to the social events (in this case, government and governmental entities associated) cannot base their decisions on knowledge for the simple reason that 'this does not exist at the moment in which they have to take their decisions'.

The Programming Approach, the Crisis of Traditional...   227

34. To the conflict between the positivist econometrics (that of the 'growth models') and that which I would like call 'Frischian econometrics' (or 'planological', but our times have not sufficiently developed—and perhaps never will—to make such a great leap forward, even in the nomenclature) has been focused on as the substantial message of this book (with an exhibition of the PAF in **Vol. III** and in other parts of the book).

35. As Myrdal used to say, absorbing the reflexive political element in the 'economics doctrine'; and as other economists, such as Frisch and Tinenger used to do by making 'political preferences' the basis of decisional models, from which political decisions were reached (more discussion on this theme is found within the present chapter).

36. Soros at this juncture feels the need to point out:

> For good order's sake, I note that my claim that all human and social constructs are deficient does not qualify as a scientific hypothesis because it cannot be properly tested. I can claim that the participants' views always diverge from reality but I cannot prove it, because we cannot know what reality would be in absence of our views. I can wait for events to show a divergence from expectations, but, as I have indicated, subsequent events do not serve as independent criterion for deciding what the correct expectations would have been because different expectations could have led to a different course of events. Similarly, I can claim that all human constructs are flawed but I cannot demonstrate what the flaw is. The flaws usually manifest themselves at some future date, but that is no evidence that they were present at the time the constructs were formed. The shortcomings of dominant ideas and institutional arrangements become apparent only with the passage of time, and the concept of reflexivity justifies only the claim that all human constructs are *potentially* flawed. That is why I present my proposition as a working hypothesis, without logical proof or scientific status. (Soros 1998, p. 20)

37. Frankly, if I had encountered the works of Soros in the final decade of the twentieth century, when the basis of this trilogy was already being developed, this basis would have been able to find an alternative vision. But the different branches from which they both originate, and the diversity that can also be one of mere language and that demarcates the vision, make this hypothesis rather superfluous. We can summarise, but one that provides an example, that the branches are Popper and Soros, and Frisch for me. But I would be keen to know if Soros would come to examine in greater

depth Frisch as I came to do with Popper in my own journey. This would be for me a wonderful occasion to make a common step forward, with others, for a renewal of the sciences and social politics.

38. Such writings are: *Open Society: Reforming Global Capitalism* (Public Affairs 2001); *George Soros on Globalization* (Public Affairs 2003); *The Bubble of American Supremacy: Correcting the Misuse of American Power* (Public Affairs 2003); *The Age of Fallibility: Consequences of the War on Terror* (Public Affairs 2006); *The New Paradigm for Financial Markets: The Credit Crisis of 2008 and What It Means* (May 2008); *Financial Turmoil in Europe and the United States: Essays* (Public Affairs 2012); and *The Tragedy of the European Union: Disintegration or Revival?* (Public Affairs 2014).

Bibliographical References to Chapter 6 (Vol. II)

Schumpeter J.A. (1942). *Capitalism, Socialism, and Democracy*. London, Allen & Unwin.

Soros, George. (1998). *The Crisis of Global Capitalism. Open Society Endangered*. London: Little, Brown and Company.

7

A Project for a New Worldwide, Strategic Methodology for Planning (*Under the Sponsorship of a Renovated University of the United Nations*)

7.1 The Construction of the 'Planning Accounting Framework' (*PAF*)[1]

7.1.1 Insufficiency of Purely Methodological Criticism

To the construction of the *Planning Accounting Framework* (PAF), and to its political management, will be dedicated all the Chapters of **Vol. III** of this Trilogy, on the traces of methods suggested by Ragnar Frisch and the other economists; recalled in the Chapters of **Vol. I** and revisited with non-defined criticism in the other Chapters of Volume II of this Trilogy. It would be important to avoid the risk that a mere criticism of the methodological basis of the neo-classical economics could be insufficient, and also, sometime dangerous, in creating a better programming basis for the managers of not experimented applications of the new economic policy itself. With such a critique we can, at most, contest the functionality and validity of the proposed solutions by different economic policies based on behaviours of uncertain effectiveness; solutions that can suggest actions through better instruments of analysis and forecast, but also worse.[2]

This critique has no positive or valid effect if the current method is not substituted with methods and applications deemed more valid. In fact, the

© The Author(s) 2019
F. Archibugi, *The Programming Approach and the Demise of Economics*,
https://doi.org/10.1007/978-3-319-78060-3_7

229

problem with the critique of a dominant economic policy—in its whole, or in respect to a single aspect—is that of rejecting a fallacious method, without suggesting its substitution.[3] To do this, it is not sufficient to demolish the hypothesis of *positivistic* rational behaviour: it is also necessary to propose *alternative methods*, whether of interpreted facts, or of economic management based on the availability of new data, implying direct interventions of operators and their agreements, instead of indirect interventions without any control or certainty that the operators will follow these up.

For these reasons, it is necessary to escape from obsolete controversies and go beyond the more generic theoretical disputes on '*market failure*' versus '*state (intervention) failure*', or '*free market*' versus '*public intervention*', and so on. Such disputes have never offered an improvement on the dull and 'Lapalissian' invention of the recurrent word of 'mixed economies' that history has already bequeathed to us.

Such disputes have dominated the scene, but with few results (even tragic at times) in the historical development of economic doctrines; instead to improve, year after year, on the progress of technology and the effectiveness of the programming approach, by constitutional representatives and by the other participants of 'civil associationism' leadership, politically selected.

On the contrary, would it not be desirable to know how to enter, for the first time in political history, with a praxeological approach, into a systematic analysis of the problems regarding each human community? Or organising a *systematic programming of actions* to advise on any field of public management by a temporary selection of a few choices, according at the same time to a set of priorities (by a selected majority of such priorities) temporarily chosen (and given the bounds of available resources, with an *ex ante* study, design and calculation of the results obtainable, and an *ex post* measurement of the results to be obtained) through the public and private political operators engaged, and the corresponding value of outcome benefit resulting from the resources employed?

And lastly, would it not be desirable that such a decision system of programmatic actions could be based on two indispensable functional aspects?

1. A new decisional system consistent with the strategic communitarian approach?
2. A new decisional system consistent with the systemic relationships?[4]

7.1.2 A New Political Decisional System Consistent with the 'Strategic' Approach (*and—in the Same Time—Fully 'Systemic', Spatially and Multi-structurally*)

The new decision system should include all sectors of actions simultaneously, in light of their interdependency, for which the community's government feels it necessary to assume entire responsibility for the welfare of the community of reference, but should also include the evaluation of others sectors of activity, which are not necessarily to be entrusted to public initiative and management, but that can be left to a private collective and free initiative and to autonomous private management without excessive public interference.

Such a system in its totality should also include household sectors and other forms of associations as the basic units of consumption and welfare of civil society in a unique and homogeneous vision of the community life and in a well-constructed framework of economic relationships, in the understanding that anything which happens in one sector has certain and measurable repercussions in the others.[5]

The overall evaluation of results, including those from 'civil society', should be guaranteed by monitoring those results carried out by a political authority. The dividing line between activity under the direct management of the state and activity that can be delegated to 'civil society' is not determined *a priori* since it is directly dependent on the capacity of the civil society of the system in question, to guarantee the minimum of essential results given by the economic state and the earnings of the community in question.

An essential requirement of the decisional system, based on the programming of actions, would be that of fixing or determining the objectives and the performance of the system itself, through a regular method of updating in the course of the management of the system itself. In the absence of those objectives, the decision system is reduced to chaos, and to ignoring or abandoning the programming approach.

The building of the PAF—to emphasise again—should aim at defining the principal objectives to be achieved in quantitative terms (according to the style of the design of the approach) in terms of 'targets' and 'stages', but at the same time also in terms of ex ante study and evaluation of instruments and the means needed to achieve the targets and stages (feasibility).

The participants' behaviour should not be presumed as rational, or as the objects of forecast and estimates, but should be the result of satisfying negotiations not for that which is desirable (as in 'wishful thinking') but—as the results of serious analysis—of the 'possible' and of compelling agreements of opposed interests: *governments* and *social parties*: and the creation of supplements to such agreements capable to assuring the respectable implementation of such agreements.

Such agreements (and related decisions) would serve also to seek the decisional commitment of the social parties in order to improve the situation in the ways described and programmed together with the government.

The PAF should include measurement, in terms of input of resources, to be employed (natural resources, capital and labour resources, technological resources); and measurement (again in monetary/and 'real', conventional terms) of the results obtained or expected (in an ex ante or ex post stage).

The aim is to obtain measurement through the PAF of the cost of each programmed action, whether in the phase of its initial selection or in its implementation phase, considering the social results or profit of the actions programmed.

At same time, it should give a value to the decisional engagement of the social parties for improving the situation in the ways described and commonly programmed.

These measurements should come whether ex ante results and expected results, from robustly evaluating planned actions, and also ex post results obtained at the end of each period of planning. Hence, the goal is to evaluate every detail of the decision-making process.

Once the government has built an appropriate PAF (a proposal of planning) and a framework sufficiently articulate and disaggregated of a Frischian kind (input-output of resources of a programmed system), this decisional system should be discussed,[6] with the best precision possible, but in the limits consistent to and quantitatively compatible with the model.[7] This kind of participation, whether in the design or in the implementation phase, should be assured politically on two levels:

1. the governmental level, according to the constitutional form of the community in question, selected in accordance with the contextual situation at a multinational and international level; and

2. the civil society level, with representations of the non-governmental associationism (profit and non-profit) and workers and professional unions of any kind of activity.

7.2 The Ridiculous Incapacity of the Current National and International, Economic Policies (*and the Irresponsibility of Governments in 'Navigating in the Fog'*)

So, would it not be desirable that such discussions of the PAF should be developed only in the case that the participants—governmental officers and representatives of civil society (unions and non-profit entities)—could express their views in a transparent way and that the free bargaining on the PAF could occur without prejudicial thinking systems (or ideologies) that could not be coherent and consistent with reality?

Furthermore, why could it not be feasible that free bargaining on the PAF could be introduced through procedures open also to alternative policies, again in programming modalities (connected to a vision of the real inter-relationship with each system) and that could be capable of orienting towards feasible solutions of the issues to be found and to a comprehensive vision of the socio-economic management of the political community of reference?

Why could it not become possible that the policies of governments and social parties, in order to replace current policies, trusting only in the automatic machineries (the 'invisible hand') of a theoretical economics, and in the presumption of standard behaviours of participants, often not agreed by participants themselves?

Are not these machineries and behaviours, in the majority of cases, influenced by the absence of adequate and unbiased information on the true state of things and overall on the effects, direct and indirect, negative and positive, from which it could be possible to obtain as a consequence of each category of action and of policy that could come from political debate and from the negotiations of the preferences? And why could this not arise from even the more limited scope of choices and very limited availabilities that different situations and the 'market' offer?

In addition, would it not be better that even a possible self-regulating automatism could arise from the debate and negotiations themselves, and could correspond to a full consideration of each interest group, and of the possible shared limitations offered by any individual situation and by the whole system?

In effect, this series of questions are less rhetorical than they seem. I consider them as the basic factors (nearly 'postulates') in order to change the current habits of the moment, which are approximate in managing political decisions, and in the hope of improving governmental capacity to achieve a certain impact on reality, and a better chance of implementation of intentional actions in effective actions.

In short, from these postulates depends a new mode of conceiving the radical reform of decision-making of governments, based on a new permanent form of in-depth, pre-ordered and coordinated study of the systemic relationship within the structures of the communities (societies and economies) under question, and under control and management (what people have called, for some time, *planning*).

It would be a question of a reform based on continuous permanent monitoring of the situation, with similar checking of temporal changes of those structures, in the absence of which any measure or political action of any kind (even that inspired exclusively to the mere *laissez-faire*) can surely determine what will be truly the result (negative or positive) of our own action.[8]

In the absence of the kind of such radical reform—the definition of strategic and priority objectives and systemic awareness of the community in question—governments will continue to 'navigate in the fog'.

On the contrary, following the current economic policies, people continue to debate and expect results, contrasting and superficially conflicting, without knowing and evaluating the structural interrelations (of any country or group of reference countries); and only debating on some pittance of 'knowledge' (or, better, 'prejudice') based only on *a-priori theoretical generic assumptions*, related to an '*idea of society*' (i.e. an '*ideology*'). I would say *prejudices*, normally older in the time of lived situation, belonging to behaviour not *current* with the historical situation and with the *unknown structure* of interests and needs newly manifested. Becoming—in such way—more as an *act of trust and faith* in those assumptions rather than a praxeological technical or 'scientific' *test of prove*.

We have reached the point of deciding to act on the basis of generic assumptions, instead of trying to decide to negotiate with the 'thinking' partners within the planning process itself, when an agreement can be made to engage people to fix future behaviour or act once selected by negotiations compatible with a shared optimising general common interest. Nobody, even an experienced economist, can run ahead safely without full knowledge of structural specifically measured data, without the support of an updated PAF, such as that described by Frisch and by the Oslo models memoranda.[9]

7.3 Organising a Political Consensus on the Planning Process and in Respect of the Practical Impossibility of Current Economic Policies to Govern the Situation

Further, the most experienced economists should have the humility to declare that they are also navigating in the fog, until the programming approach could organise the construction of a PAF.[10] And until that it could accurately be established as a workplace and 'negotiations room' to organise the explorations in technical negotiations and agreements with the participants of the 'game', that is, the political decision-makers.

The basis of all of this is the PAF, to which much reference has already been made in this trilogy and to which will be dedicated the entirety of **Vol. III**.

7.3.1 The Role of the PAF

The role of the PAF is that of supplying sufficient instruments and data formerly used to evaluate successful solutions without losing sight of various points of view and behaviour on behalf of the participants in the process, and to supply contracts/agreements that can intervene between interested parties.[11]

No one, even an experienced economist, without full specific structural knowledge, deliberately measured with data, relative to the effects of each single action on behalf of those who are taking advantage because by definition no one, without the reference framework proposed by Frisch and the Oslo models, is capable of evaluating the effects of the actions proposed on such a basis of ignorance.

This is why Frisch and Leontief warned many times, often obsessively, to avoid navigating in the fog.[12]

Perhaps, another metaphor would be more pertinent, one of a Leontiefian flavour, also in a seafaring environment (that we have used in **Vol. I**, Chap. 3): the navigators have the duty of disposing a *Nautical Chart and near perfect and complete instruments,* before venturing out to sea without adequate maps and instruments to measure the situation.

7.3.2 Using Knowledge to Plan Political Action

Without adequate and permanently updated cognitive structures, permanently monitored, through the framework mentioned, there are not valid recipes that are truly acceptable. In the absence of this kind of programming, the 'lords' of politics, ridiculously and ingenuously supporters of (or supported by) some famous presumed adviser (or some school of thinking), also continue to 'navigate in the fog', in spite of the macro-economic 'growth models', which yet Frisch was declaring old and unreliable working on aggregate structures, had already many times proved to be wrong.

In fact, in such conditions to 'navigate in the fog' becomes very dangerous, because we do not know the consequences of our actions, which are uncertain in their effects. And it would be right to 'sail in sight' with many stops, awaiting a 'clearing up', and even the development of an adequate and controlled geographical map (the suggestion of Frisch and Leontief).

Indeed, the most urgent action should be to create adequate maps of the socio-economic of all crisis areas: the PAF.

However, we must be aware that the essential way of restructuring and changing the economic policy is not that so far adopted, based on efforts still developed in the extended logic of the 'free market', as an optimal solution with weak controls on the capital markets and solutions, dictated only by the total subordination to the biggest operators of the financial markets; these are accustomed—in contrast to common savers—to casual or fabulous winnings, for proportionally very modest and paltry risks.

And, at the same time, in a growing welfare state, promoted by political competition and priorities, but without the 'public interest' control, assured by a planning system shared with every important associative sector of participants. A welfare state intended only as increasing public expenditure, producing the so-called 'fiscal crisis of the state', to which every nation-state has responded—and probably will have the opportunity of increase—according to its own financial robustness.

In effect, the financially weaker countries (among which are Italy and other Mediterranean countries) have responded according its own financial robustness, with a growing public debt, without serious control.

7.4   New Forms of Capital Formation

Within the current financial weaknesses can be found scandalous and uncontrolled cases of quantitative waste, which emerge by chance between one spending review (often erroneously conceived and practised and the other), but of which a good dose of responsibility lying with the apparent financial *laissez-faire*, which is most convenient for those who manoeuvre through the traffic.

In these weaker countries, an uncontrolled household consumerism have:

- from one side, improved, in amazing way, the level of consuming of the middle classes, evermore protected, by their privileges of income and cast, 'blinded' in their corporatism, increasingly 'armed' by their privileges of inheritance and social status;
- in reality, from the other side, these earnings are not—for a few decades by now—*used in the appropriate direction* ('canonic', as that is written in the handbook of economics): *real investments*, in *innovation and in productivity growth*, and in *industrial capitalization* (those that at their time produce *assets and employment opportunities*),

238 Volume II. Selected Testimonies on the Epistemological...

So such incomes have taken the preferred route towards the "*financialization*", that is that commerce of *financial* titles (through banks and businesses of representative bodies for *financial rent* operations), in search of maximizing income *without work*, with very distant bodies from the investments of productive real activities.

This have not allow to resolve with more austerity and spending performance, and better efficiency and ethical attitude in the public administration, with new officers well prepared in the improvement of the new methods of performances, in investments in the justice, fights to the fiscal evasion, the corruption and the criminality. Furthermore this 'consumerism' has been coeval also with a form of patrimonial sterilization of private wealth and capitals.

This has increased—beyond acceptable proportion—the distances:

- from one side, between *parasitic classes in a country*, which have significantly increased in many leading political and administrative classes of a country (the 'bureaucrats').
- from the other, the productive classes of entrepreneurs and workers (dependent or autonomous, intellectual or manual, public or private), whom are the true protagonists of social and economic development in their country, yet are forever more excluded from finance management.[13]

The classes, which I define as 'parasitic' (or 'rentiers') are those which have become such due to the legal regime based on hereditary historical lines. From my 'ethical' point of view, these hereditary regimes should have been supressed after a liberal and democratic revolution; if so, the hereditary assets—in my opinion—should have been appropriately taxed in *truly* democratic countries. These regimes, which heavily influence the overall productivity of a national system, upon which the well-being of citizens in that country depend, fail to produce goods and employment opportunities. Hence, it would be necessary to work towards their decline.[14]

Beginning with the mechanisms that push towards convergence (that which reduces and compresses inequality), the main force of convergence is the process of diffusion of knowledge and investment in education. The game of supply or demand, like the mobility of capital and labour, which constitutes a variant, can equally function in this sense, but in a more ambiguous and contradictory way.

Therefore, Piketty's findings—mentioned above—seem to confirm that which no other historical investigation confirms: not only the existence of a 'historical' mechanism that regulates the top-down relationship between the convergence and divergence of inequality in the distribution of income and wealth, but also that is useless to even look for a 'dynamic' of this phenomenon (intended in the positivist sense). And that, therefore, if we want to operate in that sense we must address ourselves only to the political will and to the consensus, democratically understood.

To be complete (though the programming approach proposed in this book would serve precisely for this reason in the future), research of this kind—founded on the hope of discovering a 'positivistic' dynamic, which is nevertheless still predominantly in the economy, even when it has been thrown out from a planning vision and agreement—none of the followers of Myrdal, Frisch, Tinbergen and other past authors tied to an approach of economic theory epistemologically overturned would have ever undertaken.

This situation, together with many other situations, present also in less capitalist countries in which capitalism had different impacts, can be different from those mentioned as typical of some of the less advanced countries (such as some Mediterranean countries, and some other Eastern Europe countries, more recently liberated from totalitarian regimes). This suggests the abandoning of any further research of recipes and policies based on 'macro-economic models' that have been more or less useful to clarify the trend of business (especially financial and commercial trends, at brief terms), but are at same time totally incapable of measuring the structural changes of the economy in their aggregated traditional phenomena in monetary values, in the medium and long term.

This kind of situation suggests other approaches to use what we call (on the traces of the economists better known in **Vol. I** of this Trilogy) the decisional use of the disaggregated models following more detailed actions, case by case, conform to every situation subject to the analysis, and covered by and intense programming analysis (done possibly with the multiple actions of the government and negotiating, possibly with the representatives of the main branches of Civil Society, with the maximum cooperation of the operators, made conscious of the existent, unavoidable, limits and bounds, of each political community).

The programming approach of each area of action, taking account of strategic and systemic limitations of the operating 'unity', is the most efficient and recommended instrument for arriving at the optimal decision by the leadership of any political community in question.[15]

So, these situations suggest rather much more integration of institutional federative policies between those single countries and stronger multinational experiences with related substantial loss of national sovereignty, which, at the moment, do not seem a prelude of great economic progress, but only occasion of conflict, enmity, hostility, antagonisms and dangerously egoistic.

7.5 A New, Universal Income Policy?

7.5.1 The Income Policy from Endogenous to Exogenous Concept

The programming approach (PA) has a first effect on *Economics*: it repels its analytical, positive use, and exalts its programming aspect. This means that people are obliged to introduce in their international models at least some 'independent' variables, simultaneous or separated, exogenously or endogenously, in any experimental use of interrelational modeling of variables, on which to build a model corresponding to that of political decision-makers in planning process, in order in their use of experimental international models among variables, on which the models such as preventive proof of outcomes are built.

All economists deserving, for studied achieved, to be acknowledged as economists, from left or rights, from any school of thinking or trend, leaving in their free-days, their language geometrical, algebraic or cybernetic, collected in a huge quantity of writing, difficult to utilize with general understanding, used only for purpose of pragmatic applications, in real situation of political choice which seem to go not beyond some political-historic experimentation, and some happy occasional application, as short game of clubs, resulting in some historical complex events for the oblivion or of ignored 'success', should be necessary ready to elaborate some normative preferences or negotiation in collective bargaining.

7.5.2 Connecting Income to Better Job Evaluation

An urgent initiative in the line of actions towards a rationalising and reduction of the economic inequalities, inherited from a past in which modern day society, despite its pretext of a welfare policy, which it still has been unable to heal or improve on a national, international, global, regional or company scale with opportune political and social strategies promoted by governments, by the world of civil society and above all by the unions in order to introduce (first, in the area of the public administration and then in the area of the companies), with a deeply innovative spirit, and the analysis and techniques of job evaluation.

Such techniques have been used in some large companies with mixed results, in relation to modernity of countries and structures and the quality of available personnel and overall in the countries in which a paternalistic tradition is not yet dominant.

Certainly each experience virtually experimental and normative, should be applied keeping in mind the inevitable spontaneous counter-effects of opposition that tended to pass systems that, although used until now, had never gotten a success on the in regard to the target of fighting the social inequality within the productive unities.

In the society of tomorrow, one should use and obtain the technical analysis of jobs for every kind of work performed in every political community, through a system of organisation of programmes and work that always conforms not to tradition and traditional competence, but to ability of a management, ever more finalised toward a technical analysis and programs of an 'engineering type' to implement—easier than the traditional one, but innovative, in comparison a confrontation on a vast scale, of jobs connected to the programming approach and adoption of special methods (now consolidated) of strategic planning.

A method destined to a diffused and operational knowledge without limitations after that it was adopted by the Congress of the United States in 1993, for a renewal of the entire federal government, and all of the 50 federal agencies, a renewal that was popularised as a 'reinvention of government'.[16]

Furthermore, these analyses of single jobs should be strictly applied to the function and coordination in the planning of the labour market connected to the introduction of methods of strategic planning in every operating community on different scales.

7.6 Towards a 'New' Economic Paradigm?

In order to understand what the new 'paradigm' is, which is also often defined as 'new economic thought', we can refer to some of the more recent writings of Joseph Stiglitz, the economist well-known for having played an important role in the USA and international economic policies, one acknowledged by academia and the media.[17]

The poor validity of models, and their low significance for any efficient future political structure of change based on them, suggests—as Joseph Stiglitz argues—a radical change in approach from positive to programmatic in the later development of economic theory.[18]

In fact, in a pithy letter to the *Financial Times* (10 August 2010), Joseph Stiglitz criticises 'economists' due to their incapacity to prevent the latest severe economic crisis, which is still ongoing:

> The blame game continues over *who* is responsible for the world recession since the Great Depression—the financiers who did such a bad job of managing risk or the regulators who failed to stop them. But the economics profession bears more than a little culpability. It provided the models that gave comfort to regulators that markets could be self-regulated; that they were efficient and self-correcting. The efficient markets hypothesis—the notion that market prices fully revealed all the relevant information—ruled the day. Today, not only is our economy in a shambles but so too is the economic paradigm that predominated in the years before the crisis. (Stiglitz 2010b)

Such a change of paradigm is something that has increasingly involved the new generations of economists, and the similarity—in some ways—with the positions of the rebel economists of the older generations (such as those to whom the method described in this book refers). This obliges me to examine as rapidly as possible if, in the position of Stiglitz (and the movement that took shape under the Institute for New Economic Thinking) can be something that could be similar to the comprehension of methodological error, common in the overall scientific community of economists, of passing from an approach of positive analysis to an approach of systematic programming, as sustained by this book.

Stiglitz rightly amused himself by ridiculing the assumptions on which the macro-economic models (that Frisch had called since the 1950s, the useless and meaningless 'growth models'—in respect of those 'decisional' models deserving only of being used in the planning processes) have been built and Federal Reserve confided to base the official policy of the American government and control of events, and that failed in warning that the 2008 crisis was coming.[19]

For instance, the assumptions that 'demand had to equal supply—and that meant there could be no unemployment' led Stiglitz to make an amusing comment: 'Right now a lot of people are just enjoying an extra dose of leisure; and if they are unhappy it is a matter for psychiatry, not economics.' Irony more than justified!

However, more than a century since our economist colleagues, called 'but institutionalists', mention many cases on which it is suitable to be ironic like this, the cases in regard for neo-classical economists have developed their econometric analysis, starting from imprudent theoretical assumptions which it was impossible to rely upon for any effective economic policy.[20]

Stiglitz continued his criticisms in a more specific way of the macro-economic models used for control of financialisation.

> It is hard for non-economists to understand how peculiar the predominant macroeconomic models were. Many assumed demand had to equal supply—and that meant there could be no unemployment. (Right now a lot of people are just enjoying an extra dose of leisure; why they are unhappy is a matter for psychiatry, not economics.). Many used 'representative agent models'—all individuals were assumed to be identical, and this meant there could be no meaningful financial markets (who would be lending money to whom?). Information asymmetries, the cornerstone of modern economics, also had no place: they could arise only if individuals suffered from acute schizophrenia, an assumption incompatible with another of the favoured assumptions, full rationality. (Stiglitz 2010b)

But here we ask: In what sense the 'information asymmetries' are to be considered 'the cornerstone of modern economics'?

Stiglitz's criticism is that of econometrics of the financial flows, where 'everything is equal to the other' and they do not occur—with an analysis more differentiated or more disaggregated, those 'asymmetric situations' that could suggest policies as much differentiated and effective.[21]

Stiglitz says:

> [B]ad models lead to bad policy: central banks, for instance, focused on the small economic inefficiencies arising from inflation to the exclusion of the far greater inefficiencies arising from dysfunctional financial markets and asset price bubbles. After all, their models said that financial markets were always efficient. Remarkably, standard macroeconomic models did not even incorporate adequate analyses of banks.
>
> No wonder former Federal Reserve chairman Alan Greenspan, in his famous *mea culpa,* could express his surprise that banks did not do a better job at risk management. The real surprise was his surprise: even a cursory look at the perverse incentives confronting banks and their managers would have predicted short-sighted behaviour with excessive risk-taking.
>
> The standard models should be graded on their predictive ability—and especially their ability to predict in circumstances that matter. Increasing the accuracy of forecast in normal times (knowing whether the economy will grow at 2.4 per cent or 2.5 per cent) is far less important than knowing the risk of a major recession. In this the models failed miserably, and the predictions of policymakers based on them have, by now, totally undermined their credibility. Policymakers did not see the crisis coming, said its effects were contained after the bubble burst, and thought the consequences would be far more short-lived and less severe than they have been.
>
> Fortunately, while much of the mainstream focused on these flawed models, numerous researchers were engaged in developing alternative approaches. Economic theory had already shown that many of the central conclusions of the standard model were not robust—that is, small changes in assumptions led to large changes in conclusions. Even small information asymmetries, or imperfections in risk markets, meant that markets were not efficient. Celebrated results, such as Adam Smith's invisible hand, did not hold; the invisible hand was invisible because it was not there. Few today would argue that bank managers, in their pursuit of their self-interest, had promoted the wellbeing of the global economy.
>
> Monetary policy affects the economy through the availability of credit—and the terms on which it is made available, especially to small-and-medium-sized enterprises. Understanding this requires us to analyse banks and their interaction with the shadow banking sector. The spread between

the Treasury bill rate and lending rates can change markedly. With a few exceptions, most central banks paid little attention to systemic risk and the risks posed by credit inter-linkages. Years before the crisis, a few researchers focused on these issues, including the possibility of the bankruptcy cascades that were to play out in such an important way in the crisis. This is an example of the importance of modelling carefully complex interactions among economic agents (households, companies, banks)—interactions that cannot be studied in models in which everyone is assumed to be the same. Even the sacrosanct assumption of rationality has been attacked: there are systemic deviations from rationality and consequences for macroeconomic behaviour that need to be explored. (Stiglitz 2010b, emphases added)

And then he concludes in more general terms:

Changing paradigms is not easy. Too many have invested too much in the wrong models. Like the Ptolemaic attempts to preserve earth-centric views of the universe, there will be heroic efforts to add complexities and refinements to the standard paradigm. The resulting models will be an improvement and policies based on them may do better, but they too are likely to fail. Nothing less than a paradigm shift will do. (Stiglitz 2010b)

And so he adds:

But a new paradigm, I believe, is within our grasp: the intellectual building blocks are there and the Institute for New Economic Thinking is providing a framework for bringing the diverse group of scholars striving to create this new paradigm together. What is at stake, of course, is more than just the credibility of the economics profession or that of the policymakers who rely on their ideas: it is the stability and prosperity of our economies. (Stiglitz 2010b)

Nevertheless, it is necessary to ask ourselves: is not what has already been done up until now—with Stiglitz in the first row—stressing the question of 'asymmetric models' with disaggregate and more realistic models?

Stiglitz, overall, does not claim that there is the need to courageously abandon phony econometrics—as Frisch attempted to do in the last 10 years of his life—driving the minds of economists (with both 'positivistic' and 'monetary' DNA) to reason in terms of the real economy?

246   Volume II. Selected Testimonies on the Epistemological...

And this reasoning in terms of the real economy should not be an instrument of labour used directly by the governments but also by civil society, and should not depend on the studies of multinational corporations that are all busy in absurd and perverse 'financial' games, without any interest in the 'physical' progress of real economic productivity?

Here, I would add, without doubt, that the '*New economic paradigm*'—about which Stiglitz speaks (and about which we still feel greatly *the absence of any kind of implementation* from the different speakers) was it not perhaps already conceived and supported fifty years ago in Oslo (Norway) in the Institute of Economics of that University, and it was put into construction by the *methodology of planning*, and more particularly by the methodology of the 'Programming approach', in the Frischian and Leontefian 'spirit' of Planning?

7.6.1 The Dispute Between the 'Growth Models'

The dispute—clear enough between both paradigms[22]—occurred, even if without many external effects,[23] taking the aspects within the econometric studies in the field of economics between the growth models concept and method on one side, and the decisional models concept and method, on the other.

As we have illustrated and explained in this book, the former is based on a positivist epistemology,[24] the latter on a programming epistemology, which the related policy makers and the academic profession do not wish to discuss.

However that framework (PAF), of which I will give technical details in **Vol. III** of this work, did not have, at Frisch's death—a great acceptance and reception, because it—following the logic of the programming approach—has been not followed from an huge quantity of real statistical data (as enquiries, polls, surveys, and so on), strongly coordinated at national, multinational and planetary scales, not yet existing, did not give impulse to the research of further data, with a constant measure of reference (real-monetary)—going beyond over-aggregated data and some misleading effects of the National Accounting System. That framework would have had need of an amount of research based on its own configu-

A Project for a New Worldwide, Strategic Methodology...   247

ration. It should be interested and extended to the detailed exploration of all basic human and social needs of world communities.

The Frischian Framework did not further elicit,[25] but nor in a re-direction of the *System of National Accounting*, that begun by the current system of economic accounting, reproduced in some OECD, countries after the end of the WW2, and later imitated—where possible, in other countries of the United Nations, built, (like that of Frisch) unfortunately on the conceptual-structural framework of the traditional *Economics*—in the sequence Quesnay-Smith-Ricardo-Marshall-Mitchell-Stone.

Leaving aside the 'dogmatic' aspects of mainstream economics, it would find a better connection with the political, institutional and democratic powers of governments, seizing back from the more privileged categories of operators the control the effect and consequence of different measures or actions, or decisions made as strictly as possible by important institutions, in a satisfying procedure of negotiations and free agreements.

Nor is it to be forgotten that the building of the PAF proceeded with the programming approach, through a permanent and innovative elaboration, which did not have clear success, because it was obliged to produce a huge quantity of statistical data, mostly non-existent and mostly to reach with enquiries, polls, and other ad-hoc surveys, in the field of social preferences, by group, and collective subjects, on their whole very far from being available and organisable, without a strong, very strong, voluntary impulse of the government authorities, congruous with first time availability for its assessment, time, that is the primary factor among the means needed for a true national planning (which are already, in themselves, the conditions for a radical change of interest of governmental action).

In sum, the *Framework* (**PAF**) of Frisch, its building, its management, are not only, an academic product destined to be published in a university paper, but overall a *political engagement*, clear and firm, of a *planning process* in the governmental decision-making method, in and with full awareness of the members of the policy rulers (members of Governments and of other *institutional bodies*) regarding:—their intentional consequence of effects, once ascertained the feasibility of its choices and the availability of the means; and—the cooperation of technicians, economists operational researchers, planners etc., to operate according the requests of the *decision-makers*, and not only to give 'advice' to them because external to the decision programming process.

The **PAF** of Frisch, now produced from the Governments, (or of Governments more or less, discussed and negotiated with the social parties (at national or multinational scale), is going by itself, beyond the aggregate behaviours and flows of revealed phenomena of traditional economic accounting (GNP), by now adapted and used (and greatly digest) across the globe. But scholars throughout the world ask if it has been 'reformed' in the sense of being richer and tied to the detailed exploration of all aspects of human and social needs in real terms.[26] And—regardless of the dogma of orthodox economics (*mainstream economics*)—that Framework would have found an easier connection with the political and democratic powers of the governments, tearing away from the hands of privileged operators of capital flows (or of the 'invisible hand') the power (less invisible) of the regulation of such flows. This, at the time, was prevented at its birth (at the end of the Sixties) with the conservative regurgitation in the economy (so-called 'Reagan's political economy'); but more for the naivety of the economists tied to their positivistic dogma of origin, than for their ability and wisdom of thought.

If we want to talk about a 'new paradigm', we must yet observe that the newness (in Frisch and his followers) was in the fact that it would not be questioned to dispose—through macroeconomic models more or less aggregate, more or less asymmetric—of better forecasting the damage of a spontaneous *laissez-faire*, with greater details on the same economic trend.

As I have said already, the contraposition between these two types of models has been the classic theme of the 1950s and 1960s of conflict between Frisch and other econometric colleagues (amply discussed in **Vol. I** of this trilogy).

In Frisch's kind of modelling, and in the programming approach about which this work is engaged, being no more about 'forecasting', that 'paradigm', or model, would be useful only for obtaining decisional simulations of feasible events, connected to the achievement of possible political or programming trends. So for the so called 'new paradigm', the priority of the economic thinking, probably would be to give simply implementation—although hard and complex could be the modalities for such implementation—to the construction and to the political use of the PAF. It is not necessary to search too far for this new economic thinking. It will sufficient open to an effective place and function to a PAF del *Frischian* **PAF** without the obstacles, the contentions, the dubiousness, the oppositions, so religiously hearth to became fast some dogmas coming from the same theory.

7.6.2 The Issue of Expections in Traditional Economic Policy, More or Less Followed by the Competents Operators

The discourse is instead—in certain limits, defined by Frisch (it can be seen in his numerous citations presented in this book)—about ....*substituting* intelligently by *laisser-faire*, and to predispose 'anticipated', strategic and feasible management of economy,[27] not the one, which makes us suppose the phrasing of Stiglitz in the quotation.

In other terms, the point is not only that '*standard models should have been classified according their capacity to make prognosis*' as Stiglitz suggests. This claim, which is as true, as obvious, in the field of *traditional economy* has been already made in the precedent pages of econometric specialist reviews or essays (using apparent authoritativeness and worships to many economists) but has not been transferred to any experimental practice in the economical politics of governments or international or worldly *Institutions*. Hence, *nowhere they were translated for building or practical usage of Governments'* **PAF** *of adequate type*, the type suggested by Frisch.

Surely, the work for constructing **PAF**, in every country as well as in the international or worldly scale, for making **PAFs** of the countries more coherent between each other, would be *immense*. It would require *united forces of dozens of dozens of economists, statisticians, political scientists and formulators of operative norms*, in enormous numbers. The individuals would disappear, would be substituted by expert accepting and high standard of cooperation to the commonly described by work program as college of direction would be recommended by staff of the United Nations Organization. This is the *real problem*, which makes the blood in veins tremble!

But we have nothing to 'conceive' new ways and new 'thoughts'. There are only few practical organizational problems and new researches, in the limits of the aims of buildings the needed PAF, national and international.

Is it all this utopian? Maybe. However we all know that, sooner or later, this is just what will happen, with the *stop and go* typical for human history, of the incessant *walk* of organization and creativity of the human intelligence. In our case the needed PAFs, also by the economists and other experts with negative resistance that restrain and sabotage them (like the un-meaningful 'sovranists', and other experts justified that believe to be the most realists, but they do not known—poor men—the first to stand out).

For Frisch, the 'growth models' *may not have any forecasting capacity*, (as Stiglitz would request them), because of being structured on a misunderstanding presupposed by real and circumstantial data and then false, for own nature.

They could change nature (from 'growth models' to '*decisional models*'), but on the basis of a *very different approach*; that would introduce in the **PAF**, also, with these *variables which could make them consistent with some control and intervention of policies, in their turn, seriously to weigh on the reality*.

However, about all this, in the real world, and in spite of the big hub-bub of economic opinions, invaded by the media and the thousand of proposals coming from the different places of thinking and also places of governments, about *some optimizing economic decisions*, without any serious proofs and certainties of results obtained, but only a sterile debate, on wrong hypothesis that have destroyed any confidence in any kind of economic reasoning, and the building itself of any PAF of experimental type, behind which mobilize a whole nation (or coalition of nations).

7.6.3 So, What May We Intend—Then—with 'New Paradigm'?

So, once we have acknowledged that there is no 'invisible hand' to be respected or violated (as Stiglitz asserts on every recent occasion), there remains only the task—for the government of the communities in question—to follow and to deepen, and render as visible as possible, the hands of all actors participating in the game, or touched by the system.

At the same time, it should be useful for the governments to encourage lines of action to monitor and evaluate what was only imagined as automatic effects, with the real and clear effects of movements occurred. In

A Project for a New Worldwide, Strategic Methodology... 251

particular, this would improve the knowledge and the real loss and gains of all participants in the game.

It should be necessary to seek to decide based on the realisation of one scenario of a programmatic type that is clear and pre-defined with the tools of an informative framework necessary and coherent with the objectives and feasibility planned.

And this should possibly be under the decisional control of the authentic constitutional representatives of the population.

In the new logic (perhaps it would be better to say new epistemology) the real and effective instrument (rather than fantastical and un-necessarily odd) to obtain this, is that of configuring multiple horizons in the short, medium and long term, an overall accounting framework of the variables at play, some of which are 'exogenous' and some 'endogenous' to the model;[28] all are interconnected and involved in the ordered development of events.[29] To this end, I must add the PAF already described by Frisch and his followers (including myself).

Some perplexities remain about what this 'new paradigm' should mean—for Stiglitz and the Institute of New Economic Thinking.

In a passage by the same scholar, he declares that:

> too many have invested into *wrong models* and they will happen heroic efforts in order to achieve complexities and refinements to the standard paradigm. The resulting models will constitute an improvement, and the policies based on them will may better. However, even they will be destined to fail (Stiglitz 2010b)

This latter observation would lead one to hope that also for Stiglitz this no longer means making more disaggregated and more 'refined' the 'standard models', but—with the programming approach that overturns that of positivism and that could represent the new paradigm—could mean progress towards decisional models connected to the existence of such a PAF, corresponding to that prefigured by Frisch in his writings of the 1960s.

So for the so called 'new paradigm' la *priorità* del pensiero economico, sarebbe probabilmente nel dare *semplice attuazione* – per quanto siano ardue e complesse le modalità di tale attuazione – alla costruzione e all'uso politico del **PAF**. Non c'è bisogno, per carità, di andare a cercare troppo

252 Volume II. Selected Testimonies on the Epistemological...

lontano, per questo '*nuovo pensiero economico*. Basterebbe dare luogo effettivo e operatività alla operatività del **PAF** *Frischiano*, senza gli ostacoli, le contestazioni, le incertezze, le opposizioni, tanto religiosamente sentite da diventare quasi dogmatiche, che provengono dalla stessa 'teoria'.[30]

The Frischian framework (PAF) is, I repeat, the same that we have described in the chapters of **Vol. I** and **Vol. III**; we will return once again at the conclusion of this chapter, in Sect. 7.7, **Vol. II**, concluding the examination of two other directions of research and work that constitute an extension of the programming approach to two other sectors of work:

A. The aggregation of the theme of the *revisitation and relaunch of the planning*, will provide a contribution, in my view to see as decisive to a new consolidated *method of planning*.

It involves:

a) the developments, even more difficult (except in the USA) of "*strategic planning*" of the secure adoption as innovation of management of the Public Administrations after the success obtained by the American federal agencies and in many other countries; (the GPRA 1993) of the 'USA Senate' for which see also Archibugi 2007).

b) a revision of the socio-economic accounting and monetary, of the social product, but also to other to other measures more reliable now for some decades developed in the sector of spatial, urban and territorial planning, by '*the theory of planning*'.

B. The divergence—quite clear between the two paradigms[31]—was consumed without great external effects without the availability of media communication—not taking the form, within increasingly hegemonic econometric studies, between the concept of 'growth models' on one hand and on the other, 'decisional models' (now amply illustrated and explained in this book). The former based on positivist epistemology and the second on a 'programmed' that the professionals did not want to know about.[32]

Nevertheless that Framework (**PAF**) of which we paid particular attention in the **Vol. III** of this book, did not enjoy a great diffusion because through the *Programming approach*, there were no further follow-ups after the death of Frisch aimed at continuous pace of research towards a constant improvement of its configuration; it did not solicit further debate, neither among the assistants of Frisch, nor in the external followers, in the vast world of researchers in other research centres around the world.[33]

Therefore, Frisch's framework is not only the academic product of research, but a political commitment, one clear and decisive for a change in the management of government in the direction of a new awareness and intentions and political results that could be achieved. To this two aspects of the technical-scientific advancement of the programming approach I will dedicate the next Chap. 8 (**Vol. II**) though *in very brief and synthetic way.*

The search for full independence from politics to understand the feasibility of its own choices and the availability of the means and the knowledge to decide.

The full availability of technicians, economists, operative researchers, planners and so on, to operate according to the demand for certain effects and consequences of political decision-makers and not only giving their own advice to political decision-makers.

Frisch's PAF, now with the government (or governments more or less cohesive in a multinational action) goes far beyond the behaviour and aggregate flows of phenomena surveyed by traditional economic accounting now adopted and in use (and digested with great approximation) in countries all around the world. For some time, scholars have asked it to be reformed in the sense that it should be enriched and connected with the detailed exploration of all aspects of human and social needs in real terms of the community.[34]

Aside from the dogma of orthodox economics (mainstream economics)—that framework would have found a simpler connection with political and democratic powers of governments, snatching it from the hands of the privileged operators the flows of capital (and the invisible hand) the power (less invisible) of the regulation of such flows.

254   Volume II. Selected Testimonies on the Epistemological...

This was impeded from being created (at the end of the 1960s) with the conservative redirection of the economy (the economic policy of Reagan) but more for the insipience of economists linked to their paradigm of a positivist origin rather than for their ability.

If we intend to speak of a 'new paradigm' we must, however, observe that the innovative feature (in Frisch and his followers) lies in the fact that it no longer means making available, through more or less disaggregated, more or less asymmetrical macroeconomic models a prediction of the possible damage of a spontaneous *laissez-faire* approach with major details on the same economic direction.

7.7   New Results Re-discovering Operational Theorems of Economic Policy (*Based on Frischian and Tinbergenian Methodology*)

The Lucas critique became the bible of mainstream economics, highly critical of economic policy. It has been shared by some generations of economists, until recently.

The first 'critique' of Lucas critique was finally contained in a book published in 2013 (see Acocella et al. 2013).

> It was based on the consideration that 'from a theoretical point of view, the Lucas critique underscores the presence of reciprocal interactions between the behavior of private agents and that of the government. In particular, the private sector plays an active rather than passive role, changing its behavior as expectations about government behavior change. The critique is a response to the fact that the traditional approach to the economic policy does not admit this sort of interaction. Once we recognize the fact that the behavioral functions of private agents can themselves change in relation to public choices, we have to accept that both government and private agents must consider the reciprocal responses to their decisions. This suggests we need a change of approach, to move from a parametric to a strategic context. The usual and easy solution is to introduce rational expectations. However, the most natural way to tackle the problem is to make use of game theory, since dynamic games are specifically structured to model strategic interactions between agents and in any case nest rational

expectations models as a particular case …' (Source: Acocella, Bartolomeo, Hughes Hallett, *The theory of economic Policy in a strategic contest*, Cambridge University Press, 2013, pp. 88–89).

The 'critique' of the Lucas critique started from the realization that rational expectations (REs) are equivalent to a strategic context. This conclusion is thus in favour of the system of Programming Approach as described in our whole Trilogy, which has as its basic intentional work a real coordination of all kinds of traditional interventions of economic policy as well as the invention of new policies, in order to respect the basic Tinbergen rule for controllability. Thus, while discovering new policy instruments such as quantitative easing, forward guidance, macro-prudential policies, this Approach requires their coordination with old instruments, such as collective bargaining with the representatives of the most important social interest groups, in a unitary coordination both internally and at an international level.

Now we must be aware of the need for an advanced step toward the rescue of the economic policy as promoted in the Tinbergen decisional modeling incrementing his deep reasonings to help with more organic and controlled solutions than those that we are offered by the Rational Expectations (REs) of the old individualistic memories, but based on an ample and effective collective bargaining.

But even numerous other American economists have shared this criticism, transforming as a reaction to a policy driven system by the conflicting objectives of gamers:

The most powerful objection leveled at the Tinbergen approach has been the Lucas critique: every policy introduced into an economy generates a reaction by the private sector or other policymakers that invalidates the premise upon which the original policy interventions were calculated. Taken literally, this means that all policies designed in a parametric context are in vain because they will have different effects than intended and perhaps no effect at all. This chapter illustrates the critique and shows that it reflects strategic interactions between rational players/policymakers, often implicitly modeled by using REs. Finally, it emphasizes that the resolution of the critique is to take the underlying policy game into account explicitly. (Source: Acocella and ass., Ibidem, 2013, pp. 83–84)

256 Volume II. Selected Testimonies on the Epistemological...

Again, explained by Nicola Acocella in another book, by himself composed, *Rediscovering Economic Policy as a Discipline*.

A better illustration of Lucas critique could perceived reading directly the full text in the book cited by Acocella and ass., pp. 83–94.

7.7.1 The Essence of the Lucas Critique

Extending the Lucas critique, (acc. the summing up of Acocella-Di Bartolmeo-Hughes-Hallett Italo-British group, remembered) is maintained among other arguments, this interesting considerations:

The analytical models used as a basis for decision models are normally the product of a combination of theory and econometric analysis that establishes the exact specification and numerical form of the behavioral functions and independent variables, as well as the values of the parameters. Econometric assessments are based on the available data about the relevant variables in past situations (characterized by the presence of certain external shocks, or certain types of policy). After testing, the model is used to forecast the consequences of particular policy changes; e.g., an increase in government spending, an optimal monetary policy design. This is, however, accomplished by taking as given and invariant the estimated values of the parameters and the form of the behavioral functions of private agents (e.g., the propensity to consume, the form of consumption function) in the new situation. But there is no guarantee that those values or functional forms would remain constant. Suppose that government spending had not been adjusted in previous years, or that any adjustment in the past had involved different forms of spending: e.g., investment in place of government consumption and transfers; or had involved certain types of government spending (teachers' salaries) rather than others (student canteens). A change in the volume and/or content of public expenditure may give rise to new forms of private behavior. For example, a program to increase the number of student canteens might change students' propensity to consume so that it differed from that estimated in econometric models based on data collected before the number of canteens was increased.

If model parameters do change, reflecting a change in the behavior of the system, but the "old" model is taken as a constraint in government decision making, the ensuing policies will not be optimal at all. They would be so

A Project for a New Worldwide, Strategic Methodology... 257

only if private behavior did not change. In other words, the constraint underlying the design of government action is not a guaranteed constraint but is likely to change as government behavior itself changes. (Source: Acocella and ass., Ibidem, pp. 84–85)

7.7.2 Deep Parameters and Rational Expectations: A Resolution?

Acknowledging the Lucas critique, there are, according Acocella and associated, a number of ways to redefine the public decision process in a more satisfactory fashion, at least at the theoretical level:

One way to circumvent Lucas' critique is to focus directly on *deep parameters* which can ensure the stability of the relation. Deep parameters are those that appear in the functions describing consumer tastes and technology, which should not change in any systematic way as a result of changes in economic circumstances and the countercyclical policies.

A shortcoming of the approach based on fixed deep parameters concerns the tendency of these parameters to drift. Lucas raised his critique at a time when Keynesian macroeconometric models were highly respected as tools for quantitative policy evaluations. Despite this, he stressed that the methods used in econometric forecasting were often found to contradict the assumption that agents' behavioral rules were fixed and, as a result, the coefficients in the more important forecasting equations were frequently adjusted. Lucas left this drift process in the coefficients unexplained. Neither macroeconomic theory nor the RE econometric models constructed after Lucas' critique explain this drift phenomenon. And, although the econometric forecasting literature has taken the issue of coefficient drift increasingly seriously, it still offers no economic explanation of it. Parameter drift is therefore a key piece of evidence that government's beliefs about the economy and its policies toward inflation and stabilization have evolved over time.

A way to derive a consistent relationship between economic targets and instruments based on deep parameters is by introducing REs. This solution is, however, just a way to circumvent the main argument against the

258   **Volume II. Selected Testimonies on the Epistemological...**

Tinbergen-Theil theory of economic policy: the existence of strategic interactions between the policymaker and other agents. It is nevertheless convenient because it implies an implicit consideration of the strategic interactions between government and private sector as REs can be introduced into the decision maker's constraints formulated in term of deep parameters only after introducing and solving the private sector's optimization problem. In a simple static context, as we shall see in the next chapter, doing this is typically equivalent to solving a Stackelberg game...

This chapter argues that drift can better be explained by formulating public decision making in an explicit strategic manner. This means considering the strategic interactions between policymakers, or between policymakers and private agents, extended perhaps to include learning and the possibility of model misspecifications. (Source: Acocella and ass., Ibidem, pp. 87–88)

7.7.3 Overcoming the Critique

[T]he Lucas critique,—maintain Acocella and ass.—is undoubtedly well founded and raises both practical and theoretical problems. At the practical level, -the amount by which parameters change in response to the change in economic policies is important. If the change is small, designing policy on the basis of previously estimated values will be broadly reliable. Obviously, reliability also depends on the data set used to estimate the parameters: the larger the set and the more it encompasses situations in which different policies were in use, the less the parameters will vary and the greater is the reliability of the model's determination of optimal policies. In the 1970s many macroeconomic relationships broke down as a consequence of major changes in the policy regime (for example, the Phillips curve) as agents adjusted their behavior and future expectations to fit the new environment.

However, from theoretical point of view the Lucas critique underscores

the presence of reciprocal interactions between the behavior of private agents and that of the government. In particular, the private sector plays an

A Project for a New Worldwide, Strategic Methodology... 259

active rather than passive role, changing its behavior as expectations about government behavior change. The critique is a response to the fact that the traditional approach to the economic policy does not admit this sort of interaction. Once we recognize the fact that the behavioral functions of private agents can themselves change in relation to public choices, we have to accept that both government and private agents must consider the reciprocal responses to their decisions. This suggests we need a change of approach, to move from a parametric to a strategic context. The usual and easy solution is to introduce REs. However, the most natural way to tackle the problem is to make use of game theory, since dynamic games are specifically structured to model strategic interactions between agents and in any case nest RE models as a particular case as we show in the next section. The rest of this book is about this strategic view of economic policy management.

Questions raised by the Lucas' critique have a specific relevance for the evolution of agents' conduct and market performance since the 1980s. The spread of economic knowledge, liberalization and international opening of markets, the rising importance of financial markets and the speed of changes in those markets all imply the formation and spread of forward-looking expectations. By their nature, these features mean that sudden changes are possible, but follow rules that are difficult to detect.

There are at least two consequences relevant for economic policy:

(a) First, economic trends are more often the outcome of conventions and "fads." In this situation only public policy can move the economy out of a liquidity trap, unemployment, and, more generally, undesired or undesirable equilibria.

(b) Public policy must take account of the active nature of private agents' conduct as well as the effects policy has on the formation of market expectations. Hence, public action should not breed expectations that make it ineffective. On the contrary, it should try to create expectations that generate desirable outcomes. How to do that is investigated in detail in Chap. 12. It reflects some necessary features of public policy that may limit the range of feasible policy, but that if used in combination with announcements ("forward guidance" in Federal Reserve language) of future policies can actually enhance their power.

In summary, the evolution of economic systems, while making public intervention more necessary, may also impose some restrictions on the range of effective policies.

The importance of financial markets in these conclusions cannot be overstated. They are the main mechanism for channeling the influence of expectations and, hence, for creating limits to or enhancements of the effectiveness of public policy. This is because expectations in financial markets change more rapidly or more sensitively than in other markets. Since financial instruments are promises rather than physical objects, by their very nature they express evaluations of the future to a larger extent than physical assets do. Nevertheless, financial assets, like physical assets, have a value in the present. At different points in the subsequent analysis we will underscore the interaction between public action and private agents' behavior through the influence of public action on private expectations. (Source: Acocella and ass., Ibidem, pp. 88–90)

Again, explained by Nicola Acocella in another book, *Rediscovering Economic Policy as a Discipline,* in the course of the publication, also at Cambridge. Without any mathematical language, but intelligently and logically expressed.

This further work, is full of good ideas in favor of a system of *Programming Approach* as described in our whole Trilogy which has as the basic intentional work, a real *coordination of all kinds of traditional intervention of economic policy,* a coordination (macro-prudential policies) at any international level, responding to a 'systemic' approach with a methodology of 'collective bargaining' directly managed by the government; at a simultaneous discussion by the representatives of the most important social interest groups, in a unitary coordination.

In the book of Nicola Acocella the ways of determining the consequences and the effectiveness of the financial crisis are specially dealt with. Searching for new rules for the public budget as defined in the following chapters (Chaps. 8 and 9) of this **Vol. II**. It is recommended that to fight inequalities, it is necessary to elaborate on the Debt Target Rules and monitoring with the strategic planning in its system of annual reporting and five year reporting as implicit in the Strategic Planning itself as applied happily at the end of the past century by the federal government (USA) (see the following Chap. 9).

One problem, do not forget that a lot of the criticism (Lucas type, see next) of the lack of control of the target of a too simple and too aggregate modelling in the case described by Tinbergen and concluding in the *critical rediscovering of the economic policy as a discipline*, even sophisticated in the academic seminars, doesn't mean to develop an alternative in terms of new escamotage against the Lucas kind of criticism, but only a new structuring of the way to bring the state agencies and also the private action to be independent again, from the state and multi-national organism but to make more coordinated and interdependent, the rules of the multi-national action, as strange as it may seem—we give the actual trends in World cohabitation.

The apparent decline of World cohabitation is a marginal effect of an unavoidable and more than certain stronger *globalization* to which mankind will be obliged *to adapt itself*. In a world that will be more and more closed and interdependent from any point of view as we have already explained a long time ago, in the *General Introduction to this Trilogy* (paragraph 10 of said introduction) and we are still in a dangerous deficit and risk, in respect to the backwardness of our United Nations planetary programs.

Again, as explained by Nicola Acocella in another book, *Rediscovering Economic Policy as a Discipline*, in the course of the publication, also by Cambridge University Press. It is without any mathematical language, but intelligently and logically expressed. This further work is full of good ideas in favour of a system of programming approach as described in our whole trilogy which has as the basic intentional work, a real coordination of all kinds of traditional intervention of economic policy, a coordination (macro-prudential policies) at any international level, responding to a 'systemic' approach with a methodology of 'collective bargaining' directly managed by the government—a simultaneous discussion by the representatives of the most important social interest groups, in a unitary coordination.

In Acocella's work, the ways of determining the consequences and the effectiveness of the financial crisis are dealt with especially. There is a search for new rules for the public budget, as defined in Chaps. 8 and 9 of **Vol. II**. It is recommended that to fight inequalities, it is necessary to elaborate on the debt target rules and monitoring with the strategic planning in its system of annual reporting and five-year reporting as implicit

262   Volume II. Selected Testimonies on the Epistemological...

in the strategic planning itself as applied happily at the end of the past century by the US federal government (see Chap. 9).

One problem, do not forget that much of the criticism of the lack of control of the *target of overly simple and aggregate modelling* in the case described by Tinbergen and concluding in the 'critical rediscovering of the *economic policy as a discipline*', even sophisticated in the academic seminar, does not mean developing an alternative in terms of new ploy against the Lucas kind of criticism, but only a new structuring of the way to make the *state agencies and also the private action independent again and to make the rules of the multi-national action more coordinated and interdependent.*

The apparent decline of world cohabitation is a marginal effect of an unavoidable and more than certain stronger globalisation to which humanity will be obliged to adapt. In a world that will be more and more closed and interdependent from any point of view, as we have already explained a long time ago, in the general introduction to this trilogy (Sect. 10 of the General Introduction to the whole trilogy, printed in **Vol. I**) and we are still in a dangerous deficit, in respect to the backwardness of our United Nations global programmes.

Notes to Chapter 7 (Vol. II)

1. I prefer to use for the acronym, for any language, the English one: Planning Accounting Framework (PAF), for any type of edition.
2. We must distrust any economic determinism on this matter: the history of the distribution of the wealth has been always a deeply political history and could not be reduced to mechanisms *merely economic.* On the other hand, I pronounce afraid and doubtful the word '*polity*', not because it could be inappropriate for the use made in itself …., but because it is the same word that allows, in name of it, to many and uncultivated and irresponsible '*newcomers' political leaders* to say so many silly ideas about the 'supremacy' of polity in respect of economics, and to do so many silly actions in name of the 'supremacy' or 'priority', in respect the Economics, easily misunderstandable words and facts, concepts and meanings, degrading inevitably the level of the dialogue and the reciprocal understanding between the people and producing great muddledness, between roles and interests, individual and community interests and preferences.

3. A good collection of such criticism is found in the essays collected by Edward Fullbrooks (2004): *A Guide to What's Wrong with Economics* and classified in seven parts: (1) Basic problems; (2) Micro nonsense; (3) Macro nonsense; (4) Ethical Voids and Social Pathologies; (5) Misuse of Mathematics and Statistics; (6) Category Mistakes Regarding Wealth; and (7) Globalist Distortions. In this anthology, 27 brilliant critics and economists participated, with rich contributions on the different aspects of the fallacy of economic theory. I am sure that each of the 27 critical aspects would be reduced to a lack of sense, if conceived in terms of the Frischian 'programming approach' (as exposed in this book), and if conceived by incorporating the overturning of the approach recommended in this book into their epistemology.

4. In their recent book, *Economic Policy in the Age of Globalisation*, Cambridge University Press, 2005, N. Acocella, G. Di Bartolomeo and A. Hughes Hallet, a well-known Anglo-Italian group of economists, reflect on the changes intervened recently in the global 'structure' of the capital and in the information communications. I consider this book a valuable tool for not forget the advantages (often ignored) of the globalisation in our epoch. In 1999, Acocella published another useful handbook, to be recommended, on the contemporary evolution of the economic policies, *Foundations of Economic Policy*: *Values and Techniques* (Cambridge University Press, 1999).

5. Of course, we are speaking about the PAF to which **Vol. III** of this book is dedicated. I refer to the next chapters of that **Vol. III** for every detail on the construction and the evaluation criteria of PAF.

6. I would say: permanently discussed, according to reasonable time procedures, which is already described in particular in **Vol. III**, Chap. 4. On the other hand, once the system is introduced, through the management of an ad hoc technically independent agency, the participants could permanently have at their disposal a tool for cognitive elaborations for simulating alternative combinations of interventions and actions to improve the capacity of study, proposal and discussion, and to be involved in real changes and more serious engagements with respect to the starting point.

The usual technique for measuring the effectiveness of results is always that of formulating (technically, but in cooperation of the representative of the parts) for any sector of political action, public and collective, by means of plans, programmes and projects ex ante, in order to measure and control ex post, (after a reasonable period of development of the actions programmed), the results obtained, (and the difficulties encountered). Consequently, comparing the difference between results expected and the results obtained—in a report—the analysis of their difference and of the factors which have been the cause of the difficulties encountered; and, analysing and evaluating such factors, decide the necessary adjustment for the next period, changing into more or less the previous targets. Obviously, all this in consideration of reducing the future gap between expectation and result, in the permanent aim to their consistence.

7. I am thinking, overall, of the workers' unions that are weaker in cognitive structures; when—in the 1960s—(in my role as chairman of an Economic Committee of the European Union, adhering to the ICFTU) I invited unions, of which I was consultant, to create some study organs in order to build a framework (of the type outlined above) in order to 'pry into the government's financial affairs' (see Archibugi 1957): this is the same framework that, in the meantime, Ragnar Frisch was elaborating in his Institute of Economics of the Oslo University ten years before receiving the Nobel Prize for Economics, but also and some time before being totally forgotten by the powerful and a-critical community of academic econometricians, see Chap. 3, **Vol. I**.

8. This, according to Keynes, would be 'pensioned off' since 1926 (see Keynes 1926).

9. Briefly already described in the chapters of **Vol. I** of this trilogy.

10. Free from easier 'positivistic' laws of the economy and equipped with a sufficient number of instruments and data, and already carefully prepared in order to assess alternative solutions of maximum results, given the constraints and the maximum agreement among interests, and given different viewpoints of the participants.

11. Leif Johansen, in his two volumes, *Lectures in Macro-economic Planning*, 1977–1978, amply quoted in this book, dealt with many of the questions of planning under of uncertainty, especially in the chapters of his second volume. He does so with an abundance of hypotheses relating to the diverse structure of the market and of the diverse reactions and liberty of behaviour by market operators. I believe that any further step in this subject cannot ignore the work of Johansen.

12. See some quotations referred in the chapters of **Vol. I**.

13. Even if the largest of entrepreneurs attempted to maintain contact with the interventions and insertions into the financial world, and to fragment themselves in financial affairs, risking losing their entrepreneurial function and passing radically into the field of financial operators, often with success, but most of the time without success yet with personal failure.

A Project for a New Worldwide, Strategic Methodology... 265

14. A young French scholar, Thomas Piketty, published a book, some years ago (*Le capital au XXIe siècle*) which received great attention to have dedicated his research—as specialist—on the theme of wealth and income inequality in the world (and its implications), passing from the nineteenth century to date across 20 countries and incorporating other historical information on the development of patrimony (using relative data from a diverse set of sources). The essential result of the accurate and surprising research confirms how for a certain number of years many people (including myself) believed that the return of capital in the most important capitalist countries not only diminishes in respect to workers but tends to grow (with the exception of a few periods of inverse trends, such as post-war periods in the USA, which would have misled Simon Kuznets, the American guru of gross national product). The principle results obtained by Piketty's research are summarised, briefly, as follows:

1. There is a need to distrust all forms of economic determinism: the story of re-allocation of wealth is always a story profoundly political and could not re-emerge in the form of purely economic mechanisms.
2. The second conclusion that constitutes—according to Piketty—the heart of his findings is that the dynamic of wealth reallocation puts into play the mechanisms that alternatively push towards convergence and divergence, and that no other natural or spontaneous process could avoid their destabilising and inegalitarian tendency in the long-term.

15. It is important to remember the structural effects of the retribution between labour and capital, which can be produced in the transition from industrial to post-industrial society (a subject on which I focused a book called '*The Associative Economics', Insight beyond the Welfare State and into Post-Capitalism* (Archibugi 2000a, Macmillan) and the effects of such a transition from an industrial society and a post-industrial society, on the functioning of the Keynesian-type model.

16. To this method, of strategic planning and to the operational guidelines of reinventing the general guidelines, Chap. 9 of **Vol. II** will be dedicated. In addition, another work of mine is in publication, in English, on strategic planning, *Introduction to Strategic Planning in the Public Domain*.

17. Joseph Stiglitz has received notable recognition and awards of the highest order as an economist: he was President of the Council of Economic Advisers of the President of the USA (under President Clinton); Vice President and Chief Economist of the World Bank; on a scientific level,

he performed his activities of research and teaching first at MIT, where he concluded his studies and then at Columbia University, receiving the Nobel Prize for Economics in 2001. From 2011 Stiglitz was elected as President of the International Economic Association. In addition to his rich biography (including books, essays and comments in the mainstream press), he found himself in a powerful position to influence the direction of political and global actions, including: (a) in 2008 as President of an International Commission of experts on the subject of 'On the Measurement of Economic Performance' and Social Progress' established as an initiative of the then French president and as co-director of two other well-known economists, Amartya Sen and Jean Paul Fitoussi; (b) in 2009 as the United Nations designated President of a Commission of international experts asked to discuss and plan a Reform of the international monetary and financial system (called the 'Stiglitz Report').

He is an ideal candidate to be assumed as an ambiguous representative of official economic theory of a positivist type and, at the same time a radical critic of the same official economics in many ways. Stiglitz found himself in strategic positions to strongly influence with his ideas the actions of governments and international organisations, in addition to implementing reform himself. But he is also in a privileged position to perceive the fallacious positions of those 'orthodox' positions of diverse schools of thought. I have the impression that his theoretical positions and methodologies have been, in recent times, progressively moving towards a more radical view (the use of the word 'paradigm' is a signal that should be increasingly clarified by him).

18. In fact, he represents an almost perfect synthesis of economic doctrine in its actual state, with all of its dissatisfactions and ambiguity. And, at the same time, he is an ideal representative of 'mainstream' economics (that is, of conventional economic theory), and—especially in recent times—an authentic, radical critic of it.

Therefore, it represents an ideal candidate to represent the scholars of official economic theory, referred to in this book as positivistic; at the same time it offers affirmations to represent the radical criticism of official economic theory under many aspects. For example, the invisible hand does not exist.

Stiglitz found himself strategically positioned to influence by means of his ideas the actions of government and international organizations, as well as his own implementation of reform. He was also in a privileged position in perceiving the fallacious positions and 'orthodox' positions from a different school of thought. I have the feeling that his theoretical and methodological positions were progressively becoming more radical in later periods (the use of the world 'paradigm' is a sign of this).

It is my conviction that he had the opportunity of expressing with great authority that which is presented as a 'new paradigm' of economic thought (as he declared he wanted to do) and, gradually, gravitating towards potentially very interesting ideas.

19. Many other governments, victims also of the subordination to tradi-tional (mainstream) economics, follow the positivist error.

20. See Geoffrey M. Hodgson, one of the most accredited scholars of 'insti-tutional' and evolutionary economics. I remember another joke from another American scholar of labour economics, Lloyd G. Reynolds, who opened his course of labour economics with the phrase (if I remember well) 'the fact that labourers are not moving from one work to another in attempt of finding a higher salary, does not say anything against the behaviour of these workers. But it does say a lot on the urgent need to consult a psychiatrist for economists that assume it was that way.'

21. The scientific contribution which motivated the assigning of the Nobel Prize to Stiglitz (2001) is 'for laying the foundations for the theory of markets with asymmetric information' (with G. Akerlof and A. Michael Spence, economists of different school). With the utmost respect for the Nobel evaluators of Stiglitz, I think that this motivation is a little restric-tive, as addressed to Stiglitz, given his important role in the knowledge of the financial factors in the evolution of real activity flows. Moreover, it should not be forgotten that at least since 50 years, some illustrious economists, like Frisch or Leontief thundered that builders of the aggre-gated models for forecasting had to distrust the behavior of the variables in the game, if they were not determined *a priori*, upon the basis of the goal to regulate and control the programmatic flows, and if they were arriving—as Frisch at the World Congress of Econometrics in Rome in 1965 has declared them as *playometrics* (see Chap. 3, **Vol. I**)—together useless and dangerous, if employed for the scoped of prognosis and pre-vention. Indeed due to their unknown 'asymmetry'. If these economists (also however granted a Nobel prize) would have been more listened and studied, and above all, utilized by the most responsiblized Governments, who are also the most informed not only about the asymmetries in financial behaviour but also fully aware of their real effect, we all would

268   Volume II. Selected Testimonies on the Epistemological...

have made serious steps forward in the *planning* technology (a 'dirty' word from the vocabulary of official **Economics**). Instead the situation was contrasted by the Governments, inspired by the thing, which Stiglitz has names 'market fundamentalism' (as was already used even by Soros) the level of control on the cognitive compatibility, which would account for the objectives, to be reached by the real economic policies and to be negotiated by the Governments as well as political forces, would have surely been greater.

22. If we now prefer to use this word.

23. And from the silence, I re-enter into conventionality, highly accelerated by the sickness and premature death of Frisch, from the strong orthodox economy, and from 'Reagonomics'. Personally, I was unable to follow the essays of Frisch, which were still in a confused editorial state, and living—in Italy—in a periphery of communication amongst economists and lacking the necessary instruments for me to be heard. Only recently was I able to order Frisch's essays (see Chap. 3, **Vol. I**) but also to my own ideas as well, a product of an abandoned philosophical culture and limited economic culture tied to my difficult Myrdalian background that was unable to find in Italy, as in the rest of the world, an easy welcome between blind students and closed horizons.

24. Among those could be there my own role, with that of my interdisciplinary Centre for Planning Studies in Rome, if my initiative agreed with the Italian government and of which to I provide with a research, Progetto Quadro, on the traces of the Frisch's programming approach (see information in **Vol. III**, Appendix 1) of this book, had not been interrupted for reasons of bigotry and political dissent by conservative governments in Italy, and for the modest cultural tenor (except some due exceptions) of the Italian Academy in the field of the social sciences.

25. I again wish to recall that Frisch—being the thinker, and not only economist, that he was—often repented in his works and in his conversations a frequent phrase: '*We have to get used to not forgetting—as economists and planners of thinking in real terms and not only monetary.*'

26. Management in which econometrics founded on alternative objectives in play could serve in finding alternatives to reaching those objectives, which compromised among participants of the game and, in general (in more praxeological terms) which new objectives should be studies, producing a 'new awareness' (cognitive effect of planning). This was the ancient argument of the 'sociology of awareness' (Karl Mannheim, *Wissensoziologie*, **Vol. II**, Sect. 2.8.2).

A Project for a New Worldwide, Strategic Methodology...   269

27. I would like not forgetting that since the most elementary visions of political science, the concept of *democracy appropriate* (until where in eighteenth century has been introduced the functional study of the Constitutions for communities of big demographic dimensions) people have almost unanimously preferred to connect to the concept of '*democracy*' to the functioning of *representativity*, rather forms of direct participation.

28. This distinction useless for the single modeling useful only for single mathematical modelling of labor only for specific models, but are no more useful when in political decisions—of all variables in gaming in their relative importance.

29. This is the most important political and technical message of Frisch (see what has already been outlined in **Vol. I**, Chap. 7).

30. As it happened in all fields of the knowledge and human progress, with all positions that in the history have seek to keep old conceptions lacking of any real historical sense, (if never they were enjoyed of it) in relation to the knowledges in the history itself lived in every field.

31. If we prefer now to use this word.

32. And from the silence returns the conventionality, strongly aided by the illness and premature death of Frisch, from the powerful orthodox economics and from 'Reaganomics'.

33. Among those could have been myself, with my Centre for Research in Planning (in Rome), if my initiative agreed with the Italian government and of which I provide some information in **Vol. III**, Appendix 1 had not been interrupted for reasons of disinterest and political dissent by conservative governments in Italy. Personally, I was not yet ready to follow up the writings of Frisch, which were in an editorial state of confusion and disorder and experiencing, as Italian, (a periphery of media communication between economists), I did not have the instruments to make myself heard (admitting that the situation has changed, but also it has not!). Only today have I managed to reorder not only the writings of Frisch (see Chap. 3, in **Vol. I**) but also my own ideas, fruit of a rejected and abandoned philosophical culture and a pained limitation of an economic culture linked to my difficult *Myrdalian background* that has not found in Italy or in all the world, an easy welcome from a discipline that is heavily defended and little open to debate.

34. I would again like to point out that Frisch, as a thinker, and not only economist, often repeated in his work and his conversations a frequent phrase 'we must get used to not forgetting—as economists and as planners—to think in real terms and not just monetary terms'.

Bibliographical References to Chapter 7 (Vol. II)

Acocella, N., Di Bartolomeo, G. and Hallet, A. H. Eds. (2013). *The Theory of Economic Policy in a Strategic Context*. Cambridge University Press.

Archibugi, Franco. (1957). 'Pianificazione economica e contrattazione collettiva', [Economic Planning and Collective Bargaining] in *Studi economici*, (Journal of the *Facoltà di Economia* of di University of Napoli, 1957).

Fullbrooks, Edward, Ed. (2004). *A guide to what's is wrong with Economics*. London: Anthem Press.

Stiglitz E. Joseph (2010a). *The 'Stiglitz Report': Reforming the International Monetary and Financial Systems in the Wake of the Global Crisis*, New Press. New York, New Press.

Stiglitz E. Joseph (2010b). http://ineteconomics.org/stiglitz-new-paradigm. Financial Time, 2010.

8

The Economics as Tool for Measuring and Improving the Communities Performance Towards a New *Social Accountability* (*in Public and Private; Economic and Social; National and Global*)

8.1 Public and Private Performance: A New Economic Language

For a political economy of today, only on the national government scale and composed of initiatives on the basis of almost all uncertainty as to the effects and results, and that have a chance to become coordinated between them in a serious way in a programming process, for a total conviction that the market still is the only way to assure the development of the economy (investment, production, labour and welfare).

I do not believe that there are other possibilities for a serious change in real growth and productivity (today, at least 80% of economic activity in a 'modern' society is in public or private services) than to rely upon public performance. For the economics of the twenty-first century, in my opinion, the only real future work will be done on the methodological and epistemological basis of the *programming approach*.

But public performance is a concept, an operating mental category, that is essential for political, social and economic thought; in reality, it is the thing that is most difficult for us to materialise, if not in an abstract and generic way, with a quantitative measure, one that can constitute a reference to the its quality and functioning as well.

© The Author(s) 2019
F. Archibugi, *The Programming Approach and the Demise of Economics*,
https://doi.org/10.1007/978-3-319-78060-3_8

272   Volume II. Selected Testimonies on the Epistemological...

Therefore, we must learn, with the new programming approach, to incorporate the need to evaluate the performance of everything in the vast world of the public decisions to be taken. The evaluation of performance, in real terms—and not in monetary terms—is the new methodology that will accompany the 'economic evaluation' and its monitoring in the programming approach.[1]

The evaluation of real (and not only monetary) performance could constitute the method, the main argument, the paradigm, of the new economics, guided by the programming approach. It will deal, in the near future, until the last corner of its main (substantial and dominant) majority of themes, the activities, researches, techniques of analysis and planning, the reflective disciplinary improvements; just in order to escape to what in this trilogy we have called the surviving of the whole economic profession, in respect of the risk of its natural demise.

Given the simple fact, that, in the entire World, in its characters still not yet well defined as 'post-industrial', we are going toward a feature of a 'world' that should be no more directed by evaluations and decisions taken on the basis of parameters exclusively monetary; (based on the 'at *Market Prices*'), rather than also those on the basis of a permanent prioritary comparison of *real* character; that is with evaluations and decisions which will be always more oriented by considerations of indicators not assumed '*at market price*', but in terms of compatible monetary evaluation and objectives in technical or physical or real terms, called '*non-market prices*'.

All this implies, in short, that we could live in a world where public evaluations and decisions will be taken on the basis *of* analysis of costs and benefits computed not only by money ('*at market-price*'), but by *others* parameters of welfare and social choice by the interested communities, in the forms and conditions considered the best in respect of social preferences, scientifically and politically sounded.

8.1.1 The 'Un-Priced Value' Question

In this Chap. 8 (**Vol. II**) I intend to synthesize the arguments with which and for which the *Programming approach*—as described in all Chapters of **Vol. I** of this Trilogy, in order to explain *itself*, needs to be based on a measuring of the goals and objectives for every community and today also at the cooperative scale trough the communities of nations, which it intends to achieve, overall in real and technical terms (and not only in monetary terms).

But as governments are responsible for the collective welfare of the whole national or multi-national community, they should negotiate and programme the objectives to be pursued by the activities of the private sector, in the spirit of full and dutiful cooperation and participation of the public plans, establishing a compatible relationship with the private sector, and vice versa.

The result is that, in the programming approach, performance becomes constituted as a new language of economics. And given the growing importance of the public sector and the need that the attention to the performance becomes treated overall in there, where it was particularly absent, the performance, renewed in the concepts of the programming approach, becomes a general problem for all societal programming.

In first place, we investigate the 'unpriced values' question.

Now, let me reproduce the *incipit*, really very synthetically expressive, of a book by two young economists (I think, not so young anymore): John A. Sinden (University of New England) and A.C. Worrell (Yale University), which have advanced, (1979) at the dawn of the *post-industrial society*, probably as a first systematic collection of methods concerning the evaluation of the transactions of any type (contractually, 'welfare erogations', donations, and so on), without references to so-called market prices (1979a):[2]

Human existence has become increasingly complex as populations have increased and standards of living have risen. The resulting pressures on environmental resources and on people have reached levels where more through planning and more effective policies are urgently needed.

Many problems are complicated by the presence of things that have not been bought and sold in markets and are therefore un-priced. People cannot decide whether such things are worth having by comparing selling price to money cost. Nor can they choose between them on the basis of comparative prices. But these decisions are still basically economic, because they arise from competing demand for scarce resources.

274   Volume II. Selected Testimonies on the Epistemological...

People can be observed making decisions about such things every day, and it is obvious that they lack of monetary prices does not prevent them from being treated as economic goods. But rational planning and policy development about unpriced good and actions require reliable evidence as to their comparatives values. So we hear planners and policy makers asking questions about the values of scenic views. California condors, improvement in health, and savings in commuting time.

Many people feel it is impossible to place values on such things. Others feel that they can only be compared by assigning monetary prices to them. We do not agree with either of these views. We believe that it is possible to determine comparative values for unpriced things and that valid comparisons can be made without always resorting to monetary prices.

People in various disciplines have tried to resolve this problem in their own areas. We have seen the published results of many of these efforts and of most of the methods that have been developed. From our perusal of them and our own experience and study we have arrived at the approach followed in this book. We are concerned with the general problem of unpriced values in policy decisions. The book attempts to assist such decisions by clarifying the nature of value, by discussing the measurement of unpriced values, and by indicating more effective ways of analyzing decisions.

We believe that economic theory can provide an appropriate basis for environmental policy. But its application to practical problems is severely restricted by its underlying assumptions, such as perfect competition.

We try to overcome this weakness as follows:

(a) rather than try to rationalize theory with complex assumptions, we rely on the basic notions of *utility*, *disutility*, and *value*. We feel that careful interpretation of these fundamental concepts can lead to a wider and more helpful application of economic principles;

(b) rather than search for optimal decisions, we search for improved decisions. A close scrutiny of available methodology appears more fruitful at this time than attempts to develop new methodology. So we try to clarify the roles and potentials of existing methods, to set them in context, and to generalize them between disciplines;

(c) rather than always search for the money values of objects, we concentrate on the nature and characteristics of problems. Policy requires the making of decisions and not the calculation of values as such. An understanding of the real nature of problems often permits a wider and simpler use of economic principles and methods.[3] (Sinden and Worrell 1979a, pp. vii–viii)

The Economics as Tool for Measuring and Improving...   275

So, these are the intentions of the authors, as recounted in their preface.[4]

Until now, I never met—30 years after its publication—another handbook containing so vast a quantity of references for the evaluation and use of un-priced values, although they are more and more important in the management of the economic policies at all levels, and render obsolete and inappropriate any economic policy, founded—as said in the previous Chap. 7—on 'paradigms' to be changed, because the damage that—with its absolute inefficiency in spite so numerous schools—it produced.[5] And that it will continue to produce if people do not change, with the programming approach, which will overturn completely the positivist approach, traditionally used during all the history of economics.

I think that the fact that in the matter of quantitative economic policy (and also in different 'economic plans' not yet practised), it is done more reference (whether at local and national levels or also international and global), the System of National Account (SNA), in its whole, expressed in limited 'monetary' reasoning and figures, without any regard and attention for the un-priced values and the complex evaluations that spring from them; this is a bad signal for economics.

Many intelligent considerations and practical solutions on the theme of the evaluation of un-priced values where the role of public action and initiative are the sources can be found in the work of Mark H. Moore, *Creating Public Value: Strategic Management in Government* (1995).[6]

Because of the structural evolution of human society, which is at the stage that several people have called it a 'post-industrial society', and the ever more forceful entry among the human needs and preferences of goods and services (mainly in the 'public domain') that are not reckonable in 'market' terms, just defined as un-priced,[7] to leave out these goods in the political choices of several planning processes, the quantitative aspect of such goods already creates by itself inadmissible negligence and an inacceptable deficit of vision on the part of institutional decision-takers and a great contradiction and fall in the dialogue, and real understanding, between different political programmes.

8.1.2 Other Directions in the Social Accounting Progress (An Interesting Proposal, Not yet Adequately Assessed, by Karl Fox)

An interesting proposal arose some time ago (1969), offered by Karl A. Fox, an American economist; though not well known, Fox nevertheless deserves a special place among the testimonies that, in this part of the trilogy I have selected for the history of the revival of the programming approach. Fox, ignored in the same circumstances with which others have been ignored, or distorted, or even misunderstood, like the economists Myrdal, Frisch, Tinbergen, Johansen, in a certain way Leontief too, are forerunners of the programming approach, for whom this trilogy claims attention, one different from those who have benefitted by the celebrity of the Nobel prize even from the academic establishment.

In the bibliographical references of this Chap. 8 (**Vol. II**), relative to the works of Karl Fox, I report the most important works of K. Fox, which were delivered in collaboration with other economists and social sciences researchers. Karl A. Fox, has been a case of cultural production very solitary in the USA (and in his State University of the Iowa), and I strongly believe it is necessary to make an action of dislodging him from his hermitage, in the advantage of developing the *new social accounting*, of which an economic science has an urgent need.[8] He became (after working as an agrarian economist in his earlier days) at the US Department of Agriculture and later dedicated himself to the study of techniques of quantitative political economy from the Rotterdam School (Tinbergen) with original contributions produced in collaboration with other scholars of econometrics of that School, that contributed to the entry of analysis in certain sectors (he dedicated himself to the study of quantitative economic policy techniques from the school of Rotterdam (Tinbergen) with original contributions produced in collaboration with other econometric scholars of that school who contributed to helping that analysis into some sectors).

8.2 Performance Measuring and Monitoring as the Main Implementation Factors in the Programming Approach

Economists, therefore, have to try urgently to introduce and measure the performances of these new goods (without 'priced' values) in the general (positive or negative) 'economic accounts' (SNA). A situation has arisen where the omission of what can still be considered an approximate self-assured use of traditional and obsolete methods has tended to become a dangerous and also outrageous abuse (from some strictly 'non-economic' viewpoint).

The scant attention given to the theoretical and practical solution to the question of un-priced values is another reason to fear the wrong and misleading effects of the traditional economic accounting (SNA), all based on statistical or simulated 'market prices'.[9]

On the contrary, people continue to trust such accounting, part of which—some affirm—is not influenced by the unpriced values question, and at the same time people still remain under the illusion that, proceeding in the use and in the improvements of the SNA, it will be possible to develop a system of accounting that is less limited and includes un-priced values.

I have the impression that this research, in the spirit and wavelength of the *Programming approach* should be directed towards a *different route*: to start from the *general goals* analysis, in order to deep the respective values and to attain a *new type* of social accounting.

For the moment the unpracticability of reforming the Unified Socio-economic accounting system has prevailed.

Several diverse systems of 'physical' accounting have arisen, separated phenomenon by phenomenon, of a technical and physical character, the prerogative of different international organisations and centres interested in separate indicators. They are periodic findings that have a 'descriptive' nature oriented towards rankings and comparisons of specific positions and phenomena, but these are often of little significance, if not analysed with current information and with an evaluation of determining and explanatory factors.

This argument, it seems to me, is the entry point in the new 'paradigm' not only in economics but in general public policy, without which *Economics*,[10] as it has been imposed in its 'positivistic' secular basis is today destined for dissolution.[11]

It is well known that economics, as a science, developed around the many reflections on the performance of things; of objectives, of 'goods' that we use, and then of the work and services that we utilise and buy or sell on the market, that we acquire through exchange and/or donation, that we perform for pleasure or obligation for any activity that we undergo, and to improve through work and study, in our lives, human relations, and in school, and we judge the level of progress in all fields in which we operate: the production of goods and services, the public order, the working of institutions (public or private), healthcare, social assistance, art, research, sports, information, entertainment, and so on.

The *'performance'* is therefore the ultimate proof of any human activity and it is assumed that this was present in every moment of the history of humanity, across centuries and within all civilisations in which any sort of performance took place, as a major factor of progress and change in both individual and collective lives.

The Programming approach—which this trilogy sets forth—is reduced to its ultimate objectives; that in search of a better performance on behalf of humanity itself, in the activities already developed and those in the process of being developed; and it seems clear that it is an inevitable tendency to care about, though this is rarely recognised, future innovation in public and private management, from the dissolution of the prevailing yet discredited economic policies of the day, and representative of the experimental cornerstone of the *Programming approach*.

Hence, I feel the duty to underline the importance of the measurement of performance in this work, from the final part of the testimonial of such an approach, attempting to examine it in terms of its explicit, key elements, beyond its technical elements (already present in the best experiences) which are nevertheless destined to slowly disperse as the programming approach, in respect to its requisites and real objectives, which will be more and more resorted to—especially once it is adopted on a total and integrated global level—the character of the post-industrial society.

In fact, it is the post-industrial society—which has been stressed throughout the trilogy—that we will need to resort to the measuring of performance as an absolute and dominant factor for ensuring a substantial shift towards the wellbeing of communities, national and international, and as a characteristic of and support for the programming approach.

A new paradigm, for a Economics' *redirection* (of which Gunnar Myrdal was talking) was that of a '*logic*' which would present itself, already at a level strictly '*non economic*', but which would also incorporate, the human, social, juridical, political implications as a whole, of any kind of *Public Program*, whatever be the geographical scale or the operational sector, with a completely *Programming approach*, (as already said many time) both:

- '**strategic**', i.e. consistent with *other objectives* of the concerned community, and
- '**systemic**', i.e. consistent with the measures of other parallel *Programs*, (in vertical or horizontal form)—spatial and structural mainly—close to the one in question.

Thus, in this Chap. 8 (**Vol. II** of our Trilogy), I will push my readers, to reflect on the argument of the *measurements of performance* by mean of the study of appropriate *Program indicators*, on which to base them, with the aim to harmonize each action, especially in the cases of '*un-priced values*'.

In this last chapter, it would not be correct to make heavy weather of the argument, entering into the techniques of the measurement of performances. It is enough to indicate the existence of the problem, and citing, in the literature, the excellent handbook by Sinden and Worrell (1979a); and to recommend an intense application of those technical tools. It is probable that a better enquiry into that literature will permit readers to discover other works and examples of applications of that Esempi which would deserve to be in the first place in the interest of the economists still engages in a ballast of questions and problems that emphasizing the great opportunity and trends of making them object of overlooking should be, in the same time, in many cases, a occasion of system evaluation for measure of the *performance* itself.

In sum, here it is sufficient to indicate the existence of the problem and to recommend an intense use of such instruments.

However, I feel to be sure to state that the eventual examples of new cases and also of related books it should be esteemed surely too little, in face of the great need—in this last 30 years—of quantity of evaluations correctly to be done, in the myriad number of cases where this kind of evaluation should be made.

I am aware, in contrast, that if the programming approach—to the partisan description of which is dedicated this trilogy—will not progress in the knowledge of scholars, under the impulsion of a systematic and strategic initiative of the planners, managers, policy-makers and decisions-takers, the supported evaluation of the un-priced values will not take place.

This will happen when the *public opinion*, influenced by the big, powerful profession of the traditional *economists,* academic and practiced, educated by the *mainspring economics,*[12] will found the way, through a new *System of general accounting,*[13] to achieve *real common targets*, established collectively and democratically, with figures and measuring roughly—(but awfully more significant of social benefits real, and in respect of traditional accounting escaping, or proxy, and misleading, *nominal* (monetary) *terms accounting*, refusing the research to catch the *real standard terms, in all parts of the world* and through *tangible performances results*, accurately measured and monitored estimation, over all, in the communities *public budgeting* (and not at all, in 'price' monetary terms with constant reference to the quantity of physical units, of good and services).

8.3 A Return to Strategic Planning?

This trilogy can be 'decorated' in its last chapter with what could be called a return to strategic planning.

It is a 'return' since the history of strategic planning developed out of the management of great production units—the corporations—but was domiciled within the context of so-called 'micro-economics', and linked to new experiences of research in the field of 'social engineering', and excluded from the larger questions of quantitative economics policy (essentially 'macroeconomics', as in Frisch, Johansen, Fox and others).

In such way, the quantitative economic policy has always brushed the technologies of econometric evaluations of the growth, on the border of validity—always more questioned by the critical econometrics itself (above all, from the negative warnings recommendations of the best mathematicians and economists); this is due to the untrustworthiness of the aggregate economic variables declared by theory and experience, both precarious and incapable of providing stable results beyond the short term.

In the meantime, with the growth of the impact of the public spending and the unstoppable advance of the role of the welfare state, connected to the growth of national gross domestic product, despite its continual loss of significance and value of the aggregate 'growth models', systematically proposed in the inconclusive and fallible evaluation of public economic policy—as seen throughout history—and combined with the 'growth in service activities' (in de-industrialised societies) and that of de-structured activities (de-localised and of the 'associative' and non-profit type), grew the perception of an economy very far from extraordinary jumps of performance (of Keynesian memory[14]), when it was expected a recovery in terms of profit and taxation which caused in terms of alterations of cost equilibrium, 'deficit spending' and a crisis of businesses.

The performances to ensure modest but secure improvements were not in the hands of the big businesses with large profit taxes, from which followed a general lowering of taxes on productivity and earnings in all advanced societies that were not at the crux between industrialisation and de-industrialisation.[15]

What I intend when I say *'return to the strategic planning'*, take the form of a pressure, from several directions and parts, in favor of a cleaner and cleaner demarcation of strategic planning in respect of traditional "management sciences"[16] (in their turn developed within the wider ambit of political science); or the trend for a more and more important and significant portion of management science to identify itself with strategic planning. All this has meant abandoning the approach that I would call "positivist"—which so much imbues all the tradition of "social sciences"—in order to adopt the "programming" approach, pragmatically addressed to "operationality", to the 'problem solving', to the strategic management. (Be aware that the process is still ongoing: people attributes several names to the new conceptual schemes).

8.4   An Overview of the Steps Ahead in the Researches of Social Accounting

The multi-disciplinary strands of the new 'demarcation' are briefly as follows.

1. Within the traditional ambit of sociology and/or political science, the new strand of research and study has been denominated 'policy science'. One of its undisputed forerunners was Harold D. Lasswell[17]; its eminent authors Charles Lindblom (1953 with Dahl) and Yehezkel Dror (1971, 1984); and later Patton and Sawicki (1986). Since 1970, the new strand created an influent international academic journal: the *Policy Science Journal* (published by Elsevier).

2. Within the traditional ambit of the training of a professional management cadre (that from the 'business schools'), 'strategic management' or 'strategic planning' has developed as an autonomous strand.[18] It continues to be developed within 'corporate planning', especially as at long term planning.[19] A new and specific development—from the managerial point of view—comes also from the world of the non-profit organisations, from this aspect related to the public domain.[20] In this ambit, the programming approach is certainly favoured, because all orientation is towards the formation of a professional figure of an action-oriented man, substantially 'operational': the managers are action-oriented and little interested in research and in academia.

3. Within the traditional ambit of 'system engineering', as we have seen, numerous strands are developed concerning the decision-making theory and processes, bordering often on a sort of social psychology of choice and decision-making.[21] Here and there, some 'positivist' approaches tend to emerge again ('How should the political man behave and make decisions?', 'What about the manager'? 'The voter'? or 'The tax-payer'? and so on). Nevertheless, the aim of the research remains of a prescriptive type.

4. Moreover, as the reader of this trilogy knows well, even traditional strands of economics and economic policy appear in the programmatic approach, as direct designers of a clear prescriptive aim. In the first place, it appears with Ragnar Frisch, the founder of the Econometric Society, who introduced, with epistemological correctness (even if without systemic treatment), the concept of programming approach.[22] Then Jan Tinbergen introduced the quantitative economic policy as the application of criteria and principles of the operational research (statistically and in business) at the scale of the

national economic policy.[23] There was also Leif Johansen, who wrote the first systemic handbook on 'macroeconomic planning' (1977–78) in two volumes, with a third volume left unfinished by the premature death of the author.

5. Some urban and land planners also participated—even without any interdisciplinary or transdisciplinary connection—in these anti-positivist overturnings of planning, at least those addressed to the building of a general methodology of planning to be taught, as knowhow, to practitioners and designers: for instance, Chapin (1965), McLoughling (1969), Chadwick (1971), Catanese and Steiss (1970) and others.

6. The operational research also influenced strategic planning at the scale of the local government agencies. A theoretical and practical experience of some interest took place in Great Britain at the Institute for Operational Research, from which were developed some interesting planning works, which found vast application.[24]

7. In this last circle of urban planners, a certain reflection on methodological and procedural issues has developed, which has come to be called planning theory, of which the highest standing representatives are Faludi[25] and Alexander.[26] And to which we have dedicated the entire Chap. 3 in **Vol. II** of the trilogy.

8. In the meantime, in the 1970s, some studies on the integration of planning took place at the United Nations organisations,[27] and on the part of individual scholars.[28]

9. From systems analysis and operational research, of which we have briefly spoken in the previous chapter, there took place during the 1960s in the United States (with some reflections in Europe) a movement—of which we have also spoken in Chap. 2—for the introduction in the decisional process of public administration (at every level: federal, state and local) of rational methods of programming, inspired by the systemic approach. This was called the Planning-Programming-Budgeting System (PPBS), which failed to take off in a systematic way, despite much political involvement (President Johnson himself issued a directive at the end of the 1960s for its introduction in the

federal agencies). The approach of the PPBS was not so different from the more recent strategic planning introduced at the federal scale (of which we will speak later). After being used in the Pentagon's strategy of military expenditure,[29] and after remarkable success obtained in some other departments (as, for instance, that of Health, Education and Welfare[30]), a connection was attempted at inter-agency level, from the then Bureau of Budget, today the Office of Management and Budget,[31] but, at that point, the premise of a systematisation of approaches, temporal and inter-sectoral, collapsed. The general 'climb' that succeeded has not been favourable and the connected initiatives—because of a certain generational turnover—were dispersed.[32]

10. In any case, the PPBS version of strategic planning continued to be practiced in the USA on a vast scale, at the level of many local public organisations and agencies,[33] and can be considered the underground river which led to the American federal development in the 1990s. At an operational public level, the PPBS was followed in the USA during the 1970s by other initiatives analogous with other evaluation methods (such as the MBO—Management by Objective and the ZBB—Zero-Base-Budgeting).[34]

11. People sought to extend the American experience of that epoch to some European countries, such as France and Italy, but with even less success.[35] The strategic planning experience, through PPBS, remained in the 1970s and 1980s at the margins in Europe more than in the USA. In Europe, the main problem of public management remained, towing the general and old problems of the macro-economic policy of financial balance.

12. But the PPBS returned to regained attention at the end of the 1980s, both as a new approach to urban and regional programming,[36] and as an instrument of cooperation between different levels of government.[37] See also the attempt to extend the operational horizon of strategic planning at a national scale. The business world has also approached the theme of international and global strategies.

The Economics as Tool for Measuring and Improving...   285

Notes to Chapter 8 (Vol. II)

1. The growth and the numerical expansion of the youth population covered by public training and education has caused an expansion of the roles of the activities connected with teaching and research, from which is also provoked the consequent development of activities and jobs always less turned to the material needs and always more to the 'intellectual' one, allows—on the scale of the main Western countries—a great hope that there will prevail political systems with bigger intellectual population, capable of understanding the importance of an active and intelligent participation to the democratic political life of the maxim number of citizens.

2. John A. Sinden and Albert C. Worrel (1979) *Unpriced Valued: Decisions without Market Prices*, A Wiley Interscience, New York.

3. The authors add to this quotation for their readers some notes about the use of their book:

> We try to put this all together in a form that will be useful to managers, planners, policy analysts, and policy makers. This is in no sense a "cookbook." But it is addressed to people who are actually working with problems, and it shows how to formulate, use, and apply the methods to such problems.
>
> The book can be used in various ways, but all readers should go through all the chapters at least once. Part I considers the nature of values, the kind of value information needed for decisions, the usefulness of comparative values, and the nature and application of basic economic concepts. Part II gives the reader an appreciation of the large number and wide range of methods that have been developed to measure unpriced values and of how each fills a special niche. Part III considers why decisions involving unpriced values are perceived as difficult and shows how appropriate I analyses can overcome this. (Sinden and Worrell, *Unpriced Values*, cited., pp. vii–viii).

4. It is very probable that a better enquiry could bring us to discover other works and examples of application of that technology concerning unpriced values. However, I think to be sure that eventual other examples should be considered rather too few in respect of the needs of these last 30 years (since Sinden and Worrel's book) and should be felt about the application of correct projectual and operational evaluations, in the myriad of cases of this type of evaluation.

5. I would suggest to my readers that they look at a further work by Edmund Phelps, *Seven School of Macroeconomic Thought* (1990) (Oxford University Press). It seems to me that Phelps doubts also of the opportunity for us to continue to speak about 'macro-economic economic policy' (an expression used indeed many time, without embarrassment and attention, also by Myrdal, Frisch, Tinbergen, Leontief and the other economists considered in **Vol. I** of this trilogy).

I think, instead, that the programming approach goes beyond any kind of distinction between 'macro', 'micro' or 'meso' economics and consists in a different 'anti-positivist' approach aimed not at 'discovering' non-existent, 'neutral', 'objective', 'claimed' norms of behaviour, but only at ascertaining the validity and operability of the conditions, possibilities, consistencies of the implementation and intentional decisions, using enough due and rightful technicality, (called 'projects' or 'plans') preferred by the representative decision-makers of any organised community (democratically and intelligibly).

6. Mark H. Moore at the Center for Non-profit Organizations at The Kennedy School of Government at Harvard University.

7. But not for this deprived of a growing essential role in the life of human societies.

8. Karl Fox, began as agrarian economist, dedicated to some econometric studies, became a fellow of Jan Tinbergen (see Karl Fox and Sengupta J.K (1969). *Optimization Techniques in Quantitative Economic Models* (Amsterdam, North-Holland). He studied the way to find alternative systems in national social accounting '*Combining Economic and Non-Economic Objectives in Development Planning: Problems of Concepts and Measurement*' In: a volume by W. Sellekaerts (ed.), (1971), See also a essay on *Economic Development and Planning,* in a vol. in honor of *Jan Tinbergen* (see bibl. ref.). Very important his opera: *Social Indicators and Social Theory. Elements of an operational system* (John Wiley, New York 1974).

9. As is well known, the SNA has its birthday in a report (1947) prepared by the Sub-Committee of the statistics of national income of the League of the United Nations, under the guidance of Richard Stone. In 1953, a first publication of the SNA has been published. A first revision was implemented in 1960, which gathered the experiences of some countries, and a second gathering in 1964, with the new contribution of data from the institution of the International Monetary Fund; in 1968, it obtained its extension with the input-output system and the 'balance sheets' and also more attention to compared estimations 'at constant

The Economics as Tool for Measuring and Improving...   287

prices'. And a greater resemblance with the accounting MPS (Material Product System) used in Urss; and lastly the 1993 and 2008 editions, again with further revision and updating, without the introduction of new concepts and measures of economic goods.

10. In my book on the *Associative Economy* (Archibugi, 2000. Macmillan), people can find the discussed issues for mistrust seriously today the arguments valid without doubt in highly industrialized structures, where and when the national economies were believing in the Keynes reasonings about the recovery, of the financial equilibrium of the 'deficit investments and spending' but this must be no more very safely expected, given the so lower productivity rates of a economy substantially 'tertiary', in a post-industrial society.

11. Many claim that this passage could have arrested in these countries the process of 'democratization' (which is already problematic in and of itself); and of creating new problems for the process of good relations between developing and developed countries. The pros and cons of this process are ties to a complex of factors that are not easily determined and, most of all, not easily controlled.

12. And also incapable to get a real role in accompanying the 'free' and disastrous management of *the profit-making measurement* of the **wealth** (of the people or f the nations') in the *real* World....

13. May be, sponsored by United Nations Organizations....

14. In my book on the associative economy (Archibugi 2000b), people can find the issues discussed (valid without doubt in highly industrialized structures) in terms of where and when the national economies were believing in the Keynes reasonings about the recovery, of the financial equilibrium of the 'deficit investments and spending', but this must be no more very safely expected, given the lower productivity rates of a economy substantially 'tertiary' in a post-industrial society.

15. Many claim that this passage could have arrested in these countries the process of 'democratisation' (which is already problematic in and of itself), and of creating new problems for the process of good relations between developing and developed countries. The pros and cons of this process are tied to a complex of factors that are not easily determined and, most of all, not easily controlled.

16. See Herbert A. Simon (1941, 1960, 1983).

17. Since 1951 a well-known collection of papers edited by Harold Lasswell in cooperation with Daniel Lerner (1951) has inaugurated reflection on the policy sciences.

18. For more updated versions of the strategic management in the field of the management science, for instance, the works of Ansoff et al. (1976), Steiner (1979), Tregoe and Zimmermann (1980).
19. Among many: Ackoff (1969), Amara and Lipinski (1983). One meaningful case is the interest of the American Committee for Economic Development, a club of industrialist inspiration (see Moskow 1978).
20. For an example, see: Bryson (1988), Koteen (1997), Allison and Kaye (1997) and Barry (1997).
21. On the point, see Fishburn (1973).
22. See various writings of Frisch, in general: *On Planning* (1958); *On the Programming Approach* (1961); *On the Forecast and Programming Methods* (1962); *On the Research of Optimisation in the National Planning Process* (1964a); *On the Decisional Approach in the Econometrics* (1964b); *On the Cooperation Between Politicians and Technicians in the Formalisation of the Political Preferences* (1971). All these writings are posthumously collected (Frisch, ed. by Lang, 1976).
23. Tinbergen's main writings on such matters are on the theory of the economic policy (1956a, b, 1963a) and on scientific programming (1964, 1967, 1969b).
24. With the special experience of Friend and Jessop (1969) and more in general, of the IOR school: Friend et al. (1974), Friend and Hickling (1987) and others like Taylor and Hawkins (1972). In the USA, they are perfecting the approaches of Ackoff and Churchman (1950).
25. See Faludi (1973a, b) and the origins of his methodological and epistemological considerations (1986a, b).
26. Among several of Alexander's contributions, see his *Introduction to Planning Theory* (1986) and a paper on 'rationality' in planning (1998).
27. UNRISD (1975, 1980); UN Centre for Housing, Building and Planning (1974). The 'Unified Approach to Planning' was the objective of the United Nations Assemblies resolutions (ECOSOC Resolution no. 1320/1968; 1409/1969; 1494/1970 and General Assembly Resolution no. 2681/1970).
28. On the problem of multidisciplinary convergence of planning, see Hermann Shaller (1976). See also a book of that period by Peter Drucker (1964) with some interesting general visions. More information about this period is included in one of my writings (Archibugi 1996).
29. See Quade and Boucher (1968), Enthoven and Smith (1970).
30. See Marvin and Rouse (1970), Rivlin (1971).

31. Carlson (1970).
32. The literature on PPBS is vast. Beyond the work already referred in **Vol. I**, Chap. 2, Sect. 1, an important contribution to the technology of the PPBS which retains its validity even today are the works of Selma Mushkin (1968 with Willcox, 1969 with Cotton). A general survey which found much audience in the time, through many re-editions, is that of Lee and Johnson (1977).
33. See the work of Washington DC's Institute of Urban Studies, under the influence of William Gorham; for instance, the tenacious works of Hatry and others (1973, 1990). Maybe we owe it to the resistance of the local administrations to continue the experience of the PPBS if today we can witness the relaunching of strategic planning on a public scale in the USA.
34. For the programme evaluation, see the handbook of Wholey Joseph S., Hatry Harry P., and Newcomer Kathrine E. editor. (1994), *Handbook of Practical Program Evaluation*.
35. In France, the programming system of expenditure was called Rationalisation des Choix Budgetaires. In Italy, a trial introduction of budget programming inspired by the American experience saw myself as witness and author (Archibugi 1970); it was dispersed in a climate of indolence and incompetence, which dominated even the part of public administration that was more interested in a planning policy. Things have not gone better in other countries, in which the competence and the economic culture were less superficial than in Italy. Other rare exceptions are the work of Malm (1975) in Sweden, and of Brunhilde Seidel-Kwem (1983) in Germany.
36. See the works of Bryson (1988) and Bryson and Einsweiler, eds (1988).
37. See in the USA, the works in the ambit of the National Academy of Public Administration and of the American Society of Public Administration; see Gage and Mandell (1990).

Bibliographical References to Chapter 8 (Vol. II)

Ackoff, R.L. (1969). "Institutional Functions and Societal Needs." *Perspectives in Planning*, 495–500.
Ackoff, R.L. and Churchman, W.C. (1950). "Purposive Behavior and Cybernetics." In: *Social Forces* 29: 32–39.
Alexander, E.R. (1986). *Approaches to Planning: Introducing Current Planning Theories, Concepts and Issues*. New York, Gordon and Breach.

290   Volume II. Selected Testimonies on the Epistemological...

Alexander Ernest, R. (1998). *Rationality Revisited: Planning Paradigms in a Post-postmodernist Perspective. Planning Theory Conference*, Oxford Brookes University, 2–4 April, School of Planning.

Allison, Michael and Kaye, J. (1997). Strategic Planning for Nonprofit Organizations: A Practical Guide and Workbook. New York, Wiley.

Amara, R. and Lipinski, A.J. (1983). *Strategic Planning. Business Planning for an Uncertain Future. Scenarios & Strategies*. Pergamon.

Ansoff Igor et alii, Ed. (1976). *From Strategic Planning to Strategic Management*. New York, Wiley.

Archibugi, Franco (1970). Rapporto sulla introduzione di un sistema di programmazione di bilancio in Italia. Roma.

Archibugi, Franco. (1996). *Towards a New Strategy of Integrations of Cities into their Regional Environments in the Countries of the European Union, (with special Respect to France, Germany, Great Britain and Italy).* [An Ongoing Report of the Study promoted by the European Commission (DGXII) presented to the 'Second United Nations Conference on Human Settlements (Habitat II)', Istanbul, June 3–4 1996]. [Available also in. www.francoarchibugi.it].

Archibugi, Franco. (2000a). *The Associative Economy: Insights beyond Welfare State and into Post-capitalism*, London, Macmillan, 2000.

Archibugi, Franco. (2000b). 'The 'programming approach': Methodological considerations based on the contributions by Frisch, Tinbergen and Leontief', paper presented to the EAEPE Conference 2000 (Berlin 2–5 November 2000). [Available also in. www.francoarchibugi.it].

Barry, W. Brian. (1997). *Strategic Planning Workbook for Nonprofit Organizations*, Amherst, H. Wilder Found., St Paul Mn.

Bryson, John M. (1988). *Strategic Planning for Public and Nonprofit Organizations: A Guide to Strengthening and Sustaining Organizational Achievement*. San Francisco, Jossey-Bass.

Bryson, John M. and Robert, C. Einsweiler. (1988). The Future of Strategic Planning for Public Purposes. *Strategic Planning: threats and opportunities for planners*. J. M. B. a. R. C. Einsweiler. Chicago, Washington DC, Planners Press: 216–230.

Carlson, J.W. (1970). The Status and Next Steps for Planning, Programming, and Budgeting. *Public Expenditures and Policy analysis*. H. R. H. a. M. J. Chicago, Rand McNally.

Catanese, A.J. and Steiss, A.W. (1970). *Systemic Planning: Theory and Application*. Lexington, MA, Heath Lexington Books.

Chadwick, George. (1971). *A Systems View of Planning: Towards a Theory of the Urban and Regional Planning Process*. Oxford: Pergamon Press. Including chapters: (a) 'Plan or Programme?' (b) 'Planning as a Conceptual System.' [Reprint, PSC, 1971] (c) 'A Mixed-Programming Strategy.' [Reprint PSC, 1971].

Dror, Y. (1971). *Design for Policy Sciences*. Amsterdam: Elsevier.

Dror, Y. (1984). Policy Analysis for Advising Rulers. *Rethinking the Process of Operational Research and Systems Analysis*. R. Tomlinson and I. Kiss. Oxford, Pergamon: 79–124.

Drucker, P.F. (1964). *Managing for Result; Economic Tasks and Risk-Taking Decisions*. New York, Harper.

Enthoven, A.C., and Smith, K.W. (1970). The Planning, Programming, and Budgeting System in the Department of Defense: An Overview from Experience. *Public Expenditures and Policy analysis*. H. R. H. a. M. J. Chicago, Rand McNally.

Faludi, A. (1973a). *Planning Theory*. Oxford, Pergamon.

Faludi, A., ed. (1973b). *A Reader in Planning Theory*. Oxford: Pergamon Press.

Faludi, A. (1986a). *Critical Rationalism and Planning Methodology*. London, Pion Press.

Faludi, A. (1986b). 'The Philosophy of Sir Karl Popper and Its Relevance to Planning Methodology'. In *Critical Rationalism and Planning Methodology*, by A. Faludi, Part II. London: Pion.

Fishburn, P.C. (1973). *The Theory of Social Choice*. Princeton, NJ, Princeton University Press.

Friend, John K., and Jessop, W. N. (1969). *Local Government and Strategic Choice: An Operational Research Approach to the Process of Public Planning*. London: Tavistock.

Friend, John K. et al. (1974). *Public Planning: The Inter-Corporate Dimension*. London, Tavistock Publication.

Friend, John, and Allen Hickling. (1987). *Planning Under Pressure: The Strategic Choice Approach*. 2nd ed. Boston: Butterworth-Heinemann.

Fox, K.A. (1967). "Functional Economic Areas and Consolidated Urban Regions of the United States." *Social Sciences Research Council* (21).

Fox, K.A. (1971). Combining Economic and Non-Economic Objectives in Development Planning: Problems of Concepts and Measurement. *Economic Development and Planning: Essays in Honour of Jan Tinbergen*. W. Sellekaerts. London, Macmillan.

Fox, K.A. (1973). Delimitations of Regions for Transportation Planning. *Perspectives on Regional Transportation Planning*. J. S. De Salvo. Lexington Books, Lexington, Mass.

Fox, K.A. (1974a). *Social Indicators and Social Theory. Elements of an Operational System*, Wiley & Sons, New York.

Fox, K.A. (1974b). Elements of an Operational System III: National and World Models and Data. *Social Indicators and Social Theory*. New York, Wiley.

Fox, K.A. (1974c). Cities and Regions. *Social Indicators and Social Theory: Elements of an Operational System*. F. K. A. New York, Wiley: Chap. 12 (chap ex liber).

Fox, K.A. (1974d). Accounts and Indicators for the Higher Education Sector. *Social Indicators and Social Theory: Elements of an Operational System*. F. K. A. New York, Wiley.

Fox, K.A. (1974e). National Goals Accounting and Policy Models. *Social Indicators and Social Theory: Elements of an Operational System*. F. K.A. New York, Wiley: Chap. 7 (chap ex liber).

Fox, K.A. (1974f). Social Science Concepts Relevant to a System of Social Accounts. *Social Indicators and Social Theory: Elements of an Operational System*. F. K.A. New York, Wiley: Chap. 2 (chap ex liber).

Fox, K.A. (1974g). Elements of an Operational System. II: Cities and Regions. *Social Indicators and Social Theory*. New York, Wiley.

Fox, K.A. (1980). "Philosophical Implications of a System of Social Accounts Based on Roger Barker's Ecological Psychology and a Scalar Measure of Total Income." *Philosophica* 25: 33–54.

Fox, K.A. (1983). "The Eco-Behavioral View of Human Societies and Its Implications for Systems Science." *International Journal of Systems Science* 14(8): 895–914.

Fox, K.A. (1984). "Behavior Settings and Eco-Behavioral Science: A New Arena for Mathematical Social Science Permitting a Richer and More Coherent View of Human Activities in Social Systems." *Mathematical Social Sciences* 7: 117–65.

Fox, K.A. (1985a). The Classification of Behavior Settings in Social System Accounts. *Social System Accounts*. F. K. A. Dordrecht, Reidel.

Fox, K.A. (1985b). *The Classification of Stocks of Physical Capital and Consumer Durables in Social System Accounts*. Dordrecht, Reidel.

Fox, K.A. (1985c). Some Broader Implications of Behavior Settings for the Social Sciences. *Social System Accounts*. F. K. A. Dordrecht, Reidel.

Fox, K.A. (1985d). Behavior Settings and Objective Social Indicators. *Social System Accounts: Linking Social and Economic Indicators Through Tangible Behaviour Settings*. F. K. A. Dordrecht, Reidel.

The Economics as Tool for Measuring and Improving... **293**

Fox, K.A. (1985e). The Usefulness of Behavior Settings for Classifying and Describing Human Activities in a Community. *Social System Accounts.* F. K. A. Dordrecht, Reidel.

Fox, K.A. (1985i). The Classification and Delineation of Communities and Regions in Social System Accounts. *Social System Accounts.* F. K. A. Dordrecht, Reidel.

Fox, K.A. (1985f). Social System Accounts Based on Behavior Settings: Some Next Steps. *Social System Accounts.* F. K. A. Dordrecht, Reidel.

Fox, K.A. (1985g). *Social System Accounts: Linking Social and Economic Indicators Through Tangible Behaviour Settings.* F. K. A. Dordrecht, Reidel.

Fox, K.A. (1985h). The Classification of Roles in Social System Accounts. *Social System Accounts.* F. K. A. Dordrecht, Reidel.

Fox, K.A. (1986a). An Eco-Behavioral Approach to Social Systems Accounting, Time Allocation Matrices and Measures of the Quality of Life. *Economic Psychology: Intersections in Theory and Application.* A. J. MacFadyen and H. W. FacFadyen. Amsterdam, Elsevier Science Publishers.

Fox, K.A. (1986b). "The Present Status of Objective Social Indicators: A Review of Theory and Measurement." *American Journal of Agricultural Economics* 68(5): 1113–1120.

Fox, K.A. (1990). *The Eco – Behavioral Approach to Surveys and Social Accounts for Rural Communities.* Ames, IOWA, Department of Economics, Iowa State University.

Fox, K.A. (1992a). *Describing and Measuring Socioeconomic Systems: Prerequisites to Planning.* (Paper Prepared for the Palermo Conference Volume from the Conference on Planning Science, Palermo, Italy, 8–12 Sept. 1992).

Fox, K.A., Ed. (1992b). *Demand Analysis, Econometrics, and Policy Models.* Iowa State University Press, Ames.

Fox, K.A. and Gosh, S. (1981). A Behavior Setting Approach to Social Accounts Combining Concepts and Data from Ecological, Psychology, Economics, and Studies of Time Use. *Social Accounting Systems.* F. T. Juster and K. C. Land. New York, Academic Press.

Fox, K.A. and Kumar, T.K. (1965). "The Functional Economic Area: Delineation and Implications for Economic Analysis and Policy." *Papers of the Regional Science Association* (15): 57–85.

Fox, K.A. and Miles, G.D. (1987). *Systems Economics: Concepts, Models and Multidisciplinary Perspectives.* Ames, Iowa State University Press.

Fox, K.A. (1987a). The Eco-Behavioral View of Human Societies: Behavior Settings, Time Allocation Matrices and Social System Accounts. *Systems Economics, Concepts, Models, and Multidisciplinary Perspectives.* F. K. A. and M. D. G. Ames, Iowa, Iowa State University Press: 118–142.

Fox, K.A. (1987b). Some Classic Examples of Systems Thinking in Several Sciences: Comment and Recommended Readings. *Systems Economics, Concepts, Models, and Multidisciplinary Perspectives*. F. K. A. and M. D. G. Ames, Iowa, Iowa State University Press: 207–237.

Fox, K.A. and Sengupta J.K. (1969a). Operations Research & Complex Social Systems. *Optimization Techniques in Quantitative Economic Models*. J. K. Sengupta and K. A. Fox. Amsterdam, North-Holland.

Fox, K.A. and Sengupta J.K. (1969b). *Optimization Techniques in Quantitative Economic Models*. Amsterdam, North Holland.

Fox, K.A., Sengupta J.K. (1973a). Economic Policy Models for Development Planning. *The Theory of Quantitative Economic Policy with Applications to Economic Growth Stabilization and Planning*. Fox K.A., Sengupta J.K. and Thorbecke E. Amsterdam, North-Holland: Chap 13 (chap ex liber).

Fox, K.A., Sengupta J.K. (1973b). *The Theory of Quantitative Economic Policy with Applications to Economic Growth, Stabilization and Planning*. Amsterdam, North Holland.

Fox, K.A., Sengupta J.K. (1973c). Introduction to Quantitative Economic Policy. *The theory of Quantitative Economic Policy with applications to Economic Growth Stabilization and Planning*. Fox K.A., Sengupta J.K. and Thorbecke, E., 1973., North-Holland, Amsterdam Chap 1 (chap ex liber).

Fox, K.A., Sengupta J.K. (1973d). National Planning Models for Developed Economies. *The Theory of Quantitative Economic Policy with applications to Economic Growth Stabilization and Planning*. Fox K.A., Sengupta J.K. and A. T. E. Amsterdam, North-Holland: Chap 14 (chap ex liber).

Fox, K.A., Sengupta J.K. (1973e). Stabilization Policy, Regional Growth and Planning. *The theory of Quantitative Economic Policy with applications to Economic Growth Stabilization and Planning*. Fox K. A., Sengupta J.K. and T. E. Amsterdam, North-Holland: Chap 12 (chap ex liber).

Fox, K.A. and Van Moeseke, P. (1973). Derivation and Implications of a Scalar Measure of Social Income. *Economic Structure and Development: Essays in Honor of J. Tinbergen*. B. H. e. alii. New York, American Elsevier.

Gage, R.W., and Mandell, M.P., Ed. (1990). *Strategies for Managing Intergovernmental Policies and Networks*. New York, Praeger.

Hatry, Harry P. et alii (1973). *Practical Program Evaluation for State and Local Government Officials*. Washington, DC, Urban Institute.

Hatry, Harry P. et alii (1990). *Monitoring the Outcomes of Economic Development Programs: A Manual*. Washington, DC, Urban Institute Press.

Koteen, Jack. (1997). *Strategic management in public and nonprofit organizations: managing public concerns in an era of limits*, 2nd ed. Westport, CT, Praeger.

The Economics as Tool for Measuring and Improving... 295

Lee R.D. Jr. and Johnson R.W. (1977). *Public Budgeting Systems*. Baltimore, University Park Press.

Lerner A.P. (1951). *Economics of employment*, McGraw-Hill company.

Malm Allan T. (1975). *Strategic Planning Systems: A Framework for Analysis and Design. Lund*, Studentlitteratur.

Marvin K. E. and Rouse, A. M. (1970). The Status of PPB in Federal Agencies: A Comparative Perspective. *Public Expenditures and Policy analysis*. Haveman R.H. and Margolis J. Chicago, Rand McNally.

McLoughlin J.B. (1969). *Urban and Regional Planning: A System Approach*. London: Faber and Faber.

Moskow, M.H. (1978). *Strategic Planning in Business and Government*.

Mushkin, Selma J., and Willcox, Marjorie. (1968). *An Operative PPB System: A Collaborative Undertaking in the States*. State-Local Finances Project: George Washington University.

Patton C. V. and Sawicki, D. S. (1986). *Basic Methods of Policy Analysis and Planning*. Englewood Cliffs, NJ, Prentice-Hall.

Quade E.S. and Boucher, W. I. (1968). *Systems Analysis and Policy Planning, Applications in Defense*. New York, American Elsevier.

Rivlin A. M. (1971). *Systematic Thinking for Social Action*. Washington, DC, Brookings Institution.

Shaller, Hermann I. (1976). *Unified planning and budgeting in a free society*. Adelphi, MD, Oakview Book Press.

Seidel-Kwem, Brunhilde (1983). *Strategische Planung in Oeffentlichen Verwaltungen*. Berlin, Duncker-Humboldt.

Simon Herbert A. (1941). *Administrative Behavior*. London, Macmillan.

Simon Herbert. A. (1960). *The New Science of Management Decision*. New York, Harper & Row.

Simon Herbert. A. (1983). *Reason in Human Affairs*. Stanford, Stanford University Press.

Sinden J. A. and A. C. Worrell (1979a). *Unpriced Values: Decisions Without Market Prices*. New York, Wiley.

Sinden J. A. and Worrell A. C. (1979b). 'Estimation of Social Values' (chap ex liber). *Unpriced Values. Decisions Without Market Prices*. Sinden J. A. and W. A. C. New York, Wiley: (Chap. 17).

Steiner H. (1979). *Conflict in Urban Transportation*. Lexington, MA, Heath Lexington Books.

Taylor, Bernard and Hawkins, K., Ed. (1972). *A Handbook of Strategic Planning*. London, Longman.

296   Volume II. Selected Testimonies on the Epistemological...

Tinbergen, Jan. (1956a). *Economic Policy: Principles and Design*. Amsterdam, North-Holland.

Tinbergen, Jan (1956b). *The Design of Development*. Rotterdam, Netherlands Economic University.

Tinbergen, Jan (1963a). *The Economic Framework of Regional Planning*. Vatican City, Pontificiae Academiae Scientiarum. (Abstract from the Proceedings).

Tinbergen, Jan (1964). '*Optimal Planning*'. In: *Central Planning*. New Haven, Yale University Press.

Tinbergen, Jan (1969b). 'International Planning of Peaceful Economic Development'. Eds. R. Jungk and J. Galtung. *Mankind 2000*. Oslo/London, Universitetsforlaget/Allen and Unwin.

Tinbergen, Jan, and Gabriella Antonelli. (1967). *Sviluppo e pianificazione*. Il Saggiatore.

Tregoe B.B. and Zimmerman, J. W. (1980). *Top Management Strategy: What It Is How to Make It Work*. New York, Simon and Schuster.

UN Centre for Housing Building and Planning (1974). *The Integration of Economic and Physical Planning*. Draft Report of a Meeting held in, New York, Sept. 1973.

UNRISD. (1975). *Report on a Unified Approach to Development Analysis and Planning*. 24th Session of UN Commission for Social Development, 6–24 Jan., 1975.

UNRISD. (1980). *The Quest for a Unified Approach to Development*.

9

Improving Human Activities and Values as a Strategy to Save Economic Performances and Improvements

9.1 A Great Opportunity: 'Reinventing Government' in the USA

The American experience of the Government Performance and Results Act (GPRA) and its implementation constitutes the institutional base for the consolidation of strategic planning as the main factor of the administrative and managerial renewal of the public sector.[1] Its establishment in the federal experience in effect made it become, with its unavoidable disciplinary and academic applications, central to the training of new public managers. In fact, the GPRA (which consists of the obligation, now routine, to prepare and continuously manage five-year Strategic Plans and Performance Plans, annually, ex ante, and Performance Reports, annually also but in this case ex post) has become the modus operandi of the managerial revolution of public affairs and of the political approach.[2]

© The Author(s) 2019
F. Archibugi, *The Programming Approach and the Demise of Economics*,
https://doi.org/10.1007/978-3-319-78060-3_9

9.1.1 The USA's GPRA Federal Law

The GPRA has all the requirements, political, historical and technical-scientific, to become the reference point for the development of a new professional discipline.

Its didactic and technical-scientific validity emerged from the definition which it prescribed for the contents and requirements of strategic planning.

According to the GPRA, the Strategic Plan of every agency or management unit of the public administration should be articulated in six parts, which by themselves represent a cognitive sequence. These parts are, according my *Introduction of Strategic Planning* (2005):[3]

1. 'A comprehensive mission statement covering the major functions and operations of the agency'; the agency is obliged to revise its mission on the basis of the existing legislation. This mission redefinition constitutes an important step in the 'reinventing' demission, therefore the way to govern.
2. A description of the 'goals and objectives' of the agency, 'including outcome-related goals and objectives, for the major functions and operations of the agency'.
3. A description of 'how' the goals and objectives are to be achieved, including a description of the 'operational processes, skills and technology, and the human, capital, information, and other resources required to meet those goals and objectives'.
4. A description of 'how' the performance goals included in the annual performance plan shall be related to the general goals and objectives in the Strategic Plan.
5. An identification of those 'key factors external to the agency' and beyond its 'control' that could significantly affect the achievement of the general goals and objectives.
6. A description of the 'program evaluations used in establishing or revising general goals and objectives', with a schedule for future program evaluations. (See F. Archibugi, *Introduction to Strategic Planning in the Public Domain*, 2005)

Also very important are the modes which the GPRA prescribed in the elaboration of the Strategic Plan:

- 'The Agency shall consult with the Congress, and shall solicit and consider the views and suggestions of those entities potentially effected by, or interested in such a plan';
- 'The functions and activities of the Strategic Plan shall be considered to be inherently Governmental functions', and that 'the drafting of Strategic Plans should be performed only by federal employees';
- the Strategic Plan 'shall cover a period of not less *five years*, forward from the fiscal year in which it is submitted, and shall be 'updated and revised at least every three years'.

But the conception of strategic planning is further specified by the GPRA through the further definition that it gives to the 'annual' Performance Plans, which it prescribes to the agencies as an annual scanning of the strategic planning.

These Performance Plans are made up of the following parts:

- they 'establish performance goals to define the level of performance to be achieved by a program activity';
- they express such goals in 'an objective, quantifiable and measurable form', unless authorised to be in alternative form;
- they briefly describe 'the operational processes, skills and technology', and the 'human, capital, information, or other resources required, to meet the performance goals';
- they 'establish performance indicators to be used in measuring or assessing the relevant outputs, service level, and outcomes, of each program activity';
- they 'provide a basis for comparing actual program results with the established performance goals'; and
- they 'describe the means to be used to verify and validate measured values'.

The GPRA clearly states that the Performance Plan (one year) 'should be consistent with the Agency's 'Strategic Plan' (five year). Consequently, a Performance Plan 'may not be submitted for a fiscal year not covered by a current Strategic Plan'.

The GPRA also states that, for the purpose of complying with a Performance Plan, 'an agency may aggregate, disaggregate, or consolidate, program activities, except that any aggregation or consolidation may not omit or minimise the significance of any program activity constituting a major function or operation for the Agency'.

Moreover, the GPRA also defines criteria, modalities and nomenclature for the prescribed measuring of the performance and for the programme indicators.

Of course, it is a basic task that every phase of strategic planning should be accompanied by a report ex post of the same plan conceived ex ante, containing analysis, measurement, assessment and updating of the different phases, reconstructing the bases of the next strategic plan.

9.1.2 The Starting 'Universal' Glossary of the GPRA

For the performance measurement, I refer to a kind of *glossary* given by the GPRA itself, as nomenclature:

'*Outcome measure*' means an assessment of the result of a program activity compared to its intended purpose;

'*Output measure*' means the tabulation, calculation, or recording of activity or effort and can be expressed in a quantitative or qualitative manner;

'*Performance goal*' means a target level of performance expressed as a tangible, measurable objective, against which actual achievement can be compared, including a goal expressed as a quantitative standard, value or rate;

'*Performance indicator*' means a particular value, or characteristic, used to measure output or outcome;

'*Program activity*' means a specific activity or project as listed in the program and financing schedules of the annual budget of the United States government;

'*Program evaluation*' means an assessment, through objective measurement and systematic analysis, of the manner and extent to which federal programs achieve intended objectives (USA, GPRA, 1993).

A definitive convergence could be obtained by the use of a kind of 'universal' *glossary* by all organs and agencies participating on the international scale in a harmonisation of certain linguistic expressions of concepts in some technical environment.

In sum, from these specifications, it is quite clear that the mechanism provided by the GPRA implies a prescription to the agencies to proceed in the identification of the appropriate programme indicators.[4] And it grafts on a transformation of the way in which decisions are taken.

The measuring definitions of the GPRA are further perfected in Office of Management and Budget (OMB) circular A-11 of 2004, in a way that deserves to be further specified here, quoting from the original text.[5]

As nomenclature, in fact the GPRA specifies that:

(a) *Strategic Goal or Strategic Objective (also General Goal)*: A statement of aim or purpose included in a strategic plan (required under GPRA) that defines how an agency will carry out a major segment of its mission over a period of time. The goal is expressed in a manner which allows a future assessment to be made of whether the goal was or is being achieved. In a performance budget/performance plan, strategic goals should be used to group multiple programme outcome goals; the program outcome goals should relate to and in the aggregate be sufficient to influence the strategic goals or objectives and their performance measures.

Effective performance budgeting and management relates program performance goals to the agency's strategic goal framework. Programs supporting a goal may be complementary, parallel (serving different populations), alternative (trying different approaches to see which works best), or competitive. Programs supporting a strategic goal can maximise their effectiveness by planning strategy together and coordinating operations. The relative strengths and effectiveness of each program should influence resource allocation to maximise the strategic goal outcome. Changing circumstances or effectiveness would be reflected in modified strategy or focus for the following year.

(b) *Performance Goal*: A target level of performance at a specified time or period expressed as a tangible, measurable outcome, against which actual achievement can be compared, including a goal expressed as a quantitative standard, value, or rate. A performance goal is comprised of a performance measure with targets and time-frames. Program performance goals are included in the performance budget and together contribute to the achievement of strategic goals. The distinction between 'long-term' and 'annual' refers to the relative timeframes for achievement of the goals.

(c) *Performance Measures*: Indicators, statistics, or metrics used to gauge program performance. Typically, program performance measures include outcome, output, and efficiency measures, because each kind of measure provides valuable information about program performance. Collectively, these measures convey a comprehensive story regarding what products and services agencies provide, how well they do so, and with what result.

(d) *Target*: A quantity or otherwise measurable characteristic that conveys how well and by when a program must accomplish a performance measure.

(e) *Outcome*: The intended result, effect, or consequence that will occur from carrying out a program or activity. With respect to programs, an outcome is an event or condition that is external to the program or activity and is of direct importance to the intended beneficiaries and/or the public.

(f) *Output*: The level of activity or effort that will be produced or provided over a period of time or by a specified date, including a description of the characteristics (e.g., timeliness) established as standards for the activity. With respect to programs, outputs refer to the internal activities of a program (i.e., the products and services delivered). Outputs should support or lead to outcomes, just as annual goals should link logically to long-term goals.

(g) *Efficiency measure*: A description of the level at which programs are executed or activities are implemented to achieve results while avoiding wasted resources, effort, time, and/or money. Efficiency can be defined simply as the ratio of the outcome or output to the input of any program.

(h) *Program assessment*: A determination, through objective measurement and systematic analysis, of the manner and extent to which Federal programs achieve intended objectives.[6]

(i) *Performance budget*: A budget presentation that clearly links performance goals with costs for achieving a target level of performance. In general, a performance budget links strategic goals with related long-term and annual performance goals (outcomes) with the costs of specific activities to influence these outcomes about which budget decisions are made. (USA, *Office of Management and Budgeting*, circular A-11, 2004)

In fact, it would not be admissible to take strategic decisions about public expenditure while ignoring the measurement of the effect of such decisions; nor to take decisions—through such measuring—without a consistency analysis of the relationship between the forecast of results and planned objectives.[7] For this reason, I think that the federal GPRA—beyond its capacities to introduce strategic planning in the administration, which seems in any case very successful—represents in itself a very good way of developing a didactic programme concerning strategic planning.

In fact, we cannot overlook that we are dealing with the six requirements of parts of the GPRA which we have been placed at the basis of strategic planning and that are inserted into national legislation. The six requirements refer to a great public organisation such as the federal government of the Unites States (and, through this act, they enter as 'routines' on the 'United States code', that is, in the banality of the administrative practice of a great country). But the novelty and quality of the act in question are surprising, even for the procedures indicated. In substance, the American legislator has imposed on the American federal administrators the regulation of every kind of action, of all the actions in a long-term perspective ('not less than five years'), and the requirement to constantly measure the feasibility of the programme, the availability of instruments and tools for their pursuit, the policies to follow, the 'rationality' of the choices, for a period of at least ten years.[8]

9.1.3 Importance and Feasibility of the GPRA

With a simple, elementary, well-constructed act, the GPRA, which has been the object for decades of political ideological disputations on the role of planning, on its temporal perspective, on its incertitude regarding the environment, and so on, has been rendered pragmatically and operationally 'standardised'. We can say that the cultural advancement recalled above, which was realised in the USA from the 1960s to the 1980s,[9] was eventually translated into a collective 'intelligence', to become the current practice of the administration.

I do not hesitate to compare this authentic revolution in the way of operating in public administration to that which has been the slow, but revolutionary, organisation of the public accounting system (with connected institutions) during a large part of the decades that, in the nineteenth century, accompanied the consolidation of the modern democratic system which still today permits the functioning and the effectiveness of most modern states.[10]

Certainly, corresponding to the revolutionary approach to the strategic planning in the field of public management is the necessary slowness in implementation. We are still at the uncertain first steps of the new system and we are still asking ourselves if it will last, or if it will be extinguished, as happened with the previous attempt.[11]

An important differentiating factor of the GPRA is the fact that it is a law, and a law which is part of the United States Code.[12] Other reforms in the USA have been introduced through presidential directives. The GPRA is not only a creation of the president, but of the entire Congress.[13]

Then there is the general consideration that important changes require much time: the staff must often readapt, and the system and processes must be readjusted.

A privileged witness observed that the information on performance and the results that federal managers use in the managerial programmes and operations form the sustaining buttress for the measurements of the GPRA performances. Some previous efforts have used this (or similar information) in a more limited way, as analysis for decisions. Even though this use is very important, data was taken for special purposes, developed and used only by a limited staff. This staff had scarce or no power over

Improving Human Activities and Values as a Strategy...   **305**

any goals or missions associated with the information. Any connection to what managers would do (or any responsibility for how they would do it) was very remote, if not quite non-existent.

And (more meaningfully), today times have changed since the PPBS experiences. In previous decades, the financing of the American federal programme—as with those of all European countries—was generally more stable, if not increasing. Today, it is decreasing, and the programmes are always more engaged with the explanation of their purposes than the demonstration of their values. Programme efficiency today counts for much more than it did in the past.

9.1.4 The Public Support for Reform of GPRA

While, on the legislative level, the cycle of the GPRA was concluding, with the bipartisan support of both Republican and Democratic senators, in January 1993 the presidential term of Bill Clinton began; the president signed the law that he found ready on his desk. The new administration immediately launched a large-scale campaign in order to give popular support to the new law and create a new body, the National Performance Review (NPR, later NPRG[14]). It was the research for a popular diffusion of the spirit of the new 'Act'—and an explanation of its meaning, intentions and new hopes. The NPR had a quick but intense life, which lasted no longer than the Clinton term. In 2001 its activity ceased with the change of tenant in the White House. The operation 'Reinventing Government', followed the first years of life and functioning of the law, served to popularise the meaning of the law and create an environment of consensus to tackle the radical change in habits and mentality needed for the application of the law.

The American experience of the GPRA has been characterised by two main aspects.[15] One is the introduction for the first time of a precise procedure of strategic planning at the level of all American agencies, and at the level of inter-agency coordination (meaning GPRA implementation). The other has been that of overturning the day-by-day operational methods at the 'front line'; reforms are 'led by the customers' and from the 'partnership of controller/controlled', which I consider political support

306 Volume II. Selected Testimonies on the Epistemological...

for the strategic planning within managing systems of public programmes (meaning the NPRG). This last address was rapidly deleted with the change of administration, but the first—the budgeting alterations of OMB—found a new impetus, by the Bush's administration itself, transforming the traditional budgeting into 'Performance Budgeting'.

9.2 The Successful Federal 'Performance Budgeting'

9.2.1 What Is a 'Performance Budget'?

This happened only in 2004, when the OMB of the President of the USA decided to ask every agency to unify the Annual Performance Plan, as prescribed by the GPRA, with the construction of the annual budget. This was made into an extension of the instructions given yearly by the OMB in a well-known circular (0–11) concerning 'the preparation, presentation and execution of the submission' of the annual budget to the OMB.[16]

Section 220 of the new circular (which is titled 'Preparation and Presentation of the Performance Budget') in fact introduces for the first time the concept of the 'Performance Budget', or budgeting, substituting what was previously provided by the GPRA under the name of the annual performance plan. This unification implied the cancellation of the Annual Performance Plan, and its absorption into the annual budget which, for this reason, became a Performance Budget.

It is opportune, even in this rapid excursus on the recent evolution of budgeting reform in the USA, to refer to the original text of that circular:

> A performance budget is a presentation that clearly links performance goals with costs for achieving targeted levels of performance. In general, a performance budget links strategic goals with related long-term and annual performance goals and with the costs of specific activities that contribute to the achievement of those goals.
>
> A performance budget starts from an overview of what the agency intends to accomplish in the budget year, structured by the goals in the agency's strategic plan. For each strategic goal, the overview would provide

background on what has been accomplished, analyses of the strategies the agency uses to influence outcomes and how they could be improved, analyses of the programs that contribute to that goal, including their relative roles and effectiveness, using *Program Assessment Rating Tool* (PART)[17] assessments when available. The overview should include expected outcomes for each strategic goal, and performance targets for the supporting programs. It should summarize how the agency expects to manage the 'portfolio' of programs for each strategic goal together to maximize the larger strategic outcome. (US-Office of Management and Budgeting 2004, Circular A)

Summary tables and text show the 'pyramid' of how program outcomes and targets support the outcomes for the strategic goals and objectives. Tables also show the full cost paid by the Agency towards each strategic goal and for each programme. Because the plan would be integrated into the Performance Budget, a separate annual performance plan would not be need to satisfy GPRA requirements. (See section 200 for further definitions of performance terms.[18])

The remainder of the Budget may be presented by bureau or other organisation, but each administrative 'entity' should start by analysing its contributions to all strategic goals, followed by a detailed analysis of supporting programs, based on PART information whenever possible. The budget request should be justified on the basis of resources needed to make planned progress toward the strategic goals.

The resources requested for each program should be the amount needed to achieve the target levels for the performance goals for the program. At a minimum, resources are aligned at the program level within this framework, and agencies are encouraged to align resources at the performance goal level. Resources should be fully costed, with centrally funded administrative services and support costs allocated to each program.

The performance budget also includes other information needed to justify the agency budget request. Section 51 [of this circular] specifies the basic justification requirements for the performance budget sent to OMB. Your agency's congressional committees may require additional information for the justification of the performance budget submitted to the Congress.

308   Volume II. Selected Testimonies on the Epistemological...

Best practice last year showed that good performance budgets are often shorter than the sum of the previous plan and budget volumes. They are more analytical and add value by explaining the relationships between past and future performance and budget cost. To make the case that they support improved management, they need to be grounded in the reality of how the programs are run and the agency is organized. This is possible even when programs in different components of an agency work on the same strategic goal. Well-organized and well-written justifications got notably better reception. (US-Office of Management and Budgeting 2004, ibidem, Circular A)

9.2.2 What Data Must Be Included in the Performance

The performance budget, however, must include the performance objective in the form of measurements of performance with time targets. This data must be prepared in order to be useful and valid for the programmes already evaluated by the PART. The OMB circular more precisely defines:

The performance budget includes performance goals (performance measures with targets and time frames) validated for programs assessed by the Program Assessment Rating Tool (PART). Every performance measure documented in an agency's PARTs does not need to be included in the agency's performance budget; however all measures included in the performance budget should meet the standards of the PART guidance. The same is true for programs not yet assessed by the PART; measures and targets included in the performance budget should meet the standards set by the PART guidance. See PART guidance for question 2.1 (of the OMB document at: http://www.OMB.gov/part/2006_part_guidance.pdf)

The performance budget displays up to six years of data for every performance goal, including for the budget year, current year, past year, and three additional past years of data. Only three years of resource data are required. Agencies need not include historical performance data for newly established goals.

As noted in section 51, the means and strategies the agency intends to use to help achieve the performance goals should also be included.

The PART assessments are conducted every year on a subset of Agency programs, prior to agency submission of its Performance Budget to

Improving Human Activities and Values as a Strategy...   **309**

OMB. Subsequently, OMB will use the current and past years' PART assessments to help make decisions as the President's Budget is formulated. The performance targets included in the PARTs and congressional justifications will need to be updated to reflect the budgetary resources and associated performance targets decided for the President's Budget. (US-Office of Management and Budgeting 2004, ibidem, Circular A)

9.2.3 What Is the Relationship Between the Performance Budget and the Strategic Plan?

It has been said that the performance budget must be organised with the same programme structure of an agency's strategic plan. The OMB document emphasises and recommends this kind of structure for the relationship between the performance budget and the Strategic Plan:

> The performance budget is organized as a hierarchy of goals structure like the agency's strategic plan. At the top of the pyramid are strategic goals, which are statements of aim or purpose that are set out in the agency strategic plan. Several agency programs may contribute to achievement of a strategic goal. If programs in different agency components contribute to the same strategic goal, the performance budget should describe how a portfolio of inter-agency programs will help attain the broadly stated aims of a strategic goal.
>
> For each strategic goal, there are usually several outcome goals, and for each outcome goal, there typically are several output goals. The outcome and output goals for programs are the performance measures and targets validated through the PART process and included in the performance budget.
>
> The annual performance report presents information on how well the agency achieved the target levels for its goals in the past year. Some of this past year information is included in the performance budget with the data for program performance measures and targets. Beginning with the report for FY 2004, all agencies will prepare an annual performance and accountability report which will satisfy all of the past-year requirements for the annual performance report. (See sections 26 and 230 [of this circular] for more information on the performance and accountability report.) Therefore, the strategic plan, performance budget and performance and accountability report together satisfy the GPRA requirements for a strategic plan, annual performance plan and annual performance report.

310   Volume II. Selected Testimonies on the Epistemological...

The congressional justification may include additional and updated past year performance data. If additional performance data is used, you should take special care in the design of your congressional justification to identify those performance goals against which actual performance will be compared in your annual performance and accountability report. (US-Office of Management and Budgeting 2004, ibidem, Circular A)

It is clear from these short quotations that the OMB fully assumed in its own role the implications of the GPRA in the structuring of the federal budget. All this took time (around five years after the first steps towards strategic planning were taken within the federal government). But at the same time, it is clear that the new Bush administration completely assumed the GPRA objectives of 'strengthening government performance and accountability'.

As we have seen, a key purpose of the Act is to create closer and closer links between the process of allocating scarce resources and the expected results to achieve with those resources. The new administration has made budget and performance integration one of the five government-wide management priorities under the President's Management Agenda.

The Executive Branch Management Scorecard tracks how well departments and major agencies are executing the five initiatives of the President's Management Agenda.

9.2.4 Improving the Evaluation Within the 'Performance Budgeting'

A central element in these initiatives is PART, elaborated by the OMB. The OMB describes the PART as a 'diagnostic tool meant to provide a consistent approach to evaluating federal programs as part of the executive budget formulation process'.

It is time that we dedicated special consideration to PART in our examination of where strategic planning is going.

The PART—the Guide of the Office of Management Budget says (OMB, March 2006)—is 'a diagnostic tool used to access the performance of federal programs and to drive improvements in program performance. Once completed, PART reviews inform budget decisions and

Improving Human Activities and Values as a Strategy... **311**

identifies actions to improve results. Agencies are held accountable for implementing PART follow-up actions, also known as improvement plans, for each of their programs.'

The PART is therefore designed to provide a consistent approach to assessing programmes across different government. PART assessments review overall program effectiveness, from how well a program is designed to how well it is implemented and what results it achieves. As such, the PART examines factors that the program or agency may not directly control but may be able to influence. For example, if a PART assessment identifies a statuary provision that impedes effectiveness, one of the follow-up actions maybe for the agency to propose legislative programmes to fix it.

The PART questions are generally written in a *Yes/No* format. A *Yes* answer must be definite and reflect a high standard of performance. *Not applicable* may be an appropriate answer when indicated by the guidance prepared by the OMB; *small extent* and *large extent* are also options for certain special questions made in cases described also by the guide of the OMB.

The OMB guide considers the PART as central to the so-called Administrations Budget and Performance Integration Initiative, because it drives a sustained focus on *results*. To earn a high part rating, a programme must use performance data to manage, justify its resources request based on the performance it expects to achieve, and continually improve efficiency—all goals of the Budget and Performance Integration Initiative.[19]

The PART process continues to aid the OMB's oversight of agencies and encourage improvements in executive budget formulation and agency programme management. The PART has helped to structure and discipline OMB's use of performance information for internal programme analysis and budget review and made its use of this information more transparent. Many agency officials state that the PART 'helped to create or strengthen an evaluation culture within agencies by providing external motivation for program review and focussed attention on performance measurement and its importance in daily program management'.[20]

Some other officials have said that the PART helped them move away from 'analysis by anecdote' and refocused their attention on the impact their programme had, instead of largely on output measures. Others echoed a similar sentiment; one indicated that the PART scores helped to create 'a new sense of urgency' about performance measures and completing the changes to performance systems that were already underway.[21]

In any case we can say that the PART was designed for, and is used in, the executive branch budget preparation and review process; as such, the goals and measures used in the PART must meet OMB's needs. Compared to the relatively open-ended GPRA planning process, any executive budget formulation process is likely to seem closed.

Independently of the technicalities of its procedures,[22] the PART has introduced at large scale—that is for all kind of public administration, at least at federal level—an organic system evaluation, permanently improving the public administration service; this is a powerful instrument to compare effectiveness between different activities and to guide any eventual policy analysis.

In this way, people hope that in a few years, the system of strategic planning will reach the point of covering all the best performances in the federal administration and arrive at the achievement of a final budget, considered through performance, which will be an instrument for making much more effective choices than before over the allocation of public money. This will constitute an effective way to reinvent government action.[23]

Now we will take a glance at the 'state of the art' concerning the application of strategic planning in some other European countries.

9.3 A Glance at Current Success and Failure of Strategic Planning

9.3.1 The Unhappy Case of the British and French Experiences

The first country in Europe which was in a condition to experiment with a wide application of the strategic planning in its public Administration, in terms similar to what was happening in the USA with the GPRA, was Great Britain. In this country, in effect—as in other countries belonging to the old British Empire with many ties of history, culture and administrative derivation (as in Australia, Canada,

Improving Human Activities and Values as a Strategy...   313

South Africa and New Zealand) has been developed—in the field of public management, academic, and political sciences, the concept of New Public Management, which is roughly that expressed in the USA with 'Reinventing Government', was developed.

In the last two decades, people have paid much attention to improving public institutions. In Great Britain, for example, a law was introduced in 1998—Comprehensive Spending Review—after several documents prepared at Tony Blair's cabinet, papers of a certain interest, concerning the basic concept of 'delivery' of public service; and as conclusion of a long period of the John Major government when important institutional reforms occurred on the number, the composition and nomenclature of governmental agencies.

The new law on the Spending Review tried to build a kind of programming of public expenditure and to define public services agreements, with the approximate indication of the results to be achieved. However, the programming has been so disorderly and confused that after two years the PSA was re-considered and a real evaluation of the result was not carried out.

Many additional new Comprehensive Spending Reviews have been passed, but the management of the PSA became uncertain until the political renouncement of the Cameron Government.

If the New Public Management was strongly flag-waved in Great Britain, it was even more so in the Commonwealth countries.

In France, many attempts at reforms developed during the second half of the twentieth century. Introducing the 'New Public Management'—not unlike other member countries of the OECD—did not achieve excellent results and included the attempt to introduce the American Planning-Programming-Budgeting System (PPBS), which in France took the name of 'Rationalisation of the Budget Choices' (Rationalisation des Choix Budgetaires).

However, a leap of quality in the application of result-based management and strategic planning occurred with the bill of 2001, called the 'Organic law concerning the financial laws' (Loi Organique des Lois Financières—LOLF), which two governments (one of the left, which launched it, one of the right, which had to manage it) have searched to apply without many differences of approach, and with a laudable bipartisan spirit.

With a law of 2001, France revolutionise was named '*the* new budget architecture of the state'.[24]

Unlike the American GPRA, the French LOLF is based more directly on a financial routine. This may be because the French constitutional ordainment does not see, as the USA does, the parliament as being directly responsible for the financial management of the country.

The GPRA was born of a bipartisan commission of the Congress, and not of the executive branch, even if it was the product of a cultural and political evolution that was permeating all the branches and activities of the administration, under the imperative of making the results of the public expenditure explicit and forcing the disclosure and public evaluation of the results of every dollar spent by the taxpayer in any direction of public expenditure.

The LOLF was created in the Ministry of Finance (now 'of the Economy, Finance and Industry', Minifie) and in the financial agencies (for instance the Court des Comptes). It is a law for the reordering of the modality of public expenditure and of the construction of the public budget but always in the traditional approach as it has been for decades, or better to say, for ever, that is, from the perspective of essentially annual terms.[25]

It is sufficient to compare the first articles of the two laws in order to immediately see the difference between the spirit of the two laws, even if the procedure, in certain ways, reaches the same goals and conclusions.

The American law is dominated by the objective which people intend to pursue; the objective of building a budget based on an effective feasibility of the goals proposed in different areas, in order to give sense to the results in connection with those goals.

The French law is concerned, rather, with the definition of the nature of public resources and the procedures required in order to decide their employment. The question of the objectives is subordinate to the question of the procedures. On the American side, in the GPRA, the first step suggested to the Agencies is to reconstruct the mandate and to build a programme structure on this mandate and to define the objectives of the strategic plan on this structure.

In short, I have the impression that the American law renders strategic planning a political fact, giving priority to the management of the financial means of the budget, whilst the French law makes strategic planning (even without mentioning it) a technical fact, to be solved within each individual agency for the improvement of its cost-result analysis and to present itself to the (annual) request of public credit with a better consciousness of the developing activities.[26]

Consequently, to understand 'Strategic planning: where is it going?' in the renewal of public management, it is sufficient to read the GPRA, which in only a few pages already represents an essential guide for any administration or federal agency, on how to build planning documents, rational and explicit at the same time.[27]

From the GPRA procedures, a general vision will not immediately emerge of all the 'missions' of the state and of the financial means at disposal. However, something else emerges: the possibility for the measurement, and the scales for that measurement—for each programme and item of the expenditure of every administration—of what people obtain against the fixed expenditure. Thus, people can instigate a process of comparison, of concrete evaluation and of the useful exemplification even at the inter-agency (inter-ministerial) level.

From the French procedure there can emerge, even more rapidly, a 'comprehensive framework' about where the money of the State goes each year (by missions, sub-missions, and even for single expenditure items). However, if a strategic planning process is not introduced soon, ministry by ministry, program by program, the ignorance will last for a long time about how that money is effectively spent. In that situation, I do not believe that strategic planning, which is the interest of this book, would go very far.[28]

The American case started with a request for the introduction of analysis and evaluation of the objectives, and of the indicators capable of measuring its achievement, in order to build a budget where it would be possible to get figures tested by the strategic planning of the agencies.

In the French case, the system started by requesting measurements of control and evaluation of the items of expenditure, during the composition of the accounting of the public budget. Therefore, as said, in France the reform started as a public budget reform, from which sprang the public agency management reform. In the USA, the reform started with new methods of agency management, through programming, from which sprang the performance budget of single agencies and from here the reform of the general budget of the confederation.

316   Volume II. Selected Testimonies on the Epistemological...

However, the two parts are destined to flow together and to merge. For instance, in France, in the years following the LOLF (2001) and in the years of its implementation, the Ministry of the Economy, Finance and Industry have multiplied the prescriptions and the guidelines (specifically, from the—intentionally created—'directorate for the reform of the budget') aimed at all public administrations, with the aim that they could adopt strategic planning methods in the programming of their activities. These methods are unique in giving a serious opportunity to know if the budget items correspond truly to a given level of performance and of each measurement. In the USA, on the contrary, people are giving ever more attention to the evaluation of agency programmes on the 'inter-agency' or 'government-wide' scale. The LOLF has in any case shaken up public management practices in France. All this is concentrated in the activities of Minifie, and a huge quantity of documents has been drawn from it, especially in the last years. And all this cannot avoid producing a great and important technical and cultural effect in the behaviour and practices of the mid-level officers of the administration.[29]

France was the traditional inspiration for the Italian reforms in the field of public administration. In my personal teaching experience at the Italian High School of Civil Officers on the matter of Strategic Planning, over the past 20 years I have met some difficulties and limited interest in my partisan attitudes in favour of the American experience of the GPRA. In Italy the cultural roots of the administrative problems are more juridical than economic, more focused on the legitimacy aspects than based on the efficiency and practical.[30]

I do not have the requisite competence in social anthropological studies and matters, but I think that the programming approach should think a lot—in its integrative approach—about unified consideration of cultural roots. Never like the actual time should need in the new public management, be open to a system of programming truly open even from this point of view.

I sincerely consider the evolution of the implementation of the GPRA in USA in the last 20 years a fortunate opportunity for many countries, countries who may wish to follow the trace of the 'American reinventing government', as an acceleration of the rhythm of their integration in the world of globalisation, profiting from the great work that some federal institutions (such as GASB and FASAB) are doing around the standards for a indicators common programming, in the engineering of the design of project.

9.3.2 Other OECD Countries

Personally, I have not the capacity to say anything about the state of business in the field of current reforms in administrative policies, oriented similarly to successful and less successful reforms in other countries and governments of the United Nations family.

9.3.3 The American Reinvention of Government

To the good fortune of non-American people, the American 'reinventing government' approach won.

I hold that such victory represents one of the most curious, great, and promising social and political reforms of all of humanity, after the discovery of the American continent, the establishment and discovery of constitutional democracy, the 'secularisation of cults', the universal affirmation of human rights, especially gender equality and those less controversial, including those tied to natural, ethnic, health and family rights.

I say social and political reform since those are directly connected to nature if not connected to anything else but that of the social nature of humans living together and in solidarity, as both beneficiaries and contributors without alternatives.

It is curious because it is a reform that involved society as a whole and does not allow for disconnection from the most extreme doctrines of solipsism. They are reforms that are still far from finding a solution without the active participation of an educated humanity aware of its rights and duties, to be defined by dialogue and cooperation, and certainly not by violence or force. Therefore, it is in this direction that many populations have already chosen, creating institutions throughout the globe with equal and open participation.

One of the greatest achievements of the reform is that of sharing values across groups and through vision and conviction.

9.4　The Increased Role of the United Nations

Proposal for the UNO Program in Public Administration and Development (see **Vol. II**, Appendix 2).

9.5　The Essentials Content of the Strategic Planning Process: General Principles

9.5.1　The Strategic Planning Process: Phases or Cycles

Keeping in mind the warnings from the previous section, we can now move on to outline the fundamental architecture of a planning process, one on which could be based both the path of a learning process concerning the method for introducing the process, and the path of action aimed at in the implementation of a strategic planning process within an individual planning unit.

The whole process that we examine is structured in six fundamental phases:

1. The identification of the subject of the mandates, of the target people and other interested parties (the so-called 'stakeholders');
2. The programme structuring;
3. The measurement of performance and the identification connected to it of the programme indicators;
4. The programme engineering, that is, the specification of action and project management;
5. The operational cost analysis and the study of their funding; the construction of programme budgeting;
6. The programme monitoring, programme revision and the feed-back process.

Where does one begin in order to build a strategic plan? To answer this question means taking the first step in learning the subject matter.

On planning as a process there are already a legion of treatments, whether didactic or operational.[31]

With strict reference to the didactic needs and opportunities of new public administration managers, we have assessed some of these treatments from which we have drawn, after much reflection, our own suggested course.

However, before delving into the description of the preferred and suggested course, it is opportune to make some other considerations of a general character about the meaning of the entire process.

In effect, such a process of planning presupposes a tension towards the future. And it presupposes that—in as much as it be different and opposed—any configuration of aspirations, wishes, needs, goals and objectives, by the related aspirants and/or decision makers (in the name of the aspirants) could be a configuration based on some value judgements.

This is a matter of judgements on possible and desired future states which are always subject to the passing of time, to the contradictions, to the reciprocal clashes and to the conflict between different holders of different interests, and so on. This is why, whatever the operationally and didactically preferred or technically suggested process, it should be accompanied by a series of cautions to be incorporated internally into the process itself.

Here we can detect some of those cautions about three peculiar points, always present in the debate on planning: those of uncertainty, of flexibility and of iteration. We will deal, in brief, with these three points as a marginal and preventive comment to the suggested process (Fig. 9.1).

9.5.2 Uncertainty in the Planning Process

The question of uncertainty in planning has been an argument that has occupied many people who have written about planning and all those who have highlighted its limits, its failures and its impossibilities. It would take too long, at this point, to summarise the whole debate, also because it has taken the direction of philosophical-type considerations, which—even if interesting per se—have been barely useful in order to improve the management capacity of the planning process.

Here we will limit ourselves to some general considerations, which, it seems to us, can give a sufficient foundation to the positive application of strategic planning.

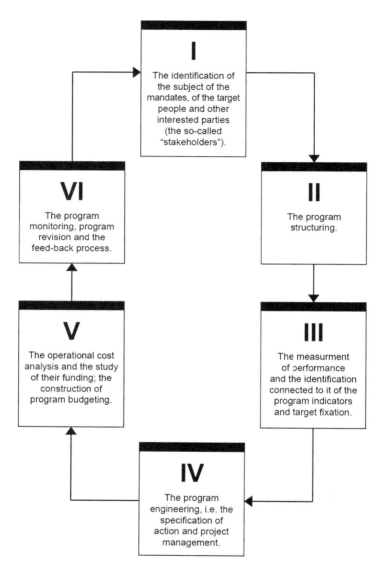

Fig. 9.1 Strategic planning cycle process. (Source F. Archibugi: Introductory lectures of Strategic Planning, High School of Public Administration, Rome (1998/9))

We will start by saying that uncertainty in respect to the future is an inherent condition of any kind of planning. There is no aspect, no moment, no type of planning which would not be subject to future uncertainty. If we have said that the future can be considered a sequence of events and planning a sequence of programmed actions acts to determine a sequence of desired events, we must also state that part of these events, programmed or not, will constitute a surprise. If experience had proved that the future consists only of unexpected events, planning would be a hopeless exercise. But experience tells us that the future is a mix of unexpected events and of foreseeable events, of events which can be displayed on a continuum of probability, of events that are displayed in a range from those that are relatively certain to those whose occurrence is totally unexpected.

One aspiration of planning can be precisely that of refining the perception of possible future events, one in connection with the other, and conceiving of events which can be controlled even without effective future explorations.

Many things can be done in respect to the future. One is to ignore it. If it is not to be ignored, it is wise to attempt to prepare for it in advance. The forecast will be successful, however, if its success is defined in-depth. To expect to anticipate a sequence of positive events in the future means to search for any failures. But to project and to work with respect of a desired sequence of events, means to 'create' the future, and it can certainly be partially successful, as many human efforts indicate. Houses are built, marriages are consummated, degrees are obtained. And, on the other hand, there are also earthquakes, floods, wars, aerial disasters, divorces, competitors who beat us and so on.

It is often appropriate to seek, first of all, to prepare the mentality of managers for an effective performance through a planning process, and to engage ourselves in those activities which are considered the most effective in such a preparation. Plans are prepared in order to assure that such a process not be ephemeral and that a valuable reflection not be lost. In order to capitalise on the effort in creating plans, specific activities are identified with the purpose of implementing such activities on the condition that the assumptions made as the base of the plans' development be accurate. But if these assumptions are later shown to be wrong, the plans should be thrown out and substituted by new plans. If the planning process has prepared the manager for a future which is meaningfully different from that prospective, owing to the uncertainty and to the incapacity to accurately determine the nature of the future, the assumptions and the planning process should both be analysed to seek to improve past performance.

Whilst it is often said that one of the main aims of planning is to acquire adequate data, it is also possible to observe competing organisations which seem to have access to the same data, but which also have totally different results.

This induces one to think that the role of data in planning could probably be less important than the way in which it is used, that is, the preparation of the minds of the leaders and managers to interpret and use the data in the effort to implement the desired events.

Therefore, the process of planning should not be defamed because of present uncertainty.

To learn from what the available information supplies to us is the most important thing, and the identification of the type of information which is necessary, but unavailable, should be considered a useful consequence of planning, given the fact that it can suggest actions seen to improve the future information flow for, or within, any subject or unity of planning.

9.5.3 Flexibility in the Planning Process

Is it possible to project a planning process that is sufficiently generic to be applied to different subjects or planning units, and sufficiently flexible to be adaptable to the particular needs of any individual planning unit?

Further, is it possible to indicate a planning process that could constitute, in spite of the affirmed flexibility, a reference frame for any type of plan projecting?

Instead of answering the question in a definitive way, perhaps it would be more appropriate to deal with the question as a matter of exploration. That is, we can assume that the framework exists and we can put further questions before it.

Does the framework confirm that every plan always has the same particular primary purpose?

Does it require that a certain course be followed, whatever may occur in the future?

Does it require activities which go beyond the given limits of time and resources?

Certainly, planning should have a primary, well-defined purpose, since success in planning is strongly related to the definition and achievement of its purpose, and limited resources are rapidly dissipated when too many purposes are aimed at with too few resources.

Certainly, planning should discover specific activities which seem to be appropriate targets for resource allocation. Otherwise, the uncertainty which would emanate from the process would be intolerable.

But the choice of the primary purpose could be left to the particular situations, and both the planning process and the plan itself will contain bifurcations, subject to choice at the appropriate moments.

Management should be heavily involved in the process of planning and decision-making as far as the process evolves; it should govern the process and the plan, rather than be governed by both of them. One of the first bifurcations in the planning processes is to determine the main planning purpose for the planning unit in question: how will this influence what is done, how it is done, and what is developed in its implementation?

9.5.4 Iteration in the Planning Process

It is generally accepted that plans require revision and that any planning process is iterative (or cyclic).

Plans would not require frequent re-consideration unless people did not make mistakes in planning. Since mistakes are considered an inefficiency factor, they are also considered something to avoid, but as long as mistakes are considered something to reproach, there will be an effort to avoid them, and as long as there is an effort to avoid mistakes, there will be a reluctance to discuss the uncertain. This is the reason why it should be opportune in the planning process to include the acceptance of mistakes. In whatever way plans could be made, to 'think the unthinkable' should be the appropriate, acceptable way to operate planning.

This does not mean that the most desirable deliberate objective of planning should be to build a plan full of mistakes. But since ideas stimulate ideas, exploration opens mental processes, and the strange and unaccustomed produces new ideas, a creative and mistake-open environment is appropriate to the exploration aspects of planning.

The generation of ideas should remain separate from the evaluation of ideas. Many ideas will seem to be poor at the end and not kept in the final plan. But unless these ideas have the possibility of existence and development, there is a great danger that the few creative ideas that should take their role in planning never surface. Thus, being open to making mistakes does not mean a deliberate acceptance of mistakes; rather, it means the suspension of discredit until an appropriate set of ideas can be developed and explored sufficiently, in order to produce a certain number of them to be inserted, at the end, into the plan.

Without new ideas, planning can rarely play the role of renovating managerial capacity, nor can there be a high probability of achieving other forms of success.

9.5.5 Planning and Evaluation

The strategic planning process of a programme identifies itself in a permanent process of evaluation of the objectives and of the means to achieve them. Every moment, every phase of the strategic planning process is imbued with moments and phases of evaluation.

Since an extended activity of research and application has been developed around the procedures, methods and techniques of evaluation (a development most of the time disjointed by the objective planning or programming process) and since in strategic planning the connection between the two processes is developed—as said—until it becomes identical, it is opportune that in such a relationship, in such a connection and such an identity, we spend, here, some general consideration in our introductive approach to strategic planning. In brief, it is opportune that one could clarify the basic concept of an evaluation aimed at planning, and of a planning permanently engaged in evaluation.

Right now, we could use some significant slogans, such as: 'Planning (or programming) and evaluation are two faces of the same coin'; or: 'As planning is inconceivable without evaluation, so evaluation is inconceivable without planning,' and so on. In as much as these slogans are appropriate in their conciseness and axiomaticity, however, it is good that they be explained more concretely in their real function. It is best that from now on in this introductory book, they be discussed and defined in more general terms.

In the strategic planning process, I insist that those evaluative moments be permanent and accompany all phases of the process itself.

In the application, however, of these evaluative moments, and related methods within the various phases of the process, we need to take into account certain aspects of the planning-evaluation relationship, which we will call 'general conditions' exactly because they can influence the efficiency and the meaning itself of the evaluation applications. These general conditions are dealt with here in a very schematic way and concern:

1. the epistemological foundations of evaluation;
2. the determinants of 'social utility';
3. the formation of social values; and
4. the current places where, in our advanced society, social utility is expressed.

It is matter of the principles of common knowledge, which are almost obvious but yet are best to recall in a concise way, as the basis for further references and applications of the strategic evaluation process within the planning framework.[32]

9.5.6 Conditions and General Limits of Strategic Evaluation

To evaluate means to give a value to something. It is difficult, therefore, not to shift—speaking of evaluation in general—to a theory of value. But we will do that in the most schematic and rapid way possible, establishing some supporting premises for our future use of the concept of evaluation in the planning process.

(a) *Concept of value*

Value is a property of things; but different from that of colour or of weight. The value of a thing derives substantially from the need or the wishes which it is capable of satisfying. The greater this capacity, the greater will be the value of the thing. This is the way our concept of 'value' has been channelled and restrained here, and it has been constrained to be identified as that of 'utility'.[33]

(b) *Variability in value*

Value is not a fixed and inherent property in things. It is, rather, a variable property, the size of which is dependent not only upon the nature of the thing in itself, but also upon who evaluates it and upon the circumstances in which it is evaluated. A thing can have different values according to different goals, in different moments, for different persons, and under different conditions (that is, the physical environment within which one evaluates it), according to the different circumstances (personal, physical, psychological, social and political) of the evaluator at the moment of evaluation.[34] One can ask: but if value is a variable propriety, how can it be a guide for decisions? The answer is implicit if we accept the idea that decisions are not and could never be general and universal decisions. They represent, always, limited choices which seem the best solution regarding the problems that we must face. Human problems tend to be specific and the decisions which concern them must be equally specific. This principle of the 'specificity' of evaluations must never be forgotten when the specificity of problems that we encounter, leads us to decide on actions that are developed over time (long-time horizons) and on problems of a general nature. For instance, social problems that do not concern specific individuals, but, on the contrary, specific communities.

(c) *Evaluation as a condition of the existence of value*

If value does not exist *per se*, but only for the utility which it produces, the utility also exists as far as, and in the moment when, it is evaluated. Neither the value nor the utility exists without evaluation; moreover, they exist only in the moment of the evaluation.

(d) *The decision as a condition of the existence of evaluation.*

On the other hand, even value gains concreteness only in context of a decision. Even when there exists a general consensus on the value (this consensus is not difficult to achieve in political life) we appreciate, truly, the value of things and of actions only in particular circumstances and situations when the values are confronted with the practical possibility to apply them, even though it limits their capacity to have worth as such. (For this reason, in political life it is in their application to circumstances that divergences of opinion and conflict of evaluation emerge.) Since values can be concretely appreciated only in the course of a decisional process, their validity depends, strongly, on the process itself. In other words, how much good the values can be as a guide to decisions, strongly depends, not on the values themselves, but on the way in which the decisions are made.

(e) *The subjects of evaluations*

However, beyond these abstract definitions that are at the basis of evaluation, we must never forget that this is always conditioned by the subjectivity of the individual who makes the evaluation; that is, the evaluation is an act which presupposes the actor, the agent and the subject (be it individual or political). Even when these last are not apparent in the way in which things are evaluated, this is because they become understated, because no action exists without an actor, nor any evaluation without an evaluator.

(f) *The evaluation as a decision and the decision as an evaluation*

As we have said above, significant values, therefore, through evaluation, are determined in the context of a choice which involves a decision.[35] In sum, values are appreciated in the cause of the decisional process which will always be circumstantial.[36] Therefore, the amount of good values have as a guide for decisions, depends, strongly—as previously stated—on how and why decisions are made.

(g) *Decisional situations*

Thus, there are decisional situations that determine the value and the utility and impact the evaluation, the choice and the decision. The decisional situation influences the evaluation process and its contents. It is from such decisional situations that many of the classical problems are born (for economic reflection): for instance, those of scarcity, those connected to the theorem of exchange, of marginal or decreasing utility of goods, and those of their 'positionality'. This has worth for the determination of value or of overall individual utility, and also for the determination of 'social' utility (of communities, of groups, and so on). Scarcity, for instance—beyond being strongly

328   Volume II. Selected Testimonies on the Epistemological...

influenced by the well-known, subjective factors—determines the relative value of things and actions on the basis of decisional situations. Even the most materially objective basic needs (food, health, shelter) and the perception of scarcity regarding them, are impacted by decisional situations, and can be the object of 'preference' (be it individual or collective).

If, from an epistemological or semantic point of view, all this has worth at the level of individual or social evaluation, we are dealing only with the social aspect of the evaluation, that is, of that evaluation that is made (1) in the name of collective and social interests, and (2) as members of a collective.[37]

Notes to Chapter 9 (Vol. II)

1. US Congress (1993). *The Government Performance and Result Act* (GPRA) and Report of the Committee on Governmental Affairs of US Senate.
2. GAO (General Accounting Office). *Executive Guide: Effectively Implementing the GPRA* (June 1996). Washington DC.
3. We reproduce a text that was published in Italian, in 2005, by the publisher Alinea, in Florence. We keep the pages of the Italian edition until an English edition is available.
4. On the concept and practice of the programme indicators, I have behind me decades of reflections, applications and suggestions. I have had the occasion to illustrate my methods (Archibugi 1992a), republished in *Social Indicator Research* (Archibugi 1996).
5. OMB (Office of Management and Budget), *Circular No. A-11. Preparation, Submission, and Execution of the Budget*, July 2004, Washington DC.
6. This list is short, but the OMB text here reproduced suggests for additional information on developing performance measures and definitions. See www.whitehouse.gov/omb/part/ for the FY 2006 PART guidance, 'Examples of Performance Measures', and 'Performance Measurement Challenges and Strategies'. OMB (Office of Management and Budget), Guide to 'Program Assessing Rating Tool'—PART (March 2006).
7. In effect, it is on the performance measuring of a programme in the sector of public activities that we have recently had an unhoped-for flowering of studies and handbooks; for the federal American agency see the handbook

Improving Human Activities and Values as a Strategy... 329

already recalled above. Moreover, even the General Accounting Office, which is a key organisation for the connection between result measuring and budget accountability, has produced many interesting 'executive guides' (that is, that people are invited to follow) for the agencies, on the matter of obtaining results evaluation. The flowering, both of the research centre and of the academic programs, to update the new needs of the public sector, of expertise and also of personal training, has been impressive in the years after the launch of the GPRA, from 1993 until today.

8. Archibugi F., www.whitehouse.gov/omb/part/ for the FY 2006 PART guidance, 'Examples of Performance Measures', and 'Performance Measurement Challenges and Strategies'.

9. Which have not themselves been exempt from the difficulties and misunderstandings encountered in the political and operational worlds.

10. The GPRA has developed in the ambit and the climate of intense debate among the public management scholars, which took place in the 1980s, and of which I will recall some works (maybe not the most important): Benveniste (1987), Bozeman and Straussman (1990), Barzelay (1992).

11. 'Will history be repeated?' is the question asked, in a lucid examination of the new bill and of its perspective, by Walter Groszyk (1995), an experienced manager of the OMB. Could the GPRA be another reform with a brief flourishing, which will soon wither? What makes the GPRA different from those previous initiatives, and why should it have success when the others did not?

12. The US Code, or simply, the Code, is a compilation of federal laws that have a current validity. The Code is 'the consolidation and codification of all the general and permanent laws of the United States [...] in force' (from the preface of the US Code, 1970). The code of the United States is published in its entirety every six years, with the cumulative updates issued every year.

13. Laws such as the GPRA—states Groszyk, one of the first gurus of GPRA—can be durable monuments for governance, but the presidential directives are more fragile. In fact, many of the previous initiatives started and finished with the presidential term. See also an acute essay by Mihm (1995–1996).

14. In 1998, the NPR was transformed into the National Partnership for Reinventing Government. The change of name was motivated by the wish to emphasise the stability of the review process. But the change to the Bush's administration led to dismantling immediately any diffusion, supporting and propaganda activity of the NPRG. Perhaps it has been the

330   Volume II. Selected Testimonies on the Epistemological...

price for a survive of the further steps of the GPRA, in rationalising and improving on its successful result of strategic planning policy, performing budgeting and self-evaluation, in full harmony with the OMB and GAO.

15. US Congress (1993). The Government Performance and Result Act (GPRA) and Report of the Committee on Governmental Affairs of US Senate.

16. OMB (2006), (Office of Management and Budget). Three Circulars: (1) for the Initial Guidance and Schedule for 2006 PART Process; (2) for the Guidance for Completing 2006 PART; (3) Updating PART Improvement Plans and Performance Data in PART-Web.

17. This is a system of evaluation previously introduced by the OMB, about which we will speak later.

18. These definitions have also been reproduced in this chapter, when we referred to the GPRA measurement definitions.

19. We will return to the meaning of the PART on the programme assessment or evaluation or below when we will deal with the relationship between planning and evaluation in the strategic planning process (Chaps. 5, 6 and 7).

20. See GAO Performance Budgeting: PART Focuses Attention on Program Performance, but More Can be Done to Engage Congress (October 2005, doc. GAO-06-28). This document is interesting because it opens the door to the way in which all the performance budgeting reforms can create a totally new way of political decision-making by Congress.

21. Ibid., p. 5.

22. In my introduction to strategic planning (under production) there will be an appendix of the PART, which will be explained more in detail in terms of the methods, criteria and implementation, including reference to the quoted OMB guide to the PART (March 2006).

23. It has been the GAO (General Accounting Office, later renamed Government Accountability) that has produced same basic document on the event 'Performance Budgeting': GAO (2004), *Performance Budgeting, Observations on the Use of OMB's Program Assessment Rating Tool for the Fiscal Year 2004 Budget*, January 2004; GAO (2005), *Performance Budgeting, Efforts to Restructure Budget to Better Align Resources with Performance*.

24. Ministère de l'Economie. *La démarche de performance: Strategie, Objectifs, Indicateurs* (2004).

25. From a certain viewpoint, we could say that the French process approaches the reform from the opposite side of the process to that taken by the American experience: from the reform of the structure of the

budget, which in the American case is the last phase (as we have seen) of the implementation of the GPRA. But we must ask ourselves: is it possible to approach the reform of the budget, and to construct a performance budget correctly, if we have not previously analysed the programs step by step, programme by programme, through first the structuring and then a new engineering of each programme, as is the process established by the GPRA?

The risk in the French case is that the new performance budgeting—even adopting a new nomenclature that is apparently more connected with the functional role of each program—remains an expression of the current action analysis and decision within each program, making superficial changes, without changing the real effectiveness of actions.

26. I have collected more information on the poor experience in other European countries about was commonly defined as new public management in a report prepared for the Italian Government in 2008. It is published only in Italian: Franco Archibugi: *Da burocrate a manager: La programmazione strategica in Italia: passato, presente e futuro* ['From bureaucrat to manager. Strategic programming in Italy: past, present and future'], Rubbettino, 2008, Soveria Mannelli. The Italian Ministry for the Public Employment is still in a basement of the Ministry and has not been distributed. It is possible that the Ministry will be happy to deliver it on demand.

27. In the French case, we cannot draw any indication from the LOLF on how to build a strategic plan. We need to wait to read some of the technical documents that the Ministry of the Economy and Finance and Industry have been progressively preparing, to have an idea of how to do this.

28. Ministère de l'Economie des Finances et de L'Industrie (2005), *Guide pratique de la déclination des programmes. Les budgets opérationnels de programme* (January 2005).

29. The LOLF has shaken up public management practices in France. All this is concentrated in the activities of the ministry and a huge quantity of documents has been drawn from it, especially in recent years. And all this cannot avoid producing a great and important technical and cultural effect in the behaviour and practices of the mid-level officers of the administration.

30. Many of my research on the meaning and utility of the public measure of performance on large scale and in many sectors could be useful for a rational and pertinent resolution of many problems scabrous of economic policy at national scale (and even more at international level). I hope that they could be used to counter the mass of disinformation and indifference under which it actually buried.

332   Volume II. Selected Testimonies on the Epistemological...

31. From handbooks in use we can point out: Bryson (1988), Gage and Mandell (1990), Kemp (1993), Koteen (1997), Mercer (1991), Seidel-Kwem (1983) and Steiner (1979). Among the handbooks prepared by the American federal agencies we can point out: US-DOE (1996a, b), US-Dept. of Navy (n.d.); US-NASA (1996). See note 30 of the previous chapter, and also the Guide in the Appendix. However, in recent years, there has been a flourishing of a large quantity of new textbooks.

32. For a greater and less apodictic discussion of them, there are many works of notable interest. Among them I recommend: Sen (1982); Sinden and Worrell (1979a); and Weiss (1972, 1992).

33. On this identity value-utility more than two centuries of reflection, of political philosophy, economic philosophy, the concept itself of political economy, and of the theory of the individual economic behaviour (*homo economicus*) have been developed from the work of Adam Smith (1776) and Jeremy Bentham (1789) to the present day. For an interesting in-depth treatment of the argument, I suggest the collection of papers edited by Hook (1967).

34. A non-conventional vision of the variables of values can be encountered profitably in the works of Charles Morris (1956). In these works, the problems magisterially discussed are: of the 'scales and dimensions of values', 'the meeting between western and eastern values', and the various determinants of value—'social', 'psychological' and 'biological'.

35. At this moment, the relationship between *choice* and *decision* around which some scholars have suggested a certain distinction, underlining that the decision is more connected to the action, is not in question (see, for instance, Lichfield 1996, pp. 27–28). Neither under discussion is the relationship between decision and action that concerns a future moment of the logical sequence which we are developing; nor is under discussion the subordinate question of whether or not the 'non-decision' may be even itself a decision (see, for instance, Jenkins 1978a, b). We limit ourselves to remembering that the value and the utility that we will deal with exist as a function of the evaluation; and that the evaluation subsists if there is an action, which, in turn, cannot but imply a decision. The problem of implementation, whether of the choice or of the decision, is not dealt with here, even if—obviously—it is very important.

36. This happens also for cases in which there is a general consensus about values. For instance, despite the fact that most agree gold has more value than steel, a producer of knives will always prefer steel as raw material, because this is better material to use for his purpose.

Improving Human Activities and Values as a Strategy... 333

37. At this point it is clear that we are keeping our distance from all the strands of analysis—central to the history of political economy—that have been concerned with the determinants of 'individual' evaluation (motivation, preference, choice, decision, and so on) and of the capacity of these determinants to explain the development and the functioning of the social economy in its entirety. And we will also keep our distance from that strand which, even if not central, has occupied a large part of the contemporary economic literature, and which is known by the name of 'the theory of social choice'. In fact, it seems to me evident that a good deal of the 'theory of social choice' is not concerned truly with 'social choice'—intended as political, or public, or collective choice, that is, of choice in the name of organised communities and of the public decision-makers—but rather of the possibilities and modalities of the aggregation of 'individual' choices, of their transformation into social choices, taking for granted that the last either derives from them, or in any case, should derive from them. The foundation of the so called 'theory of social choice' is, and will remain, however, individual choice. We will avoid here (and elsewhere) the terrain of social choice understood in such a way (limiting ourselves to recall and suggest the reading of K. Arrow's (1951) influential essay, from which the beginning of these debate strands is conventionally dated, and of the various other works to which my personal experience refers: another of Arrow's essays (1967a, b) and many works by A.K. Sen (collected in the work of 1982), the conclusion that Sen himself is believed to have given to the long debate (1986); the contribution of P.C. Fishburn (1973); and, lastly, the various papers edited in his time by B. Lieberman (1971) and, more recently, by Elster and Hylland (1986).

    To maintain distance from this approach, with the intention of being directly connected to the problems of 'public choice' does not mean adhering, without reservations, to the other well-known strand of economic reflection which goes under the name of the 'public choice' anchored itself, in spite of everything, to paradigms of individualist behaviour (even on this strand we will limit ourselves to indicate only some informative reviews; such as those of D.C. Mueller II, (updated edition of 1989) and P. Martelli (1983). But this aspect lies outside the theme and the intentions of this trilogy. For a broad and current treatment of all the aspects and directions that contemporary economics have taken in examination of the argument of the relationship between individual utility and public utility, and public *choice*, see the work of Xavier

Greffe (1997). The insertion of the question concerning the assessment of the public preferences in the wider context of the many arguments of contemporary economic policies is equally explained masterfully by Nicola Acocella (1994).

Bibliographical References to Chapter 9 (Vol. II)

Acocella, Nicola (1994). Fondamenti di politica economica. Valori e tecniche. Roma, La Nuova Italia Scientifica.

Archibugi, Franco. (1992a). *Introduction to Planology: A Survey of Developments Toward the Integration of Planning Sciences*. Rome, Planning Studies Centre.

Archibugi, Franco. (1992b). 'The resetting of planning studies', In: A. Kuklinski, ed., Society, Science, Government, Warsaw: KBN.

Archibugi, Franco. (1996). The Search for Optimal Centrality and the Abstract "Theories" of City Economics. Roma, Planning Studies Centre.

Arrow, J. Kenneth. (1951). *Social Choice and Individual Values*. New York, Wiley.

Arrow, J. Kenneth. (1967a). 'The Place of Moral Obligation in Preference Systems'. In Sidney Hook, Ed., *Human Values and Economic Policy*. New York, New York University Press.

Arrow, J. Kenneth. (1967b). Public and Private Values. *Human Values and Economic Policy*. S. Hook. New York, New York University Press.

Barzelay, Michael. (1992). *Breaking Through Bureaucracy: A New Vision for Managing in Government*. Berkeley, University of California Press.

Bentham, Jeremy. (1789). An Introduction to the Principles of Moral and Legislation.

Benveniste, Guy. (1987). *Professionalizing the Organization: Reducing Bureaucracy to Enhance Effectiveness*. San Francisco, Jossey-Bass.

Bozeman, B., and Straussman, J.D. (1990). *Public Management Strategies: Guidelines for Managerial Effectiveness*. San Francisco, Jossey-Bass.

Bryson, John M. (1988). *Strategic Planning for Public and Nonprofit Organizations: A Guide to Strengthening and Sustaining Organizational Achievement*. San Francisco, Jossey-Bass.

Elster, J., and Hylland, A. (1986). *Foundations of Social Choice Theory*. Cambridge, Cambridge University Press.

Fishburn, P.C. (1973). *The Theory of Social Choice*. Princeton, NJ, Princeton University Press.

Gage, R.W., and Mandell, M.P., Ed. (1990). *Strategies for Managing Intergovernmental Policies and Networks*. New York, Praeger.

Improving Human Activities and Values as a Strategy... **335**

Greffe, Xavier. (1997). *Economie des politiques publiques*. Paris, Dalloz.

Groszyk, Walter. (1995). *Implementation of the Government Performance and Results Act of 1993*.

Hook, Sidney, Ed. (1967). *Human Values and Economic Policy – A Symposium*. New York, New York University Press.

Jenkins, W.I. (1978a). The Case of Non-decisions. *Decision-Making: Approaches and Analysis: A Reader*. Eds. A.G. McGrew and M.J. Wilson. Manchester, Manchester University Press.

Jenkins, W.I. (1978b). *Policy Analysis: A Political and Organisational Perspective*. London, Robertson.

Kemp, L. Roger, Ed. (1993). *Strategic Planning for Local Government: A Handbook for Officials and Citizen*. Jefferson, N-C, Mc. Farland.

Koteen, Jack. (1997). *Strategic management in public and nonprofit organizations: managing public concerns in an era of limits*, 2nd ed. Westport, CT, Praeger.

Lichfield N. (1996). *Community Impact Evaluation*. London: University College of London Press.

Lieberman, Bernhardt. (1971). *Social Choice*. New York, Gordon and Breach Science Publishers.

Martelli, Paolo (1983). *La logica della scelta collettiva*. Milano, Il Saggiatore.

Mercer James L. (1991). *Strategic Planning for Public Managers*. New York, Quorum Books.

Mihm, J. Cristopher (1995–96). 'GPRA and the New Dialogue'. *The Public Manager* 24(4): 15–18.

Morris, Charles (1956). *Varieties of Human Value*. Chicago, University of Chicago Press.

Mueller Dennis C. (1989). *Public Choice II*. Cambridge, Cambridge University Press.

Seidel-Kwem, Brunhilde (1983). *Strategische Planung in Oeffentlichen Verwaltungen*. Berlin, Duncker-Humboldt.

Sen A.K. (1982). *Choice, Welfare and Measurement*. Oxford, Basil Blackwell.

Sen A.K. (1986). *Foundations of Social Choice Theory. Epilogue in Foundations of Social Choice Theory*. Cambridge, Cambridge University Press.

Sinden J. A. and A. C. Worrell (1979a). *Unpriced Values: Decisions Without Market Prices*. New York, Wiley.

Sinden J. A. and Worrell A. C. (1979b). 'Estimation of Social Values' (chap ex liber). *Unpriced Values. Decisions Without Market Prices*. Sinden J. A. and W. A. C. New York, Wiley: (Chap. 17).

Smith, Adam. (1776). *An Inquiry into Nature and Causes of the Wealth of Nations*.

336   Volume II. Selected Testimonies on the Epistemological...

Steiner H. (1979). *Conflict in Urban Transportation*. Lexington, MA, Heath Lexington Books.

US-DOE. (1996). Department of Energy, USA.

US-NASA. (1996). National Aeronautics and Space Agency, USA.

US Department of Navy. (n.d.).

Weiss Carol H. (1972). *Design of the Evaluation. Evaluation Research. Method of Assessing Program Effectiveness*. C. H. Weiss. Englewood Cliffs, NJ, Prentice-Hall.

Weiss Carol H. (1992). *Organizations for Policy Analysis*. London, Sage.

Appendices from the United Nations Organization

1. The United Nations Contribution to the Unified Approach to Planning
2. The United Nations Contribution to the Programme in Public Administration and Development

Some official documents to not forget

A Unified Approach to Planning

The idea of bringing together all the different aspects of the development of a human community into a set of viable objectives and policy approaches is at least as old as the United Nations itself.

After the end of the Second World War, in the reorganized structure of the United Nations, there arose the need to ensure new methods and meanings for the international cooperation, first of all to consider 'development' as a result of a 'unified approach to planning itself'.

© The Author(s) 2019
F. Archibugi, *The Programming Approach and the Demise of Economics*,
https://doi.org/10.1007/978-3-319-78060-3

338   Appendices from the United Nations Organization

The unified approach, as it evolved after the war, was not very clear. Since the 1970s the main organ of the United Nations, the General Assembly and the Economic and Social Commission, began to request a 'fresh exploration of a unified approach to development analysis and planning'.

The unified approach to planning has been studied in a progressive series of documents and reports that influenced some applications in the world.

However, the work of the United Nations in the field of the unified approach did not receive sufficient attention by governments and consequently was not widely diffused.

My opinion is that the current situation has obstructed the benefit of many possible addresses within the United Nations and produced waste in respect of the opportunity to obtain better advancement and allow to avoiding to fail within an disorientation surely worst in respect to that of the criteria suggested and applied by United Nations.

The political rivalry and partial economic interests of some governments have handicapped better technical and scientific cooperation on a global scale.

Become thus today more interesting a revival of cognition of the addresses of the UN work after the last more than half-secular effective decline of the international cooperation, and of relative re-consideration of the relative reconsideration of the target once elaborated.

With this purpose, I wanted with this appendix to republish in this trilogy the best 'parties and portions of documents' of the United Nations on the unified approach to planning, which are surely at the basis of many considerations developed in this trilogy.

I have selected here texts closely connected with the vision of the unified approach, dear to Gunnar Myrdal and the other economists, especially Ragnar Frisch, who researched a technical way to implement Myrdal's approach.

The two documents presented here are:

1. The two first chapters of a Preliminary Report, (UN/CN 5/477) prepared by a team (created in February 1971 by a research agency of the United Nations, UNRISD (United Nations Research Institute for

Social Development), located in Geneva, with other administrations of the United Nations itself. This report has been produced in collaboration also of the UN Commission for Latin America.

The first two sections of the report have as their titles:

1. *Styles of Development: Definitions and Criteria*
2. *Strategies*

The second document is a commentary report (on the basis of the Preliminary Report above mentioned), by a group of experts met in Stockholm, from 6 to 10 November 1972. Especially interesting is the group's composition: Amani Corea; Jacques Delors; Egbert De Vries; Gino Germani; Benjamin Higgins (Rapporteur); Ali A. Mazrui; Vilbert E. Moore; Gunnar Myrdal; Khaleeq Agma Naqvi; Josef Pajestka, George Skorov; and Inga Thorsson (Chairperson).

The writings that belong to the unified approach to planning are works that have practical strands dating back to the 1980s. The UNRISD has survived and moreover had a very poor public diffusion because the UN have stopped their use, thinking that whether their diffusion in public terms at international scale would already terminated with the work and the routine of the UNRISD itself or that the strategic address until now pursued by the United Nations were obsolete, should no more deserve to receive the same engagement. I think this a strategic mistake, one I hope will not be repeated.

Styles of Development: Definitions and Criteria

The two ways of looking at development, together with the picture of the world situation presented above, are incompatible with any supposition that development can successfully be planned for as if it were a mechanical process in which a given policy input will have everywhere the same output, and in which the status and rate of progress of different countries can be satisfactorily compared through a single quantitative indicator. Realistic discussion of the possibilities for more rational and effective action by human agents requires recognition of the existence and unavoidability of

340   Appendices from the United Nations Organization

different styles; that is, different combinations of ends and means applied to different real patterns of growth and change. It also requires the taking into account of two different kinds of limitations on styles of development—limitations in terms of internal coherence and feasibility, and limitations in terms of compatibility with human welfare and equity values. For the pursuit of this line of reasoning, the following distinctions are needed:

The real style of development refers to what is actually happening in a given national society—that is, to the empirically observable system of interrelated changes: in levels and structures of production; in the participation of different classes and groups in economic, social and political activities; in the distribution of incomes and wealth; in patterns of consumption; in institutions; in systems of values, attitudes and motivations. In this sense, the only general alternative to development is stagnation or decay, and 'underdevelopment' in the world of today very rarely consists of stagnation or decay alone; it usually involves a distorted and unacceptable form of development. It has been argued that such forms of growth and change do not deserve the label of 'development', but for present purposes the usage proposed here seems satisfactory.

The preferred style of development refers to what the national political leadership, the planning agency, or some other significant societal actor wants or expects to happen. In most societies, several preferred styles of development can be distinguished, some of them explicit and systematic, others fragmentary or implicit, inferable from the ways the state allocates resources or the ways different societal actors react to what is happening. Some preferred styles have an 'official' legally sanctioned status, others are 'counter-styles' deliberately challenging the governmental preference. In many cases it can be inferred that an overt preferred style, whether governmentally endorsed or a counter-style, masks a real preference that is quite different and less presentable in terms of values.

No detailed universal set of specifications for development or particularized 'definition' can be satisfactory; styles of development necessarily differ. But some general standard is nevertheless needed against which to assess styles of development. In the simplest terms, a style of development should be both acceptable in the importance it gives to human wellbeing and equity, and viable in terms of its compatibility with the resources of various kinds that can be mobilized by the national society as needed if it is to function and grow over the long term without breakdown.

A Unified Approach to Planning 341

Combining these aspects, the minimum criterion for assessment of a style of development (not a definition) proposed here can be summed up as the extent to which the style of development enables a society to function over the long term for the wellbeing of all its members.

Certain styles may be viable but not acceptable (for example, because they entail the continuing impoverishment or oppression of part of the society), or they may be acceptable but not viable (for example, because they neglect the requisites in productive capacity for the consumption and welfare aspirations they stimulate). A good many styles might have to be judged neither acceptable nor viable when viewed over the long term; and conversely, certain policy orientations that diminish acceptability and viability in the short term, through the sacrifices and resistances they entail, can be justified when the more distant future is taken into account. It is obviously easier to assess the acceptability of a style than it is viability, which will be affected by many contingencies that cannot be accurately weighed or foreseen, but to the extent possible the two aspects should enter jointly into any assessment.

The pattern of institutions and processes through which decisions are made (or evaded) constitutes one of the most important aspects of the real style of development. In practice, political leaders, planners, spokesmen of organized interest-groups, and so on envisage and try to apply quite different criteria and tactics so as to bring reality closer to their own preferred styles. Each may have only a distorted understanding of the rationale behind the tactics of the other parties. The national process of decision-making then consists of the interplay of conflict and consensus, pressure, bargaining, and persuasion through which the different tactics in their aggregate determine what gets done and how.

National decision-making can be expected to show widely differing degrees of coherence or diffuseness, compatibility or incompatibility with different preferred styles of development, but it always constitutes a political process dependent on the distribution of power in the national society and the form of the society's insertion into the international order. A purely technocratic national process of decision-making is not a real possibility, although the dominant forces may rely to varying degrees on 'objective' technical criteria in their choices.

342   Appendices from the United Nations Organization

The real style of development is affected by a number of objective constraints: the geographical facts of the country (its size, location, climate, topography, and so on), its available and potential resources of various kinds, its population size and density, its economic and political ties with other countries, its history and culture. Some of these can be changed or their influence countered, but the preferred style, to be viable, must take their present existence into account, as must the developmental strategy which translates this style into action.

A style of development meeting the minimum criterion set forth above requires choices, explicit or implicit, with regard to:

   (i) The extent and nature of national autonomy;
  (ii) The extent and nature of popular participation;
 (iii) The emphasis given to production in general, to specific lines and techniques of production, incentives, and forms of control over the means of production;
 (iv) The distribution of the fruits of development and mechanisms for redistribution;
  (v) The encouragement or discouragement of specific forms of individual or collective consumption of goods and services;
 (vi) The extent and nature of protection of the human environment;
(vii) The extent and nature of protection of human relationships contributing to solidarity, security, self-realization, and freedom.

These choices are complexly interdependent. If they are mutually contradictory beyond a certain point, the style will not be viable. If the choices are made in isolation from one another the probability is that they will be mutually contradictory to a dangerous degree.

The capacity to choose an autonomous style of development conditions the possibility of making choices in all the other areas. If a national society simply accepts its place in the existing international order, it may, under favourable circumstances, experience a kind of dependent 'development' over an extended period, but decisions on the main lines of production and consumption will be out of its hands, and it will be unable to tolerate forms of participation that might threaten the distribution patterns associated with these lines of production and consumption.

A Unified Approach to Planning   343

For most national societies such passively dependent development is probably not a viable style over the long term; it leads to a trap in which it cannot satisfy the expectations aroused, or in which the changing interests of the dominant power undermine its economic and political basis.

At the same time, no national society can realistically choose complete autonomy to the point of autarky. It must manoeuvre on the basis of its real situation within the international order, try to shape whatever international aid is available to its own purposes, enter into autonomy-restricting co-operative relationships with its neighbours, and be prepared to sacrifice concrete immediate advantages if it wishes to enhance its autonomy. If it tries to combine a high degree of autonomy, a high degree of reliance on external financing, and a high degree of openness to external cultural and consumption models, its style of development will probably not be viable.

Participation is one of the most complex as well as basic areas of choice. It raises the questions—very hard for political leaders and planners to face frankly—of who is doing the choosing, how choices are enforced, and whether the style of development treats participation mainly as a means or mainly as an end, an essential component of the style. When participation is willed from above it becomes mobilization, a means of getting things done. When it arises from below it usually focuses on distribution, becoming also a means, from the standpoint of the groups able to participate, of obtaining a larger immediate share of the fruits of development.

Authentic participation, heightening the participants' awareness of values, issues, and the possibility of making choices, influencing the content of development, generating new ways of doing things, and also safeguarding the participants' right to an equitable share in the fruits of development, remains an elusive aspiration—but the conversion of this aspiration into reality may well in the end prove the central requisite for a style of development enabling a society to function over the long term for the well-being of its members.

Development analysts, including many with an economic planning background, have increasingly singled out participation as a key requirement for more effective policy and planning. 'Participation', like 'planning', is sometimes treated as a mystical entity that will resolve all problems once rightly conceived and applied. It is significant that

344   Appendices from the United Nations Organization

evaluations of existing political processes of participation are generally negative. They are associated with the phenomenon of the 'soft state', corruption, allocation of resources according to the strength of political pressures, inability to maintain a consistent strategic orientation, and continual promises that the system cannot honour.

From the standpoint of many development analysts and planners, 'politics' is bad, 'participation' good. Participation is then viewed as a substitute for existing political processes, as consisting in an orderly procedure through which the competing social forces and interest groups can be educated to present more rational and manageable demands and persuaded to internalize the demands the development process will make on them.

The following propositions are relevant:

1. Authentic participation usually requires a redistribution of power;
2. Participation cannot be inserted as a 'missing ingredient' into most current real styles of development. The style itself must change, both as a result of new forms of participation and as a condition for such participation;
3. The functioning of mechanisms for participation (political movements, trade unions, co-operatives, community councils, youth clubs, and so on) depends on the setting in which they appear (or into which they are inserted). The conditions under which such mechanisms are likely to be 'successful' in terms of defined objectives can be specified with some confidence through comparative study of past experiences;
4. The higher the proportion of the population in situations of poverty and marginality, the more traumatic will be the changes in the style of development requisite for their authentic participation, and the more difficult will it be for external agents—whether or not representing the state—to undertake relevant catalytic roles;
5. The more important forms of organized participation (other than voting and political party affiliation) open to disadvantaged social groups in the past have derived from their relationship to the means of production and their clash of interests with social classes controlling the means of production: wage earners against employers; peasants against landlords.

Conflictive participation of this kind has obviously not lost its importance but in many countries today the most disadvantaged social groups—and the most rapidly growing—are 'marginal' in having only tenuous relations to production and do not confront any readily identifiable target for demands other than the state itself. They identify themselves as would-be consumers (of educational and health services as well as food and shelter) more than as producers and earners of income from defined occupations. Trade unions are irrelevant to their needs and approaches such as workers' management even more so. Their real capacities as consumers are also usually too low to allow scope for organizational forms such as co-operatives that in other settings have functioned as instruments for defence of consumer interests.

To the extent that political leaders can satisfy the modest immediate wants of such groups—or can maintain the illusion that they are going to do so—their participation can be expected to remain highly dependent and to be atomized by the attempts of individuals and families to find personal benefactors in the political party machinery or the bureaucracy of the 'service' agencies.

Up to the present, developmental preoccupations have centred heavily on production. The proposition that maximum production of goods and services is equivalent to development, no matter what is produced or how it is used, seems preposterous when stated baldly. Yet the underlying assumption in most developmental thinking about choices has not been very far from this. Even before the environmentalists began to argue that such an approach can lead to disaster for the human race (and to be heard) its narrowness had come under attack from several points of view.

It is premature to go to the other extreme of advocacy of zero growth rates. Levels of production in most of the world are much too low to be reconcilable with any acceptable style of societal development, and production objectives will unavoidably preoccupy many national societies for the foreseeable future. Acceptable and viable styles of development demand of these societies that they should direct their production much more systematically to basic human needs, and that they should seek productive techniques that minimize environmental degradation and waste of natural resources, and maximize creative involvement of their human potential.

346   Appendices from the United Nations Organization

The raising of production need not be continuous; choices of structural change may be justified even at the cost of temporary disruption and foregone production. In the longer term, the poorer national societies should multiply their per capita production several times over, depending on present levels. However, raising them by the multiples required to 'close the gap' with the present high-income societies is not necessarily relevant to the achievement of acceptable styles of development, once it is realized to what extent the incomes of the 'advanced' countries are inflated by armaments production, increasingly costly activities needed to cope with the disbenefits of the current techniques of production, and consumption artificially stimulated to keep the productive apparatus going.

Choices as to what will be produced imply a need for compatible choices as to how it will be distributed and who will consume it. In most national societies striving to develop, the choices concerning production, distribution and consumption (expressed through a multiplicity of allocations, incentives, controls and market mechanisms, the last continually interfered with but not replaced) have been far from coherent and even farther from equitable. The contradictions have become more acute as import-substitution industrialization has proceeded and as overt income redistribution measures have become more prominent in public policy. Redistribution meeting the basic needs of the masses of the population has proved incompatible with the character of the goods and services being produced, as well as with the distribution of power and with the present functioning of the societies and economies. The contradictions have appeared more acutely in industrially-produced consumer goods, in housing, and in education.

A style of development cannot be judged acceptable if it does not give a very high priority to meeting the basic physical and psychological needs of the whole population. It cannot even be judged viable over the long-term if it leaves an important part of the next generation physically and mentally stunted by malnutrition. The most easily definable and measurable of the basic needs is for food, followed by shelter, clothing, health care, rest, recreation, education, access to certain consumer goods, security from violence and oppression, and something as hard to define and measure as it is essential—human dignity, self-respect, self-realization. Such basic needs can be defined more precisely, as a guide to policy, only

A Unified Approach to Planning 347

in relation to the preferences and capabilities of specific societies; they should naturally be redefined upward as capabilities rise.

A major item in the indictment against current real styles of development consists in their failure to enable large parts of the population to meet their most obvious basic needs. Several immediate causes can be distinguished: systems of exploitation that leave the worker a share of what he produces barely sufficient for subsistence; lack of access to resources, jobs, or information; physical or psychological incapacities associated with extreme poverty; social or cultural barriers to mobility, initiative and adaptability; traditions ensuring that certain relatively defenceless groups come last in the distribution of resources within the family or community.

These factors, of widely varying importance in different national or local settings, call for many different remedies, from agrarian reform to nutritional programmes, which need not be discussed at this point. The advocacy of highest priority to the meeting of basic needs is only the first small step toward a policy.

This particular kind of emphasis on equity is emphasized here because something quite different commonly happens when equity and redistribution come to the fore in national policy debates. Urban minorities able to make themselves heard (for example, civil servants, professionals, technicians, and other components of the 'middle strata') turn equity arguments to their own advantage, by comparing their lot with international standards and with the levels of living of their counterparts in high-income countries. The 'right' to subsidized 'modern' urban housing, to free secondary and higher education, even the 'right' to own an automobile and take vacations abroad, take precedence over the right to get enough to eat, to be protected against major health risks, and to get enough elementary education to have a chance of coping with societal change. These priorities can appear to be justified by economic as well as political arguments: the groups in question are best able to give a regime effective support, and their consumption is needed to support the kind of productive structure that is emerging.

As 'development' proceeds, however, new and larger groups of claimants enter into the competition through political processes and interest-group organization, until the aggregate claims greatly exceed the resources

348   Appendices from the United Nations Organization

available to satisfy them. The middle strata are chronically frustrated by the gap between their consumption aspirations and their means of meeting them, and by the inflation through which the strain on resources is dissipated. The relative or even absolute disadvantage of the poorest strata increases.

Protection of the human environment and protection of human relationships refer partly to choices (including choices to refrain from doing certain things) aimed at avoiding or reducing the scope of negative by-products of developmental change, and partly to innovative choices aimed at enhancing the quality of the human environment and human relationships. Such choices have their own costs. They may require trade-offs against considerations of productive efficiency and often against the preferences of the population groups involved, which may be prepared to tolerate a good deal of environmental degradation and social disruption in pursuit of higher incomes and access to urban ways of life. The kinds of problems in human relationships that have to be considered are family breakdown, anomie, and alienation of youth.

Choices aimed at preserving a 'traditional' way of life, assumed to be in harmony with nature and socially integrated, are usually neither practicable nor justified in terms of the qualities of the pre-existing situation. Under conditions of rapid population growth, in particular, 'traditional' ways of life may be just as destructive of the environment and as laden with conflict and insecurity as the situations associated with rapid development. Social transformation is an essential part of development.

The nearly universal societal resistance to recognizing and paying the price of the style of development that is wanted with resulting symptoms of chronic inflation and indecisive or mutually contradictory government policies, seems to be one of the most ominous aspects of present trends, in high-income national societies as well as low-income societies. The meeting of basic human needs, the enlisting of the full human potential for development, and the obtaining of sufficient resources for genuinely productive investment, alike require a higher level of social discipline and solidarity, supporting a consumption standard that might be summed up as 'shared frugal comfort'.

One condition for the acceptance of such a standard—although far from a sufficient condition—is awareness on the part of the general public as well as political leaders and planners of the implications of present trends and the possibility of alternative futures. The climate for such a 'future-consciousness' is probably more favourable than ever before in human history. The remarkably rapid and generalized acceptance of the ideas of 'development' and 'planning' a few years ago demonstrated an unprecedented diffusion of confidence in human capacity to shape the future. The impingement on public consciousness of the implications of population and environmental trends have kept to the fore the theme of conscious and urgent choice while dispelling complacency about the future. The assessment of different styles of development in terms of acceptability and viability requires systematic exploration of images of the different possible future societies which the different styles imply. The supposition that existing societies elsewhere can substitute for such images becomes less and less plausible.

Futurological exercises and debates of the kind envisaged here do not imply that their executants have the ability or the right to specify the nature of the future society. The main tasks are to ensure that the implications of present trends and all serious alternatives are explored as far as knowledge permits.

Strategies

The national process of decision-making is the environment from which a coherent strategy or strategic orientation may or may not emerge. A strategy translates a preferred style of development into concrete choices and priorities, with specifications of the resource allocations, instruments, and institutional changes that are to be applied.

A strategy is by no means the same thing as a development plan. In various national societies the state follows strategic orientations that are not formalized in a plan; and a good many countries have 'development plans' that are very far from amounting to authentic strategies. Strategies may fail to meet the minimum criterion for acceptability if they respond to the preferences of dominant forces that give a lower priority to human welfare and equity than to other ends. Or they may fail to meet the criterion of viability because they overlook various objective requirements and constraints.

350   **Appendices from the United Nations Organization**

A unified approach to development supposes the application of a coherent strategy which takes account of the existing real style of development (and the objective constraints that partly explain the real style) and seeks to bring it closer to the preferred style.

Each of the national societies has its own set of potentialities and constraints. Problems that loom so large in some societies as to absorb most of their decision-making capacities have been partly superseded in others, and in still others are present only in embryo, probably important for the future but not justifying priority attention. The strategic options open in a society dominated by a broadly based aspiration for rapid development, in which decision-makers are overwhelmed by strong and diverse pressures, and the options open in a society in which a small elite tepidly favouring development confronts an inert traditionalist majority, are obviously very different, although basic needs may be similar.

National situations can be classified in many different ways, and for present purposes it is unnecessary to add yet another to the many existing typologies. It may be worthwhile, however, to describe briefly some of the real styles of development that must be taken into account in proposing strategies:

(i) A few relatively large countries with favourable resource endowments and with dominant elites able to maintain coherent policies of favouring investment and providing infrastructure have achieved a style characterized by vigorous economic growth, rapid urbanization, and conspicuously widening inequalities between internal regions and social classes. In these cases, one finds in the ruling elite confidence that continued high growth rates will eventually resolve the admitted deficiencies and inequities; also, usually a readiness to allocate appreciable resources to some services, reforms, and compensatory measures; but a rejection of any diagnosis pointing to the desirability of basic changes in the style itself and the power structures controlling it;

(ii) Certain other countries, similar in size and resource endowments, have lower or less sustained rates of economic growth, but similar internal inequalities. Vigorous elite groups are present but are unable to impose themselves or agree among themselves on coherent policies. Stalemated

A Unified Approach to Planning 351

styles result, in which policy continually falls into developmentally counterproductive compromises between incompatible demands, or 'pendulum' styles in which policy vacillates from one extreme to another as successive policies fail or bring about politically unmanageable resistances;

(iii) In another group of countries, usually smaller than the above but endowed with export potentials that have permitted per capita incomes higher than most of their neighbours, various historical circumstances have permitted relatively broad population strata to participate in the political process and have forced the political leaders to bargain for support through offers of extensive social services and redistributional measures. These are the countries said to have emphasized the 'social' over the 'economic'. In most examples of this style, rates of economic growth in recent years have been low, in part owing to deteriorating terms of trade and in part to insufficient productive investment. The weaknesses of the style have become obvious to the elites and to important elements of the population, particularly the educated youth, but the kind of participation that has taken shape and the range of organized interest-groups that have something to lose from reform, make it very difficult to find a politically practicable path to a different style;

(iv) Many small countries, economically dependent on a limited range of exports, with weak national integration and with internal markets too narrow to support industrialization, have highly dependent 'open' styles, in which the State has found no practicable alternative to making the best of what comes in the way of external trade, aid, investments and advice. While some have stagnated, other countries in this position have achieved high rates of growth in per capita income because of strong world markets for their exports or special relationships with an aid-dispensing power; but growth under these circumstances is precarious. These countries face particularly difficult choices relating to the limits of autonomy and the possibilities of integration with their neighbours;

(v) A few countries, most of them relatively small in population, have entered on a 'windfall' style of development through the exploitation of oil resources. In these cases, the enormous resources at the disposal of

352 Appendices from the United Nations Organization

the public sector, the limited importance of other economic activities; and the weakness of organized interest-groups, gives the ruling elite an exceptional capacity for autonomous decision-making, limited mainly by the weakness of the administrative machinery, shortages of technical skills, and the 'traditional' remoteness from developmental preoccupations of much of the population;

(vi) In certain countries, usually following upon a social revolution or a mobilizing struggle for national independence, the leadership rejects the primacy of market forces and material incentives, and combats or excludes interest-group pressures and consumption aspirations that conflict with the preferred style. The leadership assumes that increased production is essential and compatible with the style but expects this to follow upon structural transformation and raising of the qualifications and motivations of the masses of the population; production objectives are not allowed to override the central aim. It is evident that few if any national societies have been able to strive with complete consistency for a style of this kind over an extended period: contradictions appear between real forms of participation and the ideal form of participation required by the style.

Additional real styles of development, plus many hybrid forms manifesting high degrees of internal incoherence, might also be identified and the styles might be classified differently. The purpose in describing them here is not to sort the countries of the world into developmental pigeon-holes but to suggest that the reactions of political leaders and planners to recommended strategies of development differ according to the style they are committed to or find themselves constrained by. They may justifiably object to being exhorted in very general terms to do something they are already trying to do or know they are unable to do or have no intention of doing.

Subject to this proviso, certain strategic orientations can be singled out as having particularly wide applicability and particular importance for a unified approach to development. They are really reaffirmations, with some changes of emphasis, of themes already insisted on in recent years by authoritative voices in the international debate over development. The first three orientations summarized below are at the most general level; the other five deal with certain broad policy problems that almost all national societies confront.

(a) *Comprehensiveness*

The scope of a development strategy should cover the entire society. It should not restrict its vision to population groups and internal regions that can be covered by financially 'sound' investment projects, nor to the conventional sectoral public services. It should start from a comprehensive and open-minded assessment of the whole range of complementary and alternative instruments and ways of reaching its objectives, including the dynamizing possibilities of reforms in property ownership and control over the means of production, in legal systems, in educational systems, in administrative mechanisms, and in incentives for production, innovation, and self-help, as well as the allocation of material resources that are at the disposal of the state.

It should strive to maximize efficiency in the use of scarce resources, but it should be prepared for the likelihood that capital is not the scarcest resource in comparison with human qualifications and motivations; that existing installed capital in industry and elsewhere is underutilized to a very large extent; and that the combating of corruption, bureaucratism, militarism, and facade construction is more relevant to the attainment of efficiency than the competition for resources between the 'economic' and the 'social', or between different 'sectors' of production and services.

Comprehensiveness, however, can be a dangerous or illusory ideal. All governments are under continual temptation to assume more responsibilities than they can in fact carry out, and comprehensive diagnoses and evaluations of means are useful only if they lead to rational criteria for selection and concentration of efforts. Covering the entire society cannot mean according equal importance to every kind of action, frittering away attention and resources on a multiplicity of token activities, or disregarding real economic constraints through unlimited confidence in reforms intended to liberate the human potential. The strategy must seek to concentrate on key areas where the greatest overall impact can be anticipated.

(b) *Rapidity*

The strategy should aim at rapid growth and structural change, with the relative importance of the two phenomena in the short-term depending on the diagnosis. There are weighty justifications for such

354   Appendices from the United Nations Organization

an orientation: (1) the inertia and self-stabilizing traits of national institutions and structures allow small incremental changes to be absorbed without any dynamizing effect; (2) the development effort needs to be bold and inspiring enough to mobilize key sectors of the population behind it and overcome resistances from other quarters; (3) the prolongation of mass poverty and rising unemployment implied by more cautious strategies is unacceptable.

Under defined circumstances, the strategy may justifiably centre on a 'big push' for very rapid economic growth, but the argument that annual per capita growth rates of 7% or 8% are, in general, indispensable, sufficient and attainable conditions for the elimination of mass poverty and unemployment is not convincing.

The case for a strategic orientation toward rapidity of growth and structural change does not depend on the aim of 'catching up' with other countries. Development requires a transformation of human beings as well as a transformation of the system of production and leaving large parts of a national population outside the scope of this transformation is not practicable today, even if the groups in question do not seek change or if the existing style of development is unable to accommodate them. They will be involved as victims if they cannot become participants in the transformation.

The extent to which rapid economic growth will be able to incorporate widespread participation or will make additional victims depends on the capacity of a given society and economy to support it without disproportionate sacrifices, to control its content (in other words, what is produced as well as how) and to distribute its fruits with a reasonable degree of equity. In most national societies these considerations call for other kinds of 'big push'—toward structural change and redistribution of power and participation in the society—prior to or simultaneously with mobilization for rapid economic growth.

(c) *Distribution*

The strategy should specify the expected impact of its component measures on different population groups (defined by income level, occupation, relation to the means of production, urban or rural residence, geographical location, age, sex, and so on) and should continually try to assess the real impact in such terms. It should never be taken for granted that the interests of the different groups are in harmony, or that equity-oriented 'universal' services or legal rights will prove equally accessible and beneficial to the different groups. Who benefits? Who pays? Who distributes? are always relevant questions.

The real meaning of measures for income redistribution, universalization of services and subsidies to maintain a floor under levels of living is determined by the distribution and characteristics of power, participation, control of the means of production and consumer demand for and uses of the services provided in a given society. This means, for one thing, that a strategic orientation cannot realistically accord more than a supplementary role to direct measures of income redistribution. Ideally, the strategy should account for the impact of all its component measures on distribution and human welfare, along with their impact on productivity and structural change, and modify them so as to serve these aims. This, of course, is easier said than done.

(d) *Rural Development*

The importance and the difficulty of combined application of the three strategic orientations set forth above can be demonstrated in the area of rural development and agricultural policy. It is now a commonplace that this area has been neglected in the development effort of most countries in relation to industry, and that the balance must be redressed; in the Chinese formulation, development must 'walk on two legs'. In practically all of the poorer countries, and in many that are not so poor, the great reservoir of extreme poverty is in the rural areas, and this is now spilling over in increasing volume into urban settings. Almost everywhere the agricultural share in national income is far below the rural percentage of national population, and the agricultural share in investment is even lower than the share in income. For the most part, the higher the percentage of population engaged in agriculture the more inadequate is the national level of nutrition; countries with predominantly rural-agricultural populations have been increasingly compelled to import foodstuffs for the urban population and even for the rural population itself.

Meanwhile, misuse of the land, taking many forms, threatens its future capacity to support a rural population even of the present size and at present levels of poverty. The situation can be attributed in part to past national policies of squeezing resources from agriculture for the benefit of other sectors of the economy and of discriminating against small cultivators and rural workers in favour of the larger landholders (or simply accepting the discrimination inherent in pre-existing local property and power relationships).

Over the past two decades, very many governments have embarked on a wide range of rural and agricultural development programmes designed specifically to overcome rural poverty and backwardness—land tenure reform, cooperatives, community development, agricultural extension, supervised credit and, most recently, the introduction of high-yielding varieties of food grains. A good many of these activities can be dismissed as 'token', but others were allocated important financial and manpower resources and were accorded central roles in government development strategies.

A few of the later efforts can be credited with significant increases in agricultural production or with solid benefits for some previously disadvantaged sectors of the rural population, but the general record of achievement is probably farther below expectations than in any other major area of public policy. In many countries there is disquieting evidence that, to the extent that the rural development measures have worked at all, they have mostly helped minorities of the rural population (generally but not invariably the previously dominant land-owning and commercial groups) and have left the remainder relatively worse off than before.

Under present conditions, most rural change processes, whether determined by market forces by governmental drives for higher production; or by governmental intentions of promoting equity, participation and cooperation, and facilitating contact with urban centres, tend in fact to heighten inequalities and deprive part of the rural population of access to livelihood. The chief exceptions are apparently countries in which revolutionary changes have swept away not only the pre-existing rural power and property structures but also the pre-existing relationships between urban and rural.

A strategic orientation toward agricultural development, public investment and credit policies, promotion of innovation in crops and productive techniques might alleviate a number of urgent problems and remove developmental bottlenecks. It would not meet the criteria of acceptability and viability, however, unless capable of reversing the trend described above. Such a reversal cannot be achieved simply by amplifying and making more efficient the policies just named. 'Unified' rural development strategy calls also for thoroughgoing reforms in the ownership and use of land for planned changes in the factor prices of capital, labour and land to correspond with their real relative scarcity and favour agricultural employment over mechanization for an end to marketing abuses and systems for extraction of agricultural surpluses that artificially depress rural incomes; for the creation of agro-industrial complexes (and distribution systems) for the local processing of agricultural products and the generation of alternative jobs for an excess labour force; for labour-intensive public works programmes focusing on priority rural needs rather than prestige constructions.

As long, however, as the policy approaches are imposed on the rural population from outside, by administrators imbued with paternalism or preoccupied by the meeting of centrally imposed quantitative targets, something will be lacking, and the unacceptable traits of rural change will probably not be reversed. Planning for disadvantaged rural groups is not enough; other forces can continue to distort the resulting programmes or starve them of resources. What is necessary in the last analysis is the enhancement of the capacity of the rural masses to identify their own problems and defend their own interests. This is not an aim that can be 'managed' by political leaders and administrators. If it can happen at all, the process will be conflictive, as disruptive to the 'traditional' rural social order as the quite different changes that are now taking place, and unpredictable in its final outcome.

(e) *Industrialization*

Industrialization has commonly been viewed as nearly synonymous with development, and in fact a viable style of development is hardly conceivable, except in certain small and highly specialized national economies,

358   Appendices from the United Nations Organization

without considerable industrial growth. It does not follow that industrial growth of any kind and at any cost contributes to a viable style of development; assumptions of this kind have led a good many national societies into traps from which their leadership now is hard put to find a politically and economically practicable way out. The specific nature of the predicament differs depending on historical factors, resource endowment, population size, and degree of national autonomy, but the following observations are widely applicable.

Industrialization has been stimulated by price policies, import policies, foreign exchange policies, and so on, involving a continuing subsidy from agriculture. As industry has grown, the required subsidy has also increased, eventually leading to agricultural stagnation and inability to sustain further industrial growth.

The lines of industrial growth have commonly been governed by import-substitution policies—or by import-substitution necessities (for example, inability to pay for manufactured imports at previous levels because of depressed export markets). The internal market for manufactured goods is typically small and shaped by a highly uneven income distribution. The new industries thus respond to a demand for relatively expensive durable consumer goods (electrical appliances and automobiles in particular) and various luxury products.

To the extent that industries producing for this market become established, pressures mount for the maintenance of an income distribution safeguarding the market, and also for expanding it to the limits of purchasing power (or beyond) through advertising, consumer credits, and facilities for instalment buying. The potential for private saving and investment diminishes. More important, public capacity to control allocations of foreign exchange and domestic public-sector resources is narrowed by demands for a rising flow of imported inputs for the industries and for infrastructural requirements for use of their products. Instead of industrial growth contributing to an acceptable and viable style of development, the style of development has to be warped to suit the requirements of a certain kind of industrial growth.

The contradiction indicated above in the discussion of equity implications of an acceptable style is accentuated. The market can be enlarged to some extent by bringing down production costs (usually several times higher than in the industrialized countries) and by producing smaller and simpler models. It can also be enlarged by raising the incomes and increasing the numbers of the urban middle strata and the urban workers (in large part as a concomitant of the industrial growth). With possible exceptions of countries with small populations and high petroleum output, however, there is no possibility of enlarging the market for the more expensive durable goods to include the mass of the population.

The resulting dilemma is particularly acute for regimes committed to incorporating more equitable distribution of the fruits of development in their preferred style. They cannot dispense with the support of the urban strata now clamouring to enter the market for durable consumer goods— and among these are the organized workers who produce the goods and whose livelihood would be threatened by any radical change in consumption patterns. The strata that stand to benefit from a shift in the structure of industrial production (cheap bicycles and collective transport equipment instead of automobiles, cheap electrical goods instead of air conditioning equipment) are relatively passive and unaware of the possibility of an alternative. Public commitment to production of intermediate goods (steel, cement, petrochemicals, and so on) and capital equipment, as part of an import-substitution strategy, has been better justified in principle. However, the scale needed for efficient production under available up to date technologies, together with a common predisposition to identify the size and modernity of industrial plants with national prestige, have resulted in excessive costs, a good deal of unused capacity, insufficient integration with the rest of the economy, and inability to export at competitive prices.

The dependent and imitative character of the import-substitution industrial growth and the remarkably high rates of technological and managerial innovation in the world industrial centre during the same period, have left little scope either for catching up or for working out adaptations of industrial processes suited to national circumstances and relative scarcities of capital and skills. Even where national industrial growth has begun with a certain degree of autonomy it has tended to relapse into greater financial, managerial, and technological dependence on the world centre, and this is associated with a narrowing gap between the inflow of investment funds and the outflow of profits, royalties, and so on.

The above observations imply, by contraries, some of the requisites for orientation of industrial policy toward an acceptable and viable style of development. A realistic policy will have to recognize constraints imposed by the balance of payments, by external sources of investments and technology, by the structure of effective demand and of installed industrial capacity, and by competitiveness and comparative advantage in world markets; but it need not passively submit to these factors, nor accept short-term expedients that accentuate dependency and subordinate overall development strategy to the bolstering up of existing vested interests in industrial growth. The lines of growth should be appraised, and changes should be sought in relation to internal needs for products and for industrial contributions to desired societal changes. Industrial development strategy like other aspects of development strategy should aim at the reconciliation of multiple objectives even if this should be technically less convenient to the planners:

(i) Industrial development should form mutually beneficial linkages with rural-agricultural development through supply of agricultural inputs and rural consumption needs and through the processing of agricultural products rather than remain parasitic on agriculture.

(ii) Techniques organization and scale of production should be designed to raise the level of skills aptitudes and entrepreneurial talents of the people as widely as possible not simply through vocational training but through compatibilization of values and attitudes with an innovating efficiency-conscious 'industrial' way of life.

(iii) The impact of industrial products on consumption should contribute to the preferred style of development ('product policy'). That is products should be favoured that can be disseminated widely at foreseeable income levels and that support desired changes in living conditions and working methods. Lines of production responding to this criterion include: fertilizers and implements for agriculture; pharmaceuticals and personal hygiene articles for health care; paper teaching aids publications and radios for education recreation and dissemination of information; mechanical and electrical tools for small workshops and for vocational training; low-cost building materials furniture and appliances for housing; bicycles buses and trucks for transport.

A Unified Approach to Planning   361

(iv) The more important branches of industry and also the use of the mass media to stimulate consumption of products should be brought under national control—whether the tactics for doing so depend on national private capital guided by public incentives and disincentives on co-operatives and workers' management or on state ownership of the means of production or on some combination of these.

(f) *Employment*

The two most conspicuous shortcomings of current real styles of development, as already noted, are their inability to offer sufficient productive and remunerative employment to the potential labour force and their inability to relieve the extreme poverty of large parts of the national population. It is natural and justifiable that employment policy should come to the forefront of attention as offering a broad, value-oriented framework for development policy and a means of eliminating both of these shortcomings. The attempts to recast development policy in terms of employment objectives, however, have encountered several conceptual as well as practical difficulties.

The approach converts what should be primarily an important intermediate objective or means into an ultimate objective or value, and it obscures the strategic implications of the different reasons for wanting people to be employed. These reasons can be summed up as follows: means of production of goods and services; means of distribution of income; means of social integration (through work relationships) and means of self-realization (through provision of a 'meaningful' role in life). These reasons are of widely differing importance at different levels and in different styles of development, and can be satisfied by different combinations of means, among which raising the level of employment may normally be the most important but can never be the sole alternative.

In most national situations, the quest for a broad 'employment policy' leads to proposals for (among other things) changes in the factor prices of capital and labour, making the former dearer and the latter cheaper; different choices of productive technologies and product mixes; expansion of publicly financed services and public works at wage rates low enough

362   Appendices from the United Nations Organization

to make this practicable; agrarian reforms and rural development measures designed to retain as high a proportion as possible of the rural population on the land.

All of these policies may be feasible and desirable within styles of development meeting overall criteria of acceptability and viability, but in most of the countries concerned they are not compatible (except on a token scale) with the real styles of development and the real demands and expectations of the dominant social forces (and often also of the unemployed and marginalized groups).

'Unemployment' emerges as a problem demanding attention from the national authorities and separable from a generalized condition of poverty and low-productivity utilization of the labour force when a society is already in movement, with some economic growth, urbanization, educational expansion, rationalization of agriculture, breakdown of previous means of subsistence livelihood, consciousness of new opportunities obtainable through migration, and growth in the proportion of jobs that are regular and wage-paid. At this stage, unemployment cannot attain the clear-cut character that it has in an industrialized country. It is the more-or-less visible tip of an iceberg, whose dimensions can be estimated, not at all satisfactorily, through calculations of under-employment, low-productivity employment, and so on.

Any direct measures to relieve unemployment—through public works, for example—risk increasing overt unemployment, as people are attracted out of subsistence activities and become unable or unwilling to return to them. It is quite natural for a political leadership to seek painless ways to exorcize the spectre of rising unemployment but to hesitate to start on a course of action that would compel quite different national priorities and allocations of resources, and frustrate the expectations of powerful groups previously relied on for support.

The international advisory missions that have tried to formulate national employment policies have confronted a choice between recommendations adding up to radical changes in the style of development, going beyond the capacities as well as the intentions of the governments to which they are addressed, or recommendations limited to specific measures, more practicable politically but unlikely to bring about major improvements in the overall employment situation. Ability to offer a livelihood to the whole population is an essential element in any acceptable style of development. The conclusion seems justified, however, that policy concentration on raising the level of employment is not a satisfactory equivalent to a 'unified approach'.

Attention should focus on the functions of employment in the kind of social order that is aimed at, more than on employment as an end in itself. In principle, the maintenance of a satisfactory rate of economic growth and the maintenance of a level of employment fulfilling the four functions summarized above should be mutually supporting rather than competitive. The priority aim should be to enlist the full potential for meeting of basic societal needs, and to achieve authentic participation and a level of, at least, frugal comfort in the process. This can hardly be expected as long as subsistence livelihood and 'self-help' mobilization for part of the population contrast with protected high incomes and generous public services for other parts.

(g) *Education*

The economic emphasis on industrialization in development policies has been paralleled on the social side by an equally strong emphasis on educational expansion, with unexpectedly similar results. In both areas, quantitative targets for sectoral growth and standards for allocations of public resources have overshadowed, in the minds of political leaders as well as planners, questions of content and of real societal needs for and uses of output. In both areas, the demands and interests generated by what has been done threaten to dominate future development strategy and force it into an impasse.

The case for a high priority for educational expansion is well-known. Even the narrower conceptions of 'economic development' envisage education as an essential means of bringing 'human resources' into closer correspondence with developmental needs and as one of the most desirable ways of using the fruits of development to enhance welfare and equity. Broader conceptions of development imply an even higher valuation on education as a means toward cultural change and creativity and call for much higher allocations to education versus non-essential private consumption.

364 **Appendices from the United Nations Organization**

The fallacy has been to assume that expansion of existing systems of education, within existing societal structures, would ensure realization of these aims. For the most part, expansion has been governed not by the intentions of educational planners, but by the demands of consumers seeking to improve the position of their children within existing systems of rewards and status. The most vigorous demands come from the middle strata and from groups on the margin of ability to participate in the 'modern' consumer economy. The typical results include a particularly rapid expansion of secondary and higher education; a dilution of the quality of such education because of the insufficiency of qualified teachers, inability to meet costs, and lack of student interest in the content; an economically unjustified expansion of certain occupational sectors, and the emergence of growing numbers of 'educated unemployed'.

This kind of educational expansion diminishes the possibility of an acceptable and viable style of development, because of the resources it absorbs and the expectations it encourages. After a certain point, educational expansion at the higher levels may increasingly feed on itself, as the graduates, for lack of opportunities elsewhere, seek employment within the educational system and the system has to continue to grow to accommodate them. The masses of the population get disproportionately small benefits. In some cases, higher education alone eats up as much as half the public resources allocated to education, and the per capita expenditures on children who do not go beyond elementary school are necessarily minute in comparison with per capita expenditures on the favoured minorities. Those who graduate from secondary and higher institutions consider that a job is owed them fitting their certified education. Those who have acquired professional or technical skills valued on the world market may demand an income equivalent to that of their colleagues in affluent societies, thereby heightening income maldistribution in their own country (or, with lack of success in getting the high income, adding to the 'brain drain').

The contradictions in educational expansion have been visible for some time; well-reasoned recommendations for reform abound, and some of these have been officially endorsed. However, mere demonstration of the inadequacy of the present system that, at increasingly onerous costs, turns out rising numbers of 'products' for which there is no societal need, or products which the society cannot afford, does not give the recommendations the weight they need.

A Unified Approach to Planning   365

The shift to an educational policy more compatible with an acceptable and viable style of development implies a frontal clash with the population strata most strongly motivated to seek education and most capable of enforcing organized demands, and a favouring of strata lacking clearly defined educational objectives and possessing little organized strength. The contradictions of the present trends, as these affect the youth passing through the system, are indeed generating pressures for an educational revolution, but these pressures do not translate readily into viable choices concerning content and distribution of education.

Certain guidelines for educational policy within an overall strategic orientation can be proposed, in full awareness of the difficulty of their application in the absence of wider societal changes:

1. Educational policy should anticipate and support the social and economic relationships aimed at in the preferred style of development and should struggle against the perpetuation through the schools of contrary values and unrealistic expectations, whether 'traditional' or imported.
2. Educational policy should start from a formulation of the real contribution expected of education to the preferred style of development, and should give the conventional targets of school enrolment, percentage of national income devoted to education, and so on, only a subordinate place as indicators of progress, while more emphasis should be given to diagnosis of the effective functioning of education and its impact on societal change.
3. Educational policy in its developmental orientation should not restrict its vision to the school system; it should explore the relative advantages of all possible combinations of instruments for accomplishing the desired functions, including mass communications and combinations of formal schooling with productive work, voluntary services to the society, creative activity, and so on.
4. Educational policy should give highest priority to raising the basic qualifications of the whole population to function as citizens as well as producers and consumers. That is, educational policy should aim at orienting the whole society toward an acceptable and viable style of development, rather than endowing certain individuals with the

symbols of 'modernization'. The educated unemployed should be viewed as a resource for educating others, although it would be developmentally pointless for the 'teachers' to educate their 'pupils' in the values and expectations that have governed their own (misguided) education.

The main weakness in guidelines such as the above, of course, is that they personify 'policy'. In an area like education, 'policy', even if sincerely embraced by the national authorities, can do little unless it expresses the demands of major social forces convinced that education must change and prepared to sacrifice whatever stake they have in the previous system of differential advantages.

(h) *Population*

The association of high rates of population growth with poverty and marginalization within countries and as well as between countries, and the ominous long-term implications of even moderate rates of population growth, imply that demographic factors must be taken fully into account in any realistic strategy orientation. The proposition that lower rates of population growth for the world in general are indispensable, and even the proposition that zero growth rates should be aimed at for some point in the future, have gained acceptance in official quarters and informed public opinion with remarkable rapidity. Acceptance would probably be even more general were it not for a lingering identification of population size with national power and suspicion of the motives behind promotion of population control.

The place of 'population policy' within a strategic orientation toward an acceptable and viable style of development, however, raises various problems of definition. 'Population'—the human race—is the subject and object of all development policy. It would be possible, but hardly helpful, to subsume all of the topics discussed in the present report under 'population policy' and identify such policy with a 'unified approach'. In practice, international discussions of population policy have defined its scope in very inclusive terms, and then have descended rapidly to the much more limited topic of measures intended to curb fertility—mainly those labelled 'family planning'.

A revolution in attitudes and practices relating to family life and fertility is under way that will eventually no doubt embrace the whole of the world's population, although with continuing wide differences in rates and forms of change. A comprehensive strategy should support this revolution, meet demands for effective means of controlling family size, and try to foresee and adjust itself to the wider consequences of changes in the role of the family, in age structures, in the balance between active and dependent population, and other demographic variables.

For the short and medium term, however, the effectiveness of planned actions on demographic variables should not be exaggerated, or permitted to divert attention from the other requisites for acceptable and viable styles of development. Lower rates of population increase may facilitate progress toward such styles, but will not ensure it. Moreover, the strength of the case for immediate efforts to curb fertility—as well as the practicability of such efforts—depend on widely differing national circumstances.

For a good many countries the most important immediate component of 'population policy' should be measures aimed at geographical redistribution. The necessary slowing down of rates of increase and the transition to more adequate child care within smaller families, will depend very much on the changes in societal and occupational structures that should be central to a development strategy.

(i) *Spatial and Environmental Questions*

Any meaningful strategy for the spatial redistribution of developmental activities opens new channels for participation and stimulates new demands, whether intentionally or not. Conversely, any meaningful strategy for the bringing of wider population strata into the development process as agents and beneficiaries rather than victims must incorporate principles and tactics for spatial distribution.

There is now wide agreement on the general proposition that 'spatial distribution', like 'participation', must enter more prominently into development policy than heretofore. In both areas, an imposing array of guidelines, instruments and techniques has been offered for the purpose but in both areas actual achievements are meagre in relation to aspirations. It can be presumed that most current real styles of development are partly or wholly incompatible with the kinds of spatial redistribution and enhanced participation that are overtly sought. In various countries over the past quarter century national authorities have repeatedly endorsed objectives of this kind and undertaken concrete activities, while the real processes of concentration and marginalization have continued unchecked.

The conventional picture of dependent styles of development shows a concentrated growth of 'modern' productive activities, services and consumption patterns in a few large cities; more limited and specialized growth and change in other parts of the country that supply raw materials for export or the domestic urban market; stagnation or decline in still other parts of the country.

Within a development strategy that ignores the spatial dimension and concentrates on maximization of per capita income for the national population as a whole, or within a *laissez faire* approach, the spatial distribution of production incomes, and so on, may undergo various shifts, but the most general trend is toward reinforcement of the advantages of the major cities. The concentration of import-substitution industries in the cities previously benefitting from the proceeds of raw material exports is the most conspicuous example.

Such concentration has frequently been justified by economists as most 'efficient' at certain stages of growth and as leading at some future stage to enhanced capacity for the diffusion of development throughout the whole of the national territory. While not a legitimate end in itself, the spatial redistribution of developmental activities, even at some cost in productive efficiency, becomes an important means toward the achievement of more acceptable and viable styles of development to the extent that it can be demonstrated that the following conditions are present:

1. The natural resources of the entire national territory are not being rationally exploited and managed; concentrated economic growth is causing over-exploitation of some resources and disregard of others;
2. The extreme poverty of parts of the national population, concentrated in specific zones of the territory, cannot be relieved under any conditions likely to be met in practice, by out-migration to the more 'dynamic' urban centres;

A Unified Approach to Planning 369

3. The concentration of economic activities and urban population, in some zones, and the backwardness of population groups elsewhere, are associated with major environmental disbenefits and dangers in both situations (overcrowding and industrial pollution on the one hand, destruction of land resources and forests through overuse and primitive techniques on the other);
4. The pattern of spatial distribution of population, economic activities and services prevents the attainment of a satisfactory degree of national integration, and inhibits authentic popular participation in development.

These conditions do seem to be present in fact in most national settings to a degree justifying high priority to policies for the spatial redistribution of development.

The range of relevant policies is very wide, and some of the problems of selection and application have been suggested by the preceding discussion of strategic orientations and choices concerning autonomy, participation, production, distribution and consumption. A coherent policy for spatial redistribution presupposes a certain degree of national autonomy in economic and social decision-making, popular participation in development and a capacity to bring production (in structure and techniques as well as location) into closer harmony with domestic resource endowment and the priority meeting of basic human needs.

A policy for spatial redistribution cannot realistically be conceived as a remedial adjustment of general development strategy; the questions it raises are fundamental to the preferred style of development. At the same time, political leadership that accepts this proposition and tries to act on it may find that planning and decision-making in the many relevant policy areas are distributed, without any apparent logic, among units of the public administration, national legislative bodies, provincial and local units of government, semi-autonomous public corporations, and various kinds of private bodies and organized interest-groups. It is difficult to bring the activities of these dispersed decision-making centres into harmony along the lines of a national strategy. It is necessary to try to reconcile or trade-off economic efficiency, social equity, environmental

370   Appendices from the United Nations Organization

quality, political practicability, administrative costs, short-term and long-term needs and capabilities.

The 'central' decisions, even in the most 'advanced' countries, are made in settings characterized by inadequate information, conflicting interpretations advanced by different societal actors, and powerful forces of inertia or momentum deriving from what has already been done. In particular, the power of dominant interest-groups in the capital city is commonly great enough to nullify or distort most policies that clash with the capital's continued absorption of the lion's share of investment resources.

In principle, a 'unified approach' would seem to demand a comprehensive national policy for 'regionalization' of development, division of the country into a hierarchy of major regions and sub-regions according to some consistent criteria, clear guidelines in the national plan for spatial distribution of investment funds and other stimuli to development (such as tax concessions), and a network of regional and local planning bodies combining technical expertise with citizen participation.

In practice, most national administrations would probably be well-advised to settle for something a good deal more modest than 'comprehensiveness' for the foreseeable future, and to move cautiously and by stages toward more elaborate regional and local planning systems, while avoiding the other extreme of pinning their hopes on one or two showpiece regional projects. The capacity to staff and support a complex network of regional and local planning bodies cannot be improvised. Various attempts to do so rapidly and on a nationwide scale have produced ineffective paper planning mechanisms, aroused expectations that could not be met, and ended in confusion and disillusionment.

The policy approaches deriving from growth centre and growth pole theories are of particular interest for their potential contributions to spatial redistribution objectives. Their utility, however, depends on their insertion within a strategy that ensures against their becoming additional industrial enclaves with only weak linkages to the economy and society of the internal region to which they belong.

A Unified Approach to Planning 371

Historically derived distortions in spatial distribution of development can in principle be corrected by the building up of a network of growth centres having different sizes and primary functions, integrating agricultural, industrial and social services and cultural recreational activities in a rational manner, although it may not be necessary or desirable that all of the various growth-oriented activities be represented in the same centre.

The unification or integration of different 'economic' and 'social' factors of development must be tackled at the levels at which these factors interact in real terms; 'integration' in terms of national aggregates can be a futile enterprise.

372 Appendices from the United Nations Organization

The UNPAN—The Program in Public Administration and Development

From a certain viewpoint, it could be held that another field of action—undertaken this time directly by the Department of Economic and Social Affairs (DESA), managed from the headquarters in New York, and called the Program of Public Administration and Development—is also of great interest and importance.

It develops a theme, the radical reform of the way the programming approach is managed, which is a central focus on interest in this trilogy (see the themes of Chap. II-8).

This UN programme is of great interest. It corresponds to a problem considered today the key to policies involved in the crisis of economics: the problem of ensuring that there is a method for introducing the permanent capacity of plan, not in terms of political legitimacy, but in terms of performance and engineering.

I offer here the report of an international group of experts delivered to the UNPAN, as a useful starting point for a future roadmap of reform. The following report is called 'Strengthening the Administrative Capacity of the State'.

Strengthening the Administrative Capacity of the State

(a) *The Management of Change: The State as a 'Learning Organization'*

The proliferation of actors on the political scene and great diversification of interests and pursuits in society at large vastly adds to the complexity of the tasks of modern governance. This has been further compounded by the progress of globalization and modern technology, that have radically lowered or indeed eliminated some of the protective barriers which sheltered the operations of governments in the past. A world of public authorities dealing with limited numbers of clients and stakeholders and able to control events within their borders is swiftly giving way to a more complex world; a world in which the range of clients and stakeholders is vastly more diverse, and in which numerous factors, imperfectly understood, loom on the receding horizons of decision-makers.

As governments pass, in most fields of activity, from a relatively homogeneous and stable environment to one that is unstable, complex, heterogeneous and multi-faceted, they need to learn to cope with unpredictability, uncertainty and randomness. Another major challenge to governments and managers comes from the accelerating pace and the very nature of change. Describing this development, Gerald Caiden observed: 'What administrative reformers in the early 1960s did not anticipate was that they would not be able to proceed at their own pace in their own good time. The world was entering what later was to be recognized as virtually a permanent state of turbulence. The natural pace of change would so accelerate that soon everybody would be suffering from future shock as their abilities to accommodate to change would be overtaxed' (Caiden 1991).

By the late 1990s, the context for most governments and many organizations had been transformed so radically that their traditional structures and modes of operation had slipped into obsolescence. The fused pyramidal structures, hallmark of state bureaucracies, could still perform effectively conducting routine tasks in closeted environments, but they proved increasingly inept in interacting creatively with a diversified, demanding clientele or in responding swiftly to shifting opportunities and new constraints. Likewise, the five-year plans, pillars, until quite recently of the command economies but also, mutatis mutandis, a feature of policy making in many other countries were losing credibility as both a tool and process.

In a significant study of planning, which although chiefly inspired from private sector practices has relevance to government, Canadian author Mintzberg argued that, given the conditions of rapid change, planning must be continuous and incremental (Mintzberg 1994). Although it seeks to incorporate competent policy-analysis and expert advice, current strategic planning is not viewed as an essentially technocratic process It also seeks to build on clients' expectations, as well as intuition and aspiration (vision of future States). Precisely on this account, it needs to avoid the pitfalls of bureaucratic closure and a top-down approach, which tend to stifle initiative and limit participation.

374   Appendices from the United Nations Organization

Success in modern government largely depends on widening the basis of citizen participation and galvanizing support for broadly shared objectives. This, in turn, is predicated on building and maintaining an institutional framework as open to diversity as it facilitates stakeholders' contributions to policy-making and evaluation processes. This is not always easy. Not all groups of stakeholders are readily amenable to cooperation and compromise. Not all are public-spirited. Seeking to muster support and developing consensus for a given goal or vision is a most challenging task. As a process, it may prove both costly and time-consuming, even though its long-term yield may be broadly beneficial.

Flexible structures and processes are then increasingly favoured over the more traditional and bureaucratic patterns. This is so not merely on account of the nature and frequency of change in a highly volatile and turbulent global environment, but also as a result of the cumulative pressures from diverse citizens' groups, which demand to be heard. Ability to include and synergize, as well as disposition to listen and respond, are almost universally accepted as an important source of policy legitimation. Neither comes easily, as most critiques of government and organizations amply show. They call for reaffirming a unity of direction amidst many diverse and often conflicting purposes: reinforcing institutional memory. They also call for fostering a sense of continuity, consistency, stability and predictability, which structures strive to inject into the fluid, uncertain conditions in which numerous countries in today's global society live. 'Applying democracy to administration cannot fail to consolidate the State's public image by improving functional and communication channels. In this quest for democracy, citizens must be placed at the centre of public action. The return to the concept of people as citizens must mark the end of the authoritarian approach to power and the bureaucratic, technocratic and feudalistic style of management. This development, which goes beyond the conventional form of hierarchy, calls for a new style of action and conduct in the exercise of authority' (Sedjari 2000, p. 5).

Contemporary management theory highlights the value and role of learning organizations in trying to reconcile these difficult dilemmas which government must face and, furthermore, equip them to manage change effectively. In relation to developing countries and countries in transition, attention should be drawn to four areas of need, all of particular moment to the steering tasks of the State:

Management of change: The State must be in the forefront of implementing change and smoothing the path for progress. This entails pro-active measures to develop enabling policy frameworks, promote the use of new technologies, set up performance measurement and evaluation systems, overhaul administrative structures and design adequate patterns for the collection of internationally comparable, reliable and accurate data for policy-making purposes;

Administrative reform: In the light of current trends, bureaucratic structures no longer work effectively. Debureaucratization and decentralization must go in tandem with new approaches to management, exemplifying openness, adaptability, participation, flexibility, diversity and responsiveness. Many new tasks of governance require public authorities to act as mediators, advocates or promoters, actively seeking partnerships with business and non-governmental organizations, or otherwise endeavouring to engage civil society in the pursuit of developmental objectives;

Human resources development: skills constantly upgraded, leadership qualities developed, facilitation of change and fostering of a new image for the public service that call for new career structures that emphasize mobility, integrity and professionalism and the overriding claims of merit in the recruitment, placement and promotion of public servants;

Information: Timely availability of adequate, reliable, accurate and relevant data that has become a sine qua non not only of sound policy-making but also of the measurement, monitoring and evaluation of public sector performance. The United Nations Programme in Public Administration and Finance is playing a vital role in mobilizing and disseminating such information of essential importance to governments, notably through the United Nations Public Administration Network UNPAN (UN 1998, E/1998/77, pp. 1–2).

In an era of rapid change and globalization, a learning organization necessarily becomes a changing organization; that is, it learns to listen and to respond to messages that come from its environment. Furthermore, in today's global village, this never-ending process cannot, as in the past, take place under the cover of high protective barriers.

376   **Appendices from the United Nations Organization**

(b) *Enhancing Leadership Skills and Strategic Planning Capacities*

Capacity to adjust to changing circumstances and face the emerging challenges demands leadership skills and strategic planning capacities. Specifically, it calls for:

- Sound analytical and diagnostic capabilities;
- Careful scanning of the environment for possible constraints or emerging opportunities;
- Ability to galvanize and mobilize support for both the goals and course of organizational change;
- Building of the structures and culture of dialogue and mutual accommodation;
- Encompassing diversity, reconciliation of differences, promotion of consensus; and
- Management of change, in both a peaceful and effective manner.

It follows that although, under today's conditions of swift technological progress any change should incorporate extensive expert advice, a learning organization cannot consider reform in purely technocratic terms. In today's fast-moving world, a process of reform and capacity-building must also encompass clients' and partners' perspectives. It should seek to build on knowledge and expertise, but also on intuition, vision and aspirations (mission statements) because it views success as clearly predicated on:

- Inclusion, integration, participation and empowerment of all key factors, actors and stakeholders;
- Team-building, a key element of motivation; and
- Social or organizational peace and cohesion.

For analogous reasons, change and capacity-building in a learning organization cannot any longer be approached through the traditional, authoritarian and bureaucratic methods. Although they seek to inject an element of continuity, consistency and predictability, which all organizations and societies require in order to operate effectively, the structures

The UNPAN—The Program in Public Administration... **377**

and process of change in learning organizations must also induce acceptance of the following:

- A high degree of uncertainty, in an often volatile and turbulent global environment;
- Flexibility consistent with a rapid, non-linear change process in an age of discontinuity.

Swift progress and great uncertainty add an important dimension to managing change and to capacity-building, requiring leaders and managers to plan and steer the course with people, not without them, let alone in spite of them. Learning from the mistakes and lessons of past failures, there is need to address the question of what essential structures and core competencies all countries, but especially developing countries and countries with economies in transition, need to build or reinforce in order to secure sustainable progress and growth. Although much of what follows flows from what has been said, we need to be reminded that sustainable reform and capacity-building encompass far more than personnel training or human resources development. Both call for the reinforcement of institutions and their adjustment to the demands of the times in a globalizing world.

(c) *Fostering Capacity-Building*

Like the concept of 'empowerment', the term 'capacity-building' has gained a lot of currency in recent years. It is, to say the least, a very elusive concept: the composite of several elements. For the purposes of this Report, attention is drawn to three inter-related facets of this multi-dimensional issue which, aside from its importance, has acquired much topical relevance.

Capacity-building has been defined in many ways and it encompasses various dimensions. In organizational terms, one of the possible definitions of capacity is the volume and complexity of the inputs and activities which an organization is able to handle effectively in any given time. Capacity-building, accordingly, denotes an effort to expand the existing capabilities of an organization or of the State qualitatively and quantitatively. In other words, capacity-building may be defined as the co-efficient of human resources development and institution-building. Two principal dimensions may be distinguished. One is a process involving the establishment, reinforcement or reform of an organizational framework for the conduct of human activities. The other is human resources development, which includes human capital formation, the enrichment and refinement of essential management skills and requisite technical aptitudes and support for value systems conducive to the goals of cost-effective management in organizations. The two principal dimensions are complementary and mutually reinforcing. A sound institutional framework integrates and synergizes organizational members towards the accomplishment of the set goals. To be sure, the best institutional framework with limited human capacity is of as little use as a million-dollar racing car with a timid, incompetent driver at the wheel. However, the reverse is probably even worse. Nothing is more conducive to disaffection among potentially promising and competent staff than a convoluted administrative structure, which frustrates the best designs and corrupts the most efficient and best-intentioned personnel. The recent rediscovery of the complementarily of human resources development and institution-building has lent capacity-building its current importance, but also, to an extent, has shaped the ways and methods of seeking to implement it in learning organizations.

Capacity-building concerns have recently grown largely on account of increasing resource scarcity; and rapid, unanticipated changes in the external environment, occasionally leading to systems' breakdown, when action to adjust and modernize these systems is not initiated in a timely fashion and pursued effectively.

During the 1980s and early 1990s, accordingly, 'downsizing' or 'right-sizing' and 'doing more with less' became the standard mottos of reorganization. Consistent with the criticism that faulted previous practices there was also a shift of focus from the centre to the periphery and from the top to the grassroots, through a process of devolution and de-centralization. This carried in its trail emphasis on outsourcing, reliance on NGOs and other non-state actors for public service delivery, stress on priority tasks and corresponding emphasis on what were designated as an organization's core competencies.

The UNPAN—The Program in Public Administration... **379**

Emphasis on core competencies and ways in which these competencies must be deployed and leveraged to maximum effect has often been accompanied by a process of selective divestiture of secondary functions which are contracted out to partners in the private or 'third' sectors (Reschenthaler and Thompson 1998). Such focus on essentials, tied to a holistic approach and a critical review of the lessons of experience form part of the current emphasis on both 'capacity-building' and the related concept of 'the learning organization' (ibid.).

Building Cognitive Capacity in the Face of Globalization

Though few dispute the claims of the political leadership to be the final arbiters of what the public needs, many may still look askance at the role of experts in government and many more discount or fail to understand the need for policy analysts and policy advisers. Developing countries and countries with economies in transition in general have paid a heavy price for their capacity deficit in this regard. While few question the importance of expatriate expert advice, it needs to be emphasized that the value of such advice to governments is largely predicated on the availability of institutional memory at the national level, as well as on the quality of the information and know-how that governments command from indigenous sources, preferably their own.

Even the best advice received from foreign experts needs to be a complement at best to that of the government's own, which it cannot replace. Nothing can effectively replace organized policy planning on the national level. Accordingly, what matters more than the level of individual experts is the country's systemic capacity to generate ideas on major national issues and questions of global concern and institutional memory, which can instil consistency and continuity in policy direction.

Many developing countries and countries with economies in transition have seen, in recent years, the rise of independent think-tanks, whose presence in advanced societies has long been taken for granted. They play a useful part in offering a complement and check to 'official thought'. However, they are no substitute for a corps of well-organized, well-trained, professional policy-analysts and advisers in the service of the government. A constant flow of comprehensive, accurate and up-to-date

380   Appendices from the United Nations Organization

information is also essential for the government's performance of its functions, including playing its part in the management of international regimes. No government can fully 'outsource' all of its core functions to outsiders without de facto surrendering an important part of its sovereignty, credibility and prestige. What countries need most is a critical mass of expertise in government, as well as very sound organization and a degree of autonomy in the collection of data and the conduct of research (UN 1998, E/1998/77).

In many developing countries and countries with economies in transition, the dearth of expertise at the senior policy level is compounded by turnover of specialists in high demand, who find more lucrative outlets in private enterprise or international agencies, both governmental and non-governmental. The problem is further aggravated by basic flaws in the requisite support structures. To help address this issue and to assist the Member States in meeting the commitments which they made at global conferences organized by the United Nations during the past decade, the Fourteenth Meeting of the Group of Experts, which took place in New York in 1998, made a number of recommendations whose intent was to reinforce the systems of data-gathering and to enhance the quality of information available to governments for policy-making purposes. Among these recommendations was the elaboration of:

- A framework for the collection of internationally comparable data, including qualitative as well as quantitative indicators, for the purpose of measuring the changing role of the State as reflected by privatization, deregulation and decentralization;
- A framework for the exchange of information via the Internet, focusing on the provision of advisory services, particularly to least developed and geographically isolated countries, in order to improve accessibility to the Internet to strengthening capacities in public policy formation and public service management (ibid., Recommendation No. 18).

Specifically, institutional and managerial responses to globalization and diversification, should encompass:

- Dedicated think-tanks for policy planning purposes;
- Learning from global experience;

- Inclusive, participatory, decentralized decision-making bodies;
- Strengthening of the capacity to deal with and negotiate disputes and foster a culture of dialogue; and
- Focal points in departments of government to interface with outside agencies and with the public.

It has been pointed out, but it bears repeating that, under modern conditions, few major decisions of policy can be made or implemented in a political, social or economic vacuum. Important though it may be, the contribution of experts and 'technocrats' should be complemented by inputs from people representative of civil society groups. Addressing this very issue, a report on Public Administration and Globalization (Timsit and Bouckaert 2000) made the point that establishing a balance between economic efficiency and social equity is a major task of government. Inter alia, it entails such measures as the enhancement of labour union strength and support for collective bargaining. Still, according to this report, it behoves the government to develop and articulate policies and strategies expressive of the common good and of the public interest, which cannot be solely the 'product of trade negotiations among particular interests' (ibid., p. 37).

(d) *The Need for Performance Standards for Management Development*

One of the net effects of globalization is the progressive emergence and spread of global performance standards in management development and change. In the measure that such standards are developed, articulated and publicized through the relevant literature, they tend to reproduce a set of values, which often may be prevalent in a particular culture, but are certainly not universal. This is especially true of the influential literature of the past two decades. Written mostly in the English language, it records the tested practices and valuable experience, as well as belief systems of a small range of countries, economically advanced, but still comprising only a relatively small proportion of the world's population. Importing foreign standards and benchmarks, which relate to specific management traditions and sets of expectations, may be a recipe for failure, unless such standards and benchmarks are appropriately reviewed, and adapted to the local culture.

382   Appendices from the United Nations Organization

Making this point, however, is not to say that standards in certain major areas may not converge or that the setting of standards and benchmarks should not be accorded its due weight in any management culture. There is some evidence pointing to the effects of globalization on a certain convergence of standards, in the measure that behaviour norms and clients' expectations throughout the world are moving toward a common ground. However, one must acknowledge the findings of research in continental Western Europe, which stresses the profound, pervasive and persistent influence of culture on management behaviour and management techniques, both of which are culture-specific and not readily transposable from one country to another, even when they are contiguous (for example, the Netherlands and Belgium). According to this school of thought, cultural differences condition the validity of management philosophies and practices in various countries and should, therefore, be taken into account in the establishment of standards and the making of management policy.

The formulation of performance standards like the development and articulation of policy represent essential functions of the State, which cannot be surrendered or 'outsourced'. To be sure, under conditions of globalization, the exchange of information among governments will lead them, in some cases, to align methods and practices in the quest of shared objectives. However, it is incumbent on governments to establish standard setting, performance indicators and the practice of benchmarking on an institutional basis, as part of their core functions.

Though stress on performance standards has been with us for some time, it has taken on great salience in the past two decades, in part due to the effect of the new trends in management and the emphasis they have placed on results orientation. Mindful of resolution 50/225 of the United Nations General Assembly, which in paras. 7 and 9 called for enhanced effectiveness of public administration systems worldwide (UN 1996, AI RES/50/225), the Fourteenth Meeting of the Group of Experts made performance monitoring and evaluation one of the major topics of its agenda. Its report (UN 1998, E/1998/77, paras. 44–46) explores in some detail the issues in performance monitoring and evaluation and underscores their importance. The Fourteenth Meeting of the Group of Experts viewed this new significance in light of four perspectives:

The changing role of government from sole provider of services to one of founder, lender, contractor, purchaser and regulator;
- The public's right to know;
- The need to measure the outcomes of policies and programmes, and thus to act as catalyst for periodic reviews, possible reconsideration of resource allocation and the quest for performance improvements; and
- The need to go beyond the traditional forms of accountability to ensure value for money and the cost-effective pursuit of the public interest.

In light of these perspectives and the ongoing pursuit of subsidiarity through decentralization, deconcentration, devolution of responsibility and offloading or outsourcing, one must incorporate performance indicators in the formulation of policies and programmes, which serve to mobilize stakeholders' support and involvement, but also help to structure and guide the evaluation of progress and results. Seen in this light, performance measurement, monitoring and evaluation represent a necessary compass in the quest of complex objectives involving contributions from the several partners under conditions of democratic and accountable governance.

Purposes of Performance Measures

The fundamental purpose of instituting performance measures in an organization is to evaluate its performance. Briefly, they may be used in accounting for past activities, managing current operations and assessing progress toward planned objectives. One of the oldest uses of performance measures was for purposes of accountability, specifically related to the budget process. Performance measures were to be incorporated in agency budget presentations in an effort to replace:

- Workload or activity levels, such as applications processed, inventory levels, inspections carried out, students in class;
- Outputs, such as the number of children vaccinated, miles of road built, tons of trash picked up, students graduated;
- Outcomes of products or services, such as illnesses prevented, percentage of taxes collected, clean air levels achieved, accident-free workplaces attained, poverty alleviated;

384   Appendices from the United Nations Organization

- Productivity, such as cases investigated per detective, applications processed per person, emergency calls handled per dispatcher;
- Costs, such as coverage costs to build one mile of highway, educate one child, maintain one swimming pool;
- Customer satisfaction, such as numbers of complaints received over a period of time, results of surveys, use of participative processes;
- Service quality and timeliness, such as police response times, ability to contact an agency by telephone, compliance with transportation timetables, breakdown rates, service availability.

Where levels are specified for any measure, these constitute 'performance standards'.

Where reference is made to identifying and implementing best practices in order to set out a standard for comparison of results and to drive performance improvement, this is known as 'benchmarking'. When output is not directly measurable, proxies known as 'indicators' may be used. 'Performance incentives' may be used to assess individual performance in determining remuneration.

These measures are designed to assess the economy, efficiency and effectiveness with which an organization delivers its services.

Economy is concerned with the capacity of an organization to operate at the lowest possible cost and may be assessed through input measures and comparisons through benchmarking. Efficiency is the relationship between input and outputs, that is, using minimum inputs to achieve a given output, or gaining maximum outputs for a given level of input. It may be measured through output, productivity and cost measures. Effectiveness delineates the success of programmes and focuses on their results, as assessed through outcome measures. In addition, the quality of services may be assessed through process measures relating to customer satisfaction and perceptions.

While any of these measures might be used to assess an organization's performance, recent emphasis has been on quantitative effectiveness or outcomes measurement. A report of the United States General Accounting Office on Performance Budgeting has suggested a change of focus from 'ensuring that funds are spent properly' to 'managing dollars to produce agreed upon results' (United States General Accounting Office, February

The UNPAN—The Program in Public Administration...

1999, p. 3). If such a change is really taking place, it is not a trivial one. It is a move associated with administrative reforms in many European countries as well as Australia, Canada, New Zealand and the United States. Such reforms go beyond reorganization to question whether specific programme areas continue to serve a public interest; whether they should be transferred, entirely or in part, to the private or voluntary sectors; and how, if the programme continues, it might be made more efficient and affordable. In effect, programme evaluation is tied to the evaluation of the entire role of government.

(e) *The Need for Top-Level Managers*

The progress of globalization brings out a new dimension in standard setting, and in performance measurement, monitoring and evaluation: the need to elaborate and to articulate a range of shared approaches, values and methodologies, which ease communication in international dealings and make the cooperation of diverse groups more fruitful and rewarding. Referring to changing what needs to be changed, a similar remark might be made about the need for a new cadre of able and responsible top managers to face the emerging challenges and handle the global agenda in an increasingly interactive and competitive global environment.

Although technology, innovative systems and processes of work organization and user-friendly methods of public service delivery are increasingly important ingredients of the managerial response to globalization, building the capacity of the human resources represents a crucial dimension of governments' response to globalization (UN 2000, E/2000/66, pp. 12–15).

It is important to note that governments, increasingly, perform significant tasks on a supra-national level. This is true not only of entities like the European Union, which represents an advanced manifestation of this trend, but also of the formation and operation of international regimes in many fields of activities. All depend for their effectiveness on an elaborate framework of rules, processes and practices, which determine how power is exercised and governance conducted with consistency, transparency, coherence and accountability, as well as on a cadre of top level managers from the governments of Member States, who can bring this framework to life and operate effectively in the new global environment.

386   Appendices from the United Nations Organization

Attention ought to be focused on competencies needed to operate effectively on the supra-national level, and on ways of building capacity on the national level. It should be pointed out that the ability to field such a cadre of top managers and leaders conditions a country's effectiveness as an actor in inter-governmental negotiations and global regimes. With such individuals, Member States are effectively 'in the loop' and have the possibility to promote their country's interests. Dearth of such people, by contrast, may consign States to the margins and to the role of spectators of the progress accomplished by others.

> Tell me and I'll forget.
> Show me and I'll remember.
> Involve me and I'll understand. (Chinese proverb)

In view of the pressures that globalization create, 'public servants should be trained to operate on the national, sub-national and international levels and participate in leadership training. Governments should build a framework of public personnel structure, policies and career paths able to attract, retain, develop and motivate the right people and to direct their energies towards the public good' (ibid., Recommendation No. 19).

Furthermore, 'the United Nations should assist national governments in acquiring the necessary negotiating capacities to prepare for negotiations of global economic governance regimes' (ibid., Recommendation No. 15), and it 'should assist national governments in adjusting their national economic governance systems (policies and institutions) in response to globalization. This includes support for policy development and implementation capacities in developing and transition economies' (ibid., Recommendation, No. 16).

The Fifteenth Meeting of the Group of Experts drew attention to the weaknesses of the developing countries and countries with economies in transition resulting from 'the scarcity of world-wide economists and specialists with knowledge of the working of international agreements, treaties and regimes, as well as technical skills' (ibid., p. 14). Significantly, however, the Meeting took the view that analogous shortcomings could be observed in the operation of States at the national and sub-national levels. Everywhere, it may be argued, globalization and democratization have increased the pace of change, complexity and ambiguity, making demands on cadres for which they are ill-prepared.

(f) *Competencies Needed to Meet the Challenges of Globalization*

The competencies needed to meet the critical challenges of contemporary governance refer to a combination of knowledge, skills, behaviours and attitudes, which often goes beyond what was required of 'bureaucrats', or officials operating in traditional, closed system work environments. No two countries need to agree on the desired profile of a senior public manager or on the relative weight and indeed precise definition of the most often-mentioned competencies, some of which are described in the following paragraphs.

Knowledge, a substantive core, is part of the competencies that senior professional managers need to bring into their office as a basic precondition of being able to exercise effective guidance and leadership.

A component of technical knowledge will always be required. Though this may vary widely depending on a manager's assigned responsibilities, substantive knowledge is needed to grasp the issues involved in the exercise of one's duties to make intelligent choices. Traditionally, the study of law provided a common core of required technical knowledge for top public managers in many of the foremost administrative cultures.

Though this remains the case in several parts of the world, now law is complemented by the study of social sciences, especially economics. Knowledge of economics is basic not merely to the management of any given field, but also to interacting effectively with other public managers on the sub-national, national, and international levels.

Another core component of the substantive knowledge required of an effective professional public manager is, what may be described as the management of the resources assigned to his or her care. These pre-eminently include:

- Human resources;
- Financial resources; and
- Information resources.

388　　Appendices from the United Nations Organization

Most managers need not be specialists in finance, organizational theory or information management to ensure the responsible stewardship and use of the above resource. Appreciation, however, of their true value, as well as a sound understanding of all the relevant issues can greatly enhance effectiveness on the job and, therefore, should form part of pre-entry and in-service preparation for the job.

As to skills, they manifest themselves in the ways in which a manager performs his or her major roles. These comprise:

- The exercise of leadership, including managerial skills;
- Decisional roles; and
- Informational roles.

Leadership calls for vision, ability to identify and seize an opportunity, anticipate a crisis and cope with constraints effectively. It is exemplified in the persistent quest for excellence, innovative ideas and actions or behaviour, which seek constructive ways to establish and secure a country's or organization's competitive edge. Within the organization, leadership is demonstrated through building trust, communicating vision, empowering colleagues, serving as a role model and managing performance effectively.

Decision-making skills include the effective use of information, data, technologies and ideas; a clear sense of direction, priorities and needs; sound planning and good timing; and client orientation, which also means responsiveness to changes and developments in the organization's external environment.

They call for critical judgment, sagacity and discernment, courage and intuition, but also uncommon capacity to cope with ambiguity, diversity, complexity and turbulence.

In essence, information as a function of management, is effective communication. It calls for clarity of expression, verbal or written, sound knowledge of the language and ability to tailor it, in style and tone, to match the needs and expectations of a particular audience.

Culture is an important determinant of effective communication. Thus, a clear appreciation of the culture of the target audience represents a key ingredient of success in reaching out and having an impact on it. In today's diverse societies and organizations, this is no easy task. To operate effectively on the international plane, senior managers require more than vicarious knowledge of the main international languages and cultures in which they need to operate. However, even at the national and sub-national levels, the presence of diversity and the diffusion of power that have come with democratization have added to the importance of good listening skills, effective use of the media and information technologies, and above all, the need to keep the channels of communication open at all times. One of the many effects of globalization has been to enhance the value of these and other related 'soft skills', making it necessary to use in-service training, even more intensively than in the past, for the purpose of fine-tuning these valuable skills.

Furthermore, as already indicated, in an increasingly interconnected world public servants will need to master foreign languages.

In order to deal with a variety of international actors and to conduct negotiations in international fora, it will be crucial for the public servant of the twenty-first century to know more than one foreign language. Knowledge of languages should become part of public service training and lifelong learning programmes.

(g) *Public Service Professionalism*

Cutting across the range of skills and knowledge needed to build effective management in today's fast-moving world is the concept of professionalism, which, in the past few years, has made a marked re-entry into the field of management, where it had been neglected.

Suddenly, since approximately 1996, conferences and publications on public service professionalism and the related concept of public sector ethics have become legion. Much of the current interest has focused on the fight against corruption. A concern over the decline of standards and corresponding need for integrity in public life has driven the debate on the scope and significance of public service professionalism.

Professionalism in government, as in any other field, is observable through competence in ways outlined above, that is, through relevant deep knowledge and aptitudes or skills, but also through a coherent, widely shared and profoundly -internalized values system which manifests itself in the pursuit and thorough application of knowledge, the use of particular skills, and the exercise of control over practice. Indeed, it may be argued that professionalism consists in standards and values which underpin the day-to-day practices and conduct of a group. Although these values and standards must, to some extent, reflect the changing expectations of clients of the group and recipients of its services, they also represent the group's own aspirations and deep sense of its mission. Hence, their worth is an important guide and motivational tool. Historically, professionalism has played a major role in the growth and organization of major occupational groups (doctors and lawyers, for instance), as well as in providing a measure of consistency, continuity and predictability in the conduct of their activities. There is reason to believe that increasing interdependence, both at the level of government and that of civil society in the wake of globalization, has greatly enhanced the importance of consistency and predictability in inter-governmental and non-governmental relations.

It is easy to understand why kleptocracies have emerged in some cases, but more generally why the prevalence of corrupt or even mercenary behaviour has come to be perceived as an obstacle and a threat not merely to democracy and development at the national level, but also to the effective operation of the emerging system of global governance.

What may be harder to grasp, in light of the prevailing 'neo-managerial culture', is that professional ethics in any major field, be it medicine or law, teaching or architecture, sets limits to 'responsiveness' to customers' demands, requiring of professionals that they exercise instead their best professional judgement in light of best available knowledge or expertise.

At the United Nations, a recent definition and statement of the 'competencies for the future' has underscored integrity, professionalism and respect for diversity as core United Nations values for its staff. These include:

(a) pride in work and mastery of subject matter;
(b) motivation by intrinsic, professional, rather than extrinsic or personal concerns;
(c) persistence in the face of challenges and crises:
(d) resistance to 'undue' political pressure in decision-making;

The UNPAN—The Program in Public Administration...   391

(e) defence of the organization's interests, even under fire; and
(f) the legitimate use of power and authority.

Transparency: A Generalised Demand

One of the main criticisms levelled at the State in recent decades has been the fact that corrupt practices often exist and such practices are not punished. This is a very widespread problem that does not exclusively affect the developing world. These practices are not solely confined to social areas. Modern research into corruption points out that whenever there is a corrupt person in the public sector, there is someone who does the corrupting from the private sector. Corruption has to do with intra-social combinations that are often of vast scope. Some episodes of the most blatant corruption in Latin America in recent years did not occur in the public sector. The embezzlement that took place in a number of large banks in the area a few years ago, which translated into a sizable loss of resources for the countries involved, was spurred by the corrupt practices of important private bankers, often aided and abetted by the ineptitude of some public regulating bodies. The episodes of corruption that accompanied privatization processes in certain developing countries were connected to public/private interest arrangements.

Today, worldwide, there is a generalized demand to put an end to corruption. Its costs for the economies of developing countries are extremely high and the moral consequences are even worse. In the social sphere, corruption in the guise of skimming resources from policies and programmes set up to help the poorest members of society, is a true ethical crime. The State must undergo a radical transformation in this area. All anti-corruption strategies that could be effective should be brought into play, among which, the first should be the task of educating people about corruption. Spaces must systematically be created to discuss the problem in all educational venues for civil servants; clear-cut codes of ethics that can be strictly enforced must be devised. It is also necessary to make all actions taken by the State in the social area transparent to citizens. Information concerning social programmes must be complete, ongoing and totally accessible. The purpose of the programmes, the

392   Appendices from the United Nations Organization

resources to be used, sources of financing and implementation processes must constitute information that is as accessible as any other elemental administrative data, and this is precisely where IT and the Internet can make valuable contributions.

At the same time, channels should be set up so that social control of public administration can make itself felt. The entire system should also contain clear and indisputable measures for penalizing and punishing corruption.

Corruption must be transformed into an exceptional occurrence, morally penalized; but the risk of criminal prosecution should also exist. In summary, it should be difficult and dangerous to engage in corrupt practices, because of permanent controls by the preventive systems in place and monitoring by the citizens themselves, as well as by the threat of punishment.

Managing Diversity

Diversity takes on many forms. Globalization and progress bring in their wake the proliferation of preferences, sub-cultures, interest groups, religions, cults, ideologies and groups demanding recognition and protection of their identity or indeed representation in decision-making processes which impact on their status and rights.

Repression of such groups is not a viable option. It has proved counter-productive and, as experience shows, is costly economically and politically. Experience demonstrates a pressing need to strengthen the capacity of States both in accommodating and managing diversity and change. It comes as no surprise that the greater the diversity, the faster the process of change and the more vitally important the role of the State becomes in managing this process. International cooperation and the force of global example may help in building up the State's much-need ed. capacity to serve as guarantor, time-keeper, moderator and manager of a process of change involving multiple partners and stakeholders, while all along safeguarding the interests and rights of all concerned. A dynamic market economy requires an effective State, where the instruments for strengthening the nation-State obviously needed, for instance in some of the former Republics of the former Soviet Union, have to be balanced with adequate decentralized policies.

This is needed partly in response to the expectations of groups aspiring to administer their own cultures and traditions as part of the newly formed national entities. The greatest challenge, while moving into the new millennium, will prove to be the building of viable political institutions for the new nation-States of the region. Institutions should be capable of respecting the aspirations of minorities that are part of these nations, and of establishing a balance between what is dictated by economic logic and clamoured for in political expectations. The political process of the breaking up of the Soviet Union has been remarkably peaceful. However, in its aftermath, the forces of ethnicity and minority and of the periphery in relation to the centre demand political leadership to promote policies that are all inclusive, a commodity rare even in normal times and certainly harder to come by when the economic and social indicators are worsening.

'Those who applauded the lifting of the "Iron Curtain", which separated people between countries, never expected "Glass Curtains" to descend separating people within countries. The challenge now is to achieve political rights in an environment of growing economic insecurity. Human insecurity breeds human violence, making it even more necessary for economic growth to aim at enriching human development' (UNDP 1999, Human Development Report, p. 11). Training programmes on diversity and 'conflict resolution' have multiplied and spread, in several parts of the world, both in the public service and academic establishments. Still, it should be noted that the scope of such departures is, in some countries, limited to three main target group: women, minorities and people with special needs.

One cannot over-emphasize the urgency and complexity of gender mainstreaming, on the one hand, and progressive integration of hitherto underprivileged and under-represented categories of citizens, on the other. This has seldom proved an easy task. Not only special measures and facilities may be required, but also language and culture have proved in some cases to be steep barriers to surmount.

One of the many effects of globalization has been to ease the movement of peoples across borders and bring them closer together.

394   Appendices from the United Nations Organization

Proximity, however, has not invariably helped to combat or assuage stereotyping, let alone eliminate prejudice and discrimination.

Recent events in the world have brought home to some governments a sense of the diversity of their respective countries and the dangers of exclusion. Still, it would be an error to view the current stress on diversity management purely in terms of 'affirmative action', equalizing opportunities or righting historical wrongs, important though these may be.

Accommodating diversity makes good business sense in any organization. It represents a necessity primarily on account of the process of diversification present in all societies and all organizations. Such growing heterogeneity reflects more than plurality and visibility of cultures, which must be accommodated in any one workplace. On a more basic level, heterogeneity springs from the diversity of occupational groups, the product of specialization, which rapid advances in science and technology have carried in their trail.

Today, very few policies or programmes, decisions or operations can either be designed or implemented without the cooperation of many different specialties and sub-specialties. Bringing them together into a cohesive group, building them into a team, is hardly an easy task. Distinct occupational groups have often different values, divergent methodologies or problem-solving techniques, let alone competing interests. Occasionally, they exhibit what others may consider an exaggerated sense of their own relative importance. Building a balanced synthesis of many complementary but still dissimilar elements is a challenge which requires sensitivity to difference, perseverance, open mindedness, negotiating skills and capacity to reconcile conflicting views and interests.

Coping with diversity represents a reasoned response, by top managers and by the State, to the challenge of globalization and the related processes of differentiation and fragmentation, which are pronounced in most advanced societies, but present all over the world.

In fact, it constitutes an important new dimension of the functions of management, requiring new perspectives on its role, methods and mission. Particularly relevant to the needs of global management, the management of diversity calls for the investment of time and resources in building or refining the structures and a culture of dialogue and accommodation. Inclusive of both people and viewpoints, these structures and this culture endeavour to manage with differences, not in spite of or against them. Managers look to long-term progress over short-term expediency and take a broader view of the three 'Es' (economy, efficiency and effectiveness). These are obviously the antithesis of reductionist approaches and 'macho-managerialism' (Timsit and Bouckaert 2000, p. 299).

On the national as well as the international levels, the structures and the culture of dialogue and peace are clearly the mark and creation of fully democratic States. They endeavour to redress market failures and try to give a voice 'to the poor and to the future', which all too often have none (UN 1997, E/1997/86, para. 62). It has become apparent that persisting poverty and inequality between and within nations has been accompanied, in many cases, by a sharp deterioration in the prevalent conditions of life and work which 'have rendered necessary a redefinition of the role of the State' precisely in this direction (Timsit and Bouckaert 2000).

(h) *Organisational Responses for Human Resources Development*

The need for redefinition and growing interest in diversity management worldwide bring into sharp relief the critical role of the State and of its public service as guardians of the common good, charged with the critical tasks of elaborating, articulating and defending the public interest. In pluralistic societies, let alone the global community, these tasks need to be accomplished through democratic processes of dialogue and consensus.

These processes, in turn, require elaborate structures, but also special skills—already discussed at length above—and a mindset which senior managers especially will need to develop and internalize. How to acquire this mindset and high-level skills could be the subject of debate at national, regional and interregional fora, although in the last analysis, countries may opt to formulate their own specific responses to this generic challenge.

Many regional initiatives since 1997 suggest that the revaluation of public service professionalism including ethics must be included in this response. A synthesis of the outcomes of these several UN-sponsored activities is provided in a document published by the Department of Economic and Social Affairs under the title 'Professionalism and Ethics

396   Appendices from the United Nations Organization

in the Public Service: Issues and Practices in Selected Regions' (UN 2000, STIESAlPAD/SER.E/5). It has been rightly argued that, in a way, there is not one single profession of government, but many.

'Governments employ all kinds of persons such as doctors, meteorologists, teachers, lawyers, public security personnel, as well as those whose field of expertise does not easily fit under any single heading. Yet government professionals have certain attributes in common. They work in a common institutional and legal framework, which offers its own constraints and opportunities. They share a commitment to use their skills for the public good, in public service as against private gain, for fixed remuneration. They are subject to public accountability for their actions' (UN 1999, STIESA/PAD/SER.E/3, p. 80).

How governments recruit and under what conditions they employ their personnel are institutional issues, where wide diversity of practice may be observed. Obviously, there is no one-best-way, and 'no-one-size-fits-all'. In many parts of the world, patterns in public employment have long been bound with tenure and the concept of careers. The growth of political pluralism during the nineteenth and twentieth centuries reinforced this trend. For reasons related as much to political probity as to the proper working of the administrative system, civil service reforms have promoted the separation between political functions and civil service posts. The latter were progressively brought into career structures, one of whose main objectives was to buffer public servants from external political pressures and to safeguard their 'neutrality'.

To be sure, respect for this neutrality and lack of political tampering with the public service have been variously observed in different parts of the world. More recently, however, both 'career' and 'permanence' have come under attack from several quarters. Among the arguments put forward in favour of the abandonment of this traditional doctrine, the diversification and changing configuration of personnel requirements in the public sector stand out as incontrovertible. The civil service profile in most countries today bears no relation to its counterpart before the Second World War. What is more, it is constantly changing. With efforts on the way to curb public expenditures and calls to privatize or outsource large sectors of activity, several governments and public organizations have come to regard permanent contracts or 'tenure' as an obstacle to change, or as an obstruction to rapid response. At times of resource scarcity, constraints on 'trimming down' redundant personnel are both found unacceptable to some and accentuate the feeling that permanent appointments provide strong disincentives to work hard and to adjustment.

Accordingly, many governments and intergovernmental organizations are currently experimenting with innovative approaches which seek to redefine the scope of the public sector, change the traditional structures of public organizations and introduce more flexible, often private-sector-inspired modalities for the employment of personnel in the public sector. It should be pointed out that success of such experiments in one country does not necessarily mean they would work in others. Uncritical acceptance of foreign policy transfers, as we have seen, has often led to unhappy consequences. There are, nevertheless, important ways in which comparison of civil service reforms in different parts of the world could prove extremely useful by shedding light on factors which contributed to the success of reforms. Such factors are, for instance, the presence of a well organized market for high-level skills, a developed and expanding private sector, a culture of respect for the rule of law and a generally supportive legal and institutional framework. With the analysis of outcomes, cross-cultural comparisons should explore the factors which contributed to the success of policies and shaped these final outcomes.

After more than two decades of experiments with change, it would be very useful to proceed with an objective analysis of benefits and costs and try to demonstrate the strengths and weaknesses, advantages and disadvantages of the policies pursued: what worked and what did not; where, how and, most importantly, why.

States' responses to the challenge of globalization ought to accord priority to the enrichment of the stock of competencies available to governments for purposes of management and policy-making. However, the value of a structured institutionalized approach should not be overlooked. Governments need to build 'a framework of public personnel structures, policies and career paths able to attract, retain, develop and motivate the right people and motivate their energies towards the public good' (UN 2000, E/2000/66, Recommendation No. 19). Furthermore, 'governments should take urgent concerted per measures to reinforce the ethics infrastructure of their respective countries and to introduce a comprehensive set of mechanisms, including merit pay and performance benchmarks, to deal with corruption and generally raise the standards of public life, nationally and globally' (ibid., Recommendation No. 20).

The role of infrastructures and institutional frameworks is to act as the key determinant of the nature and levels of the competencies and values that a country wants to foster both in the public service and public life in general. Notwithstanding cultural differences, most countries would agree in including, in the latter, objectivity, equity, tolerance, intellectual courage, integrity and, even more importantly today, commitment to democracy, and respect for human rights and for the rule of law. Although it would be risky to generalize, it may be fair to argue that countries find it hard to nurture and sustain such values and competencies in the public service in the absence of certain conditions, which need to be highlighted:

- An institutional framework and a professional cadre for human resources management and development ensuring for the service a measure of coherence, consistency, transparency, credibility and predictability;
- A culture of respect for service to society and to the State, and for recognition of merit.

Many developing countries and countries with economies in transition are facing serious problems in this regard. For example, due to the paucity of pay, which is so low in some countries and so rarely disbursed, public servants are forced to choose between service to their country and meeting their family's basic needs. Experience throughout the world corroborates the dictum that a 'cheap public servant can cost the State a lot'.

However, increasing salary levels of public officers would not yield proper results and might be counterproductive if it were not accompanied by a commensurate rise in training levels. Raising performance levels demands concerted action. In turn, such action demands a truly professional management of public sector human resources and a holistic approach to their sustained development. The former would require building a cadre of top-level professionals. The latter would entail well-coordinated action through (a) pre- and in-service training; (b) mobility and rotation; (c) ending the patronage system, where it exists; and (d) recruitment, posting and promotion strictly on the basis of merit (with

The UNPAN—The Program in Public Administration... **399**

allowances for affirmative action). In this regard, it would be advisable that 'the State stop being an employer of last resort' (ibid., p. 14).

To give substance to this approach in concrete terms, the Meeting of the Group of Experts recommended 'the proclamation of a United Nations Public Service Day, which would celebrate the value and the virtue of service to the community on the local, national and global levels, with prizes to be awarded by the Secretary-General for contributions made to the cause of enhancing the role, prestige and visibility of public service' (ibid., Recommendation No. 3).

It may be worth exploring, in the framework of the United Nations Programme in Public Administration and Finance, other measures to enhance the prestige accorded to public service worldwide and the relative autonomy of the public service profession. For too long and in too many countries, public employment has been viewed as instrumental to extraneous ends and human resource management subordinated to short-term considerations unrelated to the goal of sound overall performance in the public service.

Specifically, in several countries, a spoils system still prevails. Positions at all levels, though paid from public funds, are virtually appropriated by the political leadership and used for electoral purposes or the exercise of patronage. The effects of 'clientelism' are compounded, in most cases, by the tendency to use the public service as a means or as an instrument to combat or conceal unemployment. The negative effects of such practices have been manifold and visible. Not only have they contributed to inflating staff costs and adding to tax burdens on citizen taxpayers, but they have also tended to 'debase the civil service coin'. A once prestigious profession, it has gradually become the butt of attacks and derision from many quarters.

Efforts to enhance the role, professionalism, performance, ethical values and standards in the public service ought to begin by addressing this issue. Whatever must be done to further job creation, using the public service is not the way. Staffing, recruitment, posting, promotion, career development and remuneration practices must follow objective principles with only the prestige, performance and integrity of the service in mind.

Though policies will vary from one country to another, one thing seems certain: that policies and practices of human resources management and development must rest in professional hands. How to recruit,

400   **Appendices from the United Nations Organization**

retain, develop and motivate professionals, at various levels, is an issue that must be addressed.

A complex of activities which seeks to apply the lessons of international practice, international cooperation in institution-building and human resources development conveys a powerful message. The means available, in terms of knowledge, science, technology and know-how open immense possibilities for the world as a whole. Building a public service worthy of a democracy is well within the reach of most governments. Will the determination to use these possibilities prove commensurate to the challenge of the times?

(i) *Technology and Reform*

It has become apparent that globalization has invested reform with new meaning. Once an occasional task of bureaucrats and politicians, it is fast becoming a recurrent event and a facet of the process of modernization. Increasingly, however, two new dimensions are added. One dimension is the progressive exposure of previously veiled structures to public view and growing public scrutiny; the other may be termed the 'internationalization' of administrative change. On both fronts, major strides have been made in recent years. Most governments now welcome an exchange of information and some indeed accept a measure of convergence of administrative practice, notably as a prerequisite of their accession to wider regional groups (for example, the acquis communautaire, required for future membership of the European Union).

Reflective of the effects of technological progress in accelerating the transition from a closed to an open systems approach and in promoting transparency of government operations, this new exposure of national administration to domestic civil society and international scrutiny is welcome on the whole. It fosters sensitivity to public expectations and may serve to reinforce greater respect for professionalism in the public service. There are nevertheless also potential downsides. One is a certain risk that the responsibility for administrative action may be dangerously diffracted and that accountability may suffer, as a result. The other is the tendency to exaggerate the scope for meaningful comparisons and policy transfers.

Capacity-reinforcement must therefore be understood in broad strategic terms as a long-term endeavour, indeed a continual task of shaping, redefining and revamping institutions with the help of evolving technologies and refining human competencies in this light. The potential is enormous. But how to ensure that progress driven by modern technologies follows the paths of reason and serves the public interest is the challenge that public institutions at the national, sub-national and international levels must face.

Information Technology: Its Promise and Potential for Reform

It carries in it the prospect of major reforms in the whole field of governance and public administration. These could take shape and form in any of the following ways:

- More efficient and effective public management;
- More accessible and better information for the public;
- Better delivery of services; and
- Building partnerships for interactive and participative governance.

Though in the 1960s and 1970s computers were already widely used by governments to improve the efficiency and effectiveness of their operations, it is since the 1980s that information technology has been applied more massively, not only on the operational, but also on the tactical or managerial and strategies levels. Innovations, in the form of Management Information Systems and Decision Support Systems, are gradually transforming the processes of governance.

Thus, they have made governments in most developed countries the largest single users of IT and predominant consumers of IT products in many developing countries.

Information systems have greatly improved effectiveness, efficiency and productivity in government. For example, an integrated network-based national revenue management system will collect information speedily and effectively, enable revenue officers to receive cases more quickly and also automate and modernize the tax collection process. Furthermore, it

402   Appendices from the United Nations Organization

will empower the treasury department to collect taxes more productively, which is, of course, a benefit to government and the country.

A significant concomitant of computerization is the exploitation and utilization of government data/information resources. The process of computerizing government business is de facto a process of exploitation of government information resources. It is well known that one of the primary activities of government is record-keeping. On the operational level especially, government authorities collect, process, maintain and update various kinds of data on individuals, families and organizations. As a result, the government becomes the largest public information owner and manages vast resources of data.

In many developing countries, the government is frequently the only producer and manager of relevant economic and social data.

Information is a valuable resource. However, it must be developed so that it can better serve users. The traditional means for obtaining and disseminating information were books, journals, indexes, libraries and archives. Favoured today, by contrast, are digitization and computerization of data and information in such forms as digitized documents, digitized images, audios and videos, databases, data mining and data warehousing. Thus, large amounts of data/information can be effectively, promptly and easily stored, reprocessed, retrieved and transmitted widely.

In this and other ways, IT facilitates government information services. In democratic societies, one of the government's principal responsibilities is to report on its affairs to its citizens. The administration has the duty to inform individuals of their rights and obligations and to maintain good relations with them. An individual citizen's understanding of the public service depends not on its outcomes only, but also on the way in which he or she is informed. Therefore, to make information accessible and intelligible to the public is a critical component of government services to citizens and a powerful means to facilitate popular participation in the processes of government.

IT is changing the ways of public information. Electronic distribution of government documentation and increasing public access to government information are being developed very quickly in many countries. Many governments have set up websites and connected databases and information systems to the Internet, thus enabling the public to search, locate, view and download government reports, studies, computer software, data files and databases. IT promotes the sharing of information resources and makes governments able to provide more and better information services cost-effectively.

By improving public access to information, IT has helped to foster transparency and accountability in government. In the past two decades, IT has also played a major role in helping to spread the concept of a more efficient and responsive public sector, based on 'service management'. Emphasis on this concept has also led to extensive use of IT tools for measuring the effectiveness and efficiency of public services.

IT has made a start at changing the modalities of public service delivery. For centuries, the notion that citizens might actively participate in all public affairs and make substantive inputs in policy decisions remained a distant prospect. Now government websites, e-mail and other means could turn such participation into a reality. Electronic polling, for instance, by either public or private institutions, will probably take place in the very near future. If family computers are connected to a national or local information infrastructure and wired up to government websites, a two-way communication system will have been established. At the local community level, an Intranet may also be set up.

This Intranet may be used to sample opinions in a quick and painless fashion. Questions put on an administration's website would appear on the computer screens of all the households connected to it. Viewers could click the icon which they select on the screen, and thus a poll is taken. Each household on the network could then be briefly scanned; the choices and results accumulated would appear in a matter of a few seconds.

Electronic referenda and electronic voting may also happen eventually. An on-line voter guide could provide the public with current information about elections. Consultation on national issues may take place and elections, either local or national, could be conducted through the Internet. The voting can take place wherever the voter is, provided that electronic votes are properly designed. It goes without saying that such electronic polls, referenda and voting systems must meet political as well as technical requirements of accuracy, reliability and eligibility, when required.

In the public and private sectors, IT is rapidly changing not merely work processes and ways of doing business, but also forms and structures

404   **Appendices from the United Nations Organization**

in organizations. For example, with the Internet and on-line databases, all kinds of information text, graphics, images, voice or video can be accessed and handled by many individuals concurrently.

Accordingly, it is possible to carry out activities and workflows at different posts simultaneously if computers and information networks are in place. Knowledge management systems, with the help of a search engine on the Internet can capture the knowledge of specialists and non-specialists for routine decision-making. Delegation of authority to lower levels of responsibility within an organization thus becomes a distinct possibility. Traditional hierarchical organizational structures based on pyramidal flows of information could be rendered obsolete. IT has the potential to bring about significantly altered organizational structures previously based on hierarchical distribution of information, diminish the value of departmental boundaries, and change the way decisions are taken and communicated.

Since the mid-1980s, accordingly, the focus of IT has shifted, from the quest for efficiency and productivity by automating routine tasks, to the achievement of effectiveness in terms of new approaches to traditional tasks and solutions to new tasks. State agencies and enterprises in many countries are currently engaged in restructuring their organizations in manners more appropriate to the new IT environment. In this process, they are removing layers of traditional management, compressing job categories, creating work teams, training employees in multi-level skills, simplifying business processes and streamlining administration. The outcomes of this re-engineering have demonstrated the scope for administrative reform as well as shown that, ultimately, decisions on the pace and extent of such reform depend on the quality of top management.

Delivering on Promises: Coping with the Digital Divide

The paradigm of a knowledge-based economy is not an impossible dream for the developing countries. Still, moving to a knowledge-based economy may not be either feasible or meaningful for all countries, especially in the short term. 'It is important to note that bridging the "digital divide" is not simply an issue of building an information infrastructure, nor of buying and handing out computers and modems to everyone in a society. Indeed, moving to a knowledge-based economy and becoming integrated into the globalization process involves more than just acquiring and using IT. Specific policy choices, the ability to absorb new technologies and success in creating a national "IT culture" are also important variables. It should also be noted that in some developing countries there are major technical problems. For example, in many rural areas of South Africa and in the rest of Africa, electricity is a scarce or even unavailable commodity' (Thornhill 2000, p. 13).

These critical prerequisites highlight the crucial role that only States can play. The initiative must come from duly empowered governments acting in cooperation with civil society. Governments need to articulate a vision and a strategy based on the situation in their respective countries. They must then galvanize the needed political will, commit the resources and mobilize for action that will eventually lead their countries to integration in the process of globalization and the emerging information-based global system.

With a keen sense of priorities, governments must be aware of the advantages and pitfalls of IT. Notwithstanding the widely acknowledged potential of IT, evidence of its impact is still limited, particularly in developing countries. It is also instructive to note that IT-based concepts such as e-government and e-commerce, in which all internal activities as well as external relations with partners are conducted substantively through electronic means, have yet to become a widespread reality. The problems in achieving and measuring the immediate impact on productivity and competitiveness are common to both the public and private sectors.

For national governments, the most important and immediate task is the formulation and implementation of a coherent national.

IT strategy which clarifies priorities, maps out an action plan over the short, medium and long term, and establishes roles for both the public and private sectors. In many developed countries, such a national IT strategy exists only implicitly because of the high level of understanding of IT and the existence of numerous specialized institutions with substantial experience in IT. However, for all countries, an explicit IT strategy is required which would serve to catalyse inducements of acquisition and diffusion of IT.

406   **Appendices from the United Nations Organization**

The information revolution poses significant challenges to States not only in the developing countries but also in the developed world. By way of simplification, it may be said that governments are confronted with the following challenges:

- To introduce IT in the public sector, to train civil servants, to enhance the efficiency of service delivery through the use of IT, and to improve effectiveness, accountability and citizen participation;
- To elaborate policies, which ensure computer training and affordable access to information technology for the disadvantaged groups in society;
- To encourage, through appropriate measures, on-the-job training and re-training, as well as to promote life-long learning in the public sector;
- To elaborate policies aimed at creating safety nets for those laid off as a consequence of the introduction of IT in the workplace;
- To assist countries, particularly developing countries, in building or improving their capacity to access, manage and exchange the information that is so critical for efficient public sectors and effective policy development.

In this sphere of activity, as in other areas, the progress of technology and globalization has served to accentuate the importance of democratic, efficient States acting singly or in unison through inter-governmental organizations. IT has also enhanced the need for highly skilled professionals in the service of the government. Ultimately, to quote an ancient dictum: 'the measure of all things is Man' (that is, men and women).

Bibliography

Ackoff, R.L. (1960). "Systems, Organizations and Interdisciplinary Research." In *General Systems Yearbook*, Society for General Systems Research 5: 1–18.

Ackoff, R.L. (1969). "Institutional Functions and Societal Needs." *Perspectives in Planning*, 495–500.

Ackoff, R.L. and Sasieni, M.W. (1968). *Fundamentals of Operations Research*. New York: John Wiley and Sons.

Ackoff, R.L. and Emery, F.E. (1972). *On Purposeful Systems*. Chicago: Aldine-Atherton, 1972.

Ackoff, R.L. (1974). *Redesigning the Future: A Systems Approach to Societal Problems*. New York: Wiley.

Ackoff, R.L. (1992). *Scientific Method: Optimizing Applied Research Decision*. New York: Wiley.

Ackoff, R.L. and Churchman, W.C. (1950). "Purposive Behavior and Cybernetics." In: *Social Forces* 29: 32–39.

Ackoff, R.L. and Gharadjedaghi, J. (1986). A Prologue to National Development Planning. New York: Greenwood Press.

Acocella, Nicola (1994). Fondamenti di politica economica. Valori e tecniche. Roma, La Nuova Italia Scientifica.

© The Author(s) 2019
F. Archibugi, *The Programming Approach and the Demise of Economics*,
https://doi.org/10.1007/978-3-319-78060-3

408   Volume II. Selected Testimonies on the Epistemological...

Acocella, N. and Di Bartolomeo, G., Ed. (2011). *Theoretical issues in the provision of global public goods*. Rome: Università La Sapienza Publishing House.

Acocella, N. and Di Bartolomeo, G. (2004). "Non-neutrality of Monetary Policy in Policy Games," *European Journal of Political Economy* 20: 695–707.

Acocella, N. and Di Bartolomeo, G. (2005). '*Controllability and non-neutrality of economic policy: The Tinbergen's approach revised*'. (Working Paper No. 81), Public Economics Department, University of Rome, 'La Sapienza'.

Acocella, N. and Di Bartolomeo, G. (2006). 'Tinbergen and Theil meet Nash: Controllability in policy games'. *Economics Letters* 90: 213–218.

Acocella, N., Di Bartolomeo, G. and A. Hughes Hallett (2005). 'Dynamic Controllability with Overlapping Targets: A Generalization of the Tinbergen-Nash.'

Acocella, N., Di Bartolomeo, G. and A. Hughes Hallet (2012). *The theory of economic policy in a strategic context*. Cambridge, Cambridge University Press.

Acocella, Nicola, *Rediscovering Economic Policy as a Discipline*. Cambridge, Cambridge University Press.

Alexander, E.R. (1986). *Approaches to Planning: Introducing Current Planning Theories, Concepts and Issues*. New York, Gordon and Breach.

Alexander Ernest, R. (1998). *Rationality Revisited: Planning Paradigms in a Post-postmodernist Perspective. Planning Theory Conference*, Oxford Brookes University, 2–4 April, School of Planning.

Alexander, E.R., ed. (2006). *Evaluation in Planning. Evolution and Prospects*. Aldershot (England, GB): Ashgate.

Allison, Michael and Kaye, J. (1997). Strategic Planning for Nonprofit Organizations: A Practical Guide and Workbook. New York, Wiley.

Altshuler, A. (1965a). 'The Goals of Comprehensive Planning'. *Journal of the American Institute of Planners*, 31 (1965).

Altshuler, A. (1965b). *The City Planning Process: A Political Analysis*. Ithaca, NY: Cornell University Press, 1965.

Amara, R. and Lipinski, A.J. (1983). *Strategic Planning. Business Planning for an Uncertain Future. Scenarios & Strategies*. Pergamon.

Ansoff Igor et alii, Ed. (1976). *From Strategic Planning to Strategic Management*. New York, Wiley.

Archibugi, Daniele and David Held, Ed. (1995). *Cosmopolitan Democracy. An agenda for a New World Order*. Cambridge, Polity Press/Blackwell.

Archibugi, Daniele, Ed. (2003). *Debating Cosmopolitics*. London, Verso.

Archibugi, Daniele. (2011). *European Democracy and Cosmopolitan Democracy*. Ventotene, Altiero Spinelli Institute for Federalist Studies.

Archibugi, Daniele., Koenig-Archibugi, M. and Marchetti, R., (2012). *Global Democracy. Normative and Empirical Perspectives*, Cambridge University Press.

Archibugi, Daniele (2012). 'From peace between democracies to global democracy'. In: Archibugi D, Koenig-Archibugi M, and Marchetti R, Global Democracy etc.

Archibugi, Daniele and Filippetti, Andrea (2012). *Innovation and Economic Crisis. Lessons and prospects from the economic downturn*. USA, Routledge.

Archibugi, Daniele and Filippetti, Andrea Eds. (2015). *The Handbook of Global Science, Technology and Innovation*. Oxford, Wiley Blackwell.

Archibugi, Franco. (1957). 'Pianificazione economica e contrattazione collettiva', [Economic Planning and Collective Bargaining] in *Studi economici*, (Journal of the *Facoltà di Economia* of di University of Napoli, 1957).

Archibugi, Franco (1970). Rapporto sulla introduzione di un sistema di programmazione di bilancio in Italia. Roma.

Archibugi, Franco. (1971). *Un Quadro contabile per la pianificazione nazionale*, [An accounting frame for the national planning] in: V. Cao-Pinna, ed., Econometria e Pianificazione [Econometrics and Planning], Etas-Kompass, Milano.

Archibugi, Franco. (1974). A System of Models for the National Long-Term Planning Process, UN-ECE Seminar on *The Use of Systems of Models in Planning*, UNECE Conference, Moscow, 2–11 Dec 1974 (Revised version: *The Configuration of a System of Models as an Instrument for the Comprehensive Management of the Economy*, Paper for the 'XII International Input-Output Conference', Seville, 1993.

Archibugi, Franco. (1992a). *Introduction to Planology: A Survey of Developments Toward the Integration of Planning Sciences*. Rome, Planning Studies Centre.

Archibugi, Franco. (1992b). 'The resetting of planning studies', In: A. Kuklinski, ed., Society, Science, Government, Warsaw: KBN.

Archibugi, Franco. (1996). 'Program Indicators: Their Role and Use in the Integrated Social or Community Programming.' In: *Social Indicator Research, An International and Interdisciplinary Journal for Quality-of-life Measurement* 39(3).

Archibugi, Franco. (1996a). The Search for Optimal Centrality and the Abstract "Theories" of City Economics. Roma, Planning Studies Centre.

Archibugi, Franco. (1996b). *Towards a New Strategy of Integrations of Cities into their Regional Environments in the Countries of the European Union, (with special Respect to France, Germany, Great Britain and Italy)*. [An Ongoing Report of the Study promoted by the European Commission (DGXII) presented to the 'Second United Nations Conference on Human Settlements (Habitat II)', Istanbul, June 3–4 1996]. [Available also in. www.francoarchibugi.it].

Archibugi, Franco. (1998). 'Planning Theory: Reconstruction or Requiem for Planning?' (Presented to the Planning Theory Conference, Oxford 2–4 April 1998). [Available also in. www.francoarchibugi.it].

Archibugi, Franco. (1999). *Introductory lectures of Strategic Planning*, High School of Public Administration, Rome.

Archibugi, Franco. (2000a). *The Associative Economy: Insights beyond Welfare State and into Post-capitalism*, London, Macmillan, 2000.

Archibugi, Franco. (2000b). 'The 'programming approach': Methodological considerations based on the contributions by Frisch, Tinbergen and Leontief', paper presented to the EAEPE Conference 2000 (Berlin 2–5 November 2000). [Available also in. www.francoarchibugi.it].

Archibugi, Franco., Ed. (2004). *The Performance-based Management: Its Training Implications in the Public Sector*. Rome, Planning Studies Centre.

Archibugi, Franco. (2008a). *Planning Theory. From the Political Debate to the Methodological Reconstruction,* Springer.

Archibugi, Franco. (2008b). *Da burocrate a manager: La programmazione strategica in Italia: passato, presente e futuro* [From burocrate to manager. The strategic programming in Italy: past, present and future], Rubbettino, Soveria Mannelli.

Arendt, Hannah. (1993). What is Politik?

Argyris, Chris. (1974). Theory in Practice: Increasing Professional Effectiveness.

Arrow, J. Kenneth. (1951). *Social Choice and Individual Values*. New York, Wiley.

Arrow, J. Kenneth and Debreu G. (1954). 'Existence of an Equilibrium for a Competitive Economy' *Econometrica* 22(3): 265–290.

Arrow, J. Kenneth. (1960). 'The Work of Ragnar Frisch, Econometrician'. Econometrica a.28(April).

Arrow, J. Kenneth. (1967a). 'The Place of Moral Obligation in Preference Systems'. In Sidney Hook, Ed., *Human Values and Economic Policy*. New York, New York University Press.

Arrow, J. Kenneth. (1967b). Public and Private Values. *Human Values and Economic Policy*. S. Hook. New York, New York University Press.

Arrow, J. Kenneth. (1981). 'Real and Nominal Magnitudes in Economics' In: D. Bell and I. Kristol, Eds. *The Crisis in Economic Theory etc*. New York, Basic Books.

Arrow, J. Kenneth, and Boskin M.J. (1988). 'The Economics of Public Debt?'. In *Proceedings of a Conference Held by the International Economic Association*, Stanford, CA, Macmillan Press.

Arrow, J. Kenneth. (1994). "Methodological Individualism and Social Knowledge." *American Economic Review* 84(No. 2): pp. 1–9.

Bibliographic of Vol. II 411

Arrow, J. Kenneth. et alii (1998). 'Social Choice Re-Examined'. Proceedings of the IEA conference held at Schloss Hernstein, Berndorf, (near Vienna, Austria), Macmillan.

Atkinson, A.B. (1999). *The Economic Consequences of Rolling Back the Welfare State.* Cambridge, MA, MIT Press.

Baier, K. (1967). *Welfare and Preference. Human Values and Economic Policy.* New York, New York University Press.

Banfield, Edward C. (1961). *Political Influence,* The Free Press of Glencoe, New York.

Banfield, Edward C. (1968). *The Unheavenly City.* Boston: Little Brown.

Barone F. (1977). *Il neo-positivismo logico* [The logical neo-positivism] Bari, Laterza.

Barry, W. Brian. (1997). *Strategic Planning Workbook for Nonprofit Organizations,* Amherst, H. Wilder Found., St Paul Mn.

Barzelay, Michael. (1992). *Breaking Through Bureaucracy: A New Vision for Managing in Government.* Berkeley, University of California Press.

Baumol, J. William. (1968). *Economic Theory and Operations Analysis.* Englewood Cliffs, NJ: Prentice-Hall.

Baumol, J. William. (1969). *Welfare Economics and the Theory of the State.* Second ed. Welfare and the State Revisited. Cambridge: Harvard University Press.

Beer, A. Stafford. (1966). *Decision and Control: The Meaning of Operational Research and Management Cybernetics.* London: Wiley.

Beer, A. Stafford. (1974). *Designing Freedom.* London: Wiley.

Bell, D.E., Raiffa, H. and Tversky, A. (eds.) (1988). *Decision Making: Descriptive, Normative and Prescriptive Interactions.* Cambridge, Cambridge University Press.

Bell, Daniel. (1965). *The End of Ideology: On the Exhaustion of Political Ideas in the Fifties: With a New Afterword.* New York, Free Press.

Bell, Daniel. (1973). *The Coming of Post-Industrial Society: A venture in social forecasting.* New York, Basic Books.

Bell, Daniel. (1979). *The Cultural Contradiction of capitalism.* London, Heinemann.

Bell, Daniel. (1980). The Winding Passage. Sociological Essays and Journeys. (1991).

Bell, Daniel. (1981). Models and Reality in Economic Discourse. *The Crisis of Economic Theory.* D. Bell and I. Kristol. New York, Basic Books.

Benne, K.D. (1985). 'The Current State of Planned Changing in Persons, Groups, Communities and Societies' In: Bennis. W. G. e. alii. *The Planning Change.* New York, College Publishing: 68–82.

412   Volume II. Selected Testimonies on the Epistemological...

Benner T. et alii (2005). "Multisectoral Networks in Global Governance: Towards a Pluralistic System of Accountability". In: Held D. and Koenig-Archibugi M. Global Governance and Public Accountability.

Bennis, W.G., Kenneth, D. Benne, and Robert, Chin, eds. (1961). The Planning of Change. New York: Holt, Rinehart and Winston.

Bennis, W.G. (1966). 'Theory and Method in Applying Behavioural Science to Planned Organizational Change'. In: *Operational Research and the Societal Sciences*, edited by J. R. Lawrence, London: Tavistock Publications.

Bentham, Jeremy. (1789). An Introduction to the Principles of Moral and Legislation.

Benveniste, Guy. (1987). *Professionalizing the Organization: Reducing Bureaucracy to Enhance Effectiveness*. San Francisco, Jossey-Bass.

Bergson, Abram. (1966). *Essays in Normative Economics*. Cambridge, MA, Belknap Press of Harvard University Press.

Berle, Adolf A. Jr. and Means, G. (1932). *The Modern Corporation and Private Property*, Harcourt, Brace & World.

Berlin, Isaiah. (1938). *Karl Marx: His Life and Environment.*

Berlin, Isaiah. (1967). *Does Political Theory Still Exist?*

Berlin, Isaiah. (1989). *Against the Current: Essays in the History of Ideas.*

Berlin, Isaiah. (2003). *Freedom and Its Betrayal.*

Berlinski, D. (1976). *On System Analysis: An Essay Concerning the Limitations of some Mathematical Methods in the Social, Political, and Biological Sciences.* Cambridge, MA: MIT Press.

Bernstein, Richard J. (2010). *The Pragmatic Turn.* Oxford: Polity Press.

Black, M. (ed.) (1961). *The Social Theories of Talcott Parsons.* Englewood Cliffs, NJ: Prentice-Hall.

Blaug, M. (1992). *The Methodology of Economics: Or, How Economists Explain.* Cambridge: Cambridge University Press.

Bolan, R. (1973). 'Community Decision Behaviour: The Culture of Planning'. In *A Reader in Planning theory.* Oxford, Pergamon.

Bourdeau, Louis. (1882). *Théorie des sciences: Plan de Science intégrale*, Paris, p. 463.

Boyd, Gavin, Ed. (1995). *Competitive and Cooperative Macromanagement: The Challenges of Structural Interdependence.* Aldershot, UK, Elgar.

Bozeman, B., and Straussman, J.D. (1990). *Public Management Strategies: Guidelines for Managerial Effectiveness.* San Francisco, Jossey-Bass.

Bryson, John M. (1988). *Strategic Planning for Public and Nonprofit Organizations: A Guide to Strengthening and Sustaining Organizational Achievement.* San Francisco, Jossey-Bass.

Bibliographic of Vol. II

Bryson, John M. and Robert, C. Einsweiler. (1988). The Future of Strategic Planning for Public Purposes. *Strategic Planning: threats and opportunities for planners.* J. M. B. a. R. C. Einsweiler. Chicago, Washington DC, Planners Press: 216–230.

Bunge, Mario. (1962). *Intuition and Science.* Prentice-Hall.

Carlson, J.W. (1970). The Status and Next Steps for Planning, Programming, and Budgeting. *Public Expenditures and Policy analysis.* H. R. H. a. M. J. Chicago, Rand McNally.

Carnoy, M. (2000). *Sustaining the New Economy. Work, Family, and Community in the Information Age.* New York, Russel Sage Foundation.

Catanese, A.J. and Steiss, A.W. (1970). *Systemic Planning: Theory and Application.* Lexington, MA, Heath Lexington Books.

Chadwick, George. (1971). *A Systems View of Planning: Towards a Theory of the Urban and Regional Planning Process.* Oxford: Pergamon Press. Including chapters: (a) 'Plan or Programme?' (b) 'Planning as a Conceptual System.' [Reprint, PSC, 1971] (c) 'A Mixed-Programming Strategy.' [Reprint PSC, 1971].

Chapin, F. Stuart Jr. (1965). 'A Model for Simulating Residential Development.' *Journal of the American Institute of Planners*: 120–125.

Checkland, P.B. (1981). *Systems Thinking, Systems Practice.* New York, Wiley.

Chestnut, Harold. (1965). *Systems Engineering Tools.* New York: Wiley.

Chestnut, Harold. (1967). *Systems Engineering Methods.* New York: Wiley.

Choukroun, Jean-Marc and Roberta, M. Snow, Ed. (1992). *Planning for human systems,* [Essays in honor of Russell L. Ackoff.] Busch Center, Wharton School of the University of Pennsylvania. Philadelphia, University of Pennsylvania Press.

Churchman, C. W. (1961). *Prediction and Optimal Decision.* Englewood Cliffs, NJ: Prentice-Hall.

Churchman, C. W., and Emery, F. E. (1966). 'On Various Approaches to the Study of Organizations'. In: J. R. Lawrence ed., *Operational Research and the Social Sciences.* London: Tavistock.

Churchman, C. W. (1957). *An Introduction to Operations Research.*

Churchman, C. West. (1968). *The Systems Approach.* New York, Delta.

Churchman, C. West. (1979). The Systems Approach and Its Enemies. New York, Basic Books.

Churchman, C. West and Verhulst, M. (1960). *Management Sciences.* New York, Pergamon Press.

Cohen, Gerald A. (1995). *Self-Ownership, Freedom, and Equality.* Cambridge University Press.

Cohen, Gerald A. (2008). *Rescuing Justice and Equality.* Cambridge, MA, Harvard University Press.

Cohen, Gerald A. (2010). *Socialismo, perché no?* [Socialism why not?] Milano, Ponte alle Grazie.

Commission on Growth and Development. (2008). *The Growth Report: Strategies for Sustained Growth and Inclusive Development.* Washington, DC, World Bank.

Croce, Benedetto. (1938). History as Thought and Action.

Cullingworth, Barry., and Caves, Roger W. (2003). *Planning in the U.S.A.* London, New York, Routledge.

Dahl, Robert A. (1959). *La politique de la planification.*

Davidoff, P. (1965). 'Advocacy and Pluralism in Planning.' In *Journal of the American Institute of Planners* Vol. 31 (1965).

Davidoff, P., and Reiner, T.A. (1992). 'A Choice Theory of Planning'. *Journal of the American Institute of Planners*. Vol. 28.

de Finetti, Bruno. (1906–1984). Best known for his important studies on the 'theory of probability' ('Theory of Probability', 1974).

de Finetti, B. (1969). *Un Matematico e l'Economia*, [A mathematician and the Economics], Angeli, Milano, 1969.

de Finetti, B. (ed.) (1973a). '*Requisiti per un Sistema Economico Accettabile in Relazione alle Esigenze della Collettività*', [Requirements for an Acceptable Economic System in Relation to the Needs of the Collectivity]. Milano: Angeli.

de Finetti, Bruno. (1973b). 'The Utopia as necessary presupposition, etc.' in *Requirements for an acceptable economic system etc.* [ed. de Finetti, pp.13–15].

de Finetti, B. (note 12) – in a Seminar promoted by the Italian CIME (Mathematical Economics) in Urbino (20–25 September 1971).

de Finetti, Bruno. (2015). *Un matematico tra Utopia e Riformismo*. Roma, Ediesse.

Dewey, John. (1925). *Experience and Nature.*

Dewey, John. (1929). 'The Quest for Certainty: A Study of the Relations of Knowledge and Action', *The Journal of Philosophy*, 1930.

Dewey, John. (1944). Some questions about Value, *The Journal of Philosophy*, Vol. 41 (17).

Debreu, Gerard. (1952). *A Social Equilibrium Existence Theorem*. Santa Monica, CA, Rand Corporation.

Drewnowski, J. (1974). *On Measuring and Planning the Quality of Life*, Mouton, The Hague, 1974.

Dror, Y. 'A Choice Theory of Planning' In: *International Review of Administrative Sciences*, No. 29 (1963a): 46–58.

Dror, Y. "The Planning Process: A Facet Design." In: *International Review of Administrative Sciences* 29 (1963b).

Bibliographic of Vol. II 415

Dror, Y. (1967). 'Comprehensive Planning: Common Fallacies Versus Preferred Features' In *Essays in Honour of Professor Jac. P. Thijsse*, edited by Van Schlagen F., 85–89. The Hague: Mouton.

Dror, Y. (1971). *Design for Policy Sciences*. Amsterdam: Elsevier.

Dror, Y. (1984). Policy Analysis for Advising Rulers. *Rethinking the Process of Operational Research and Systems Analysis*. R. Tomlinson and I. Kiss. Oxford, Pergamon: 79–124.

Drucker, P.F. (1954). *The Practice of Management*. New York, Harper.

Drucker, P.F. (1964). *Managing for Result; Economic Tasks and Risk-Taking Decisions*. New York, Harper.

Drucker, P.F. (1993). *Post-Capitalist Society*. New York, Harper Collins.

Drucker, P.F. (1996). *The Executive in Action*.

Dugger, W.M. (1988). An Institutionalist Theory of Economic Planning. *Institutionalist Theory and Policy*. T. M.R. New York. Vol. Ii of Evolutionary Economics: 231–257.

Dyckman, J.W. (1964). 'State Development Planning: The California Case.' *Journal of the American Institute of Planners* XXX, No. 2 (1964): 144–152.

Dyckman, J.W. (1970). Social Planning in the American Democracy. *Urban Planning in Transition*. E. E. New York, Grossman.

Edvarsen Kare, N. (2001). *Ragnar Frisch: An Annotated Bibliography*. Department of Economics, University of Oslo, DE-UO.

Edwards, W. (1961). 'Behavioural Decision Theory', *Annual Review of Psychology*, No. 12, pp. 473–498.

Edwards, W. (1972). 'Social Utilities' *The Engineering Economist Sumner Symposium,* IV: 119–129.

Eisler, Riane. (2007–2008). *The Real Wealth of Nations*, Berrett- Koehler.

Elster, J., and Hylland, A. (1986). *Foundations of Social Choice Theory*. Cambridge, Cambridge University Press.

Elster, Jon and Slagstad, Rune, Ed. (1988). *Constitutionalism and Democracy*. Cambridge, Cambridge University Press.

Eltis, W.A. (1973). *Growth and Distribution*. London, Macmillan.

Enthoven, A.C., and Smith, K.W. (1970). The Planning, Programming, and Budgeting System in the Department of Defense: An Overview from Experience. *Public Expenditures and Policy analysis*. H. R. H. a. M. J. Chicago, Rand McNally.

Etzioni, Amitai. (1961). *A Comparative Analysis of Complex Organizations*. New York, Free Press.

Etzioni, Amitai. (1964). *Modern Organizations*. Englewood Cliffs, NJ, Prentice Hall.

Etzioni, Amitai. (1967). 'Mixed-Scanning: A 'Third' Approach to Decision Making'. In: *Public Administration Review.*

Etzioni, Amitai. (1968). *The Active Society: A Theory on Societal and Political Process.* New York, Free Press.

Etzioni, Amitai. (1969). *Indicators of the Capacities for Societal Guidance.* New York.

Etzioni, Amitai. (1983). *Bureaucracy and Democracy: A Political Dilemma.* Boston, Routledge and Kegan.

Etzioni, Amitai. (1988). *The Moral Dimension: Toward a New Economics.* New York, The Free Press.

Etzioni, Amitai. (1991). Beyond Self-Interest. *Policy Analysis and Economics: Developments, Tensions, Prospects.* D. Weimer. London, Kluwer.

Faber, M., and Seers, D. (1972). *The Crisis in Planning (Vol. 1: The Issues, Vol. 2: The Experiences).* London, Chatto & Windus for Sussex University Press.

Falk, R.A. (2012). 'The promise and perils of global democracy' In: Archibugi D, Koenig-Archibugi M. and Marchetti R., *Global Democracy etc.*

Faludi, A. (1973a). *Planning Theory.* Oxford, Pergamon.

Faludi, A., ed. (1973b). *A Reader in Planning Theory.* Oxford: Pergamon Press.

Faludi, A., and Voogd, H., eds. (1985). *Evaluation of Complex Policy Problems.* Delft: Delfsche Uitgevers Maatschappij.

Faludi, Andreas. (1978). *Essays on Planning Theory and Education.* Oxford, Pergamon Press.

Faludi, A. (1985). 'A decision-centred view of environmental planning', in *Landscape Planning*, Vol. 12.

Faludi, A. (1986a). *Critical Rationalism and Planning Methodology.* London, Pion Press.

Faludi, A. (1986b). 'The Philosophy of Sir Karl Popper and Its Relevance to Planning Methodology'. In *Critical Rationalism and Planning Methodology*, by A. Faludi, Part II. London: Pion.

Faludi, A., and Waterhout, B. (2002). *The making of the European spatial development perspective: No Masterplan.* London, New York, Routledge.

Farkas, J. (1984). 'Change in the Paradigms of Systems Analysis'. In: Tomlison and Kiss, eds. *Rethinking the Process of Operational Research and Systems analysis.* Oxford, Pergamon.

Fellner, William and Haley, B.F. (1950). *Readings in the Theory of Income Distribution.* London, George Allen and Unwin Ltd.

Feyerabend, Paul. (1979). *Against Method. Outline of an Anarchistic Theory of Knowledge.* London.

Fishburn, P.C. (1973). *The Theory of Social Choice.* Princeton, NJ, Princeton University Press.

Fisher, Irving. (1948). *The Money Illusion*, Garzanti.

Fitoussi, J.P., and Rosanvallon, P. (1996). *Le nouvel age des inegalities*. Paris, Editions du Seuil.

Fitzgerald, K.V.E., and Wuyts, M., Eds. (1988). *Markets Within Planning: Socialist Economic Management in the Third World*. London, Frank Cass.

Fleurbaey, M. (1996). *Theories economiques de la justice*, Paris, Economica.

Fleurbaey, M. et alii (1998). eds. *Freedom in Economics*. London, Routledge.

Fleurbaey, M. and Mongin, P., co-ed. (1999). *L'economie normative*, (Special issue).

Fleurbaey, M. (2006). *Capitalisme ou Democratie? L'alternative du XXIeme siecle*. Paris, Grasset.

Fleurbaey, M. (2008). Fairness, *Responsabilité and Welfare*. Oxford University Press.

Florida State of, G. C. (1992). *A Strategic Plan for Florida: 1992–1996* update. Tallahasse, FL, Executive Office of the Governor.

Foley, D. L. (1964). 'An Approach to Metropolitan Spatial In: M. M. Webber, ed. *Explorations into Urban Structure*. Philadelphia, University of Pennsylvania Press.

Foley, D.L. (1973). 'British Town Planning: One Ideology or Three? In: Faludi A. ed. A *Reader in Planning theory'*. Oxford, Pergamon.

Forsyth, Murray, Ed. (1989). *Federalism and Nationalism*. Leicester, Leicester University Press.

Fox, K.A. (1967). "Functional Economic Areas and Consolidated Urban Regions of the United States." *Social Sciences Research Council* (21).

Fox, K.A. (1971). Combining Economic and Non-Economic Objectives in Development Planning: Problems of Concepts and Measurement. *Economic Development and Planning: Essays in Honour of Jan Tinbergen*. W. Sellekaerts. London, Macmillan.

Fox, K.A. (1973). Delimitations of Regions for Transportation Planning. *Perspectives on Regional Transportation Planning*. J. S. De Salvo. Lexington Books, Lexington, Mass.

Fox, K.A. (1974). *Social Indicators and Social Theory: Elements of an Operational System*. New York, Wiley. [Chapters titles]: (a) 'Social Science Concepts Relevant to a System of Social Accounts'. (b) 'National Goals Accounting and Policy Models'. Chap. 7. (c) 'Social Indicators and Models for Cities and Regions'. Chap. 8. (d) 'Cities and regions' Chap. 12. (e) 'National World Models and Data'. Chap. 13. (f) 'National Goals Accounting and Policy Models'. (g) 'Accounts and Indicators for the Higher Education Sector'.

Fox, K.A. (1974a). *Social Indicators and Social Theory. Elements of an Operational System*, Wiley & Sons, New York.

Fox, K.A. (1974b). Elements of an Operational System III: National and World Models and Data. *Social Indicators and Social Theory*. New York, Wiley.

418   Volume II. Selected Testimonies on the Epistemological...

Fox, K.A. (1974c). Cities and Regions. *Social Indicators and Social Theory: Elements of an Operational System*. F. K. A. New York, Wiley: Chap. 12 (chap ex liber).

Fox, K.A. (1974d). Accounts and Indicators for the Higher Education Sector. *Social Indicators and Social Theory: Elements of an Operational System*. F. K. A. New York, Wiley.

Fox, K.A. (1974e). National Goals Accounting and Policy Models. *Social Indicators and Social Theory: Elements of an Operational System*. F. K.A. New York, Wiley: Chap. 7 (chap ex liber).

Fox, K.A. (1974f). Social Science Concepts Relevant to a System of Social Accounts. *Social Indicators and Social Theory: Elements of an Operational System*. F. K.A. New York, Wiley: Chap. 2 (chap ex liber).

Fox, K.A. (1974g). Elements of an Operational System. II: Cities and Regions. *Social Indicators and Social Theory*. New York, Wiley.

Fox, K.A. (1980). "Philosophical Implications of a System of Social Accounts Based on Roger Barker's Ecological Psychology and a Scalar Measure of Total Income." *Philosophica* 25: 33–54.

Fox, K.A. (1983). "The Eco-Behavioral View of Human Societies and Its Implications for Systems Science." *International Journal of Systems Science* 14(8): 895–914.

Fox, K.A. (1984). "Behavior Settings and Eco-Behavioral Science: A New Arena for Mathematical Social Science Permitting a Richer and More Coherent View of Human Activities in Social Systems." *Mathematical Social Sciences* 7: 117–65.

Fox, K.A. (1985). *Social System Accounts: Linking Social and Economic Indicators Through Tangible behaviour Settings*. Dordrecht, Reidel Publishing Company. Included chapters: (a) 'The Classification of Stocks of Physical Capital and Consumer Durables 'Linking Social and Economic Indicators through Tangible Behavior. (b) 'The Classification of Roles in Social System Accounts'. (c) 'Social System Accounts Based on Behavior Settings: Some Next Steps'. (d) 'The Classification and Delineation of Communities and Regions in Social System Accounts'

Fox, K.A. (1985a). The Classification of Behavior Settings in Social System Accounts. *Social System Accounts*. F. K. A. Dordrecht, Reidel.

Fox, K.A. (1985b). *The Classification of Stocks of Physical Capital and Consumer Durables in Social System Accounts*. Dordrecht, Reidel.

Fox, K.A. (1985c). Some Broader Implications of Behavior Settings for the Social Sciences. *Social System Accounts*. F. K. A. Dordrecht, Reidel.

Bibliographic of Vol. II 419

Fox, K.A. (1985d). Behavior Settings and Objective Social Indicators. *Social System Accounts: Linking Social and Economic Indicators Through Tangible Behaviour Settings.* F. K. A. Dordrecht, Reidel.

Fox, K.A. (1985e). The Usefulness of Behavior Settings for Classifying and Describing Human Activities in a Community. *Social System Accounts.* F. K. A. Dordrecht, Reidel.

Fox, K.A. (1985i). The Classification and Delineation of Communities and Regions in Social System Accounts. *Social System Accounts.* F. K. A. Dordrecht, Reidel.

Fox, K.A. (1985f). Social System Accounts Based on Behavior Settings: Some Next Steps. *Social System Accounts.* F. K. A. Dordrecht, Reidel.

Fox, K.A. (1985g). *Social System Accounts: Linking Social and Economic Indicators Through Tangible Behaviour Settings.* F. K. A. Dordrecht, Reidel.

Fox, K.A. (1985h). The Classification of Roles in Social System Accounts. *Social System Accounts.* F. K. A. Dordrecht, Reidel.

Fox, K.A. (1986a). An Eco-Behavioral Approach to Social Systems Accounting, Time Allocation Matrices and Measures of the Quality of Life. *Economic Psychology: Intersections in Theory and Application.* A. J. MacFadyen and H. W. FacFadyen. Amsterdam, Elsevier Science Publishers.

Fox, K.A. (1986b). "The Present Status of Objective Social Indicators: A Review of Theory and Measurement." *American Journal of Agricultural Economics* 68(5): 1113–1120.

Fox, K.A. (1990). *The Eco – Behavioral Approach to Surveys and Social Accounts for Rural Communities.* Ames, IOWA, Department of Economics, Iowa State University.

Fox, K.A. (1992a). *Describing and Measuring Socioeconomic Systems: Prerequisites to Planning.* (Paper Prepared for the Palermo Conference Volume from the Conference on Planning Science, Palermo, Italy, 8–12 Sept. 1992).

Fox, K.A., Ed. (1992b). *Demand Analysis, Econometrics, and Policy Models.* Iowa State University Press, Ames.

Fox, K.A. and Gosh, S. (1981). A Behavior Setting Approach to Social Accounts Combining Concepts and Data from Ecological, Psychology, Economics, and Studies of Time Use. *Social Accounting Systems.* F. T. Juster and K. C. Land. New York, Academic Press.

Fox, K.A. and Kumar, T.K. (1965). "The Functional Economic Area: Delineation and Implications for Economic Analysis and Policy." *Papers of the Regional Science Association* (15): 57–85.

Fox, K.A. and Miles, G.D. (1987). *Systems Economics: Concepts, Models and Multidisciplinary Perspectives.* Ames, Iowa State University Press.

420   **Volume II. Selected Testimonies on the Epistemological...**

Fox, K.A. (1987a). The Eco-Behavioral View of Human Societies: Behavior Settings, Time Allocation Matrices and Social System Accounts. *Systems Economics, Concepts, Models, and Multidisciplinary Perspectives*. F. K. A. and M. D. G. Ames, Iowa, Iowa State University Press: 118–142.

Fox, K.A. (1987b). Some Classic Examples of Systems Thinking in Several Sciences: Comment and Recommended Readings. *Systems Economics, Concepts, Models, and Multidisciplinary Perspectives*. F. K. A. and M. D. G. Ames, Iowa, Iowa State University Press: 207–237.

Fox, K.A. and Sengupta J.K. (1969a). Operations Research & Complex Social Systems. *Optimization Techniques in Quantitative Economic Models*. J. K. Sengupta and K. A. Fox. Amsterdam, North-Holland.

Fox, K.A. and Sengupta J.K. (1969b). *Optimization Techniques in Quantitative Economic Models*. Amsterdam, North Holland.

Fox, K.A. et alii, (1973a). *The Theory of Quantitative Economic Policy with applications to Economic Growth, Stabilization and Planning*. Amsterdam, North Holland.

Fox, K.A. et alii, (1973b). 'Economic Policy Models for Development Planning'. Chap 13 in: Fox K.A. et alii, *The theory of Quantitative Economic Policy etc*, (see above).

Fox, K.A. et alii, (1973c). 'Introduction to Quantitative Economic Policy'. [Chap 1 in: Fox K.A. et alii The theory of Quantitative Economic Policy, etc. see above].

Fox, K.A. et alii, (1973d). 'National Planning Models for Developed Economies'. Chap 14 in: Fox K.A. et alii, The Theory of Quantitative Economic Policy etc. (see above), Amsterdam, North-Holland.

Fox, K.A. et alii, (1973e). 'Stabilization Policy, Regional Growth and Planning'. Chap 12 in: Fox K. A., et alii, The Theory of Quantitative Economic Policy etc. (see above) Amsterdam, North-Holland.

Fox, K.A., Sengupta J.K. (1973a). Economic Policy Models for Development Planning. *The Theory of Quantitative Economic Policy with Applications to Economic Growth Stabilization and Planning*. Fox K.A., Sengupta J.K. and Thorbecke E. Amsterdam, North-Holland: Chap 13 (chap ex liber).

Fox, K.A., Sengupta J.K. (1973b). *The Theory of Quantitative Economic Policy with Applications to Economic Growth, Stabilization and Planning*. Amsterdam, North Holland.

Fox, K.A., Sengupta J.K. (1973c). Introduction to Quantitative Economic Policy. *The theory of Quantitative Economic Policy with applications to Economic Growth Stabilization and Planning*. Fox K.A., Sengupta J.K. and Thorbecke, E., 1973., North-Holland, Amsterdam Chap 1 (chap ex liber).

Bibliographic of Vol. II 421

Fox, K.A., Sengupta J.K. (1973d). National Planning Models for Developed Economies. *The Theory of Quantitative Economic Policy with applications to Economic Growth Stabilization and Planning.* Fox K.A., Sengupta J.K. and A. T. E. Amsterdam, North-Holland: Chap 14 (chap ex liber).

Fox, K.A., Sengupta J.K. (1973e). Stabilization Policy, Regional Growth and Planning. *The theory of Quantitative Economic Policy with applications to Economic Growth Stabilization and Planning.* Fox K. A., Sengupta J.K. and T. E. Amsterdam, North-Holland: Chap 12 (chap ex liber).

Fox, K.A. and Van Moeseke, P. (1973). Derivation and Implications of a Scalar Measure of Social Income. *Economic Structure and Development: Essays in Honor of J. Tinbergen.* B. H. e. alii. New York, American Elsevier.

France, *Ministère de l'Economie. La demarche de performance: Strategie, Objectifs, Indicateurs* (2004).

Friedmann, John. (1964). 'Regional Development in Post-Industrial Society', *Journal of the American Institute of Planners* XXX, No. 2 (1964): 90–100.

Friedmann, John. (1965). 'A response to Althusser: Comprehensive Planning as a Process.' *Journal of American Institute of Planners* 31 (1965).

Friedmann, John. (1987a). *Planning in the Public Domain: From Knowledge to Action.* Princeton, NJ: Princeton University Press.

Friedmann, John. (1987b). 'The Terrain of Planning Theory.' In *Planning in the Public Domain: From Knowledge to Action.* [Reprint-PSC, 1987].

Friend, John K., and Jessop, W. N. (1969). *Local Government and Strategic Choice: An Operational Research Approach to the Process of Public Planning.* London: Tavistock.

Friend, John K. et al. (1974). *Public Planning: The Inter-Corporate Dimension.* London, Tavistock Publication.

Friend, John, and Allen Hickling. (1987). *Planning Under Pressure: The Strategic Choice Approach.* 2nd ed. Boston: Butterworth-Heinemann.

Frisch, Ragnar. (1957). *Oslo Decision Models.* Oslo, University of Oslo Institute of Economics.

Frisch, Ragnar. (1958). 'Generalities on Planning', In: *'L'Industria'*, ottobre-dicembre 1958.

Frisch, Ragnar. (1959a). 'A Complete Scheme for Computing All Direct and Cross Demand Elasticities in a model with Many Sectors.' *Econometrica* 27: 117–196.

Frisch, Ragnar. (1959b). *The Principle of Recurrent Planning.* [with, J. Berqvall, O. Dahlem, G. Gerdner and B. Lumdstom]. Stockholm, 67–74.

Frisch, Ragnar. (1959c). *Unbounded Optimalization in Economic Policy.* Oslo, University of Oslo Institute of Economics.

422   Volume II. Selected Testimonies on the Epistemological...

Frisch, Ragnar. (1961). The Oslo REFI Interflow Table. Memorandum, Oslo, University of Oslo Institute of Economics.

Frisch, R. (1962). 'Preface to the Oslo Channel Model: A Survey of Types of Economic Forecasting and Programming. In: R. C. Geary, ed., Europe's Future in Figures. Amsterdam, North-Holland. [republished. In: F. Long ed., *Economic Planning Studies*, Reidel, Dordrecht (see), 1976, (pp. 87–127).

Frisch, R. (1963a). 'An Implementation System for Optimal National Economic Planning Without Detailed Quantity Fixation from a Central Authority, Part 1, Prolegomena', Memorandum, DE-UO, Sept 1963. Second preliminary printing. [Republished. In: F. Long ed. *Economic Planning Studies* (1976) pp. 129–174].

Frisch, Ragnar. (1963b). *Selection and Implementation: The Econometrics of the Future*. Vatican City, Pontificiae Academiae Scientiarum. (*Memorandum*, DE-UO).

Frisch, Ragnar. (1964). A Generalized Form of the REFI Interflow Table. *Problems of Economic Dynamics and Planning: Essays in Honour of Mickal Kalecki*. P. A. e. a. Baran. Warsaw, Polish Scientific Publishers (Pergamon Press): 133–156.

Frisch, R. (1965). 'General Outlook on a method of advanced and democratic macroeconomic planning', (paper presented at CIME Study Week, L'Aquila, 29 Agosto–7 Settembre 1965). In: de Finetti ed., *Mathematical Optimization in Economics*, Roma: Cremonese Edizioni 1966.

Frisch, Ragnar. (1970a). 'Cooperation between politicians and econometricians on the formalization of political preferences'. In: Frisch Ragnar, (Frank Long ed.), *Economic Planning Studies*. 1976 (see).

Frisch, Ragnar. (1970b). *Econometrics in the Midst of Analytical and Social Turmoils*. Scientists at Work. (With: T. Dalenius, G. Karlsson and S. Malmquist. Stockholm, Almqvist & Wiksell.

Frisch, Ragnar. (1970c). *Econometrics in the World of Today. Induction, Growth and Trade*. [Essays in Honour of Sir Roy Harrod. Eds. W. A. Eltis, M. F. Scott and J. N. Wolfe.] Oxford, Clarendon Press: 152–166.

Frisch, Ragnar. (1971). 'Communication and Developing Countries.' In: *Socio-Economic Planning Sciences,* 5 (No. 4 – August).

Frisch, Ragnar. (1976a). *Economic Planning Studies*. A Collection of Essays edited posthumous, by Frank Long, D. Reidel Publishing Company.

Frisch, Ragnar. (1976b). 'From Utopian Theory to Practical Applications: The Case of Econometrics'. In *Economic Planning Studies*, ed. by F. Frank Long, Reidel Publishing Company.

Fullbrooks, Edward, Ed. (2004). *A guide to what's is wrong with Economics*. London: Anthem Press.

Bibliographic of Vol. II 423

Fuller, Steve. (1988). *Social Epistemology*. Bloomington, IN, Indiana University Press.

Gage, R.W., and Mandell, M.P., Ed. (1990). *Strategies for Managing Intergovernmental Policies and Networks*. New York, Praeger.

Galbraith, J.K. (1990). *A Short History of Financial Euphoria*. Knoxville, TN, Whittle Direct Books.

Garrigou-Lagrange, A. (1976). *Systèmes et structures*. Paris, Dalloz.

Gershuny, Jonathan. (1978). *After Industrial Society? The Emerging Self-Service Economy*. London, Macmillan.

Gharadjedaghi, J., and Russel, L. Ackoff. (1986). *A Prologue to National Development Planning*. New York, Greenwood Press.

Gordon, L. Gerald. (1993). *Strategic Planning for Local Government*. Washington, ICM.

Gottinger, W. Hans., and Leinfellner, W., Ed. (1978). *Decision Theory and Social Ethics*. Dordrecht, Reidel.

Greffe, Xavier. (1981). *Analyse economique de la bureaucratie*. Paris, Economica.

Greffe, Xavier. (1990). *La valeur économique du patrimoine: la domande et l'offre de monuments*. Paris, Anthropos.

Greffe, Xavier. (1992). *Societes postindustrielles et redeveloppement*. Paris, Hachette.

Greffe, Xavier. (1997). *Economie des politiques publiques*. Paris, Dalloz.

Greffe, Xavier. (1999). *Gestion Publique*. Paris, Dalloz.

Gross Bertram, M. (1964). *The Managing of Organisations*, Vols. 1 and 2. New York, The Free Press of Glencoe.

Gross, B.M. (1965). '*Space-Time and Post-Industrial Society*.' (Paper presented at the Paper presented to 1965 Seminars of Comparative Administration Group of the American Society for Public Administration), Syracuse University.

Gross, B.M. (1966a). 'Activating National Plans.' In: *Operational Research and the Social Sciences*, edited by J. R. Lawrence. London: Tavistock.

Gross, B.M. (1966b). 'The State of the Nation: Social Systems Accounting.' In: *Social Indicators*, edited by R. A Bauer. Cambridge: MIT Press.

Gross, B.M. (1967). 'Social Goals and Indicators for American Society' In: *The Annals of the American Academy of Political and Social Science*, I and II.

Gross, B.M. (1969). *Social Intelligence for America's Future*. Boston: Allyn and Bacon.

Groszyk, Walter. (1995). *Implementation of the Government Performance and Results Act of 1993*.

Hall, A.D. III (1962). *A Methodology for Systems Engineering*. Princeton, Van Nostrand.

Hall, A.D. III (1969). 'Three-Dimensional Morphology of System Engineering.' IEEE *Trans. Syst. Sci. Cybern.* SSC 5(2): 156–160.

Hansson Sven Ove. (1998). *Decision Theory, an brief Introduction*. Stockholm: Royal Institute of Technology Deptm. of Philosophy and History of Technology (KTH).

Harsanyi, J.C. (1962). 'Measurement of Social Power, Opportunity Costs and the Theory of Two Persons Bargaining Games', *Behavioural Science*, 7 (67–80).

Hatry, Harry P. et alii (1973). *Practical Program Evaluation for State and Local Government Officials*. Washington, DC, Urban Institute.

Hatry, Harry P. et alii (1990). *Monitoring the Outcomes of Economic Development Programs: A Manual*. Washington, DC, Urban Institute Press.

Haveman, Robert H. and Margolis, Julius (1970). Public Expenditures and Policy Analysis. Chicago, Markham Rand McNally.

Healey, P., McDougall, G. and Thomas, M.J., Eds. (1982). *Planning Theory: Prospects for the 1980s*. Oxford: Pergamon Press.

Healey Patsy. (1990). 'The City and the Environment: Problems and Perspectives of Urban Policy'. (Paper Presented at the European Conference "Environment and Urban Development, Bremen, 24–26 January).

Healey Patsy. (1992). 'Planning Through Debate. The Communicative Turn in Planning Theory', *Town Planning Review* 63(2).

Heilbroner, R.L. (1985). *The Nature and Logic of Capitalism*. New York, Norton.

Heilbroner, R.L. (1993). *21st Century Capitalism*. New York, Norton.

Heilbroner, R., and Milberg, W. (1995). *The Crisis of Vision in Modern Economic Thought*. USA, Cambridge University Press.

Held, David, and Mathias Koenig-Archibugi. (2003). *Taming Globalization. Frontiers of Governance*. Cambridge, Polity.

Held, D., and Koenig-Archibugi, M. (2005). *Global Governance and Public Accountability*. USA, Blackwell Publishing.

Henderson, Hazel. (1995a). *Paradigms in Progress Life Beyond Economics*. USA, Berrett-Koehler.

Henderson, Hazel. (1995b). "Beyond GNP". In: *Paradigms in Progress Life Beyond Economics. USA, Berrett-Koehler, 1995*.

Henderson, Hazel. (1999a). *Beyond Globalization. Shaping a Sustainable Global Economy*, Kumarian Press.

Henderson, Hazel. (1999b). "Globalization: The Current Dilemmas". In: Henderson Hazel *Beyond Globalization etc*.

Henderson, Hazel. (1999c). 'From Economics to Systems Thinking'. In: Henderson Hazel *Beyond Globalization etc*.

Henderson, Hazel, and Ikeda Daisaku (2002). *Planetary Citizenship*. Tokyo, Middleway.

Bibliographic of Vol. II   **425**

Hicks, J. (1979). *Causality in economics*. Oxford, Basil Blackwell.

Hirschman, Albert O. (1970). *Exit, Voice and Loyalty*: Responses to Decline in Firms, Organisations and States. Cambridge, MA: Harvard University Press.

Hirschman, Albert O. (1977). *The Passion and the Interests*. Princeton, NJ: Princeton University Press.

Hirschman, Albert O. (1986). *Rival Views of Market Society and Other Recent Essays*. New York: Viking.

Hirschman, Albert O. (1991). *The Rhetoric of Reaction: Perversity, Futility, Jeopardy*. Cambridge, MA: Belknap Press.

Hodgson, Geoffrey M. (1988). *Economics and Institutions. A Manifesto for a Modern Institutional Economics*, Polity Press.

Hodgson, Geoffrey M. (2004). 'Can Economics Start From Individual Alone? In: Edward Fullbrook, ed. *A Guide to What's Is Wrong with Economics*, F. Edward. London, Anthem Press: 57–67.

Hodgson, Geoffrey M. 'Can Economics Start from the Individual Alone' in Edward Fullbrook ed., 2005.

Hook, Sidney, Ed. (1967). *Human Values and Economic Policy – A Symposium*. New York, New York University Press.

Hout, W. (1993). Capitalism and the Third World: Development, dependence and the world system, Hants, Edward Elgar.

Hudson, W.D. (1969). *'The Is-Ought Question'. A Collection of Papers on the Central Problem in Moral Philosophy*. London: Macmillan, 1969.

Hume, David, (1739). *Treatise of the Human Nature*.

Hunt, E.K. (1990). Social Economics: A Socialist Perspective. In: Social Economics: Retrospect and Prospect. A. M. Lutz. London, Kluwer. 1990.

Hutchison, T.W. (1964). *'Positive' Economics and Policy Objectives*. London, George Allen & Unwin Ltd.

Hylland, A. and Elster, J. (1986). *Foundations of Social Choice Theory*. Cambridge, Cambridge University Press.

Isard, W. et al. (1969). *General Theory: Social, Political, Economic, and Regional with Particular Reference to Decision-Making Analysis*. Cambridge, MA, MIT Press.

James, W. (1907). *Pragmatism: A New Name for Some Old Ways of Thinking*.

Jencks, C. (1992). *The Post-Modern Reader*. London, Academy Editions.

Jessop, Bob. (1982). *The Capitalist State: Marxist Theories and Methods*. Oxford, Blackwell.

Jessop, Bob. (1990a). "Regulation Theories in Retrospect and Prospect." In: *Economy and Society* 19(2): 153–216.

Jessop, Bob. (1990b). *State Theory: Putting the Capitalist State in Its Place*. Cambridge, Polity.

Jessop, Bob. (1993). 'From the Keynesian Welfare to the Schumpeterian Workfare State'. In: R. Burrows and B. Loader eds, *Towards a Post-Fordist Welfare State?*. London, Routledge.

Jessop, Bob, Ed. (2000). *Regulation Theory and the Crisis of Capitalism*. Series No. 6. Cheltenham, UK, Edward Elgar.

Jessop, Bob. (2007). *State Power: A Strategic-Relational Approach*. Cambridge, Polity.

Jessop, Bob. (2014). *Towards A Cultural Political Economy. Putting Culture in Its Place in Political Economy*. Cheltenam, E.Elgar.

Jessop, Bob. (2016). *The State. Past, Present, Future*. Cambridge, Polity.

Jenkins, W.I. (1978a). The Case of Non-decisions. *Decision-Making: Approaches and Analysis: A Reader*. Eds. A.G. McGrew and M.J. Wilson. Manchester, Manchester University Press.

Jenkins, W.I. (1978b). *Policy Analysis: A Political and Organisational Perspective*. London, Robertson.

Jessop, W.M., and Friend, J.K. (1969). *Local Government and Strategic Choice: An Operational Research Approach to the Process of Public Planning*. London, Tavistock.

Joas, H. (1993). *Pragmatism and Social Theory*. Chicago: University of Chicago Press.

Johansen, L. (1977/1978). *Lectures on macroeconomic planning: Vol. 1. General Aspects; Vol. 2 Centralization, Decentralization, Planning under uncertainty*. Amsterdam: North-Holland.

Johansen, L. (1979). "The Bargaining Society." *Kyklos* 32.

Jones S.G., Ocampo J.A., and Stiglitz E. Joseph, Ed. (2010). *Time for a Visible Hands: Lessons from the 2008 World Financial Crisis*. Oxford, Oxford University Press.

Kahler, M. (2005). 'Defining Accountability Up: The Global Economic Multilaterals'. In: Held D. et alii, *Global Governance and Public Accountability*. (see).

Kahneman, D., and Tversky, A. (2013). *Prospect Theory: An Analysis of Decision Under Risk. A Handbook of the Fundamentals of Financial Decision-Making*.

Kalecki, M. (1986). *Selected Essays on Economic Planning*. New York, University of Cambridge.

Kaufmann, A. (1968). *Le tecniche decisionali: introduzione alla praxeologia*. [Decisional techniques. Introduction to Praxiology.]. Milano, Il Saggiatore.

Keeney, R.L., and Raiffa, H. (1976). *Decisions with Multiple Objectives*.

Kemp, L. Roger, Ed. (1993). *Strategic Planning for Local Government: A Handbook for Officials and Citizen*. Jefferson, N-C, Mc. Farland.

Kindleberger, Charles. (2000). *Manias, Panics and Crashes*.

Kettl Donald F., Ed. (1994). *Reinventing Government? Appraising The National Performances Review.* Washington, DC, Center for Public Management, Brookings Institution.

Kettl Donald F. and DiJulio John J., Eds. (1995). Inside the Reinvention Machine: Appraising Governmental Reform. Washington, DC, Brookings Institution.

Kindler J. and Kiss I. (1984). Future Methodology Based on Post Assumption. *Rethinking the Process of Operational Research and Systems Analysis.* R. Tomlinson and I. Kiss. Oxford, Pergamon.

Klappholz, K (1964). Value Judgements and Economics, *British Journal for the Philosophy of Science*, 15 reprinted in Hausman, 1984; pp: 267–292.

Kleinknecht, A and Mandel, E (1983). *Historical Capitalism with Capitalist Civilization.* London: Verso.

Kleinknecht, A., Mandel, E and Wallerstein, I. (1992). *New Findings in Long Wave Research.* London, Macmillan.

Koenig-Archibugi M. (2005). 'Transnational Corporations and Public Accountability'. In: Held D. and Koenig-Archibugi M. *Global Governance and Public Accountability.* (see).

Kol J. and de Wolff, P. (1993). 'Tinbergen's Work: Change and Continuity.' *De Economist* 141 (No. 1): 1–28. [Includes a bibliographic catalog of the works of J. Tinbergen] (Reprint, by 'Erasmus Centre for Economic Integration Studies', University of Rotterdam).

Koopmans, T.C. (1963). On the Concept of Optimal Economic Growth, Pontificia Accademia Scientiarium.

Koteen, Jack. (1997). *Strategic management in public and nonprofit organizations: managing public concerns in an era of limits*, 2nd ed. Westport, CT, Praeger.

Kristol I. (1981). Rationalism in Economics. *The Crisis in Economic Theory.* D. Bell and I. Kristol. New York, Basic Books.

Korten David C. (1999). *The Post- Corporate World, Life After Capitalism.* USA, Kumarian Press, Berrett – Koehler.

Kotarbinski T. (1965). *Praxiology: An Introduction to the Science of Efficient Action.* Oxford, Pergamon Press.

Kuhn, A. (1963). The study of society-A unified approach, Richard D. Irwin, Inc., The Dorsey Press, Inc.

Lange O. (1960). 'Fundamentals of Economic Planning'. In O. Lange ed. *Essays on Economic Planning.* Calcutta, Indian Statistical Institute/Statistical Publishing Society.

Lasswell Harold D. and Lerner, D., Ed. (1951). *The Policy Sciences: Recent Developments in Scope and Method.* Stanford, Stanford University Press.

Lawrence J.R., Ed. (1966). *Operational Research & the Social Sciences*. London, Tavistock Publications.

Lee C. (1973). *Models in planning: an introduction to the use of quantitative models in planning*. Oxford, Pergamon.

Lee R.D. Jr. and Johnson R.W. (1977). *Public Budgeting Systems*. Baltimore, University Park Press.

Leontief W. (1976a). 'National Economic Planning: Methods and Problems.' In: Leontief W. and H. Stein (eds) *The Economic System in an Age of Discontinuity: Long-range Planning or Market Reliance*, New York University Press. Republished in Essays in Economics, Vol. 2, *Theories, Facts and Policies*, Blackwell, Oxford, 1977.

Leontief, Wassily (1976b). 'An Information System for Policy Decision in a Modern Economy'. In: *Forging America's Future,* [Strategies for National Growth Development. Washington, DC, Report of 'The Advisory Committee on National Growth Policy Process'. Vols. 3].

Leontief W. (1987). 'The Ins and Outs of Input-Output Analysis.' In *Mechanical Engineering* (1987).

Lerner A.P. (1951). *Economics of employment*, McGraw-Hill company.

Levitt Steven D. e Dubner Stephen J. (2005). *Freakonomics il calcolo dell'incalcolabile.* Milano, Sperling and Kupfer Editori.

Lewis C.I. (1946). An Analysis of Knowledge and Valuation, Open Court.

Lichfield N. et al., (1975). *Evaluation in the Planning Process*. Oxford: Pergamon Press.

Lichfield N. (1975). "A Comparison of the Planning Balance Sheet with the Goals Achievement Matrix Method of Evaluation." In: *Evaluation in the Planning Process*, edited by Lichfield N. et alii, Kettle P. and Whitebread M. Oxford: Pergamon Press.

Lichfield N. and Darin-Drabkin H. (1980). *Land Policy in Planning*. London: Allen & Unwin.

Lichfield N. (1990). 'Plan Evaluation Methodology: Comprehending the Conclusions' In: *Evaluation Methods for Urban and Regional Plans*, edited by D. Shefer and H. Voogd. London: Pion.

Lichfield N. (1996). *Community Impact Evaluation*. London: University College of London Press.

Lichfield N. et al., Ed. (1998). *Evaluation in Planning: Facing the Challenge of Complexity*. Dordrecht, Holland: Kluwer Academic Press.

Lieberman, Bernhardt. (1971). *Social Choice*. New York, Gordon and Breach Science Publishers.

Bibliographic of Vol. II 429

Lilienfeld R. (1978). *The Rise of Systems Theory: An Ideological Analysis*. New York, Wiley.

Lindblom Charles E. and David Baybrooke. (1963). *A Strategy of Decision: Policy Evaluation as a Social Process*. Free Press.

Lindblom Charles E. (1965). *The Intelligence of Democracy*. New York: Free Press.

Lindblom Charles E. (1968). *The Policy Making Process*. Englewood Cliffs, NJ: Prentice Hall.

Litterick, David (2002). The Billionaire who broke the Bank of England, *The Telegraph*, 13th September.

Long F. 'Ragnar Frisch: Econometrics and the Political Economy of Planning.' *American Journal of Economics and Sociology* 38 (1978): pp.141–53.

Luce R. D. and Raiffa H. (1957). *Games and Decisions*. New York, Wiley.

Lutz, A. Mark, Ed. (1990). *Social Economics: Retrospect and Prospect*. London, Kluwer Academic.

Malm Allan T. (1975). *Strategic Planning Systems: A Framework for Analysis and Design. Lund*, Studentlitteratur.

Mannheim, Karl (1950). *Freedom, Power & Democratic Planning*. London, Routledge & Kegan Paul.

Mandel, Ernest (1975). Der Spaetkapitalismus. Frankfurt, Suhrkam.

Mandelbaum S.J. (1995). *Open Moral Communities*. Berkley, University of California Press.

Mandelbaum S.J., L. Mazza and R. W. Burchell. Eds. (1996). *Exploration in Planning Theory*. Piscataway, NJ, Transaction Publisher.

March J.G. and Simon, H. (1958). Organizations. New York: Wiley.

March J.G. and J. P. Olsen. (1984). 'The New Institutionalism: Organizational Factors in Political Life.' In *American Political Science Review* (1984).

March J.G. (1988). *Decisions and Organizations*. Oxford: Basil Blackwell.

March J.G. and Olsen, J.P. (1989). Rediscovering Institutions: *The Organizational Basis of Politics*. New York: Free Press.

March J.G. (1999). *The Pursuit of Organizational Intelligence*. Oxford, Blackwell.

March J. G. and Mie Augier (2008). 'Realism and Comprehensioning Economics: A Footnote to an Exchange Between Olive E. Williamson and Herbert A. Simon', In: *Journal of Economic Behaviour and Organization* 66 (2008) 95–105.

Marcuse, Herbert (1968). *La fine dell' utopia*. [tr.it.:The end of Utopie], Bari, Laterza.

Marcuse, Herbert (1966). Ragione e rivoluzione. Hegel e il sorgere della "teoria sociale". [Reason and Revolution. Hegel and the arising 'social theory'] Bologna, il Mulino.

Martelli, Paolo (1983). *La logica della scelta collettiva*. Milano, Il Saggiatore.

Marschak J. (1974). *Economic Information, Decision and Prediction*. Dordrecht: Reidel.

Marvin K. E. and Rouse, A. M. (1970). The Status of PPB in Federal Agencies: A Comparative Perspective. *Public Expenditures and Policy analysis*. Haveman R.H. and Margolis J. Chicago, Rand McNally.

Mazza L. (1995). *Ordine e cambiamento, regole e strategia*. [Order and Change. Rules and strategy] Paper to the seminar 'The city and its sciences', Perugia (Italy).

Mazza L. (1998). *Designers of the future: certainty, flexibility and time in land use planning*. (Conference, 2–4 April 1998, Oxford Brookes University, Oxford, School of Planning).

McClelland, D. C. et alii (1953). *The Achievement Motive*. New York, Appleton-Century-Crofts.

McClelland D.C. (1961). *The Achieving Society*. Princeton, NJ, Van Nostrand.

McLoughlin J.B. (1969). *Urban and Regional Planning: A System Approach*. London: Faber and Faber.

McLoughlin J.B. and Thornley, J. (1973). *Some Problems in Structure Planning: a Literature Review*. London, CES (Centre for Environmental Studies).

McLaughlin, Kate et al., Eds. (2002). New Public Management: Current Trends and Future Prospects. London, Routledge.

Meade George H. (1934). (posthumous), *Mind, Self and Society*. Chicago, University of Chicago Press, pp. xxxvii–xxxviii; 328.

Meade James E. (1968). *The Theory of Indicative Planning*. Manchester: Manchester University Press.

Meade James E. Agathopia: *The Economics of Partnership*. Aberdeen: Aberdeen University Press, 1989.

Meade James, E. Liberty, *Equality and Efficiency*. London: Macmillan, 1993.

Menger, Karl (1871). Principles of Economics, Vienna.

Mercer James L. (1991). *Strategic Planning for Public Managers*. New York, Quorum Books.

Meyerson, Martin and Banfield, Edward C. (1955). *Politics, Planning, and the Public Interest: The Case of Public Housing in Chicago*. New York: Free Press.

Meyerson, Martin. (1956). 'Building the Middle-Range Bridge to Comprehensive Planning', *Journal of the American Institute of Planners* XXII (1956).

Michalos Alex C. (1978). *Foundations of Decision-Making*. Ottawa, Canadian Association for Pub. in Philosophy. Department of Philosophy of Carleton University.

Michalos A.C. (1995). *A Pragmatic Aproach To Business Ethics*. Thousand Oaks, Sage Publications.

Mihm, J. Cristopher (1995–96). 'GPRA and the New Dialogue'. *The Public Manager* 24(4): 15–18.

Mill, J. Stuart (1994). 'On the definition and method of political economy'. In: *The Philosophy of Economics. An Anthology.* Editor D. M. Hausman. Cambridge, Cambridge University Press: 52–68.

Millikan, F. Max (1969). *National Economic Planning.* New York, National Bureau of Economic Research.

Ministère de l'Economie des Finances et de L'Industrie (2005). *Guide pratique de la dèclination des programmes. Le budgets opérationnels de programme.*

Minsky, Human, (1986). *Stabilizing an unstable economy,* 1986.

Mishan Edward J. (1976). *Cost-Benefit Analysis: An Introduction.* New York: Praeger.

Mishan Edward J. (1981). *Introduction to Normative Economics.* New York: Oxford University Press.

Moore Mark H. (1995). *Creating Public Value. Strategic Management in Government.* Cambridge, MA, Harvard University Press.

Morris, Charles (1956). *Varieties of Human Value.* Chicago, University of Chicago Press.

Moskow, M.H. (1978). *Strategic Planning in Business and Government.*

Mueller Dennis C. (1989). *Public Choice II.* Cambridge, Cambridge University Press.

Mushkin Selma J. and Willcox Marjorie (1968). *An Operative PPS System: A Collaborative Undertaking in the States.* State-Local Finances Project: George Washington University.

Mushkin Selma J. and Cotton John F. (1969). *Sharing Federal Funds for State and Local Needs; Grants-in-aid and PPB Systems.* New York, Praeger Publishers.

Myrdal G. (1933). *The Political Element in the Development of Economic Theory.* [English Edition, London: Routledge, 1953].

Myrdal, Gunnar. (1944). *An American Dilemma: the Negro Problem and Modern Democracy.* New York, Harper & Brothers.

Myrdal, Gunnar (1951). *The Trend Towards Economic Planning.* The Manchester School of Economic and Social Studies. First published: January 1951.

Myrdal, Gunnar (1958). *Value in Social Theory; a Selection of Essays on Methodology.* ed. Paul Streeten, NewYork, Harper and Brothers.

Myrdal, Gunnar (1968). *Asian Drama; An Inquiry into the Poverty of Nations.* New York, Twentieth Century Fund.

Myrdal, Gunnar (1973). *Against the Stream: Critical Essays on Economics.* New York, Pantheon Books.

Myrdal G. (1969). *Objectivity in Social Research.* Gerald Duckworth. London 1970.

432   Volume II. Selected Testimonies on the Epistemological...

Myrdal G. (1972). 'How Scientific are the Social Sciences?' *Cahiers de l'ISEA, Serie H.S. 14.*

Myrdal, Gunnar (1970). *The Challenge of World Poverty; a World Anti-Poverty Program in Outline.* New York, Pantheon Books.

Nagel, Ernest (1961). *The Structure of Science, Problems in the Logic of Scientific Explanation* (2nd ed. Hacket, 1979).

Nagel, Ernest. (1967). Preference, Evaluation, and Reflective Choice. *Human Values and Economic Policy. A Symposium.* H. Sidney. New York, New York University Press.

Nanz P. and Steffek J. (2005). "Global Governance, Participation and the Public Sphere". In: Held D. and Koenig-Archibugi M. *Global Governance and Public Accountability.*

Newcomer E. K., Ed. (1997). *Using Performance Measurement to Improve Public and Nonprofit Programs.* San Francisco, Jossey-Bass Publisher.

Newcomer E. K. and Wholey S. J. (1989). *Improving Government Performance: Evaluation Strategies for Strengthening Public Agencies and Programs.* San Francisco, Jossey-Bass.

Notturno, Mark A. (2000). *Science and the Open Society: The Future of Karl Popper's Philosophy.*

NPR, Al Gore (1993). *From Red Tape to Results: Creating a Government that Works Better and Costs Less;* (Report of the National Performance Review). New York, NPR.

NPR. (1994). *Mission-Driven, Results-Oriented Budgeting* (Accompanying Report of the NPR). Washington, DC, NPR.

NPR. (1996a). *Reaching Public Goals: Managing Government for Results: Resource Guide.* Washington, DC, NPR.

NPR. (1996b). *Reinvention's Next Steps: Governing in a Balanced Budget World.* (A Speech by Vice President Al Gore and Supporting Background Papers). Washington, DC, NPR.

NPR, Bill Clinton & Al Gore. (1997). Blair House Papers. Washington DC, NPR.

NPR, and F. B. Consortium. (1997). *Serving the American Public: best Practices in Customer Driven Strategic Planning.* Washington, DC, NPR.

OMB. 2004 (Office of Management and Budgeting, USA).

Ozbekhan H. and G. E. Talbert, Ed. (1969). *Business and Government Long-Range Planning: Impacts Problems Opportunities.* Providence, RI, Institute of management Sciences.

Paris, Chris, Eds, (1982). *Critical Readings in Planning Theory.* Oxford, Pergamon.

Parsons T. & Shils E. A. (1951). *Toward a General Theory of Action*. Cambridge, MA, Harvard University Press.

Parsons T., R. F. Bales & E. A. Shils, (1953). *Working Papers in the Theory of Action*. Glencoe, IL, The Free Press.

Parsons T. & N. J. Smelser (1957). *Economy and Society, A Study in Integration of Economic and Social Theory*. Routledge and Kegan Paul, London.

Parsons T., ed. (1961). *Theories of Society*. Glencoe, IL, The Free Press.

Patton C. V. and Sawicki, D. S. (1986). *Basic Methods of Policy Analysis and Planning*. Englewood Cliffs, NJ, Prentice-Hall.

Peirce C.S., *Reasoning and the Logic of Things*. The Cambridge Conferences Lectures of 1898.

Perloff Harvey S. (1957). *Education for Planning: City, State, and Regional*. Baltimore: John Hopkins University Press.

Perloff Harvey S. (1969a). *The Quality of the Urban Environment: Essays on "New Resources" in an Urban Age*. Baltimore, John Hopkins Press.

Perloff Harvey S. (1969b). A Framework for Dealing with Urban Environment. *The Quality of the Urban Environment. Essay on "New Resources" in an Urban Age*. H. S. Perloff. Washington, DC, Resources for the Future Inc.

Peterson, Lorna. (1985). Strategic and Lorn-lange Planning for Public Administrators: a selective Bibliography. Monticello, III.

Phelps, Edward (1990). *Seven Schools of Macroeconomic Thought*, Oxford University Press.

Piaget J. and Garcia R. (1971). *Understanding Causality*. New York, Norton, 1974.

Pigou, Arthur Cecil (1912). *The Economics of Welfare*.

Piketty, Thomas (1997). *L'economie des inegalites*. Paris, La Decouverte.

Piketty, Thomas (2013). *Le capital au XXIe siecle*. Paris, Seuil.

Popper Karl R. (1945). *The open society and his enemies* [Vol. 1 The spell of Plato; Vol. 2 The high tide of prophecy: Hegel, Marx and the aftermath.].

Popper Karl R. (1959). *The logic of scientific discovery*. London, Hutchinson.

Popper Karl R. (1972). *Objective knowledge – An evolutionary approach* (orig. 1942). Oxford, Clarendon Press.

Popper Karl R. (1974). *Unended Quest An Intellectual Autobiography*. London and New York, Routledge Classics.

Quade Edward S. (1975). *Analysis for Public Decisions*. New York, American Elsevier.

Quade E.S. and Boucher, W. I. (1968). *Systems Analysis and Policy Planning, Applications in Defense*. New York, American Elsevier.

Raiffa, Howard (1988). Bell David, and Tversky Amos, *Decision making. descriptive, normative, and prescriptive interactions*. Cambridge. Cambridge University Press.

Reinhart, Carmen M. & Rogoff, Kenneth S. (2008). *This Time is Different: A Panoramic View of Eight Centuries of Financial Folly.*

Rivlin A. M. et alii (1970). 'The Planning, Programming and Budgeting System in the Department of Health, Education and Welfare: Some Lessons form Experience'. In: *Public Expenditures and Policy analysis*. Chicago, Rand McNally: (chap. 21).

Rivlin A. M. (1971). *Systematic Thinking for Social Action*. Washington, DC, Brookings Institution.

Rivlin A. M. (1973). 'Measuring Performance in Education'. In: *The Measurement of Economic and Social Performance*, New York, Columbia University Press.

Rivlin A. M. (1974). 'Social Experiments: Their Uses and Limitations.' In: *Monthly Labour Review.*

Rizzo M.J. (1978). Praxeology and Econometrics: a critique of positivist economics. *New Directions in Austrian methodology*. L.M. Spadaro. Kansas City, Sheed Andrews & McMeel.

Robbins, Lionel (1994). 'The nature and significance of economic science'. In: D. M. Hausman ed. *The Philosophy of Economics. An Anthology*. Cambridge, Cambridge University Press.

Robinson Ira M. (1972). *Decision-making in Urban Planning: An Introduction to New Methodologies,* Beverly Hill, CA, Sage.

Robson W. A. (1976). *Welfare State and Welfare Society*. London, Allen and Unwin.

Roemer J. (1993). 'A pragmatic theory of responsibility for the egalitarian planner'. *Phil.&Publ.Affairs* 10, 146.

Roemer J. (1996). *Theories of distributive Justice*. Cambridge, MA, Harvard University Press.

Ruffolo G. (1967). *La grande impresa nella società moderna*. [The great corporation in the modern society], Laterza, Bari.

Ruffolo G. (2008). *Il capitalismo ha i secoli contati*. [The capitalism cannot be survive but for centuries] Torino, Einaudi.

Sabattini, Gianfranco (2009). *Welfare State* nascita, evoluzione e crisi. Prospettive di riforma [Birth, evolution and crisis. Perspective of reform]. Milano, Franco Angeli.

Sanderson, S (1955). *Civilizations and World Systems*. London, Sage.

Sassen, Saskia (1998). *Globalisation and its Discontents. Essays on the new mobility of people and money*. New York, The New Press.

Bibliographic of Vol. II   **435**

Schumpeter J.A. (1911). *Theorie der Wirtschaftlichen Entwicklung* (1st ed. 1911, English ed., 3th ed. 1934, Oxford University Press.

Schumpeter J.A. (1959). *History of economic analysis*. New York, Oxford University Press.

Schumpeter J.A. (1942). *Capitalism, Socialism, and Democracy*. London, Allen & Unwin.

Scholte J. A. (2005). 'Civil Society and Democratically Accountable Global Governance'. In: Held D. and Koenig-Archibugi M. *Global Governance and Public Accountability.* (see).

Shackle G.L.S. (1962). *Economics for pleasure*, University Press of Cambridge.

Shackle G.L.S. (1973). *Epistemics and Economics: A Critiques of Economic Doctrines*, Cambridge University Press, Cambridge.

Shaller, Hermann I. (1976). *Unified planning and budgeting in a free society*. Adelphi, MD, Oakview Book Press.

Shils, Edward A., and Henry A. Finch. (1949). Max Weber on the Methodology of the Social Sciences. *Glencoe* 111: 73rT.

Seidel-Kwem, Brunhilde (1983). *Strategische Planung in Oeffentlichen Verwaltungen*. Berlin, Duncker-Humboldt.

Sen A.K. (1982). *Choice, Welfare and Measurement*. Oxford, Basil Blackwell.

Sen A.K. (1986). *Foundations of Social Choice Theory. Epilogue in Foundations of Social Choice Theory.* Cambridge, Cambridge University Press.

Sen, Amartya. (1970). "The impossibility of a Paretian Liberal." *Journal of Political Economy* 78.1: 152–157.

Sen, Amartya (1999). *Developpement as Freedom* [tr.francaise *Un novueau modele economique* Odile Jacob 2003]. Paris, Alfred Knopf.

Sen, Amartya (2009). *The Idea of Justice* [tr.fr.*L'idee de justiceFlammarion* 2012]. Londres, Penguin Books.

Shannon, T (1989). An introduction to the World System Perspective, Oxford, Westview Press.

Shils, Edward A. & Finch, Henry (1949). *The Methodology of the Social Sciences.*

Simon Herbert A. (1941). *Administrative Behavior*. London, Macmillan.

Simon, Herbert. A. (1957). *Models of Man. Social and Rational.* New York, Wiley & Sons Inc.

Simon Herbert. A. (1960). *The New Science of Management Decision.* New York, Harper & Row.

Simon Herbert. A. (1962). 'The Architecture of Complexity.' In: *Proceedings of the American Philosophical Society* (106).

Simon Herbert. A. (1969). *The Sciences of the Artificial.* Cambridge, MA, MIT Press.

Simon Herbert. A. (1983). *Reason in Human Affairs*. Stanford, Stanford University Press.

Sinden J. A. and A. C. Worrell (1979a). *Unpriced Values: Decisions Without Market Prices*. New York, Wiley.

Sinden J. A. and Worrell A. C. (1979b). 'Estimation of Social Values' (chap ex liber). *Unpriced Values. Decisions Without Market Prices*. Sinden J. A. and W. A. C. New York, Wiley: (Chap. 17).

Slaugter, Anne-Marie (2005). 'Disaggregated Sovereignty: Towards the Public Accountability of Global Government Networks'. In: Held D. et alii *Global Governance and Public Accountability*.

Smith, Adam. (1759). *The Theory of Moral Sentiments*.

Smith, Adam. (1776). *An Inquiry into Nature and Causes of the Wealth of Nations*.

Soros, George. (1998). *The Crisis of Global Capitalism. Open Society Endangered*. London: Little, Brown and Company.

Sprigge, Sylvia (1941). *History as the Story of Liberty*, Tim Allen & Unwin, London.

Steiss A. and Catanese A. J. (1970). *Systemic Planning: Theory and Applications*. Lexington, MA, Lexington Books.

Steiner H. (1979). *Conflict in Urban Transportation*. Lexington, MA, Heath Lexington Books.

Stiglitz, E. Joseph and B.C. Greenwald (2014). *Creating a Learning Strategy: A New Approach to Growth, Development and Social Progress*. New York, Columbia University Press.

Stiglitz, E. Joseph (1996). *Whither Socialism*. Cambridge MA, MIT Press.

Stiglitz E. Joseph (2010a). *The 'Stiglitz Report': Reforming the International Monetary and Financial Systems in the Wake of the Global Crisis*, New Press. New York, New Press.

Stiglitz E. Joseph (2010b). http://ineteconomics.org/stiglitz-new-paradigm. Financial Time, 2010.

Stiglitz, E. Joseph (2012). *The Price of Inequality: How Today's Divided Society Engenders Our Future*. New York, Norton & Co.

Taylor Frederick W. (1911). *The Principles of Scientific Management*. New York, Harper & Bros.

Taylor, Bernard and Hawkins, K., Ed. (1972). *A Handbook of Strategic Planning*. London, Longman.

Theil H. (1961). *Economic Forecasts and Policy*. Amsterdam, North-Holland.

Theil H. (1963). *Decision Rules and Simulation Techniques in Development Programming*. Vatican City, Pontificiae Academiae Scientiarum. Seminar Proceedings.

Theil, H. et al. (1964). *Optimal Decision Rules for Government and Industry*. Amsterdam, North-Holland.

Thomas, Huw, and Healey, Patsy. (1991). *Dilemmas of Planning Practice*. Avebury Technical, Aldershot.

Tinbergen, Jan. (1952). *On the Theory of Economic Policy*. Amsterdam, North-Holland.

Tinbergen, Jan et alii (1954). with P. J. Verdoorn and H. J. Witteveen. *Centralization and Decentralization in Economic Policy Amsterdam,* North-Holland Publishing Company.

Tinbergen, Jan. (1956a). *Economic Policy: Principles and Design*. Amsterdam, North-Holland.

Tinbergen, Jan (1956b). *The Design of Development*. Rotterdam, Netherlands Economic University.

Tinbergen, Jan (1959a). 'La planification de la politique economique' *Revue Internationale des Sciences Sociales* (3): 365–376.

Tinbergen, Jan (1959b). 'La valutazione oggettiva delle mansioni e il mercato del lavoro' [the Job Evaluation and the Labor Market] *Politica Sindacale* (Anno II – N. 1. Febbraio): 9–19.

Tinbergen, Jan (1961a). "Do Communist and Free Economies Show a Converging Pattern?" Soviet Studies XII(4): 333–341.

Tinbergen, Jan (1961b). 'The Relevance of Theoretical Criteria in the Selection of Investment Plans'. In: J Tinbergen ed. *Investment Criteria and Economic Growth*. New York, Asia Publishing House.

Tinbergen, Jan (1962). *Mathematical Models of Economic Growth*. New York, McGraw-Hill.

Tinbergen, Jan (1963a). *The Economic Framework of Regional Planning*. Vatican City, Pontificiae Academiae Scientiarum. (Abstract from the Proceedings).

Tinbergen, Jan (1963b). *Project Appraisal: A Traditional Approach*. Calcutta, Statistical Publishing Society U.P.: 3–41.

Tinbergen, Jan (1964). '*Optimal Planning*'. In: *Central Planning*. New Haven, Yale University Press.

Tinbergen, Jan (1966a). 'Some Refinements of the Semi-Input-Output Method.' *Pakistan Development Review* (VI).

Tinbergen, Jan (1966b). *Development Planning*. New York, McGraw Hill.

Tinbergen, Jan (1968). 'Wanted: A World Development Plan.' In: *International Organization* (22).

Tinbergen, Jan (1969a). Gunnar Myrdal on Planning Models. Bangkok, UN Asian Institute for Economic Development and Planning.

438   Volume II. Selected Testimonies on the Epistemological...

Tinbergen, Jan (1969b). 'International Planning of Peaceful Economic Development'. Eds. R. Jungk and J. Galtung. *Mankind 2000.* Oslo/London, Universitetsforlaget/Allen and Unwin.

Tinbergen, Jan (1970a). "A positive and a normative theory of income distribution.", The Review of Income and Wealth (Series 16, Number 3): 221–234.

Tinbergen, Jan (1970b). *The Use of Models: Experience and Prospects.* Stockholm, Les Prix Nobel en 1969: 244–252.

Tinbergen, J. (1971a). *Two Approaches to the Future: Planning Vs. Forecasting,* [mimeo].

Tinbergen, J. (1971b). Comment faut-il étudier l'avenir?, pp. 1–2.

Tinbergen, Jan, and Gabriella Antonelli. (1967). *Sviluppo e pianificazione.* Il Saggiatore.

Tomlinson, Rolfe and Kiss Istvàn, Ed. (1984). *Rethinking the Process of Operational Research and Systems Analysis.* Oxford, Pergamon.

Tregoe B.B. and Zimmerman, J. W. (1980). *Top Management Strategy: What It Is How to Make It Work.* New York, Simon and Schuster.

UN Centre for Housing Building and Planning (1974). *The Integration of Economic and Physical Planning.* Draft Report of a Meeting held in, New York, Sept. 1973.

UNRISD. (1970). *Studies in the Methodology of Social Planning.* Geneva, Unrisd.

UNRISD. (1973). *Regional Disaggregation of National Policies and Plans.* Paris and The Hague, Mouton.

UNRISD. (1975). *Report on a Unified Approach to Development Analysis and Planning.* 24th Session of UN Commission for Social Development, 6–24 Jan., 1975.

UNRISD. (1980). *The Quest for a Unified Approach to Development.*

UNRISD. (2003). 'Recherches pour le changement social: Rapport du 40éme anniversaire de L'UNRISD.' UNRISD, p. 141.

US-DOE. (1996). Department of Energy, USA.

US-NASA. (1996). National Aeronautics and Space Agency, USA.

US Department of Navy. (n.d.).

Vercellone, Carlo, Ed. (2003). *Sommes-nous sortis du capitalisme industriel?* Paris, La Dispute/SNEDIT.

Verma, Niraj (1998). *Similarities, Connections, and Systems.* Lanham, MD, Lexington Books.

von Hayek F. A. (1954). *Capitalism and the Historians.* Chicago, The University of Chicago Press.

Bibliographic of Vol. II   **439**

von Mises L. (1933). *Grundprobleme der Nationaloekonomie Untersuchungen Über Verfahren, Augaben Und Inhalt Der Wirtschafts Und Gesellschaftslehre.* Wien, 1933. (English transl.: *Epistemological Problems of Economics*, 1960) (Last edition. by New York University Press, 1978).

von Mises L. (1960). *Epistemological Problems of Economics.* Princeton: Van Nostrand, 1960.

von Mises L. (1957). *Theory and History. An interpretation of social and Economic Evolution*, Yale University Press. (Last reprint 2007 by 'L.von Mises Institute', Alabama 2007).

von Mises L. (1962). *The Ultimate Foundation of Economic Science. An Essay on Method.* Van Nostrand, (Princeton, etc, 1962).

von Mises L. (1951). *Socialism.* New Haven, CT, Yale University Press.

von Mises L. (1949). *Human Action.* New Haven, Yale University Press.

Wallerstein, I (1976). *The Modern World System*, (Capitalist Agriculture, etc).

Wallerstein, I (Mercantilism) etc. New York, Academic Press, etc.

Wallerstein, I (1996). *The Age of Transition: Trajectory of the World System, 1945–2025.* London, Zed Press.

Wallerstein, I. (1979). *The Capitalist World-Economy,* Cambridge University Press.

Wallerstein, I (1982). *World-Systems Analysis: Theory and Methodology.* Beverly Hills: Sage.

Wallerstein, Immanuel (2000). *The essential Wallerstein.* New Press.

Wallerstein and Hopkins, *The Age of Transition: Trajectory of the World-System, 1945–2025.* London: Zed Press, 1996.

Warfield J. N. (1976). *Societal Systems: Planning, Policy and Complexity.* New York: Wiley.

Webber, M. M. et alii, ed. (1964a). *Explorations into Urban Structure.* Philadelphia: University of Pennsylvania Press.

Webber M. M. (1964b). 'The Urban Place and the Non-Place Urban Realm.' In: *Explorations into Urban Structure, etc.* edited by M.M. Webber et alii. Philadelphia, University of Pennsylvania Press.

Webber M. M. (1968). 'The Post-City Age.' In *Daedalus*, Fall: 1091–1110.

Webber M. M. (1973). 'Dilemmas of a General Theory of Planning.' *Policy Sciences 4.*

Webber M. M. (1978). 'A Difference Paradigm for Planning.' In: *Planning Theory in the 1980's a Search for Future Directions*, edited by R. W. Burchell et al. New Jersey: Rutgers University.

440 Volume II. Selected Testimonies on the Epistemological...

Weber Max. (1975). 'Subjectivity and determinism'. In: A. Giddens, ed., *Positivism and Sociology*, London: Heinemann.

Weber Max. (1949). *The Methodology of the Social Science*. Edited by E.A. Shils and H.A. Finch (eds). Glencoe: The Free Press.

Weber Max. (1864–1920). 'Objectivity and understanding in economics', in Hausman D.M. Editor, *The Philosophy of Economics. An Anthology*, 1996 (chapter 2).

Weiss Carol H. (1972). *Design of the Evaluation. Evaluation Research. Method of Assessing Program Effectiveness*. C. H. Weiss. Englewood Cliffs, NJ, Prentice-Hall.

Weiss Carol H. (1992). *Organizations for Policy Analysis*. London, Sage.

White A.G. (1986). *Strategic Management: A Selected Bibliography*. Monticello III.

Wholey Joseph S., Hatry Harry P., and Newcomer Kathrine E. editor. (1994). *Handbook of Practical Program Evaluation*. San Francisco, Jossey-Bass Publisher.

Wilbur C. and R. Harrison. (1978). 'The Methodological Basis of Institutional Economics.' *Journal of Economic Issues*, No. 12, March: 61–90.

Williams Colin C. and Windebank, J. (1998). *Informal Employment in Advanced Economies: Implications for Work and Welfare*. London, Routledge.

Zauberman A. (1967). *Aspects of Planometrics*. London, University of London, The Athlone Press.

Zurn M. (2005). 'Global Governance and Legitimacy Problems'. In: Held D. and Koenig-Archibugi M., *Global Governance and Public Accountability*.

Index[1]

Ability, 22, 28, 57, 59, 111, 140n2, 193, 197, 241, 244, 254, 362, 374, 376, 388, 405, 349, 364
Acceptability, 341, 349, 357, 362
Acceptable style of development, 345, 363
Acceptance, 39, 41, 88, 147n3, 323, 324, 348, 349, 366
Achievement commodity, 141
Acocella, N., 258, 260, 261, 263n4
Action
    categories of, 7
    nexus between knowledge and, 69
Action-oriented analysis, programming approach as, 109–110

Adaptive subsystem, 138
Administrations Budget and Performance Integration Initiative, 311
Administrative reformers, 373, 375
Administrative science, 151–155, 163–171
Administrative theory, 133
Advanced vision of consequences, 96–97
AESOP, 123n52
Affection commodity, 140
Affirmative action, 394
Agency
    'goals and objectives' of, 298
    programs, 308, 309
Agrarian reform, 347
Agricultural policy, 355

---

[1] Note: Page numbers followed by 'n' refer to notes.

© The Author(s) 2019
F. Archibugi, *The Programming Approach and the Demise of Economics*,
https://doi.org/10.1007/978-3-319-78060-3

442 Index

Agricultural share
  in investment, 355
  in national income, 355
Agro-industrial complexes, 357
Alexander, E.E., 80
Alexander, E.R., 80, 119n29
American agencies, 305
American case, 315, 331n25
American Economic Association, 26
American federal programme, 305
American government, 243
American GPRA, 314
American law, 314
American legislator, 303
American Planning Association,
  117n19
American Planning-Programming-
  Budgeting System (PPBS),
  284n9, 284n10–12, 289n30,
  289n31, 305, 313
American reinventing government,
  316, 317
Analytic, 9
Annual Performance Plan, 306
Annual performance report, 309
Anti-corruption strategies, 391
Anti-positivist programming
  approach, 120n36
a-priori categories, 6–7
Aristotle, 69, 160, 173n18
Arrow, J.K., 22, 142, 333n37
Aspects of Planometrics (1967), 67n22
Attention, 77–79, 276, 284n12,
  363, 386
Attitudes, 18, 135–137, 367, 387
Authentic participation, 343, 344
Authentic strategies, 349
Authoritative voices, 352
Axiomaticity, 325
Axioms, 5, 56, 135

Bad models, 244
Barone, F., 22
Becker, G., 27
Beer, A.S., 174n25
Behavioural theories, 72
Bell, D., xxi, 20–28, 30, 33n13, 33n14
Bell, D.E., 54, 65n16, 65n17
Bell-Raiffa-Tversky (BRT), 54–56,
  58–59
Benchmarking, 384
Berle, A.A., Jr., 171n2
Bernstein, R.J., 115n2
Blair, T., 313
Blaug, M., 36–44, 46, 64n2, 65n13
Bounded rationality, xxiii, 163–168
  case of programming language,
    166–167
  imprecision and relativity of,
    163–165
British experiences, unhappy case of,
  312–317
Budget and Performance Integration
  Initiative, 311
Budget architecture of the state, 314
Budget presentation, 303
Bunge, M., 173n18
Bypass Controversial Terms, 43–45

Caiden, G., 373
Canonic principle of programming
  approach, 11
Capacity-building, 377, 378
Capacity-reinforcement, 401
Capital formation, new forms of,
  237–240
Capitalism, 183
  global system of, 180–182

Capitalism, Socialism and Democracy (1942), 180, 222n11
Casuistics, relaxation of assumptions and multiplication, 134–137
Catanese, A.J., 283
Catastrophe, mathematical theory of, 73
Causality, 5–6
Cause-and-effect-chains, 96
Central decisions, 370
Centre for Planning Studies, 268n24
Chadwick, G., 283
Chapin, F.S., Jr., 283
Chinese formulation, 355
Citizen participation, 374
Civil associationism, 230
Civil service profile, 396
Civil service reforms, 397
Civil society, 231, 233, 239, 241, 246, 405
Clientelism, 399
Clinton, B., 305
Co-efficient
    of human resources development, 378
    of transformation, 22
Coeteris paribus abuse, 73
Cogent-approach, to flexibility, 99
Cognition, 5, 8, 38, 97, 108, 187, 195, 197, 198, 202, 203, 338
Cognitive capacity in globalization, 379–381
Cognitive sphere, 70
Coherent policy for spatial redistribution, 369
Collective bargaining, 98–99, 261
Community, 75, 78, 100, 139, 226n32, 231
    of planning theorist, 79–82

Community performance, economics as tool for measurement and improvement, 271–284
Comprehensive framework, 315
Comprehensive mission statement, 298
Comprehensiveness, 353, 370
Comprehensive Spending Review, 313
Comprehensive strategy, 367
Computerization of data, 402
Computerizing government business, 402
Concept of value, 326
Conciseness, 325
Conference of Palermo, 119n33
Conflictive participation, 345
Conflict resolution, 393
Congressional justification, 310
Congress of the United States, 241
Consultation on national issues, 403
Contemporary economic theory, 27
Contemporary management theory, 374
Context planning, 11
Contradictions, 346, 358, 364, 365
Conventional economic theory, 48, 266n18
Conventional sectoral public services, 353
Core competencies, emphasis on, 379
Corea, A., 339
Corruption, 391, 392
Cost-effective management in organizations, 378
Creative destruction, 27
Crisis, 179–181
    of economic theory, 180
    of welfare, 179
Critical 'non-positivist' sociology, 33n14

444 Index

Critical rationalism, 119n34
  spirit of, 100–103
Critical-rationalist methodology, 109
Critical thought, 74
Criticism methodology, 229–230
Culture, 26, 311, 381, 388, 394, 395, 398
Customer satisfaction, 384

Darwinian nature, 21
de Finetti, B., xxi, xxviiin5, 15–17, 19, 20, 32–33n11
De Vries, E., 339
Debate method (job planners), 76
Debate (new methodology), 80
Debreu, G., 22, 142
Debureaucratization, 375
Decentralization, 375
Decisional analysis, 2
Decisional models, 243
  dispute between growth models and, 246–249
  logical foundations of, 1–3
Decisional situations, 327–328
Decisional system, 231
Decision-making process, 232
Decision-making skills, 388
Decision-making theory, 282
Decision models, 62
Decisions, to programmes and plans, 95–96
Decision Support Systems, 401
Decision theory, 35–64
  descriptive vs. normative, 36, 49
  new trichotomy in, 53
  prescriptive approach, 63
  traditional methodological debate on economic decision theory, 36

Deep parameters, 257–258
Definitive convergence, 301
Delors, J., 339
Department of Economic and Social Affairs (DESA), 372
Descriptive (deterministic) analysis, 2, 61
Descriptive approach, 55
  in modern decision theory, 49–53
  and normative approach, dichotomy between, 36–49, 54–60
Descriptive models, 59
Determinist approach, 1, 3, 15
Determinist crisis, 2
Deterministic analysis, 2
Development, 354, 373
  analysts, 343
  of economic theory, 242
  industry, 361
  of Planning Accounting Framework, xxv
  rural, 355–357
  spatial distribution of, 371
  styles of, 339–349, 352, 361, 367–369
  of welfare state, 49
Developmental activities, spatial redistribution of, 367
Developmental pigeon-holes, 352
Dialectical cognitive process, 114n1
Digitization of data, 402
Disadvantaged rural groups, planning for, 357
Distinct occupational groups, 394
Distribution, 26, 42, 239, 340–343, 346, 354, 358
Diversification, 380
Diversity, 392–395

DNA, 71, 116n14
  of positivist approach, 74–75
Domestic public-sector resources, 358
Dror, Y., 282
Drucker, P.F., 172n4, 172n6
Dutch planning, 98
Dutch urbanisation, 84
Dynamic market economy, 392
Dynamizing possibilities of
  reforms, 353

Econometric Society, 282
Economic and Social Commission, 338
Economic crises, management of,
  183–184
Economic decision theory, traditional
  methodological debate on, 36
Economic development policy,
  technical-scientific discovery
  influence of, vii
Economic efficiency, 381
Economic general theory, 131–146
  economic neo classical school,
    needs of realism, 131
  Isard general theory, 132, 142, 144
  non-economic commodities, 137
  planning accounting frame, 142
Economic innovation, 27
Economic language, 271–273
Economic neo classical school, needs
  of realism in, 131–132
Economic policies, 233–235
  management of, 259
  operational theorems of, 254–262
Economics, 184
  as tool for measuring and
    improving community
    performance, 271

epistemological basis of, 3–4
radical criticism of, 212–213
Economic theory, 25, 26, 74, 116n9,
  119n30, 239, 242, 244,
  263n3, 266n17
  as 'Fiction,' 20–23
  'Utopia' role as requirement in,
    15–17
Economic thinking, performance
  revolution in, xxvi–xxviii
Economy, 8, 12, 13, 16, 18, 21,
  24–26, 116n15, 239, 242,
  244, 245, 254, 271, 281, 354,
  356, 359, 364, 384, 404
Economy subsystem, 138
ECOSOC, 121n43
Education, 363–366
  vs. non-essential private
    consumption, 363
Educational policy, 365
Educational revolution, 365
Effectiveness, 90–95, 384
Effective performance budgeting and
  management, 301
Efficiency measure, 302, 384
Egalitarian principle, 48
Electronic distribution of government
  documentation, 402
Electronic polling, 403
Electronic referenda, 403
Electronic voting, 403
Empirical indirect inference, 72
Employment, 361–363
Empowerment, 377
The End of Ideology (Bell), 33n13
Engineering designer, 74
Enlightenment commodity, 141
Entrepreneurialism, 152
Environmental planning, 83, 84
Epistemics & Economics (Shackle), 25

446   Index

Epistemological planning, 15
Essays in Economics, 13–14
European countries, 305, 331n26, 385
European Union, 385
Evaluation
   as decision, 327
   existence of, 326–327
   subjects of, 327
Ex ante evaluation, 112–114
Ex ante results, 232
Ex ante stage, 232
Executive Branch Management
   Scorecard, 310
Experience, 5, 8–10, 77, 80, 98,
   104–107, 274, 280, 321,
   392, 398
Ex post evaluation, 112–114
Ex post results, 232
Ex post stage, 232

Fallibility, 201
   to feasibility form, 207–212
Faludi, A., xxii, 76–79, 83, 84,
   86–107, 117n18, 117n19,
   119n29, 119n34, 120n36,
   120n37, 121n38, 121n39,
   122n44, 122n45, 123n47,
   123n51, 124n53
Faludi, S., 283
Family planning, 366
Feasibility
   from fallibility to, 207–212
   of plans, 202–207
Federal budget, 310
Federal Reserve, 243, 244
Fiction, economic theory as, 20–23

Fifteenth Meeting of the Group of
   Experts, 386
Financial Times, 242
Fiscal crisis of the state, 237
Flexibility, in strategic planning
   process, 322–323
Forecast analysis, 2
Forecasting approach, 2
Foreign policy transfers, 397
Fostering capacity-building, 377–381
Fourteenth Meeting of the Group of
   Experts, 380, 382
Fox, K.A., 276
France, 289n33, 313–316, 331n29
Frankfurt School, 69, 115n4
Free market, 236
   vs. public intervention, 230
French case, 315, 331n25, 331n27
French constitutional ordainment, 314
French experiences, unhappy case of,
   312–317
French law, 314
French procedure, 315
Friedmann, J., 80, 118n26, 156, 158,
   160, 162, 163, 173n16, 173n17
Friend, J.K., 122n46
Frisch, R., xxv, xxixn9, 1, 10, 14, 19,
   32n5, 33n11, 62, 146, 167,
   171n1, 195, 204, 222n12,
   235, 236, 239, 245–249, 251,
   253, 264n7, 268n23, 268n24,
   269n29, 269n32, 270n34,
   276, 282, 286n5, 338
Frisch's pyramid, 96–97
*From Planning Theory to Planning
   Methodology*, 87–90
Function of management, 388
Fused pyramidal structures, 373

Garcia, R., 173n18
General Assembly, 338
General social system, 138–139
General theory, 132, 134, 138, 139, 141
General Theory of Action, 138
Germani, G., 339
Glass Curtains, 393
Global capitalism, 181
without public planning, criticism of, 213–214
Global community, 53, 395
Globalization, 372, 380, 392, 393, 400, 405, 406
effects of, 381, 382
era of, 375
progress of, 385
Global performance standards in management development, 381–385
Global scale, 79, 179, 338
Global system of capitalism, 180–182
Goal-attainment subsystem, 138
Government Performance and Results Act (GPRA), 297, 329n10, 331n25
federal law, 298–300
importance and feasibility of, 304–305
public support for reform of, 305–306
'Universal' Glossary of, 300–303
Government professionals, 396
Great Britain, 283, 313
Great Depression, 242
Greenspan, A., 244
Growth models, 1, 204, 243
and decisional model, dispute between, 246–249

Hallmark of state bureaucracies, 373
Hansson, S.O., 50–52, 64n1
Heterogeneity, 394
Hickling, A., 122n46
Higgins, B., 339
Historical Capitalism with Capitalist Civilization, 181
Homo economicus, 53
Human agents, 339
Human beings, transformation of, 354
Human capital formation, 378
Human civilization, 7
Human existence, 273
Human insecurity, 393
Human mind and of history, logical structure of, 6–10
Human resources development, 375, 378
organizational responses for, 395–400
Hume, D., 36
the Hume guillotine, 64n3

IIASA, 110, 124n57
Import-substitution industrial growth
concentration of, 368
dependent and imitative character of, 359
Import-substitution strategy, 359
Income policy, from endogenous to exogenous concept, 240
Indeterminacy, 189, 192–194
Indicators, 277, 279, 315, 384
Industrial development strategy, 360
Industrial growth, lines of, 358

448   Index

Industrialization, 357–361
  in development policies, emphasis on, 363
Infinite improvement, 210
Information revolution, 406
Information systems, 375, 401, 402
Information technology, 401–404
Innovative choices, 348
Innovative systems, 385
Institute for New Economic Thinking, 242, 245
Institute for Operational Research (IOR), 101, 122n46, 283
Institutional constraints, 18, 19
Institutional framework, 398
Institutional memory, 379
Institutions and processes, 341, 393
Integrated network-based national revenue management system, 401
Integrative subsystem, 138
Interactive vision of reality, 196–200, 203–205
Inter-agency coordination, 305
Interest-group organization, 347
Intergovernmental organizations, 397
Internal market for manufactured goods, 358
International advisory missions, 362
International cooperation, 392
Internationalization of administrative change, 400
International Monetary Fund (IMF), 286n9
International order, 343
Internet, 402, 404
Interpretative economic theory, 26–28
Intranet, 403

Introduction of Strategic Planning (2005), 298
Investment, agricultural share in, 355
Iron Curtain, 393
Irrationality, 57, 58
Isard general theory, 132–137, 146
  and planning accounting frame (PAF), 142–144
  between positivist methodology and programming approach, 144–146
Isard, W., xxiii, 131–146
is-statement, 38, 39, 43, 46
Iteration, in strategic planning process, 323–324
IT strategy, 405

Jessop, W.M., 122n46
Job evaluation, 241
Johansen, L., 264n11, 276, 283
Journal of Economic Methodology, 223n18

Keynesian theory, 26
Kleinknecht, A., 181
Kleptocracies, 390
Knowledge, 69–74, 235, 238, 241, 251, 253, 267n21, 387
  activistic basis of, 4–6
  of economics, 387
  of languages, 389
  to plan political action, 236–237
  of praxeology, 4
Knowledge–action nexus, 69–74

Index 449

Knowledge-based economy, 404, 405
Knowledge management systems, 404
Koopmans, T.C., 22
Kuznets, S., 265n14

Laissez-faire, 234, 237, 254, 368
Land and urban planners,
    contribution of, 74–86
Land-use planning, 75, 78
Lange, O., 22
Language of mathematics, over-
    simplification in abuse of, 19–20
Lapalissian invention, 230
Large-scale management, 77
Lasswell, H.D., 282
Leadership skills, 352, 376–377, 388
Learning organizations, 375, 377
Leontief, W., xxv, xxixn9, 1, 12–14,
    286n5
Lerner, A.P., 22
Levels of production, 345
Library of the Planning Studies
    Centre, 31n4
Limitations on styles of
    development, 340
Lindblom, C., 282
Local planning systems, 370
Logical action, 24
'Logical confusion,' 38–39
Logical foundations of decisional
    models, 1–3
Logical positivism, 5, 198
    programme's feasibility and
        relationship with, 205–207
    to theory of reflexivity, 186–196
LOLF, 314, 316, 331n27, 331n29

Long-term forecasting, 11
Love-tendered commodity, 141
Lucas critique, 254–259

McLoughlin, J.B., 283
Macro-economic models, 239, 243,
    244, 248, 254
Macroeconomic planning, 283
Mainstream economics, vi, xix–xxvi
Major, J., 313
Management, 82, 139, 152, 172n6,
    209, 241, 247, 252, 253,
    263n6, 268n23, 313, 314,
    323, 387
Management Agenda, 310
Management culture, 382
Management Information Systems,
    401
Management of change, 375
Management policy, 382
Management sciences, as context,
    151–154
Managerialism, 152, 153, 171n2
Mandel, E., 181, 220n8, 220n9
Man is action, characteristic feature
    of, 7
Mannheim, K., xxi
Manufactured goods, internal market
    for, 358
Market failure *vs.* state (intervention)
    failure, 230
Market prices, viiin2, 242, 272, 273
Marschak, J., 32n10
Marshall, A., 27
Mathematical theorem, 22, 164
Mathematical theory, of catastrophe, 73

450 Index

Maximisation, 133
Mazrui, A.A., 339
Means, G., 171n2
Measurement, 6, 91, 232, 278, 304, 318
Meeting of the Group of Experts, 399
Member States, 380, 385
Menger, K., 22
Meta-disciplinary approach, 2
Meta-disciplinary message, 76
Methodological argument, 212
Methodological judgements *vs.* value judgements, 39–42
The Methodology of Economics, 36
Methodology of Social Sciences, 64n9
Micro-economics, 280
Mill, J.S., 36
Mintzberg, Henry, 373
Mirandola, Pico della, 104
Mobilization, 343, 363
Models and Reality in Economic Discourse, 22
Modern decision theory
 descriptive and normative approach in, 49–53
 new trichotomy in, 53–63
Modern democratic system, 304
Modern economic science, 179
Modern government, 374
Modern technology, 372
Modern productive activities, 368
Monetary policy, 244
Moore, M.H., 275
Moore, V.E., 339
More realism, 132–134
Multi-disciplinary strand of new demarcation, 281–284
Multi-national community, 273

Multi-national system, 214
Mushkin, S.J., 289n32
Myrdal, G., 3, 24, 45–49, 62, 223n20, 227n35, 239, 276, 286n5, 338, 339

Nagel, E., 39–42, 64n6, 66n20
Naqvi, K.A., 339
National Accounting System, 246
National authorities, 366
National economic plan, 12
National industrial growth, 359
National "IT culture," 405
National Partnership for Reinventing Government, 329n14
National Performance Review (NPR), 305
National population, 368
National process of decision-making, 341, 349
National situations, 350, 361
National society, 340, 342, 343, 350
Naturalist support invasion, 72
Natural phenomena, 186–190
Neo-classical economists, 243
Neo-managerial culture, 390
Newcomer, E.K., 172n9
New economic paradigm, 242–246
New paradigm, 245,250–254
New Public Management, 313
Nexus, between knowledge and action, 69–74
Neyman-Pearson theory, 39
Nicola, A., 334n37
Non-critical social positivism, 73
Non-critical thought, 74

Non-economic commodities, 137–142
Non-essential private consumption, education *vs.*, 363
Non-protagonist actor, 71
Non-rational behaviour, 25
Non-rationality, 57
Normative approach
  dichotomy between descriptive approach and, 36, 54–60
  in modern decision theory, 49–53
Normative models, 59, 63
Normative nature, 72
Normative (or prescriptive) analysis, 2, 61
Normative standard, 21
Normative theory, 89
NPR, *see* National Performance Review

Objectivity in Social Research, 65n14, 223n20
OECD countries, 313, 317
Office of Management and Budget (OMB), 301, 306, 307, 309–312
Official economic theory, 266n18
On-line databases, 404
On-line voter guide, 403
Open society, 186, 187, 211
Operational research, 2, 47, 74, 75, 77, 110
Operational sphere, 70, 75
Operational theorems of economic policy, 254–262
Optimisation, 167–168, 174n29
Organisational responses for human resources development, 395

Organisational science, as result-based science, 154–155
Organizational framework, 378
Organizational terms, 377
Organized interest-groups, 351
Organized participation, 344
Oslo models, 235, 236
Ought-statement, 38
Outcomes measurement, 300, 384
Output measure, 300
Overturning approach, 100
Ozbekhan, H., 174n23

Paradox, 72
Pareto-optimality, 27
Parsons, T., 138
PART, *see* Program Assessment Rating Tool
Participation, 195, 343, 344
Participation commodity, 140
Pattern-maintenance subsystem, 139
Patton, C.V., 282
Performance budget, 301, 303, 306–308
  data included in, 308–309
  evaluation of, 310
  vs. strategic plan, 309–310
Performance goal, 300, 302
Performance incentives, 384
Performance indicator, 300
Performance measure, 302, 308, 383
Performance plan, 299–301
Performance standards, 382
Period of progress in planning theory, 75–76
Phelps, E., 286n5

452   Index

Philanthropy, 223n17
Physical design, 74
Physical planning, 72
Piaget, J., 173n18
Piketty, T., 239, 265n14
Plan-making, 97
Planning, 85
 design for worldwide strategic
   methodology for, 229–262
 of methodology, 73
Planning accounting framework
   (PAF)
 construction of, 229–233
 Isard general theory and, 142
 role of, 235–236
Planning agency, 97, 340
Planning designer, 74
Planning for disadvantaged rural
   groups, 357
Planning in the Public Domain, 156
Planning methodology, 90–95,
   100–103
 ex ante and ex post evaluation in,
   112–114
 indispensable ingredient of
   rationality in, 98–99
 steps in, 103–114
Planning problem, 77, 78, 105
Planning process, political consensus
   on, 235–237
Planning-Programming-Budgeting
   System (PPBS), 283, 284,
   289n32, 289n33
Planning quantification, operational
   requirement of, 110–112
Planning theorists, 77–79, 82–83,
   117n18, 120n37
 community of, 79–82
 DNA of, 74–75

Planning theory, xxii, xxixn8, 71, 283
 period of progress in, 75–76
 to planning methodology, 87–90
Planning theory movement, 74–86
Planology, 1, 64, 82, 105, 144
Planometrics, 61
Plan political action, knowledge to,
   236–237
Plato, 69
Pluralistic societies, 395
Policy approaches, 327, 357, 370
Policy driven system, 255
Policy for spatial redistribution, 369
Policymakers, 244, 245
Political consensus, on planning
   process, 235–237
Political decisional system, with
   strategic approach, 231–233
Political leaders, 343, 345, 349, 351,
   352, 363
Political participation, design and,
   194–196
Political science, 62, 133, 156,
   163–171
Political thinking, performance
   revolution in, xxvi–xxviii
Polity subsystem, 138
Popper, K.R., 69, 87–89, 95, 100,
   105, 119n34, 120n36,
   122n45, 185, 186, 195, 198
Popperian philosophy, 100
Population, 366–367
Positive analysis, 2, 28, 111, 169, 242
Positive economics, 47, 48
Positive knowledge, 70–71
Positive–normative dichotomy, 36, 39
Positive theory, 89, 92
Positivist approach, 1, 82
 damage done by, 71–74

Positivist science, 153
Positivist-scientific, 181
Post-industrial society, 273, 275, 278
Post-Second World War, 77, 100
Power commodity, 140
Power of dominant interest-groups, 370
PPBS, *see* Planning-Programming-
  Budgeting System
Pragmatic realism, 29–31
Pragmatism, 69, 74, 81, 115n2
Praxeological approach, 81, 230
Praxeology, xxviiin1, 8–10
Predictive activities, 2
Preferred style of development, 340
Prescriptive analysis, 2, 67n21
Prescriptive approach, 63–64
Prescriptive models, 59, 64
Price system, 22, 26
Price theory, 26
Private performance, 271–273
Privileged witness, 304
Proceduralism, integration of,
  83–86
Productivity, 238, 271, 281, 287n12,
  384, 404, 405
Progetto Quadro, 268n24
Program activity, 299, 300
Program assessment, 303
Program Assessment Rating Tool
  (PART), 307–312
Program evaluation, 310–312
Program in Public Administration and
  Development (UNPAN), 372
Programmatic activities, 2
Programme efficiency, 305
Programme's feasibility *vs.* logical
  positivism, 205–207
Programming Accounting
  Framework (PAF), 182

Programming approach, 1–3, 26,
  63–64, 69–74, 82, 88,
  151–155, 167–171, 175n38,
  198, 202–203, 211, 271–273,
  275, 276, 278, 372
  as action-oriented analysis,
    109–110
  bounded rationality concept in,
    166–167
  collective decision and action-
    centred analysis, 69–114
  vs. forecasting, 10–14
  performance measuring and
    monitoring as implementation
    factors in, 277
  postulates in, 107–109
Programming knowledge, 70–71
Programming nature, 72
Program performance goals, 302
Progressive dialectic of ideas, 30
Protagonist actor, 71
Protection of human environment
  and relationships, 348
Public Administration, 312
Public Administration and
  Globalization, 381
Public agency management reform,
  315
Public authorities, 92–95, 372, 375
Public consciousness, impingement
  on, 349
Public environmental measures, 84
Public information, 402
Public intervention *vs.* free market, 230
Public management, 79
Public organizations, 155, 396
Public performance, 271–273
Public planning, effectiveness
  of, 194

454 Index

Public sector, vii, 153, 172n5, 273, 297, 352, 369
  cultural origins of managerial planning in, 155–163
Public service professionalism, 389–395
Pyramidisation, 86

Quality of services, 384
Quantitative effectiveness, 384

Radical criticism of economics, 212–213
Radical fallibility, 209
Radical reform, 234
Raiffa, H., 54, 65n17
Rapid change, era of, 375
Rapidity, 353–354
Rational *a-priorisms*, 3
Rational expectations (REs), 254, 255, 257–258
Rationalisation of the Budget Choices, 313
Rationalism, vi
Rationality, 73, 74, 83, 162–163
  indispensable ingredient of, 98–99
  in planning, 91–95
Rational planning, 70, 71, 73, 86–103
A Reader in Planning Theory (1973), 76
Realism, 29–31, 57
Realistic policy, 360
Realistic validity, illogicality of, 60–63
Real style of development, 340
Reciprocal influence, 70
Rectitude commodity, 140

Rediscovering Economic Policy as a Discipline, 261
Redistribution meeting, 346
Reductionism, 161
Reflexivity, 201
Reform, 234, 266n17, 305, 306, 313, 315, 317, 347, 385, 400–406
Regional planning systems, 370
Reinhart, C.M., 222n11
Reinvention of government, 241
Relative decisional models, 1
Repression, 392
Research
  level of, 72
  steps in, 281–284
Resources, 18, 22, 24–26, 29, 230, 307, 342, 345, 402
Respect commodity, 140
Result-based science, organisational science as, 154–155
Results-based management, 155
Return to strategic planning, 280–285
Revolutionary approach, 304
Reynolds, L.G., 267n20
Risk management, 244
Rogoff, K.S., 222n11
Romanticism, 162–163
Rotterdam School, 276
Ruffolo, G., 172n2, 222n11
Rural-agricultural development, 360
Rural-agricultural populations, 355
Rural development, 355–357
Rural population, 356

Samuelson, P., 27
Sanctions commodity, 141

Index **455**

Sawicki, D.S., 282
Scale of production, 360
Scarcity, 327
Scepticism, 30
Schumpeter, J.A., 27, 180
Science, 70, 154
Scientific Congress of Planning, 118n25
Scientific management, 162
'Scientific' propositions, 38–39
Scientific research, 72, 76
Scientific utopism, 15
Scope for organizational forms, 345
Second World War, 337, 396
Seek productive techniques, 345
Sen, A.K., 333n37
Service quality and timeliness, 384
Shackle, G.L., 25
Short-term memory, 98
Simon Herbert, A., 167
Sinden, J.A., 273, 279
Situational opportunity, 47
Skill commodity, 140
Smith, A., 21, 27, 193–194, 244
Social accounting progress, directions in, 276–277
Social Acts, borrowing, 138–139
Social control of public administration, 392
Social conventions, 26
Social engineering, 77, 280
Social equity, 369, 381
Social groups, 345
Socialist, 180
Sociality commodity, 140
Social phenomena, 186–190
Social positivism, 72, 73
Social revolution, 352
Social transformation, 348
Social utility, 327

Societal actors, 340
Socio-economic accounting system, 277
Socio-economic management, 233
Socio-economic mechanisms, 12
Socio-economic planning, 72
Socio-economic policy, 11
Sociologists of knowledge, 41
Sociology, 72, 133
Sociology of knowledge, xxi, 69, 81
Solidarity commodity, 139–140
Solow, R.M., 26
Soros, G., xxiv, 183, 185, 187–201, 203, 204, 205, 207–213, 222n13
Sound institutional framework, 378
Soviet Union, 224n22, 393
Spatial distribution
    of development, 371
    of population, pattern of, 369
Spatial redistribution of developmental activities, 367
Spontaneous order, xiii, 22, 73
Stakeholders, 318, 374, 383
Standard models, 244, 251
Standard mottos of reorganization, 378
State agencies, 261, 392, 404
Statistical Abstract or the *Census of Manufacture*, 12
Steiss, A.W., 283
Stiglitz Report, 266n17
Stiglitz, E.J., xxvi, 242–245, 251, 265–266n17, 266n18, 267n21
Strategic planning capacities, 376–377
Strategic planning process, 70, 171, 298
    conditions and general limits of, 325–328
    evaluation of, 324
    flexibility in, 322–323
    functions and activities of, 299

456 Index

Strategic planning process (*cont.*)
   iteration in, 323–324
   phases/cycles, 318–320
   success and failure of, 312–317
   uncertainty in, 319–322
Strengthening the Administrative
   Capacity of the State, 372–406
Structure plans, 122n46
Subsidiarity, ongoing pursuit of, 383
Substantial interaction, 70
Substantive core, 387
Substantive knowledge, 387
Substantivism, integration of, 83–86
Synthetic, 9
System engineering, 2, 282
Systemic approach, 156–162
System of National Account (SNA),
   275, 277, 286n9
Systems of exploitation, 347
System theory, 156, 157

Tabula rasa, 184–186
Taylor, F.W., 174n24
Taylorism, 174n24
Technical knowledge, 387
Techniques organization, 360
Technocratic national process of
   decision-making, 341
Technology, 385, 400–406
Teleology, 5–6
Territorial planning, 72
Theories of Society, 138
Theory of decision, 2
Theory of planning, 29, 82, 83, 89,
   92, 103, 174n23

Theory of Reflexivity, 186–196
Theory of social choice, 333n37
Thurow, L., 27
Tinbergen, J., 1, 11, 31n4, 32n5,
   276, 282, 286n5
Tinbergen, N., 239, 262
Trade unions, 345
Traditional economic policy,
   expections issue, 249–250
Traditional economics, crisis of,
   179–214
   criticism of global capitalism
      without public planning, 213
   fallibility, 201, 207
   feasibility of plans, 202
   global system of capitalism, 180
   interactive vision of reality, 196
   logical positivism to theory of
      reflexivity, 186
   management of economic crisis, 183
   radical criticism of economics, 212
   reflexive concept of truth, 196
   reflexivity, 201
Tabula Rasa, 184
Traditional hierarchical
   organizational structures, 404
Traditional rural social order, 357
Training programmes on diversity, 393
Transformation of human beings, 354
Treasury bill, 245
A Treatise of Human Nature (1739), 36
Trilogy, 2, 338
Truth, reflexive concept of, 196–200,
   203–205
Tversky, A., 54, 65n17
2008 crisis, 243
Two-way communication system, 403

Uncertainty in strategic planning process, 319–322
UN Commission for Latin America, 339
Unemployment, 243, 354, 362, 399
Unified approach, 78, 337–371
  to planning, 82, 288n25, 338
Unified Approach to Development Analysis and Planning, 121n43
Unified rural development strategy, 357
Unique methodology, integration of proceduralism and substantivism in, 83–86
United Nations, 380, 386, 390
United Nations Development Programme, 78
United Nations General Assembly, resolution 50/225 of, 382
United Nations Programme in Public Administration and Finance, 375, 399
United Nations Public Administration Network (UNPAN), 375
United Nations Public Service Day, 399
United Nations Research Institute for Social Development (UNRISD), 118n25, 121–122n43, 339
United States, 241, 283, 300
United States General Accounting Office on Performance Budgeting, 384
Universal income policy, 240–241

Universal societal resistance, 348
Un-priced values, questions, 272–275
UN programme, 372
UNRISD, *see* United Nations Research Institute for Social Development
UN-sponsored activities, 395
Urban minorities, 347
Urban planning, 74, 75, 77
US Code, 329n12
US Department of Agriculture, 276
US federal government, 262
Utopian approach, 15, 16, 19
Utopian point of view, 17
Utopian rationality, 28
Utopia role, as requirement in economic theory, 15–17
Utopic fiction, xxi

Value
  concept of, 326
  existence of, 326
  variability in, 326
Value-free judgements, 38–39
Value judgements, 16, 18
  methodological judgements vs., 39–42
Value system, 26, 378
Variability in value, 326
Variable attitudes, 135
Viability, 349
Viable styles of development, 345
Vigorous elite groups, 350
von Hayek, F.A., 22
von Mises, L., xx, xxviiin3, 3–4, 8

458 Index

Wallerstein, I., 180, 181
Weber, M., 26, 43–45, 158
Welfare state, 237
Well-being commodity, 140
Wertfreiheit, 44
White House, 305
Wiener Circle, 117n18
Windfall style of development, 351

World markets, 360, 364
Worldwide strategic methodology for planning, 229–262
Worrell, A.C., 273, 279

Zero growth rates, 345, 366
Zero-sum game, 27

CPSIA information can be obtained
at www.ICGtesting.com
Printed in the USA
LVHW042116291119
638954LV00008B/585/P